BTEC First Travel Atlas
UK & Europe Edition

ISBN: 1-84690-005-0

First published in 2006

© 2006 Columbus Travel Publishing
Pages 6-12, 15-21 & 144 © Edexcel Limited 2006

Distributed by:
Pearson Education Limited
Edinburgh Gate
Harlow
Essex CM20 2JE
www.longman.co.uk

• Cartographic Editor: *David Burles*.

• Production Editor: *Brian Quinn*.

• Additional Cartography: *Anderson Geographics Ltd, Berkshire*.

• Contributors: *Patrick Fitzgerald, Tony Peisley, Patrick Thorne, Penny Locke, Graeme Payne, Jon Gillaspie, Bill la Violette, Ned Middleton, Sachiko Burles, Carol Spencer, Hayley Dalton, Lucy Stewart*.

• Continental Introductions: *Brian Quinn*.

• Cover Design: *Antonio Manuel of Nexus Media Communications*.

• Printed by: *Croxsons, Chesham*.

• Founding Editor: *Mike Taylor of the University of Brighton*.

• Publisher: *Pete Korniczky*.

This publication has been created from a wide range of sources and where appropriate these have been credited on the relevant maps, charts or articles. The publishers would like to thank all the many organisations and individuals who have helped in the preparation of this edition, with particular thanks to Ian Alexander of Battlefiels Tours; Bill Adams of Safari Consultants; Isobel Falk of JLA; Keith Wright of Amusement Business; Brad Smith of Foremost West; John Knighton of African Pride; Maria Hinayon of ACI; Kate Pirie and Natalie de la Porte of Southern Skies Marketing; John Douglas of Malawi Tourism; John Haycock of Africa Explorer; David Ezra of the Saltmarsh Partnership; Maria Polk of Tours.com; Cathy Keefe of Travel Industry Association of America; Graham Johnson; Dirk Triep of the German National Tourist Office; Theresa Mancini of IACO; Olaf Schoonhoven of the World Travel School; Ivo Siebens of KHM; Ann Tack of Spermalie Hotel & Tourism School; Jeff Bertus of Bertus Leisure; Elliot Frisby of Visit Britain; Simon Hampton and Anne-Marie Hansen of Kuoni; Jane Voss; Dan Josty; Steve Jackson; Leila Carlyle; and Michael Knop. Apologies to organisations or individuals omitted from this list in error.

▶ *See also...* Country Contents (3); Thematic Contents (4-5); Countries A-Z (108-116); Index (117-143)

The listings above refer to a selection of related themes.

General Contents

This General Contents provides a summary of the main subjects and areas covered in this atlas. For clarity, many of the individual countries and topics covered are not listed separately here. Many countries have focus maps which give detailed coverage of areas of particular importance. For further help with locating countries or topics, see the Country Contents (3), the Thematic Contents (4-5) and the navigation panels which appear at the top of every page and which refer to a selection of related themes.

Country Contents

This section lists the countries in Europe as they have been defined for the purposes of this book. For more information on what is and what is not a country – a less clear-cut matter than might be supposed – please see the World Pointers section on page 24, the introduction to the Countries A-Z section on page 108 or the Columbus *World Travel Dictionary*. Countries are here prefixed with a dot. Only one page number has been given per entry and this generally refers to where a map of the entire country can be found; more detailed maps may appear on the subsequent page/s. A selection of other names is also given here, in *italics*. If preceding ≈, this is not, or no longer, the official name of the country: the official or current name follows the symbol. If preceding >, this is politically part of another country: the 'mother' country follows the symbol. (For ease of reference, the page number has been given where this is different from that of the 'mother' country). If preceding Δ, this is a geographical area or informal term: the countries it comprises follow the symbol. The list of such ambiguities could be many times longer and only those regarded as being the most important for the purposes of this atlas have been included here. For further help with locating places, see the General Contents (2), the Thematic Contents (4-5), the World Political map (28-29), Appendix 1: Geographical Definitions (100), Countries A-Z (108-116), the Index (117-143) and the navigation panels which appear at the top of every page and which refer to a selection of related themes.

Names preceded by > are politically part of another country; by ≈ are old/unofficial titles; by Δ are geographical areas. *See also introduction above.*

4 Contents

Country Contents

▶ *See also...* General Contents (2-3); Thematic
Contents (6-7); World Pointers (10); Countries A-Z
(202-210); Index (211-256)

The listings above refer to a selection of related themes.

Thematic Contents

This Thematic Contents gives page references for a selection of the topics covered in the Atlas. The abbreviations SIs and CSs mean that the theme is covered in the section introductions or the country sections. For further help with locating topics, please see the General Contents (2), the Country Contents (3), the Index (117-143) and the navigation panels which appear at the top of every page and which refer to a selection of related themes.

KEY TO TOPOGRAPHIC MAPS

Communications

✈ Airport *main international gateways and domestic hubs*

━━━━ Motorway/expressway or equivalent *focus maps only*

━━━━ - - - - - Main road • Road in tunnel

┅□┅ - - - - - Main passenger railway, with station • Railway in tunnel

━━━━ Dedicated high-speed rail line *focus maps only*

. . . . Ferry route *selected passenger routes: focus maps only*

Boundaries & boxes

━━━━ - - - - - International boundary • Disputed international boundary

- - - - - Internal administrative boundary *sometimes shown as solid line for clarity*

━━━━ National park, wildlife reserve

▭ Area featured in a focus map

Settlement

● ○ ○ ○ ○ Towns and cities *size of dot is determined by population; darkest red indicates a city with over one million inhabitants*

■ ■ □ □ □ National capital/capital of overseas territory *named in CAPITAL LETTERS*

Built-up area *larger scale focus maps only*

∴ ▪ Archaeological site, ruins • Important building/s (e.g castle, temple)

◆ Other place of interest (e.g. park, reserve, natural feature) *focus maps only*

Physical features (see individual map pages for elevation tints)

△ ▽ Mountain peak • Land depression *with altitude in metres*

= Pass, canyon *with altitude in metres*

River, with waterfall, with dam • Seasonal river

◯ ◯ ◯ Lake • Seasonal lake • Salt lake

━━━━ Canal

Coral reef

Introduction

The BTEC First Atlas: UK and Europe edition is an invaluable resource for teaching and assessing students working towards BTEC First Certificate and Diploma in Travel and Tourism.

The UK and Europe edition of the BTEC First Atlas has been specifically designed for *Unit 3: UK Travel and Tourism Destinations* and *Unit 4: European Holiday Destinations*. The following teaching sessions are for planning and developing lessons, enabling students to get full use out of the atlas. The sessions also show how activities can be combined to develop students' knowledge and understanding of UK and European geography. Blank maps of the UK and Europe have been provided for use in the teaching sessions and are found on pages 13 and 14 of this atlas. 'Test yourself' quizzes are also included, starting at page 15. The answers can be found on page 144.

Important note: The sessions published in this supplement have not been designed to form part of the assessment for the units mentioned and should not be used in this way. These sessions do not cover all of the content that has been set out in the specification. When teaching and assessing students for these units, please refer to guidance published in the specification for this qualification with the publication code BF017274. This and other support materials for this qualification can be obtained from the Edexcel website www.edexcel.org.uk.

Teaching sessions

> United Kingdom

• Teaching topic:
The UK and its regions

Session objectives:

- To understand the location of the UK nations, their capitals and their regions
- To check understanding with *UK Quiz 1 – UK regions*

Guidance

An interactive session is recommended using large-scale blank outline maps displayed to encourage group participation. Students' own UK holiday experiences should be shared and locations plotted on a map.

Students can then move on to structured map work, using the atlas to determine the location of significant tourist destinations in the UK. On a blank UK map, and using the map on pages 58/59, ask students to identify England, Scotland, Wales and Northern Ireland and their capital cities. Using the same, or a new blank map, ask students to identify and locate the regions of the UK that attract high numbers of tourists. The maps on page 61 are a good starting point.

TV travel programmes can be used for additional visual and factual input. Some tourist boards are able to provide promotional videos for educational purposes and may also be willing to offer guest speakers. Details of tourism regions can be found on page 60 of this atlas

• Teaching topic:
Tourist destinations: UK towns and cities

Session objectives:

- To understand the factors affecting the appeal of historical and cultural towns and cities (including spa towns)
- To understand what is on offer in UK towns and cities for tourists
- To find out the location of key UK towns and cities which attract tourists

Guidance

Devise practical activities to help students become proficient and independent in using brochures, leaflets, guidebooks, trade manuals and websites to locate information on UK destinations. These tools should be used specifically to examine the factors affecting the appeal of historical, cultural and spa towns or cities for different types of visitors.

Get students to investigate specific locations, taking into account visitor attractions, topography, facilities, arts and entertainment, sightseeing and transport links. Initial focus should be on a tourist town or city in the locality. This should be followed by paired work to investigate different town or city destinations across the UK, culminating in short presentations.

Using the map on pages 58/59, ask students to identify

towns and cities that appeal to tourists. For each location students should summarise what the main appeal is for inbound and domestic tourists.

The following is an example list of UK towns and cities with appeal to tourists:

Bath, Belfast, Buxton, Canterbury, Cardiff, Cheltenham, Edinburgh, Glasgow, Harrogate, Inverness, Liverpool, London, Londonderry, Manchester, Oxford, Stirling, Stratford-upon-Avon, York

Many UK towns and cities have their own marketing teams that may be able to provide guest speakers or additional information.

• Teaching topic:
Tourist destinations: UK seaside resorts

Session objectives:

- To understand the factors affecting the appeal of UK seaside resorts

- To find out what UK seaside resorts have to offer tourists

- To design posters to promote a UK seaside resort

- To find out the locations of popular UK seaside resorts

- To check understanding with *UK Quiz 2 – UK seaside resorts*

Guidance

Develop research activities, using the internet, guidebooks, holiday brochures and leaflets, to examine the factors affecting the appeal of UK seaside resorts for different types of visitors. This should take into account visitor attractions, topography, facilities, arts and entertainment, sightseeing and transport links. The group will benefit from individual students selecting different seaside resorts for investigation.

Ask students to design and display posters to promote the appeal of a seaside resort for a specific type of visitor.

Using the map on page 60 ask students to locate popular seaside resorts. For each one located students should state their appeal (this could include areas of natural beauty, built visitor attractions, events and festivals).

The following are examples of UK seaside resorts:

Aberdour, Aberystwyth, Ballycastle, Barmouth, Blackpool, Brighton, Llandudno, Margate, Newquay, Portrush, Scarborough, South Wold, Tenby

Many seaside resorts have their own marketing teams who can provide guest speakers or additional information.

• Teaching topic:

Tourist destinations: UK islands, countryside and coastal areas

Session objectives:

- To understand factors affecting the appeal of islands, countryside and coastal areas

- To understand what islands, countryside and coastal areas have to offer tourists

- Design fact sheets about islands, countryside and coastal areas

- Check understanding with *UK Quiz 3 – Transport links to islands, the countryside and coastal areas* and *UK Quiz 4 – National Parks of England Scotland and Wales*

Guidance

Develop research activities, using the internet, guidebooks, holiday brochures and leaflets, to examine the factors affecting the appeal of islands, countryside and coastal areas, for different types of visitor. This should take into account visitor attractions, topography, facilities, arts and entertainment (where applicable), sightseeing and transport links. Additional activities could be organised to investigate accessibility of tourist islands from the mainland.

Compile fact sheets to make up a display on a wide variety of islands, countryside and coastal areas.

Use maps on pages 58/59 to locate islands. Ask students to note what features each island has that might help its appeal to inbound and domestic tourists. *The following are examples of UK islands:*

Arran, Guernsey, Isle of Wight, Mull, Skye, St. Marys

Use maps on pages 58, 59, 60, 61 and 64 to locate countryside and coastal areas that appeal to tourists *The following are examples of UK countryside areas:*

Cadir Idris, Chiltern Hills, Forest of Dean, Lake District, Loch Lomond, Loch Ness, Mourne Mountains, New Forest

The following are examples of UK coastal areas:

Chesil Bay, Gower Peninsula, Lizard Heritage Coast

Many National Parks have visitor centres which may be able to provide videos for educational purposes, guest speakers or additional information.

• Teaching topic:

Transport: UK airports

Session objectives:

- To locate major international air gateways for inbound tourists

- To understand locations of UK airports and their 3-letter codes

- To check understanding with *UK Quiz 5 – Airports and their 3-letter codes*

Guidance

Using the map on page 62, locate the major international air gateways into the UK for inbound tourists. Although almost every airport has international flights, students could focus on Heathrow, Gatwick, Manchester, Glasgow International and Belfast International. Using a variety of sources students should identify where inbound tourists may arrive from into these airports.

Students can then locate on a blank map all the airports in the UK, with their 3-letter codes. Ask students to make observations about the locations of the airports and how this could affect the appeal for both inbound and domestic tourists in specific areas.

• Teaching topic:
Transport: UK seaports

Session objectives:

- To know locations of major seaports in the UK

- To know the names of ferry operators and types of vessels operating to, from and within the UK

- To check understanding with *UK Quiz 6 – UK seaports and their destinations*

Guidance

Using the map on page 62, ask students to identify major seaports in the UK on a blank map. *The following are examples of UK seaports:*

Aberdeen, Dover, Fishguard, Harwich, Holyhead, Liverpool, Portsmouth, Ryde, Stranraer, Troon

For six of these seaports ask students to research the number and names of the ferry services operating, and their destinations. Ask them to find out what type of vessel operates (for example, car carrying, high speed) and how they think this might affect the appeal for inbound and domestic tourists.

There should be at least one example of:

1. a route within the UK (for example, Portsmouth to Ryde),

2. a route from mainland UK to the Republic of Ireland (for example, Fishguard to Rosslare),

3. a route from the UK to continental Europe (for example, Harwich to Hook of Holland).

> Europe

For the purposes of this unit, Europe is considered to be all of continental Europe west of the Urals and including the Republic of Ireland, the Canary Islands, the Azores and Cyprus. It does not include any part of the United Kingdom including the Channel Islands or the Isle of Man.

The term 'holiday destination' can refer to a specific city or town that is an established holiday destination, such as Madrid, St. Moritz or Benidorm. It could also be a small island or a distinct area, for example Ibiza or Côte d'Azur, or a specific city or town within that area, for example San Antonio or Nice. Countryside areas can include lakes and mountains such as the Italian Lakes or the Black Forest.

• Teaching topic:
Countries of Europe

Session objectives:

- To gain a general overview of the geography of Europe

- To gain an understanding of the variety of resorts in Europe

- To develop skills in using an atlas and other types of reference material

Guidance

Using a blank map of Europe ask students to locate European countries, noting which ones are in the EU and which are in the Eurozone. The maps on pages 44 and 46 may be helpful in this exercise.

Using statistics, brochures or other sources ask students to identify which countries are popular with ex-UK tourists and why.

Working in groups, students can then be allocated different European countries to investigate using tour operators' brochures, websites and the atlas. This enables different groups to produce and present annotated maps to identify a wide range of holiday destinations within different European countries. The maps should highlight the variety of holiday destinations and transport gateways within individual countries. A wide range of destinations should be located within each country chosen, including (where appropriate) at least one each of summer sun, winter sun, winter sport, countryside, city break and cruise areas. Airports and passenger ferry ports should also be identified.

• Teaching topic:
Summer and winter sun destinations

Session objectives:

* To identify and locate summer and winter sun destinations

* To find out about natural attractions and how they might affect the popularity and appeal of summer and winter sun destinations

* To check understanding with *Europe Quiz 1 – Summer sun destinations*

Guidance

Ask students to research popular summer and winter sun destinations using brochures. *The following are examples of summer sun destinations:*

Algarve, Croatia, Gumbet, Ibiza, Limassol, Salou, Santorini

The following are examples of winter sun destinations:

Gran Canaria, Lanzarote, Tenerife

Students can locate summer and winter sun destinations on a blank map, using maps found on pages 76-95.

Ask students to research natural attractions (for example beaches and lakes) and climate (for example average temperature and rainfall) and say how these affect the popularity of winter and summer sun destinations. The climate map on page 45 might be useful.

• Teaching topic:
Winter sports and countryside destinations

Session objectives:

* To find out about significant geographical features in Europe and activities that might be associated with these

* To know locations for winter sports in Europe and the physical factors that affect their appeal

* To find out about countryside areas and their appeal to ex-UK tourists

* To check understanding with *Europe Quiz 2 – Areas of European countryside*

Guidance

On a blank map ask students to identify significant geographical features in Europe (for example forests, lakes, volcanic areas, areas of wilderness, sub-tropical forests and glacial lakes). The maps on pages 44 and 54 identify some of the most significant ones. Ask students to identify what types of activities may be popular in these areas.

Using brochures, students should identify and locate popular European winter sport destinations. The map on page 57 might be helpful in this exercise. *The following are examples of winter sports destinations:*

Are, Flaine, Meribel, Poiana Brasov, Soldeu, Vogel

Ask students to explain what physical factors might affect the appeal of winter sport destinations (for example altitude, number of runs or distance from airport).

Using the map on page 54 identify and research six countryside areas in Europe. For each one they should locate them on a map and describe the natural features that would appeal to ex-UK tourists.

• Teaching topic:
City breaks

Session objectives:

- To find out the locations of city break destinations in Europe

- To learn about how low-cost airlines and flight times can contribute to the popularity of city break destinations

- To understand the importance of arts and culture on the appeal of city breaks

- To learn about the negative impacts of too much tourism on European cities

- To check understanding with *Europe Quiz 3 – Low-cost carriers and their destinations*

Guidance

Students should locate major European city break destinations on a blank map. *The following are examples of major European city break destinations:*

Brussels, Krakow, Madrid, Paris, Prague, Rome, Tallinn

Using route maps of low-cost airlines, and other sources, ask students to identify popular European city breaks that are served by low-cost carriers.

Develop research activities using the internet, guidebooks, *World Travel Guide*, holiday brochures and leaflets to examine the traditions, culture and image of a variety of European holiday destinations.

Ask students to use guidebooks (such as the *Rough Guides*) to find out about traditions, arts and culture that cities are famous for. They should imagine they are making a bid to have the city named as European City of Culture 2014. What are the main highlights of the city they would like to bring to the judges attention? TV travel programmes can be used for additional visual and factual input.

Newspaper articles, especially bad press (for example, about crime level, loutish behaviour or sporting clashes) should be reviewed to prompt discussions about image. Ask students to consider which cities have a negative image because of crime or too much tourism.

The map on page 39 indicates flying times from London. Students should note which of the destinations they have found are within two hours flying time of London. Ask students to consider how far people would be willing to travel for a city break, and which city breaks are popular with UK tourists and why.

• Teaching topic:
European cruise areas

Session objectives:

- To find out about the European cruise areas and their appeal to tourists

- To check understanding with *Europe Quiz 4 – Cruise areas: ports of call*

Guidance

Using the map on page 40/41, ask students to locate the major European cruise areas on a blank map. Using cruise brochures, ask students to explain how cruises in major European areas might appeal to different types of tourists.

• Teaching topic:
Transport: European airports

Session objectives:

- To know the location of major air gateways in Europe

- To check understanding with *Europe Quiz 5 – Airports and their 3-letter codes*

Guidance

On a blank map, ask students to locate key airports in Europe with flights to and from the UK, noting their 3-letter codes. The map on page 38 locates some of these.

Using airport websites, ask students to identify scheduled and charter routes to and from these airports to the UK.

• Teaching topic:
Transport: European sea ports

Session objectives:

- To know the locations of major seaports and ferry routes from the UK to Europe

- To check understanding with *Europe Quiz 6 – European seaports and their destinations*

Guidance

Using the map on page 62, ask students to identify major seaports in Europe with links to the UK on a blank map. *The following are examples of European sea ports which link to the UK:*

Calais, Bilbao, Esbjerg, Rotterdam, Zeebrugge

For six of these seaports ask students to research the number and names of the ferry services which operate from the port, and their destinations. Ask them to find out what type of vessel operates (for example car carrying, high speed) and how they think this might affect the appeal to ex-UK tourists.

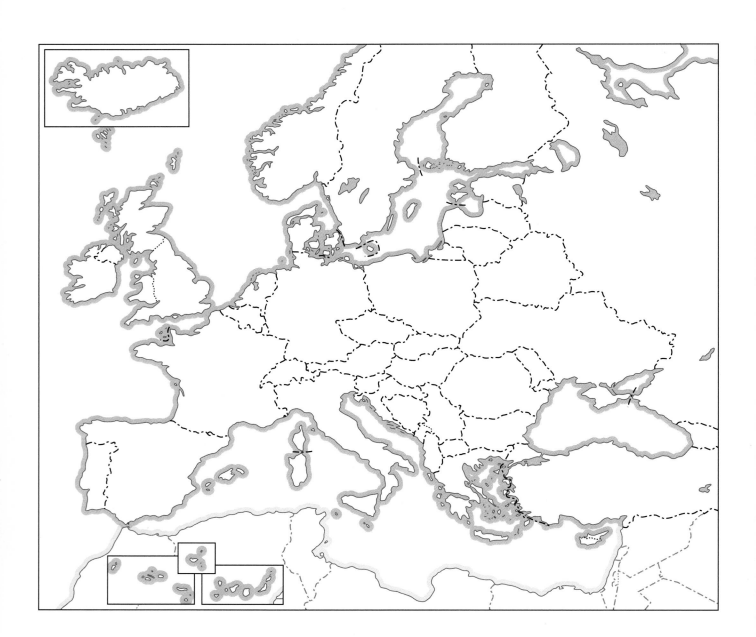

Quizzes

Answers to all UK and European quizzes can be found on page 144

> United Kingdom

■ UK Quiz 1 – UK regions

Match the description to the region it describes.

Question	Answer
1 This area of England is home to two National Parks and the UK's surfing capital.	☐
2 These are all islands that are part of the Inner Hebrides.	☐
3 This Northern Ireland county is home to the Giants Causeway.	☐
4 The Heart of England is the birthplace of which famous English playwright?	☐
5 Gatwick, Heathrow and Stansted are all located in this region.	☐
6 Glamorgan and Pembrokeshire are counties in which area of the UK?	☐
7 Loch Lomond and Loch Tay are two of the many lochs found in this area of the UK.	☐
8 Lowestoft, South Wold and Cromer are all in this English Tourist Board region.	☐
9 This county is home to the Mourne Mountains.	☐
10 Although nearer France these islands are British dependencies.	☐

A Shakespeare	D East of England	G South Wales	J County Down
B Scottish Lowlands	E Southeast England	H The Channel Islands	
C Antrim	F West Country	I Mull, Jura and Islay	

■ UK Quiz 2 – UK seaside resorts

Name the seaside resort to which the fact relates.

Fact   **Resort**

1   This English seaside resort is home to a famous pavilion built for King George IV.   _____

2   Dolphins are often spotted near this Welsh seaside resort in Cardigan Bay.   _____

3   This Cornish seaside resort is home to the China Clay Trials and near to
    the Eden Project.   _____

4   This seaside resort is home to the famous 'pleasure beach' amusement park.   _____

5   This seaside resort is home to the world's longest pier.   _____

6   This Welsh beach is sometimes referred to as the unofficial capital of the
    Llyn Peninsula.   _____

7   This seaside resort in Northern Ireland is well known for its Ould Lammas Fair.   _____

8   This seaside resort has its own Tate gallery.   _____

9   This popular Isle of Wight beach has a pier, a small airport and its own
    dinosaur museum.   _____

10 This Yorkshire seaside resort is famous for its fair held each May.   _____

■ UK Quiz 3 – Transport links to islands, the countryside and coastal areas

What is the closest city, and therefore transport gateway to these areas?

1   Peak District   ☐

2   New Forest   ☐

3   Lough Neagh   ☐

4   The Trossachs   ☐

5   Jersey   ☐

6   Gower Peninsula ☐

7   Lake District   ☐

8   Norfolk Broads   ☐

9   Isle of Wight   ☐

10 Land's End   ☐

A	Lancaster	D	Sheffield	G	Southampton	J	Penzance
B	Stirling	E	Lowestoft	H	Swansea		
C	St. Helier	F	Ryde	I	Belfast		

■ UK Quiz 4 – National Parks of England, Scotland and Wales

Label the National Parks on the map.

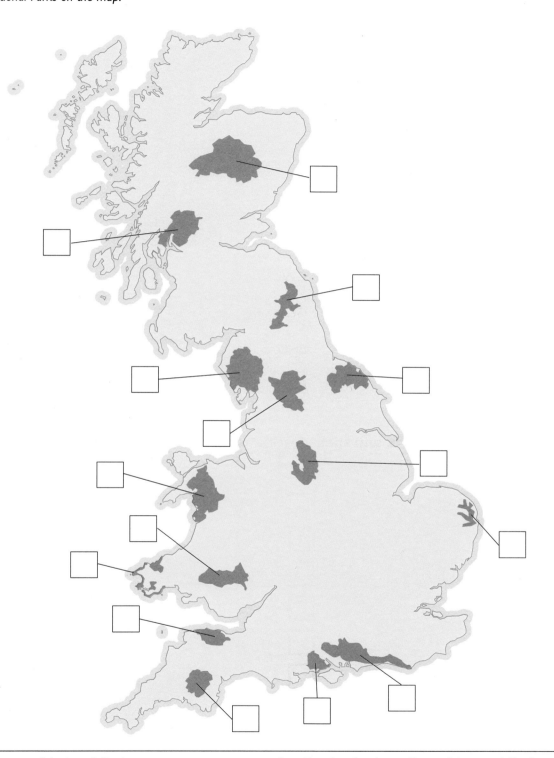

A	Cairngorms National Park	I	Pembrokeshire Coast National Park
B	Loch Lomond National Park	J	Brecon Beacons National Park
C	Northumberland National Park	K	Exmoor National Park
D	Lake District National Park	L	Dartmoor National Park
E	Yorkshire Dales National Park	M	New Forest National Park
F	North York Moors National Park	N	Broads Authority National Park
G	Peak District National Park	O	South Downs Proposed National Park
H	Snowdonia National Park		

■ UK Quiz 5 – Airports and their 3-letter codes

Complete the table.

	Airport	3-letter code
1	London Heathrow	
2	Londonderry	
3	Edinburgh	
4	London Stansted	
5	Leeds Bradford	
6		BHX
7		CWL
8		GLA
9		BHD
10		BOH

■ UK Quiz 6 – UK seaports and their destinations

Match the UK seaport with its destination.

Seaport

1 Dover ☐

2 Harwich ☐

3 Portsmouth ☐

4 Holyhead ☐

5 Ullapool ☐

6 Belfast ☐

7 Southampton ☐

8 Liverpool ☐

9 Newhaven ☐

10 Plymouth ☐

A	Stranraer	D	Roscoff	G	Stornoway	J	East Cowes
B	Bilbao	E	Dun Laoghaire	H	Douglas		
C	Dieppe	F	Calais	I	Esbjerg		

> Europe

■ Europe Quiz 1 – Summer Sun Destinations

The following summer sun destinations are all located on islands. Name the island, the country to which it belongs and the sea that it is in.

Resort	Island	Country	Sea/Ocean
1 Lindos			
2 Kavos			
3 Paphos			
4 Kyrenia			
5 Alcudia			
6 Funchal			
7 Sliema			
8 Alghero			
9 Porto Vecchio			
10 Molyvos			

■ Europe Quiz 2 – European Countryside Areas

Describe the natural features of these European countryside areas and suggest activities that tourists could do while they are there. The first one has been done for you.

Area	Natural features	Activities
1 The Dolomites, Italy	*Mountains and lakes, with snow in winter*	*Skiing in winter, walking, cycling in summer*
2 The Black Forest, Germany		
3 Gauja, Latvia		
4 Mount Teide, Tenerife, Spain		
5 Trakai, Lithuania		
6 The Pyrenees, Spain		
7 Wolinski, Poland		
8 Sumava, Czech Republic		
9 Hamra, Sweden		
10 Wicklow Mountains, Ireland		

■ Europe Quiz 3 – **Low-cost carriers and their destinations**

The following are airports served by low-cost carriers. For each one, identify the major town or city nearby and which airlines operate there.

	Airport	**Nearby town or city**	**Airlines**
1	Ciampino		
2	Bratislava		
3	Sabiha Gokcen		
4	Brescia		
5	Beauvais		
6	Reus		
7	Mulhouse		
8	Schonefeld		
9	Treviso		
10	Torp		

■ Europe Quiz 4 – **Cruise areas: Ports of call**

In which body of water are the following ports?

	Port	**Body of water**
1	Bergen	
2	Crete	
3	Dubrovnik	
4	Porto	
5	Palma de Mallorca	
6	Istanbul	
7	Stockhlom	
8	Tromso	
9	Tallinn	
10	Gibraltar	

■ Europe Quiz 5 – **Airports and their 3-letter codes**

Complete the table.

	Airport	3-letter code
I	Paris Orly	_____
2	Faro	_____
3	Palma, Majorca	_____
4	Cork	_____
5	Mikinos	_____
6	_____	AGP
7	_____	ADB
8	_____	LCA
9	_____	PRG
10	_____	KRK

■ Europe Quiz 6 – **European seaports and their UK destinations**

Match the European seaport with its UK destination.

I	Cuxhaven	☐
2	Bergen	☐
3	Cork	☐
4	Kristiansand	☐
5	St. Malo	☐
6	Cherbourg	☐
7	Zeebrugge	☐
8	Dunkirk	☐
9	Santander	☐
10	Granville	☐

A	Swansea	D	Kingston upon Hull	G	Plymouth	J	Poole
B	Weymouth	E	Harwich	H	Newcastle		
C	Dover	F	Lerwick	I	St. Helier		

▶ *See also...* World Political (28-29); Travel Indicators (34-35); Europe Introduction (42-43)

The listings above refer to a selection of related themes. For more information, see the Contents (2-5).

Key facts

Number of Countries	226
Area ('000 sq km)	135,477
Population ('000)	6,450,988
Population Density (per sq km)	48
Gross National Income (US$m)	39,659,845
Visitor Arrivals ('000)	766,000
Visitor Receipts (US$m)	601,726

GNI figures are for 2004. Population figures are taken from the most recent reliable source. Travel figures (UNWTO) are based on overnight stays, not same-day visitors, and are for 2004. For more information see the Countries A-Z section from page 202.

World

There are many opinions as to how big the worldwide travel business really is. Like all service-based sectors it has no physical product that can be weighed or counted. Many problems of definition follow from this – an airline pilot or a travel agent is clearly part of the industry; but what about a small-town taxi driver, or the owner of a convenience store that also sells local souvenirs? Different countries and organisations will take different views on such points. Despite such challenges, widely accepted estimates are produced by several respected bodies. One such, the World Travel and Tourism Council, suggests that 10.6% of the world's GDP and 8.3% of the world's jobs depend directly or indirectly on travel and tourism, making it the world's largest industry: in the 1960s it was not even in the top ten. The World Tourism Organisation further suggests that travel is the world's fastest growing one, with an annual average increase in receipts of 9% between 1984 and 2000. Various projections put the real growth per year at around 4 to 5% between 2006 and 2015. By any estimate, travel is clearly big business – a multi-trillion dollar industry, driven by people's frequent desire to be elsewhere.

The *World Travel Atlas*, now in its tenth edition, provides a unique overview of the travel industry in the early 21st century. The focus maps which complement the conventional regional and country plates offer detailed, travel-specific coverage of the most-visited areas. A large number of themes, ranging from economic indicators to UNESCO World Heritage Sites and from ski resorts to time zones, are covered throughout the book, supplemented with detailed appendices. There are also six continental introductions, which provide an overview of each region, a discussion of some of the key travel-related issues, a summary of the main travel destinations and a selection of statistics. Themes covered here include low-cost airlines, the cruise industry, intra-regional travel patterns, the changing role of the travel agent, responsible tourism, regional economic change, the internet, the problems of the major airlines, globalisation and niche markets. Many of the maps and charts are new to this edition and all pre-existing ones have been updated. Another first-time feature is the navigation aid panel at the top of each page which refers to maps or charts of related interest. There is also are also two additional contents providing thematic and country-by-country overviews of the numerous topics that the *World Travel Atlas* addresses. Overall, the book's aim is to provide a clear, balanced and accurate picture of the world for a wide range of readers in the travel industry and elsewhere.

Past, present and future

Apart from 1982 (due mainly to the Gulf War) and 2001 (due mainly to the 11 September terrorist attacks), visitor numbers and travel receipts have risen in every year since accurate records began in 1950. Aviation figures go back even further than that: in 1926 the US domestic air travel market involved some 8,000 passengers, about the number that took to the skies for domestic flights in America every seven minutes in 2005. As for international flights from the USA in 1926, there were none recorded. It was not until 1946 that US international departures broke through the one million mark. They have increased by an average of about one million per year ever since.

By whatever means of transport, Europe remained comfortably the most-visited continent in 2005. What is encouraging for the global health of the industry is that, while Europe's market is still growing, arrivals to other regions – notably Asia – are growing at a faster pace. The WTO's Tourism 2020 Vision forecasts that worldwide international arrivals are likely to exceed 1.56 billion by 2020. Under this model, Europe will remain the most-visited region, but with a market share reduced from 60% in 1995 to 46% in 2020. As regards outbound travel, Europe will continue to dominate, but Asia will, by 2020, have doubled its number of visitors compared to 1995 whereas those of the Americas will only have increased by 50%. The report goes on to predict that long-haul travel will grow at a faster rate than regional travel during this period.

The leading countries in the travel-numbers league seem to have their positions assured, for the next few years at least. The six top countries in terms of visitor arrivals were the same in 2004 as in 1997, with France comfortably in the lead and the chasing pack bunched some way behind them, occasionally changing their positions from year to year. On the other three basic indicators, the Germans travel more and (having recently overtaken the USA) spend the most, while the Americans receive the most money. The most significant medium-term change is likely to be the emergence of China, not only as a destination but also as a source of travellers. The increase in number of countries being granted Approved Destination Status, the relaxation of travel restrictions and China's rapidly growing prosperity have already led to international departures more than doubling between 2000 and 2004. By many estimates, China will be supplying more tourists than any other country by 2010.

Travel remains something of an exclusive market: the 11 most visited countries accounted for over 50% of all tourist arrivals in 2004. It is also something of a crowded one: in 41 of the world's countries the annual visiting population in 2004 exceeded the native one, on four occasions (Andorra, Macau, the British Virgin Islands and Aruba) by a factor of more than 10.

Prospects for 2006 and beyond appear good on the basis of recent performance and medium-term trends,

although there are several potential problems ahead. The WTO has identified terrorism, rising oil prices and the spread of the H5N1 avian flu virus as three of the most important factors which could disrupt the industry during the coming years.

Travel trends

2005 was another record year for the travel industry with visitor arrivals reaching 808 million according to the WTO, an increase of 5.5% and over 40 million travellers compared to 2004's 766 million. All this was despite a catalogue of problems including natural disasters, health scares, terrorism and oil price rises, all seemingly striking at the very heart of the industry. The strongest continental growth was recorded in the less mature markets, with Africa (10% up) leading the way: further good news for an industry which, like any other, is seeking to diversify its appeal. Even the airlines prospered better than many would have predicted a couple of years ago, with RPKs (revenue passenger kilometres) of IATA members up by nearly 8%. Still more surprisingly, many observers predict that the aviation industry as a whole will return to profit by the end of 2007. It was another excellent year for many niche markets: cruising, for example, attracted double the number of travellers in 2005 than ten years earlier. New holiday options are constantly being offered and new ways of doing business developed. In addition, a new ethical dimension is being added, with an increased emphasis on responsible and sustainable tourism. All things considered, the travel business is clearly both very adaptable and very robust.

An important area of the industry, but one that is often overlooked, is domestic tourism. The extent of this is for obvious reasons very hard to quantify. Although this generates no new revenue from foreign countries, it at least keeps money flushing through a national economy and keeps travel-related businesses healthy even at times when people are, for whatever reason, disinclined to venture abroad. Around 95% of all trips taken by Americans are domestic, according to TIA – 'See America First' was first used as a slogan by the National Parks Service in 1906 and has been popular ever since – while the UK Tourism Survey estimates that over 126 million such journeys were made in Britain in 2004. Many national tourist offices now devote a good part of their budget to encouraging their own citizens not to travel abroad.

Special-interest holidays have been growing steadily in recent years and the trend shows no sign of slowing. Adventure holidays, cruising, winter sports and city

■ Visitor arrivals

The world's 25 most visited countries in 2004 (millions)
Source: WTO

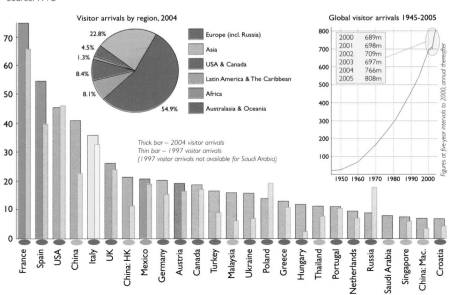

Visitor arrivals by region, 2004

- 22.8% Europe (incl. Russia) — 54.9%
- 4.5% Asia
- 1.3% USA & Canada
- 8.4% Latin America & The Caribbean
- 8.1% Africa
- Australasia & Oceania

Thick bar – 2004 visitor arrivals
Thin bar – 1997 visitor arrivals
(1997 visitor arrivals not available for Saudi Arabia)

Global visitor arrivals 1945-2005

2000	689m
2001	698m
2002	709m
2003	697m
2004	766m
2005	808m

Figures at five-year intervals to 2000, annual thereafter

France, Spain, USA, China, Italy, UK, China: HK, Mexico, Germany, Austria, Canada, Turkey, Malaysia, Ukraine, Poland, Greece, Hungary, Thailand, Portugal, Netherlands, Russia, Saudi Arabia, Singapore, China: Mac., Croatia

- In economic terms, international travel and tourism receipts are classified as exports, and international tourism expenditure as imports. According to the WTO, travel and tourism is one of the top five export categories for over 80% of countries.
- In 2004, Air France-KLM carried 47,190,000 international passengers, more than any other airline. Delta carried the most domestic passengers (79,289,000).
- 19 countries received over 10 million international visitors in 2004. 60 others received over 1 million.
- 17 countries supplied more than 10 million international travellers in 2004. 40 others supplied more than 1 million.
- 17 countries received in excess of US$10billion from international travel in 2004. 46 others received in excess of US$1billion.
- 14 countries spent in excess of US$10billion on international travel in 2004. 28 others spent in excess of US$1billion.
- The biggest travellers, the Germans, have, on average, 35 vacation days a year: Americans have only 13.
- The world's population grew from 1.6 billion to 6.1 billion during the 20th century and is expected to exceed 7 billion by 2015.
- In an average year, Carnival Cruise lines puts 10 million chocolate mints on their guests' pillows.
- Saudi Arabia is the most generous aid donor measured by contributions as a proportion of national income.
- 41 countries (including France, Hong Kong, Portugal, UAE, Ireland, Singapore and many Caribbean states) receive annually more visitors than their population.
- According to ACI, the world's airlines carried 6.7% more passengers in June 2005 than in June 2004.
- Over 55% of cruises in 2005 were in the Caribbean or the Mediterranean.
- The first commercial flight took place in 1914.
- More people are killed on the roads of the USA in an average six-month period than have been in all commercial aviation accidents since 1960.
- The WTO predicts that international travel arrivals will exceed 1.5 billion by 2020.
- And finally, a few thoughts from some other travellers:

   'Like all travellers, I have seen more than I remember and remembered more than I have seen.'
   (Benjamin Disraeli)

   'Maps encourage boldness. They're like cryptic love letters. They make everything seem possible.'
   (Mark Jenkins)

   'The traveller sees what he sees – the tourist sees what he has come to see.'
   (GK Chesterton)

   'The destination is never a place, but a new way of seeing things.'
   (Henry Miller)

   'Everywhere I go, I find a poet who has been there before me.'
   (Sigmund Freud)

breaks are four of the most important and travel agencies able to offer specialist advice and services in these areas have benefited. Travellers are also becoming more discriminating, demanding and adventurous, a trend fuelled by the internet. In Europe, for example, the low-cost airlines are offering a complete one-stop range of short-break options – flights, hotels, car-hire and insurance – through their web-sites. Many of these involve destinations that ten years ago would have been almost unknown, and the list is growing. The number of European city breaks doubled between 2000 and 2004, and many cities have seen year-on-year growth of over 30% in this period.

The low-cost airlines are one sign of change, and of a kind that few would have predicted 15 years ago. In fact, the distinction between low-cost and other kinds of airlines is already starting to blur. With varying degrees of success, many traditional carriers now compete on cost, and some have started up their own low-cost operations. The business model of successful entrants into any market is usually based on a mixture of addressing the failings of the incumbents and utilising new technology, and the new breed of airlines have exploited both. Furthermore, it is easier to start with a blank slate, free of long-established and possibly outdated labour contracts, marketing perceptions and partnership arrangements, than it is to adapt an

existing business. Low-cost airlines have been highly successful in re-defining the travel business.

So to has the internet, the other major force for change of recent years. Numerous statistics, some of which are reported elsewhere in this book, testify to the internet's dramatic growth as a medium for travel information and bookings, and appear to suggest an irreversible trend towards direct sales. The reality is rather more complex. The more successful agencies are now making use of the internet as a 24-hour marketing and sales tool, while at the same time ensuring that their levels of knowledge (often in specialist areas) and customer service keep pace with consumers' increasing expectations. In the same way, many on-line companies are looking to provide a human face to their services by using retail outlets. In time, these developments are likely to blur the distinction between 'on-line' and 'traditional' travel suppliers. Throughout the travel industry, as in others, the companies that thrive will do so because they manage to provide the best and most cost-effective service to their customers.

■ Big spenders

The 20 countries whose residents spent the most on international travel in 2004.
Source: WTO/IMF/World Bank

	Expenditure (US$ millions)	GNI (US$ millions)	Expenditure as % of GNI
■ Germany	72,271	2,488,974	2.9%
■ USA	65,635	12,150,931	0.5%
■ UK	55,930	2,016,393	2.8%
■ Japan	38,129	4,749,910	0.8%
■ France	28,636	1,858,731	1.5%
■ Italy	20,544	1,503,562	1.4%
■ China	19,100	1,676,846	1.1%
■ Netherlands	16,539	515,148	3.2%
■ Canada	16,017	905,629	1.8%
■ Russia	15,730	487,335	3.2%
■ Belgium	13,954	322,837	4.3%
■ China: HK	13,258	183,516	7.2%
■ Spain	12,156	875,817	1.4%
■ Austria	11,416	262,147	4.4%
■ Sweden	10,123	321,401	3.1%
■ Korea, Rep.	9,499	673,036	1.4%
■ Australia	9,407	541,173	1.7%
■ Switzerland	8,797	356,052	2.5%
■ Norway	8,428	238,398	3.5%
■ Taiwan	8,170	317,070	2.6%

■ Visitor receipts

The 25 countries that received the most from international travel in 2004 (US$ millions)
Source: WTO

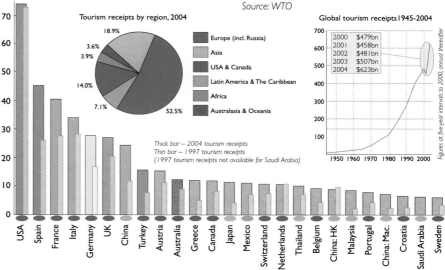

Tourism receipts by region, 2004

- Europe (incl. Russia) — 52.5%
- Asia — 18.9%
- USA & Canada — 14.0%
- Latin America & The Caribbean — 7.1%
- Africa — 3.9%
- Australasia & Oceania — 3.6%

Thick bar – 2004 tourism receipts
Thin bar – 1997 tourism receipts
(1997 tourism receipts not available for Saudi Arabia)

Global tourism receipts 1945-2004

2000	$479bn
2001	$458bn
2002	$481bn
2003	$507bn
2004	$623bn

Figures at five-year intervals to 2000, annual thereafter

(Bar chart countries: USA, Spain, France, Italy, Germany, UK, China, Turkey, Austria, Australia, Greece, Canada, Japan, Mexico, Switzerland, Netherlands, Thailand, Belgium, China: HK, Malaysia, Portugal, China: Mac., Croatia, Saudi Arabia, Sweden)

The reasons for travelling, the means by which the arrangements are made, the choice of possible destinations and the activities to engage in one arrived are all more numerous than ever before. Business trips or beach holidays, cruises or kayaking, safaris or skiing – they are all available somewhere, as long as one has the necessary leisure time and disposable income.

Travel and wealth

Sadly, many people in the world are currently no more than spectators of this glamorous industry. According to the World Bank, the percentage of the population in developing countries who live on a purchasing power parity of less than US$2 a day (defined as describing what US$2 will actually buy in that country, rather than what it will buy in the USA) was 62.1% in 1990 and had only fallen to 55.6% by 2000 and 52.9% in 2004. This is over 3.4 billion people. In subsistence economies, leisure time as it is understood in the developed world is non-existent. For such people, international leisure travel is an impossibility.

As beneficiaries, directly or otherwise, of the leisure time and spending of others, however, travel and tourism becomes rather more relevant. For many countries, incoming travel represents a large, if not the largest, source of foreign exchange and jobs. The infrastructure required is generally less damaging or divisive than that needed for an industrial operation, there is less danger of its being sold out to a foreign government or corporation and at least as good a chance of the wealth it creates reaching the local economy. Moreover, the 'product' itself is generally already in place, in the shape of beaches, jungles, temples or local culture. The demands of tourism have in many cases reversed trends of destruction and development; without tourists, many national parks and game reserves would not be financially viable. The world's number-one industry may have its share of faults and cause its share of problems, but it also has much to be proud of.

Ethical tourism

All forms of travel have an impact on the planet, as do the creation and maintenance of what visitors expect on arrival: while mass tourism can cause change and disruption to the destination societies, and not always for the better. All sectors have been forced to become more aware of the effects of their transient presence. A number of organisations such as the The International Ecotourism Society, The Pro-Poor Partnership, Tourism Concern, The Travel Foundation and Just a Drop, sometimes in conjunction with major airlines and bodies as the WWF, ABTA, PATA, AITO

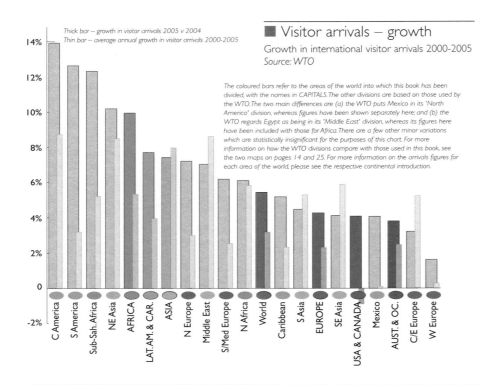

Thick bar – growth in visitor arrivals 2005 v 2004
Thin bar – average annual growth in visitor arrivals 2000-2005

■ Visitor arrivals – growth

Growth in international visitor arrivals 2000-2005
Source: WTO

The coloured bars refer to the areas of the world into which this book has been divided, with the names in CAPITALS. The other divisions are based on those used by the WTO. The two main differences are (a) the WTO puts Mexico in its 'North America' division, whereas figures have been shown separately here; and (b) the WTO regards Egypt as being in its 'Middle East' division, whereas its figures here have been included with those for Africa. There are a few other minor variations which are statistically insignificant for the purposes of this chart. For more information on how the WTO divisions compare with those used in this book, see the two maps on pages 14 and 25. For more information on the arrivals figures for each area of the world, please see the respective continental introduction.

Chart categories (left to right): C America, S America, Sub-Sah. Africa, NE Asia, AFRICA, LAT. AM. & CAR., ASIA, N Europe, Middle East, S/Med Europe, N Africa, World, Caribbean, S Asia, EUROPE, SE Asia, USA & CANADA, Mexico, AUST. & OC., C/E Europe, W Europe

and the EU, have emerged in recent years, all in their different ways dedicated to the idea of improving, or at least mitigating, the impact of travel. An increasing number of awards, such as Tourism for Tomorrow, are designed to motivate good practice, and newspaper travel supplements frequently devote their entire edition to the subject of ethical tourism. In a world dominated by globalisation, it is increasingly hard to be know how much expenditure will benefit the community, or even the country, being visited. To pick but one example, in 2005 nearly 75% of Kenyan hotels were foreign-owned, as were all of the charter airlines serving the country. Such statistics suggest that the benefit of tourism is not being equally shared.

Fortunately, steps are being taken to address these problems. Many operators have become involved in projects ranging from water conservation to sponsorship of schools. Local bodies, like ASSET in the Gambia, have emerged in recent years to offer representation, business training and marketing advice to small local businesses such as local guides and restaurants which depend on visitors. Bodies ranging from national tourist offices to small hotels are increasingly keen to stress their ethical credentials. There is certainly no shortage of innovative ideas in this area. The challenge for the industry as a whole is to reconcile growth with sustainability and responsibility, in all the ways these terms are now used, while at the same time offering value for money. So far, the signs are encouraging, but much still remains to be done.

World pointers

This section provides information or definitions for a selection of the global events, industry trends and technical terms which are directly or indirectly relevant to today's travel business, many of which are referred to throughout this Atlas. This list is not intended to be exhaustive, but merely an Editor's selection. More information on these and many other points may be explored in more detail elsewhere in this book, or in the *World Travel Guide* and the *World Travel Dictionary*, also published by Columbus Travel Guides.

11 Sept 2001 • The date on which Islamic terrorists hijacked four planes in the USA and destroyed the twin towers of the World Trade Centre in New York and damaged the US Defense Pentagon building in Virginia with the loss of around 3,000 lives. Often referred to as 9/11. For the travel business not least, the scars have been psychological as much as physical and plunged airlines in particular into a sharp decline. On a wider level, the event has served to redefine the nature and focus of US foreign policy.

Adventure travel • Originally, this was a general terms for a type of holiday, such as trekking, white-water rafting or jungle expeditions, which involved a fairly high level of physical exertion and often an element of danger. Increasingly, the term covers a wider field: skiing, diving, cycling and walking holidays are now often referred to in this way.

AIDS • Acquired Immune Deficiency Syndrome, a loss of cellular immunity as a result of viral infection generally through sexual fluids and blood, which leaves the body vulnerable to a wide range of often fatal infections. The first reported case was in December 1980. Estimates as to how many people are, or will be, infected vary greatly, but many experts predict over 40 million worldwide by 2007. The majority of cases are in sub-Saharan Africa.

Bird flu • The common name for avian influenza, a viral disease believed until 1997 not to be transmittable to people. The H5N1 strain of the disease has

been identified as causing human deaths initially in south-east Asia and increasingly elsewhere. The first confirmed avain case in the UK was in April 2006. The World Health Organization has warned of the risk of a global pandemic.

Climate change • The effects of industrial pollution and in particular the burning of fossil fuels has, according to most estimates, caused measurable increases in average global temperatures and sea levels. Travel and tourism, along with many other industries, is now taking some steps to redress these potentially very serious problems. Most remedies are, however, seemingly incompatible with economic growth.

Concorde • The world's first and, to date, only supersonic passenger aircraft. An Anglo-French co-operative venture, it made its maiden flight in March 1969: regular trans-Atlantic services started in May 1976. Only 20 were ever built, though the original plan was for over 300. On 25 July 2000, an Air France Concorde crashed on take-off from Paris with the loss of 113 lives. Services were resumed the following November. British Airways and Air France announced in April 2003 that all Concordes would be withdrawn from service and the last scheduled flight landed at London Heathrow on 24 October 2003.

Continents • There are anything between five and eight of these depending on which source one consults. The six divisions used in this

atlas have been created to make the title easy to use and have no political or other significance.

Countries • As with continents (qv), there is no clear definition as to how many countries there are in the world. Many 'countries' have varying degrees of connection with an independent state which might in some cases amount to practical independence. In other cases, a conflict has created differing views as to the 'country's' status. French Guiana, Gibraltar, Jersey, Guam, Palestine, the Cook Islands, Taiwan, Western Sahara and Bonaire all provide different examples of this ambiguity. For travel purposes the distinction is often unimportant but can lead to confusions with paperwork such as visas. The most important examples are Hong Kong and Macau which, though now part of China, are still regarded as separate destinations by, for example, the World Tourism Organization for statistical purposes.

Cruising • One of the fastest-growing sectors within the travel business, and one of the areas which has shown continued growth throughout the problematic years of the early 21st century. In 1985 there were 2.75 million worldwide cruise passengers: this had risen to 4.5 million in 1990, to 11 million in 2000 and to 14 million in 2005. The industry is developing additional itineraries and introducing new ports of call, particularly in the Indian sub-continent and the Far East.

Eco-tourism • Tourism which respects the environment being visited. (The term is often used in conjunction with the overlapping concepts of 'fairtrade tourism' and 'responsible tourism' (qv) and also other more general terms such as 'ethical tourism' (qv).)

Ethical tourism • The increasingly popular type of, and attitude to, travel which seeks to ensure that tourism development and activity respects the geographical and social environment. This includes involving local communities in

the creation and management of tourism projects, sharing the socio-economic benefits fairly with them, and ensuring that any development makes as much use as possible of sustainable local resources. (The term is often used in conjunction with the overlapping concepts of 'responsible tourism' and 'fairtrade tourism' (qv) and also other terms such as 'ethical tourism' (qv). Such terms are often used interchangeably, but all convey a similar attitude.)

Euro • The common currency of 12 of the members of the European Union, introduced in January 2002 and replacing the previously used local currencies. Other countries, notably the UK, may join in the future.

European Capital of Culture • An initiative, formerly known as the European City of Culture, run by the EU since 1985 to reflect, promote and celebrate Europe's cultural diversity. Until 1999, one city a year was selected, but in the millennium year of 2000 there were nine (Avignon, Bergen, Bologna, Brussels, Cracow, Helsinki, Prague, Reykjavik & Santiago de Compostela). Since then, the cities have been/will be: 2001 – Oporto & Rotterdam; 2002 – Bruges & Salamanca; 2003 – Graz; 2004 – Genoa & Lille; 2005 – Cork; 2006 – Patras; 2007 – Luxembourg & Sibiu; 2008 – Liverpool & Stavanger. The UK's only previous representative was Glasgow in 1990.

European Union expansion • In 1957, there were six founding members of the then-European Economic Community: from mid-2004 the European Union had 25 members and now, for the first time, has a frontier with Russia. Several other countries including Bulgaria, Romania and Turkey are waiting to join.

Fair-trade tourism • Tourism which is developed and operated in partnership with local communities, and which is designed to be at least partly for their social and economic benefit. This will include ensuring a fair remuneration for

Conclusion

Change, renewal and growth appear to be the three words that best sum up the prospects for the travel business. The world is changing fast, and the best companies are adapting to it. Few industries have such a solid record of performance stretching back several decades to help underpin their future. The desire for new destinations and new experiences seems to be insatiable. Public demand for new ethical standards is growing and will shape future supply. The industry has long since shifted away from its traditional commission-driven pattern of package holidays and monopolistic airlines. It is also shifting away from its well-established Europe-North America axis. To a certain extent, every traveller has become their own travel planner. Do any certainties remain?

Quite possibly not. It seems more than likely that entrepreneurial companies and new technology will continue to challenge all our current preconceptions about travel. So – what's next? Space tourism? In fact, it already exists. Denis Tito was the first (in 2001). Others have followed since, and many more plan to boldly go in the future. Low-cost space tourism, booked through the internet? Now there's a thought…

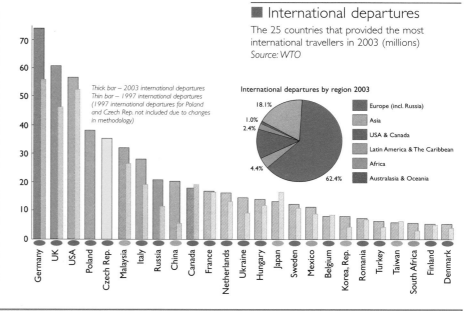

■ International departures

The 25 countries that provided the most international travellers in 2003 (millions)
Source: WTO

Thick bar – 2003 international departures
Thin bar – 1997 international departures
(1997 international departures for Poland and Czech Rep. not included due to changes in methodology)

International departures by region 2003

- Europe (incl. Russia) — 62.4%
- Asia — 18.1%
- USA & Canada — 4.4%
- Latin America & The Caribbean — 2.4%
- Africa — 1.0%
- Australasia & Oceania

---

workers, maximising the level of local (rather than foreign) ownership of the tourism facility, encouraging the use of local suppliers of products and services (such as food and tour guides) and establishing sustainable relations between all parties involved. (The term is often used in conjunction with the overlapping concepts of 'responsible tourism' and 'ecotourism' (qv) and also other terms such as 'ethical tourism' (qv).)

GDP and GNI • In crude terms, GDP (Gross Domestic Product) is the value of the wealth produced by a nation – 'the gross value of all resident producers in the economy' as the part of the World Bank's definition puts it. GNI (Gross National Income) is increasingly used in many publications, including this one. The two measures are broadly comparable: in essence, GNI also includes income derived by residents of the country in question from abroad, such as from external investments.

High-speed rail • Many countries, particularly in Western Europe and Japan, have invested massive sums in dedicated high-speed lines and trains offering city-to-city services at speeds in excess of 200 kph. The network is constantly expanding and major projects are being planned in many countries, including China and the USA. New Maglev (magnetic levititation) trains represent the new generation, and should run at over 550kph. In Europe, the low-cost airlines have provided considerable competition.

Indian Ocean tsunami • The devastating tidal wave resulting from an undersea earthquake near Northern Indonesia on 26 December 2004. Over 200,000 people were killed and 500,000 left homeless, mainly in Thailand, Indonesia, Sri Lanka, India, the Maldives and the coastal regions of East Africa.

Internet • On-line sales and information services have revolutionised the travel business in recent years, and the trend is increasing. There are countless statistics to illustrate this, and the growth in web usage generally. It took radio 38 years and TV 13 years to build an audience of 50 million in the US: the internet

achieved this in three and a half years. The internet had over one billion worldwide users in April 2006.

Iraq war • After years of diplomatic stand-off and unsuccessful UN attempts to locate Iraq's alleged weapons of mass destruction, US-led coalition forces began attacking the country on 20 March 2003. The war itself, and in particular its protracted count-down, caused a slump in the travel industry worldwide, although the relatively quick resolution of the initial phase of the conflict saw a fairly quick recovery in airline bookings. Despite elections in 2005, the long-term future of Iraq and the nature of its government remains uncertain, as does the question as to whether the intervention will have calmed or inflamed the volatile situation in the Middle East.

Long-haul charters • The introduction of medium-sized wide-body aircraft such as the Boeing 767 and Airbus A300 in the 1990s facilitated the growth of package holidays to destinations further afield such as Goa, Sri Lanka and the Maldives. These areas suddenly became very affordable and, as a consequence, have rapidly developed as a result of the arrival of charter flights from Europe. Many local authorities are currently reviewing the desirability of receiving such flights.

Low-cost airlines • The terms 'budget' and 'no-frills' are also often used. The concept began in the USA in 1971 when Southwest Airlines started services between Dallas and San Antonio. Numerous other airlines have since followed suit, including Jet Blue, Ryanair and easyJet. Their low prices and commercial flexibility result from following very precise and efficient business models.

Mega cruise ships • Any ship with a gross registered tonnage of 100,000 is regarded as mega. The first of these arrived in the late 1990s as *Voyager of the Seas* owned by Royal Caribbean Line at GRT 142.000 GRT: it took 21 million man-hours to build and is (so far) the only cruise vessel with its own zip-code (33132-2028). These massive ships of up to 22 decks high have become resorts at

sea opening the cruise market to a much wider audience. On 12 January 2004, Cunard Lines' 150,000 GRT *Queen Mary 2* entered service on the traditional transatlantic scheduled route. RCI's 156,000 GRT *Freedom of the Seas* made its maiden voyage in June 2006.

MICE • 'Meetings, incentives, conferences and exhibitions', which have in recent years become a distinct and increasingly important part of the the global travel business.

Olympic Games • Last held in Athens in August 2004. The next Olympics (the 29th) will be in 2008 in Beijing.

Pets Travel Scheme • Introduced in 2000, this allows cats and dogs to travel between the UK and a number of European and long-haul destinations (though currently not North America) without the need for quarantine on arrival back in the UK. Pets must be micro-chipped, be issued with an appropriate pet passport, and have a valid vet's certificate certifying vaccination against rabies.

Responsible Tourism • The increasingly important principle that guides touristic development and behaviour, particularly in respect of developing countries, with the aim of ensuring that its impact is as positive as possible. Exact definitions vary, but the Cape Town Declaration of 2002 provides possibly the most comprehensive summary. Its key points are that responsible tourism should: minimise negative economic, environmental, and social impacts; involve local people positively and generate economic benefits for them; contribute to the conservation of natural and cultural heritage; offer more rewarding experiences for tourists through more connections with local people and a greater understanding of local cultural, social and environmental issues; and provide access for physically challenged people. (The term is often used in conjunction with the overlapping concepts of 'fairtrade tourism' and 'eco-tourism' (qv) and also other more general terms such as 'ethical tourism'(qv).)

SARS • Severe Acute Respiratory Syndrome, an air-borne virus which causes flu-like symptoms and sometimes

death. The first reported case was in Hanoi in February 2003 and it rapidly spread to other parts of Asia, and to Canada, causing havoc in the travel industry for several months.

Set Jetter • A person who makes holiday destination decisions based wholly or partly on being able to visit the sets or locations of films or novels. By some estimates, up to one in four outbound travellers from the UK could be so described.

Travel statistics • There are a multitude of these available. organisations, cities, states, countries and regions all produce their own, for a variety of purposes; while the most authoritative global figures are compiled by the World Tourism Organization (WTO or, more formally, UNWTO to distinguish it from the Would Trade Organization), which is based in Madrid. Statistics concerning movement of people and money as a result of travel can most conveniently be divided into inbound and outbound, of which the former are generally more complete and reliable. Because of the time spent collating and analysing them, many statistics are not published for months or even years after the period to which they refer and historical data is often revised retrospectively. Comparisons between figures produced by different organisations may be misleading due to possible different methodologies used or time periods covered.

USSR • The Union of Soviet Socialist Republics (also known as the Soviet Union). Dominated by Russia, it came into being in 1922 in the aftermath of the Russian Revolution and Civil War. During the early 1990s it fragmented into 15 independent states in Eastern Europe and Central Asia. All of the former states apart from the three Baltic republics formed the Commonwealth of Independent States in 1991 which still retains some co-ordinating powers.

World Cups • Many sports, notably rugby, cricket and football, organise regular international tournaments, usually every four years. Flights and accommodation for such events may need to be booked months or even years in advance.

The listings above refer to a selection of related themes.
For more information, see the Contents (2-5).

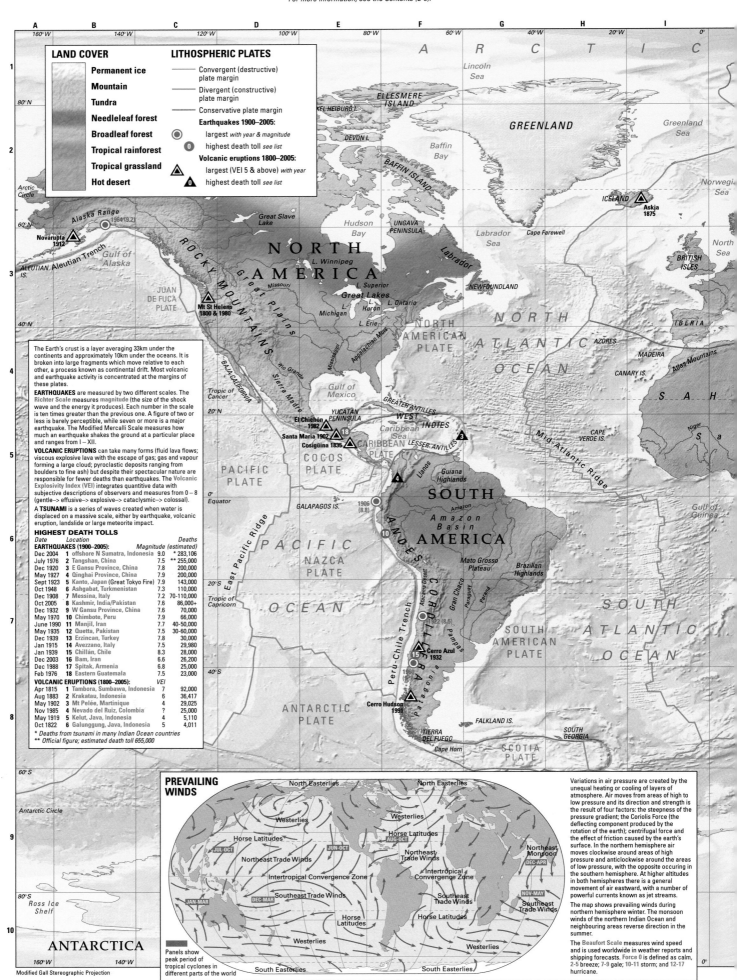

LAND COVER

- Permanent ice
- Mountain
- Tundra
- Needleleaf forest
- Broadleaf forest
- Tropical rainforest
- Tropical grassland
- Hot desert

LITHOSPHERIC PLATES

—— Convergent (destructive) plate margin
—— Divergent (constructive) plate margin
—— Conservative plate margin

Earthquakes 1900–2005:
◎ largest *with year & magnitude*
⓪ highest death toll *see list*

Volcanic eruptions 1800–2005:
▲ largest (VEI 5 & above) *with year*
▲ highest death toll *see list*

The Earth's crust is a layer averaging 33km under the continents and approximately 10km under the oceans. It is broken into large fragments which move relative to each other, a process known as continental drift. Most volcanic and earthquake activity is concentrated at the margins of these plates.

EARTHQUAKES are measured by two different scales. The Richter Scale measures magnitude (the size of the shock wave and the energy it produces). Each number in the scale is ten times greater than the previous one. A figure of two or less is barely perceptible, while seven or more is a major earthquake. The Modified Mercalli Scale measures how much an earthquake shakes the ground at a particular place and ranges from I – XII.

VOLCANIC ERUPTIONS can take many forms (fluid lava flows; viscous explosive lava with the escape of gas; gas and vapour forming a large cloud; pyroclastic deposits ranging from boulders to fine ash) but despite their spectacular nature are responsible for fewer deaths than earthquakes. The Volcanic Explosivity Index (VEI) integrates quantitive data with subjective descriptions of observers and measures from 0 – 8 (gentle→ effusive→ explosive→ cataclysmic→ colossal).

A **TSUNAMI** is a series of waves created when water is displaced on a massive scale, either by earthquake, volcanic eruption, landslide or large meteorite impact.

HIGHEST DEATH TOLLS

EARTHQUAKES (1900–2005):

Date		Location	Magnitude	Deaths (estimated)
Dec 2004	1	offshore N Sumatra, Indonesia	9.0	* 283,106
July 1976	2	Tangshan, China	7.5	** 255,000
Dec 1920	3	E Gansu Province, China	7.8	200,000
May 1927	4	Qinghai Province, China	7.9	200,000
Sept 1923	5	Kanto, Japan (Great Tokyo Fire)	7.9	143,000
Oct 1948	6	Ashgabat, Turkmenistan	7.3	110,000
Dec 1908	7	Messina, Italy	7.2	70-110,000
Oct 2005	8	Kashmir, India/Pakistan	7.6	86,000+
Dec 1932	9	W Gansu Province, China	7.6	70,000
May 1970	10	Chimbote, Peru	7.9	66,000
June 1990	11	Manjil, Iran	7.7	40-50,000
May 1935	12	Quetta, Pakistan	7.5	30-60,000
Dec 1939	13	Erzincan, Turkey	7.8	30,000
Jan 1915	14	Avezzano, Italy	7.5	29,980
Jan 1939	15	Chillán, Chile	8.3	28,000
Dec 2003	16	Bam, Iran	6.6	26,200
Dec 1988	17	Spitak, Armenia	6.8	25,000
Feb 1976	18	Eastern Guatemala	7.5	23,000

VOLCANIC ERUPTIONS (1800–2005):

Date		Location	VEI	Deaths
Apr 1815	1	Tambora, Sumbawa, Indonesia	7	92,000
Aug 1883	2	Krakatau, Indonesia	6	36,417
May 1902	3	Mt Pelée, Martinique	4	29,025
Nov 1985	4	Nevado del Ruiz, Colombia	?	25,000
May 1919	5	Kelut, Java, Indonesia	4	5,110
Oct 1822	6	Galunggung, Java, Indonesia	5	4,011

* Deaths from tsunami in many Indian Ocean countries
** Official figure; estimated death toll 655,000

PREVAILING WINDS

Panels show peak period of tropical cyclones in different parts of the world

North Easterlies
Westerlies
Horse Latitudes
Northeast Trade Winds
Intertropical Convergence Zone
Southeast Trade Winds
Horse Latitudes
Westerlies
South Easterlies
Northeast Monsoon
Southeast Trade Winds

JUL-OCT · JUN-OCT · AUG-OCT · DEC-APR · JAN-MAR · DEC-MAR · NOV-MAY

Variations in air pressure are created by the unequal heating or cooling of layers of atmosphere. Air moves from areas of high to low pressure and its direction and strength is the result of four factors: the steepness of the pressure gradient; the Coriolis Force (the deflecting component produced by the rotation of the earth); centrifugal force and the effect of friction caused by the earth's surface. In the northern hemisphere air moves clockwise around areas of high pressure and anticlockwise around the areas of low pressure, with the opposite occuring in the southern hemisphere. At higher altitudes in both hemispheres there is a general movement of air eastward, with a number of powerful currents known as jet streams.

The map shows prevailing winds during northern hemisphere winter. The monsoon winds of the northern Indian Ocean and neighbouring areas reverse direction in the summer.

The Beaufort Scale measures wind speed and is used worldwide in weather reports and shipping forecasts. Force 0 is defined as calm, 2-5 breeze; 7-9 gale; 10-11 storm; and 12-17 hurricane.

Modified Gall Stereographic Projection

The listings above refer to a selection of related themes. For more information, see the Contents (2-5).

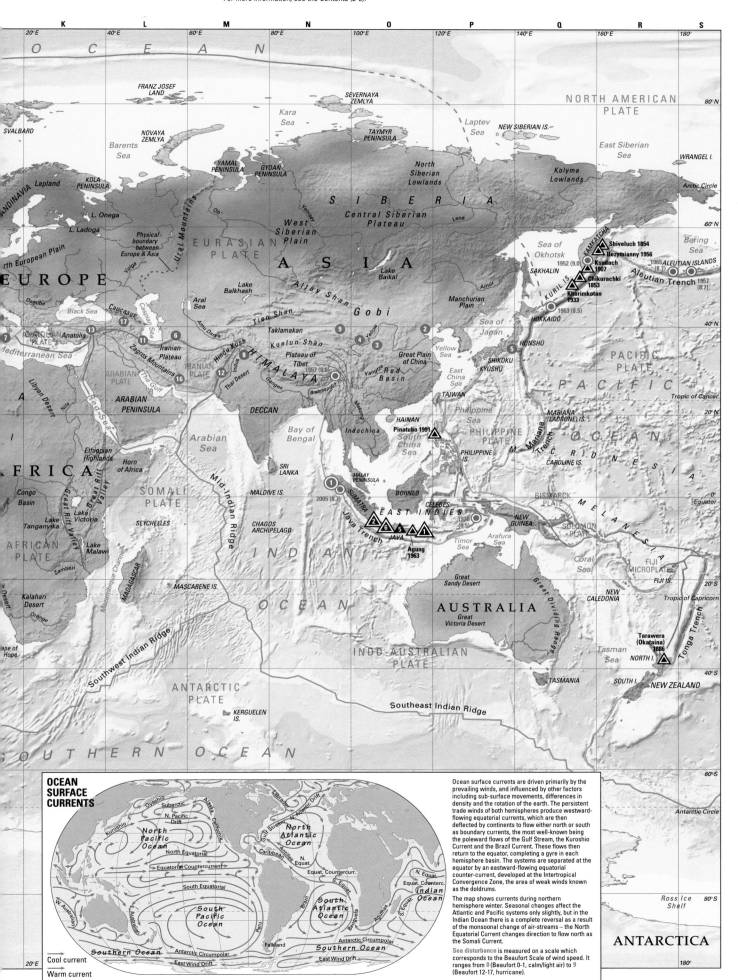

OCEAN SURFACE CURRENTS

Ocean surface currents are driven primarily by the prevailing winds, and influenced by other factors including sub-surface movements, differences in density and the rotation of the earth. The persistent trade winds of both hemispheres produce westward-flowing equatorial currents, which are then deflected by continents to flow either north or south as boundary currents, the most well-known being the poleward flows of the Gulf Stream, the Kuroshio Current and the Brazil Current. These flows then return to the equator, completing a gyre in each hemisphere basin. The systems are separated at the equator by an eastward-flowing equatorial counter-current, developed at the Intertropical Convergence Zone, the area of weak winds known as the doldrums.

The map shows currents during northern hemisphere winter. Seasonal changes affect the Atlantic and Pacific systems only slightly, but in the Indian Ocean there is a complete reversal as a result of the monsoonal change of air-streams – the North Equatorial Current changes direction to flow north as the Somali Current.

Sea disturbance is measured on a scale which corresponds to the Beaufort Scale of wind speed. It ranges from 0 (Beaufort 0-1, calm/light air) to 9 (Beaufort 12-17, hurricane).

Cool current
Warm current

▶ *See also...* World Physical (26-27); City Nicknames (106-107); Countries A-Z (108-116)

The listings above refer to a selection of related themes.
For more information, see the Contents (2-5).

ALB.   - ALBANIA
AUS.   - AUSTRIA
AZ.   - AZERBAIJAN
B.-H. - BOSNIA-HERZEGOVINA
BELG. - BELGIUM
CRO.   - CROATIA
HUNG. - HUNGARY
LIE.   - LIECHTENSTEIN
LUX.   - LUXEMBOURG
MAC.   - FORMER YUGOSLAV REPUBLIC OF MACEDONIA
MO.   - MONTENEGRO
NETH. - THE NETHERLANDS
PAL.   - PALESTINE NATIONAL AUTHORITY REGION
         (West Bank & Gaza)
S.   - SAN MARINO
SLOV. - SLOVENIA
SWITZ. - SWITZERLAND
UAE   - UNITED ARAB EMIRATES
V.   - VATICAN CITY
SE.   - SERBIA MONTENEGRO

ARCTIC C

ELLESMERE ISLAND

AXEL HEIBURG I.

PARRY IS

DEVON I.

BANKS I.

VICTORIA I.

BAFFIN ISLAND

Greenland
(Denmark)

Jan Mayen
(Nor.)

Arctic Circle

ICELAND

Nuuk

Reykjavik

Faroe is.
(Den.)

Alaska
(US)

Anchorage

60° N

C A N A D A

Edmonton

Calgary

Vancouver

Winnipeg

Seattle

Québec

Montreal

Ottawa

Toronto

Detroit

Chicago

Halifax

Boston

New York

Philadelphia

Washington DC

St-Pierre
et Miquelon
(Fr.)

UNITED
KINGDOM

Dublin

IRELAND

London

Amsterdam

BELG.

Brussels

Paris

Be

FRANCE

MONACO

ANDORRA

Channel Is.

40° N

UNITED STATES
OF AMERICA

Denver

San Francisco

Los Angeles

San Diego

Phoenix

Dallas

Houston

New Orleans

Monterrey

Guadalajara

MEXICO

Gulf of
Mexico

Miami

Nassau

BAHAMAS

Havana

CUBA

Bermuda
(UK)

NORTH
ATLANTIC
OCEAN

Azores
(Port.)

PORTUGAL

Lisbon

Madrid

SPAIN

Gibraltar (UK)

Ceuta (Sp.)

Algiers

Rabat

MOROCCO

Melilla (Sp.)

Madeira
(Port.)

Casablanca

Canary Is.
(Sp.)

Laâyoune

WESTERN
SAHARA

ALGERIA

20° N

Hawaii
(US)

Tropic of Cancer

Mexico City

Belmopan

BELIZE

Kingston

JAMAICA

HAITI

Turks &
Caicos Is.
(UK)

Cayman Is.
(UK)

DOMINICAN
REPUBLIC

Puerto
Rico (US)

British
Virgin Is. (UK)

Virgin Is. (US)

Anguilla (UK)

St Maarten (Neths.) & St-Martin (Fr.)

St-Barthélemy (Fr.)

ANTIGUA & BARBUDA

Guadeloupe (Fr.)

DOMINICA

Martinique (Fr.)

ST LUCIA

BARBADOS

ST VINCENT & THE GRENADINES

GRENADA

TRINIDAD & TOBAGO

Guatemala City

GUATEMALA

HONDURAS

Tegucigalpa

San Salvador

EL SALVADOR

Managua

NICARAGUA

Aruba (Neth.)

Netherlands
Antilles

ST KITTS
& NEVIS

Montserrat
(UK)

Caribbean
Sea

San José

COSTA
RICA

PANAMA

Panama City

Caracas

VENEZUELA

Georgetown

Paramaribo

Cayenne

French
Guiana (Fr.)

GUYANA

SURINAM

Medellín

Bogotá

COLOMBIA

São Pedro e São Paulo
(Brazil)

NOUAKCHOTT

MAURITANIA

MALI

NI

CAPE VERDE

Dakar

SENEGAL

Banjul

GAMBIA

Bissau

GUINEA-BISSAU

Conakry

GUINEA

Freetown

SIERRA LEONE

Monrovia

LIBERIA

CÔTE
D'IVOIRE

BURKINA

Bamako

Ouagadougou

Nian

Abu

Porte

TOGO

Accra

Yamoussoukro

Mal

EQUATORIAL G

São Tomé

SÃO TOM
E PRÍNCIP

Libre

PACIFIC

KIRIBATI

INTERNATIONAL DATE LINE

0° Equator

OCEAN

Galápagos Is.
(Ec.)

ECUADOR

Quito

Lima

PERU

B R A Z I L

Manaus

Belém

Fortaleza

Fernando de Noronha
(Brazil)

Recife

Salvador

Brasília

Belo Horizonte

Ascension
(UK)

Tokelau
(NZ)

American
Samoa
(US)

Cook
Islands
(NZ)

Niue
(NZ)

French Polynesia
(Fr.)

20° S

Tropic of Capricorn

La Paz

BOLIVIA

Sucre

PARAGUAY

Asunción

Rio de Janeiro

São Paulo

Trindade e
Martin Vaz
(Brazil)

SOUTH
ATLANTIC
OCEAN

St Helena
(UK)

Pitcairn Is.
(UK)

Easter I.
(Chile)

Córdoba

Porto Alegre

URUGUAY

Juan
Fernández Is.
(Chile)

Santiago

CHILE

ARGENTINA

Buenos
Aires

Montevideo

Tristan da Cunha
(UK)

Gough I.
(UK)

Falkland Is.
(UK)

South Georgia
(UK)

8 ▶

South Sandwich Is.
(UK)

Antarctic Circle

9 ▶

ALEXANDER I.

ANTARCTIC
PENINSULA

BERKNER I.

10 ▶

A N T A R C T I C A

■ Capital city
○ Other city
   For reasons of space, capital cities for some
   smaller countries have not been shown here: see
   the respective country maps or the Countries A-Z
   section on pages 108-116.
   For more information on the symbols used on
   other political and physical maps, see the Key to
   Topographic Maps on page 5.

Modified Gall Stereographic Projection

The listings above refer to a selection of related themes.
For more information, see the Contents (2-5).

▶ See also... Europe Climate (45); Regional Climate Terms (104)

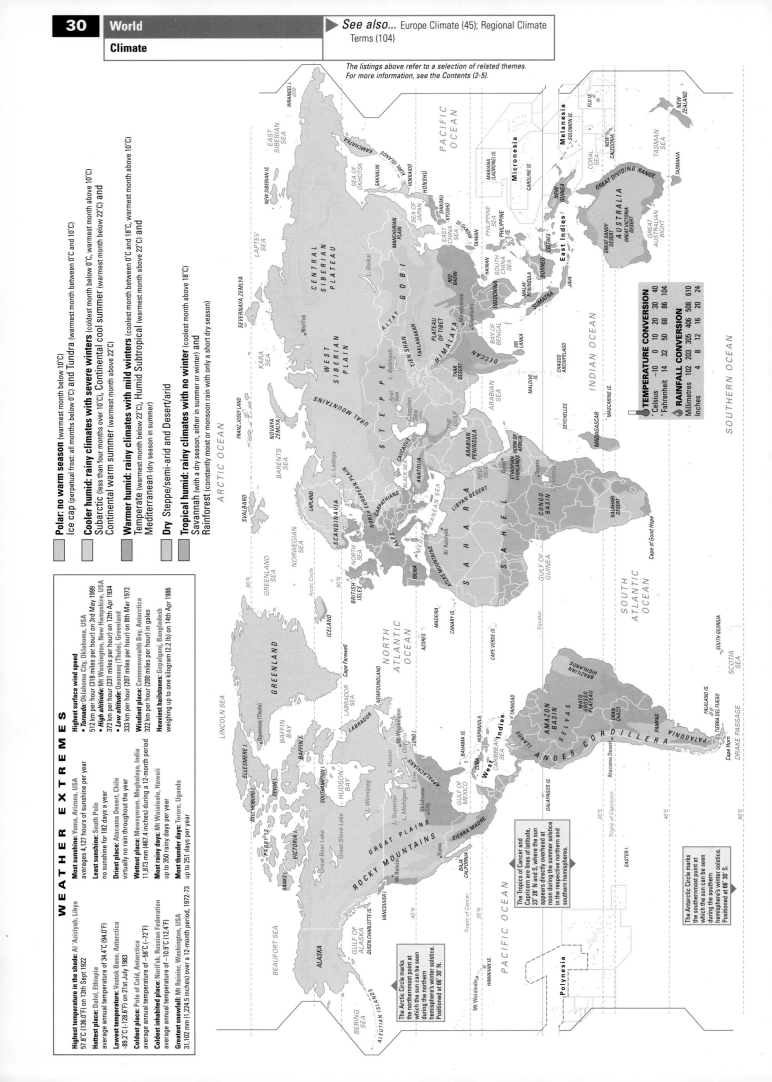

The listings above refer to a selection of related themes. For more information, see the Contents (2-5).

Polar: no warm season (warmest month below 10°C)
Ice cap (perpetual frost: all months below 0°C) and Tundra (warmest month between 0°C and 10°C)

Cooler humid: rainy climates with severe winters (coldest month below 0°C, warmest month above 10°C)
Subarctic (less than four months over 10°C), Continental cool summer (warmest month below 22°C) and Continental warm summer (warmest month above 22°C)

Warmer humid: rainy climates with mild winters (coolest month between 0°C and 18°C, warmest month above 10°C)
Temperate (warmest month below 22°C), Humid Subtropical (warmest month above 22°C) and Mediterranean (dry season in summer)

Dry Steppe/semi-arid and Desert/arid

Tropical humid: rainy climates with no winter (coolest month above 18°C)
Savannah (with a dry season, either in summer or winter) and Rainforest (constantly moist or monsoon rain with only a short dry season)

TEMPERATURE CONVERSION
°Celsius	-10	0	10	20	30	40
°Fahrenheit	14	32	50	68	86	104

RAINFALL CONVERSION
Millimetres	102	203	305	406	508	610
Inches	4	8	12	16	20	24

WEATHER EXTREMES

Highest temperature in the shade: Al 'Aziziyah, Libya
57.8°C (136.0°F) on 13th Sept 1922

Hottest place: Dalol, Ethiopia
average annual temperature of 34.4°C (94.0°F)

Lowest temperature: Vostok Base, Antarctica
-89.2°C (-128.6°F) on 21st July 1983

Coldest place: Pole of Cold, Antarctica
average annual temperature of -58°C (-72°F)

Coldest inhabited place: Noril'sk, Russian Federation
average annual temperature of -10.9°C (12.4°F)

Greatest snowfall: Mt Rainier, Washington, USA
31,102 mm (1,224.5 inches) over a 12-month period, 1972-73

Most sunshine: Yuma, Arizona, USA
averages 4,127 hours of sunshine per year

Least sunshine: South Pole
no sunshine for 182 days a year

Driest place: Atacama Desert, Chile
virtually no rain throughout the year

Wettest place: Mawsynram, Meghalaya, India
11,873 mm (467.4 inches) during a 12-month period

Most rainy days: Mt Waialeale, Hawaii
up to 350 rainy days per year

Most thunder days: Tororo, Uganda
up to 251 days per year

Highest surface wind speed
• **Tornado:** Oklahoma City, Oklahoma, USA
512 km per hour (318 miles per hour) on 3rd May 1999
• **High altitude:** Mt Washington, New Hampshire, USA
372 km per hour (231 miles per hour) on 12th Apr 1934
• **Low altitude:** Qaanaaq (Thule), Greenland
333 km per hour (207 miles per hour) on 8th Mar 1972

Windiest place: Commonwealth Bay, Antarctica
322 km per hour (200 miles per hour) in gales

Heaviest hailstones: Gopalganj, Bangladesh
weighing up to one kilogram (2.2 lb) on 14th Apr 1986

The Arctic Circle marks the northernmost point at which the sun can be seen during the northern hemisphere's winter solstice. Positioned at 66° 30' N.

The Tropics of Cancer and Capricorn are lines of latitude, 23° 28' N and S, where the sun appears directly overhead at noon during the summer solstice in the respective northern and southern hemispheres.

The Antarctic Circle marks the southernmost point at which the sun can be seen during the southern hemisphere's winter solstice. Positioned at 66° 30' S.

The listings above refer to a selection of related themes.
For more information, see the Contents (2-5).

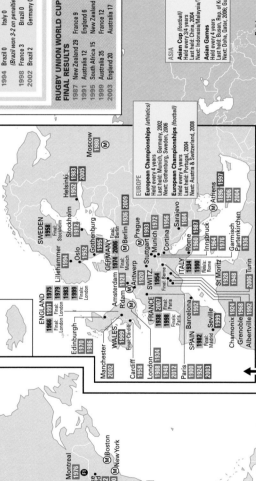

MAJOR INTERNATIONAL SPORTING EVENTS

■ SUMMER OLYMPICS
The first modern Olympic Games, founded by Frenchman Baron de Coubertin, were held at Athens in 1896. They are held every four years, and a Paralympic Games is held in conjunction with the main Games. An extra Olympics held in 1906 celebrated the tenth anniversary of the 1896 Games. The next Games, the 29th Olympiad, will be held in Beijing in 2008 and the 2012 Games will be in London.

■ WINTER OLYMPICS
The first separate Winter Games took place in 1924 at Chamonix, France. The Games originally took place in the same year as the Summer Games, but are now held in between. The next Winter Olympics are due to be held in Vancouver in 2010.

■ COMMONWEALTH GAMES
Originally the British Empire Games, first held in 1930 at Hamilton, Ontario. Renamed the British Empire and Commonwealth Games in 1954, the British Empire and Commonwealth Games in 1970 and the Commonwealth Games in 1978. Held every four years, the next Games are due to be held in in New Delhi in 2010.

■ WORLD ATHLETICS CHAMPIONSHIPS
The World Athletics Championships were first held in Helsinki in 1983, and at four-year intervals until 1991. They are now held every two years. The next Championships are due to be held in Osaka in 2007 and Berlin in 2009.

■ FOOTBALL WORLD CUP
Association Football's premier event. Brazil kept the Jules Rimet Trophy after winning it for the third time in 1970. The teams now compete for the FIFA World Cup. Held every four years, the next competition is due to be hosted by South Africa in 2010.

■ CRICKET WORLD CUP
The venue of the first Cricket World Cup in 1975 was England. Played every three to five years, it was not until 1987 that the competition was held outside England. The next World Cup is due to be held in the West Indies in 2007.

■ RUGBY UNION WORLD CUP
The first Rugby Union World Cup was held in 1987 and is now held every four years, with the next competition in France in 2007.

FOOTBALL WORLD CUP FINAL RESULTS

1930	Uruguay 4	Argentina 2
1934	Italy 2	Czechoslovakia 1
1938	Italy 4	Hungary 2
1950	Uruguay 2	Brazil 1
1954	FR Germany 3	Hungary 2
1958	Brazil 5	Sweden 2
1962	Brazil 3	Czechoslovakia 1
1966	England 4	FR Germany 2
1970	Brazil 4	Italy 1
1974	FR Germany 2	Netherlands 1
1978	Argentina 3	Netherlands 1
1982	Italy 3	FR Germany 1
1986	Argentina 3	FR Germany 2
1990	FR Germany 1	Argentina 0
1994	Brazil 0	Italy 0
	(Brazil won 3-2 on penalties)	
1998	France 3	Brazil 0
2002	Brazil 2	Germany 0

RUGBY UNION WORLD CUP FINAL RESULTS

1987	New Zealand 29	France 9
1991	Australia 12	England 6
1995	South Africa 15	New Zealand 12
1999	Australia 35	France 12
2003	England 20	Australia 17

FIFA WORLD RANKINGS

	May, 2003	May, 2004	May, 2005	May, 2006
1	Brazil	Brazil	Brazil	Brazil
2	France (2=)	France	Czech Rep.	Czech Rep.
3	Spain (2=)	Spain	Argentina	Netherlands
4	Argentina	Netherlands	Netherlands	Mexico
5	Germany	Germany	France	USA
6	Netherlands	Mexico	Netherlands	Spain
7	England	England	England	Portugal
8	Turkey	USA	Spain	France
9	Mexico	Portugal	Portugal	Argentina
10	USA (10=)	Czech Rep.	Italy	England
11	Denmk. (10=)	Italy	USA	Denmark
12	Czech Rep.	Cameroon (12=)	Greece	Italy
13	Italy	Spain	Sweden	Cameroon
14	Portugal	Denmark	Denmark	Italy
15	Ireland	England (12=)	Ireland	Sweden
16	Costa Rica	Nigeria	Ireland	Egypt
17	Cameroon	Belgium	Japan	Germany
18	Paraguay	Iran	Uruguay	Greece
19	Sweden	Rep. of Korea (19=)	Iran	
		Denmark (19=)	Japan	
			Portugal	

CRICKET WORLD CUP FINAL RESULTS
1975 West Indies (291-8) beat Australia (274) by 17 runs
1979 West Indies (286-9) beat England (194) by 92 runs
1983 India (183) beat West Indies (140) by 43 runs
1987 Australia (253-5) beat England (246-8) by 7 runs
1992 Pakistan (249-6) beat England (227) by 22 runs
1996 Sri Lanka (245-3) beat Australia (241) by 7 wickets
1999 Australia (133-2) beat Pakistan (132) by 8 wickets
2003 Australia (359-2) beat India (234) by 125 runs

SOME OTHER SPORTS: ANNUAL EVENTS

CYCLING
Major tours:
Giro d'Italia (Tour of Italy);
Tour de France;
Tour DuPont, USA;
Vuelta d'España (Tour of Spain).
Classics:
Belgium:
Flèche Wallonne;
Liège-Bastogne-Liège;
Tour of Flanders.
France:
Grand Prix des Nations;
Paris-Nice;
Paris-Roubaix.
Italy:
Milan-San Remo;
Tour of Lombardy.
Paris-Brussels.

HORSE RACING
English Classics:
1,000 & 2,000 Guineas,
Newmarket;
St Leger, Doncaster;
Derby & Oaks, Epsom.
Triple Crown, USA:
Belmont Stakes, NY;
Kentucky Derby, Louisville;
Preakness Stakes,
Baltimore.
Other major races:
Cheltenham Gold Cup, UK;
Dubai World Cup;
Grand National, Aintree,
UK;
Irish Derby, The Curragh;
Japan Cup, Tokyo;
Melbourne Cup, Australia;
Prix de l'Arc de Triomphe,

Paris, France;
Royal Ascot, UK.

GOLF
Majors:
British Open; US Open;
US Masters; US PGA
Championship.
Principal international tournament:
Ryder Cup (every 2 yrs).

MOTOR RACING
Circuits which have held
a Formula One race since
1990 are marked ①.
Other major races:
Indianapolis 500, USA;
Le Mans 24-hour, France.
Major rallies:
Lombard RAC, UK;

Monte Carlo;
Safari Rally, Kenya.

MARATHON
Major marathons Ⓜ:
Athens, Berlin, Boston,
Chicago, London, Moscow,
NY, Prague, Rotterdam.

TENNIS
Grand Slam:
Australian Open,
Melbourne;
French Open, Roland
Garros, Paris;
US Open, Flushing
Meadow, New York;
Wimbledon, UK.
Principal international tournament:
Davis Cup.

ASIA
Asian Cup *(football)*
Held every 3/4 years
Last held: China, 2004
Next: Indonesia/Malaysia/Thailand/Vietnam, 2007
Asian Games
Held every 4 years
Last held: Busan, Rep. of Korea, 2002
Next: Doha, Qatar, 2006; Guangzhou, China, 2010

WORLDWIDE
Pan-Arab Games
Last held: Algeria, 2004
Next: Libya, 2007
Universiade
(World University Games)
Held every 2 years
Last held: İzmir, Turkey, 2005
Next: Bangkok, Thailand, 2007

EUROPE
European Championships *(athletics)*
Held every 4 years
Last held: Munich, Germany, 2002
Next: Gothenburg, Sweden, 2006
European Championships *(football)*
Held every 4 years
Last held: Portugal, 2004
Next: Austria & Switzerland, 2008

AFRICA
African Cup of Nations
(football)
Held every 2 years
Last held: Egypt, 2006
Next: Ghana, 2008
All-Africa Games
Held every 4 years
Last held: Abuja, Nigeria, 2003
Next: Algiers, Algeria, 2007

AMERICAS
Copa America *(football)*
Held every 2/3 years
Last held: Peru, 2004
Next: Venezuela, 2007
Pan-American Games
Held every 4 years
Last held: Santo Domingo,
Dominican Rep., 2003
Next: Rio de Janeiro,
Brazil, 2007

Map location markers (selection):

Auckland 1950 1990; Christchurch 1974
Brisbane 1982; Sydney 2000 1938 (Final: Sydney); Melbourne 1956 2006 (Final: Melbourne) — **AUSTRALIA & NEW ZEALAND** 1987 1992 (Final: Auckland); Perth 1962; Adelaide — **AUSTRALIA** 2003 (Final: Sydney)

Sapporo 1972; Nagano 1998; Tokyo 1964 1991; Osaka 2007; Suzuka — **JAPAN & REP. OF KOREA** 2002 (Final: Yokohama, Japan)
Seoul 1988; Beijing 2008; Shanghai
Kuala Lumpur 1998; Sepang
Delhi 2010 — **INDIA & PAKISTAN** 1987 (Final: Calcutta, India); **INDIA, PAKISTAN & SRI LANKA** 1996 (Final: Lahore, Pakistan)
Bahrain
Kyalami, Johannesburg — **SOUTH AFRICA** 1995 (Final: Johannesburg) 2003 2010 (Final: Johannesburg)

Moscow 1980
Helsinki 1952 1983 2005 (Final: Stockholm); Stockholm 1912 1958 (Final: Stockholm); **SWEDEN** 1958; Gothenburg 1995
Oslo 1952; Lillehammer 1994
Berlin 1936 2009; Prague; **GERMANY** 1974 2006 (Final: Berlin); Stuttgart 1993; Munich 1972; Cortina 1956; Garmisch-Partenkirchen 1936
Amsterdam 1928; R'dam; Antwerp 1920; Sarajevo 1984; Innsbruck 1964 1976; Athens 1896 1906 2004; Rome 1960 1987 (Final: Rome); **ITALY** 1934 1990 (Final: Rome); St Moritz 1928 1948; Turin 2006; Monza, Italy
ENGLAND 1966 (Final: London) 1908 1948 2012 (Final: London); London 1908 1948 2012; Edinburgh 1970 1986; **FRANCE** 1938 1998 (Final: Paris); Paris 1900 1924 2003; **WALES** 1999 (Final: Cardiff); Cardiff 1958; Manchester 2002; Barcelona 1992; Berne (Final: Berne); Seville 1999 (Final: Madrid); **SPAIN** 1982 (Final: Madrid); Chamonix 1924; Grenoble 1968; Albertville 1992

Vancouver 1954 2010; Victoria 1994; Squaw Valley 1960; Los Angeles 1932 1984; Salt Lake City 2002; Phoenix; Edmonton 1978 2001; Calgary 1988; Montreal 1976; Hamilton 1930; Lake Placid 1932 1980; Indianapolis; Chicago; St Louis 1904; Atlanta 1996; Boston; New York; Kingston 1966; **UNITED STATES** 1994 (Final: Los Angeles); **MEXICO** 1970 1986 (Final: Mexico City); Mexico City 1968; **WEST INDIES** 2007

BRAZIL 1950 (Final: Rio de Janeiro); Interlagos, São Paulo; **URUGUAY** 1930 (Final: Montevideo); Buenos Aires; **ARGENTINA** 1978 (Final: Buenos Aires); **CHILE** 1962 (Final: Santiago)

Ⓕ A1 Ring, Spielberg, Austria
Ⓕ Spa-Francorchamps, Belgium
Ⓕ Le Castellet, France
Ⓕ Magny Cours, France
Ⓕ Nürburgring, Germany
Ⓕ Hockenheim, Germany
Ⓕ Budapest, Hungary
Ⓕ Imola, Italy
Ⓕ Monza, Italy
Ⓕ Monte Carlo, Monaco
Ⓕ Estoril, Portugal
Ⓕ Barcelona, Spain
Ⓕ Jerez de la Frontera, Spain
Ⓕ Istanbul, Turkey
Ⓕ Donington Park, UK
Ⓕ Silverstone, UK

See also... World Flight Times (39); Russian Republics (99)

The listings above refer to a selection of related themes. For more information, see the Contents (2-5).

This table provides time differences compared to the Universal Time Co-ordinate (UTC), now the generally accepted term for Greenwich Mean Time (GMT). Time differences , in hours and (sometimes) minutes, are coloured by whether the 'normal' (non Daylight Saving) time in the main part of the country is ahead (red) or behind (blue) UTC. Countries that use UTC are in green.

Several countries span more than one time zone. In some cases (such as the USA) these zones have names which are widely understood. In others (such as Russia) a list of the main cities within each zone has been considered more useful. The names used to describe these zones here do not necessarily follow any official term, even where one exists. Countries may change their time arrangements without reference to any international body, although alterations usually only affect Daylight Saving Time (see below) rather than the 'normal' time. One exception to this was in 2000 when part of Kiribati moved its time forward to UTC+14 in order to be the first place on earth to see in the new millennium.

Daylight Saving Time (DST) was first introduced in some European countries during the First World War, but the idea did not become firmly or widely accepted until 1960s. Today it is used in some or all of about 70 states, generally outside the tropics. Clocks are advanced by one hour in spring and put back one hour in autumn. While many countries change their clocks on predictable days from year to year, others do not. There is no universal agreement on the subject and countries, or regions within them, may make any arrangements they see fit, often at short notice. Some countries, most notably the USA, have extendied the period of DST as an energy-saving measure, and others may follow suit . All information may thus be subject to change.

The dates between which DST is effective are shown in the 'DST change' column. For the reasons described above, these may alter from year to year. The letters M, A, S, O and N refer to March, April, September, October and November. The abbreviations Su, Th, etc refer to the day of the week. The initial number (or L, for last) refers to the incidence of that day in the month. Thus LSuM-LSuO (by far the most common period, and one which applies throughout Europe) means the Last Sunday in March to the Last Sunday in October. In some cases, particularly countries in the Middle East which use different calendars, dates cannot accurately be predicted and so more general ranges have been given. Sometimes DST is not observed throughout all of the area in question. The more important of these are referred to in this column.

For reasons of space, information has not been included on several minor dependencies and overseas territories .

Country	Time	(DST time)	DST change
Afghanistan	+4.30		
Albania	+1	(+2)	LSuM-LSuO
Algeria	+1		
American Samoa	-11		
Andorra	+1	(+2)	LSuM-LSuO
Angola	+1		
Anguilla	-4		
Antigua & Barbuda	-4		
Argentina	-3		
Armenia	+4	(+5)	LSuM-LSuO
Aruba	-4		
Australia – *Western*	+8		
– *Central*	+9.30	(+10.30)	LSuO-LSuM (SA)
– *Eastern*	+10	(+11)	1SuO-LSaM *(not QL)*
Austria	+1	(+2)	LSuM-LSuO
Azerbaijan	+4	(+5)	LSuM-LSuO
Bahamas	-5	(-4)	LSuM-LSuO
Bahrain	+3		
Bangladesh	+6		
Barbados	-4		
Belarus	+2	(+3)	LSuM-LSuO
Belgium	+1	(+2)	LSuM-LSuO
Belize	-6		
Benin	+1		
Bermuda	-4	(-3)	1SuA-LSuO
Bhutan	+6		
Bolivia	-4		
Bonaire	-4		
Bosnia-Herzegovina	+1	(+2)	LSuM-LSuO
Botswana	+2		
Brazil – *Western*	-5		
– *Central*	-4	(-3)	3SuO-3SaF
– *Eastern*	-3	(-2)	3SuO-3SaF
– *Fernando de Noronha*	-2		
British Virgin Islands	-4		
Bulgaria	+2	(+3)	LSuM-LSuO
Burkina	UTC		
Burundi	+2		
Cambodia	+7		
Cameroon	+1		
Canada – *Newfoundland*	-3.30	(-2.30)	1SuA-LSuO
– *Atlantic*	-4	(-3)	1SuA-LSuO
– *Eastern*	-5	(-4)	1SuA-LSuO
– *Central*	-6	(-5)	1SuA-LSuO *(not SK)*
– *Mountain*	-7	(-6)	1SuA-LSuO
– *Pacific*	-8	(-7)	1SuA-LSuO
Cape Verde	-1		
Cayman Islands	-5		
Central African Republic	+1		
Chad	+1		
Channel Islands	UTC	(+1)	LSuM-LSuO
Chile – *incl. Juan Fernandez*	-4	(-3)	2SuO-2SaM
– *Easter Island*	-6	(-5)	2SuO-2SaM
China – *incl. HK & Macau*	+8		
Colombia	-5		
Comoros	+3		
Congo (DR) – *Western*	+1		
– *Eastern*	+2		
Congo, Republic	+1		
Cook Islands	-10		
Costa Rica	-6		
Côte d'Ivoire	UTC		
Cuba	-5	(-4)	LSuM-LSuO
Curaçao	-4		
Cyprus	+2	(+3)	LSuM-LSuO
Czech Republic	+1	(+2)	LSuM-LSuO
Denmark – *Mainland*	+1	(+2)	LSuM-LSuO
– *Faroes*	UTC	(+1)	LSuM-LSuO
Djibouti	+3		
Dominica	-4		
Dominican Republic	-4		
East Timor	+9		
Ecuador – *Mainland*	-5		
– *Galapagos*	-6		
Egypt	+2	(+3)	LFrA-LThS
El Salvador	-6		
Equatorial Guinea	+1		
Eritrea	+3		
Estonia	+2	(+3)	LSuM-LSuO
Ethiopia	+3		
Falkland Islands	-3	(-4)	3SuA-1SaS
Fiji Islands	+12		
Finland	+2	(+3)	LSuM-LSuO
France	+1	(+2)	LSuM-LSuO
French Guiana	-3		
Fr. Polynesia – *Gambier*	-9		
– *Marquesas*	-9.30		
– *Papeete*	-10		
Gabon	+1		
Gambia, The	UTC		
Georgia	+4		
Germany	+1	(+2)	LSuM-LSuO
Ghana	UTC		
Gibraltar	+1	(+2)	LSuM-LSuO
Greece	+2	(+3)	LSuM-LSuO
Greenland – *Eastern*	-1	(UTC)	LSuM-LSuO
– *Central*	-3	(-2)	LSuM-LSuO
– *Western*	-4	(-3)	LSuM-LSuO
Grenada	-4		
Guadeloupe	-4		
Guam	+10		
Guatemala	-6		
Guinea	UTC		
Guinea-Bissau	UTC		
Guyana	-4		
Haiti	-5		
Honduras	-6		
Hungary	+1	(+2)	LSuM-LSuO
Iceland	UTC		
India	+5.30		
Indonesia – *Western*	+7		
– *Central*	+8		
– *Eastern*	+9		
Iran	+3.30		
Iraq	+3	(+4)	A-O; dates vary
Ireland	UTC	(+1)	LSuM-LSuO
Israel	+2	(+3)	M-O; dates vary
Italy – *incl. San Marino, Vat.*	+1	(+2)	LSuM-LSuO
Jamaica	-5		
Japan	+9		
Jordan	+2	(+3)	M-O; dates vary
Kazakhstan – *Western*	+4		
– *Central*	+5		
– *Eastern*	+6		
Kenya	+3		
Kiribati – *Christmas Is.*	+14		
– *Phoenix Is.*	+13		
– *Gilbert Is. (incl. Tarawa)*	+12		
Korea, DPR (North)	+9		
Korea, Republic (South)	+9		
Kuwait	+3		
Kyrgyzstan	+6		
Laos	+7		
Latvia	+2	(+3)	LSuM-LSuO
Lebanon	+2	(+3)	LSuM-LSuO
Lesotho	+2		
Liberia	UTC		
Libya	+2		
Liechtenstein	+1	(+2)	LSuM-LSuO
Lithuania	+2	(+3)	LSuM-LSuO
Luxembourg	+1	(+2)	LSuM-LSuO
Macedonia, FYR	+1	(+2)	LSuM-LSuO
Madagascar	+3		
Malawi	+2		
Malaysia	+8		
Maldives	+5		
Mali	UTC		
Malta	+1	(+2)	LSuM-LSuO
Marshall Islands	+12		
Martinique	-4		
Mauritania	UTC		
Mauritius	+4		
Mexico – *Central*	-6	(-5)	1SuA-LSuO
– *Mountain*	-7	(-6)	1SuA-LSuO
– *Pacific*	-8	(-7)	1SuA-LSuO
Micronesia – *Yap, Chuuk*	+10		
– *Kosrae, Pohnpei*	+11		
Moldova	+2	(+3)	LSuM-LSuO
Monaco	+1	(+2)	LSuM-LSuO
Mongolia – *Central/Eastern*	+8	(+9)	
– *Western*	+7	(+8)	
Montenegro	+1	(+2)	LSuM-LSuO
Montserrat	-4		
Morocco	UTC		
Mozambique	+2		
Myanmar (Burma)	+6.30		
Namibia	+1	(+2)	1SuS-1SuA
Nauru	+12		
Nepal	+5.45		
Netherlands	+1	(+2)	LSuM-LSuO
New Caledonia	+11		
New Zealand – *N & S Is.*	+12	(+13)	1SuO-3SuM
– *Chatham Island*	+12.45	(+13.45)	1SuO-3SuM
Nicaragua	-6		
Niger	+1		
Nigeria	+1		
Niue	-11		
Northern Mariana Is.	+10		
Norway	+1	(+2)	LSuM-LSuO
Oman	+4		
Pakistan	+5		
Palau	+9		
Palestine NAR	+2	(+3)	M-O; dates vary
Panama	-5		
Papua New Guinea	+10		
Paraguay	-4	(-3)	3SuO-2SuM
Peru	-5		
Philippines	+8		
Poland	+1	(+2)	LSuM-LSuO
Portugal – *incl. Madeira*	UTC	(+1)	LSuM-LSuO
– *Azores*	-1	(UTC)	LSuM-LSuO
Puerto Rico	-4		
Qatar	+3		
Réunion	+4		
Romania	+2	(+3)	LSuM-LSuO
Rwanda	+2		
Russian Fed. – *Kaliningrad*	+2	(+3)	LSuM-LSuO
– *Moscow, St Pet, Astrakh.*	+3	(+4)	LSuM-LSuO
– *Samara, Izhevsk*	+4	(+5)	LSuM-LSuO
– *Perm, Yekater'g, Surgut*	+5	(+6)	LSuM-LSuO
– *Omsk, Novosibirsk*	+6	(+7)	LSuM-LSuO
– *Tuva, Norilsk, Abakan*	+7	(+8)	LSuM-LSuO
– *Bratsk, Irkutsk, Ulan-Ude*	+8	(+9)	LSuM-LSuO
– *Yakutsk, Tynda, Mirnyy*	+9	(+10)	LSuM-LSuO
– *Vladiv'k, Khab'k, Sak'n*	+10	(+11)	LSuM-LSuO
– *Magadan, Chirskiy*	+11	(+12)	LSuM-LSuO
– *Kamchatka, Anadyr*	+12	(+13)	LSuM-LSuO
St Eustatius	-4		
St Kitts & Nevis	-4		
St Lucia	-4		
St Maarten	-4		
St Pierre et Miquelon	-3	(-2)	1SuA-LSuO
St Vincent & the Gren.	-4		
Saba	-4		
Samoa	-11		
São Tomé e Príncipe	UTC		
Saudi Arabia	+3		
Senegal	UTC		
Serbia	+1	(+2)	LSuM-LSuO
Seychelles	+4		
Sierra Leone	UTC		
Singapore	+8		
Slovak Republic	+1	(+2)	LSuM-LSuO
Slovenia	+1	(+2)	LSuM-LSuO
Solomon Islands	+11		
Somalia	+3		
South Africa	+2		
Spain – *incl. Balearic Is.*	+1	(+2)	LSuM-LSuO
– *Canary Islands*	UTC	(+1)	LSuM-LSuO
Sri Lanka	+5.5		
Sudan	+3		
Surinam	-3		
Swaziland	+2		
Sweden	+1	(+2)	LSuM-LSuO
Switzerland	+1	(+2)	LSuM-LSuO
Syria	+2	(+3)	A-O; dates vary
Taiwan	+8		
Tajikistan	+5		
Tanzania	+3		
Thailand	+7		
Togo	UTC		
Tonga	+13		
Trinidad & Tobago	-4		
Tunisia	+1		
Turkey	+2	(+3)	LSuM-LSuO
Turkmenistan	+5		
Turks & Caicos Islands	-5	(-4)	1SuA-LSuO
Tuvalu	+12		
Uganda	+3		
Ukraine	+2	(+3)	LSuM-LSuO
United Arab Emirates	+4		
United Kingdom	UTC	(+1)	LSuM-LSuO
United States – *Eastern*	-5	(-4)	*see note**
– *Central*	-6	(-5)	*see note**
– *Mountain*	-7	(-6)	*see note* (not AZ)*
– *Pacific*	-8	(-7)	*see note**
– *Alaska*	-9	(-8)	*see note**
– *Aleutian/Hawaii*	-10		
US Virgin Islands	-4		
Uruguay	-3	(-2)	2SuO-2SuM
Uzbekistan	+5		
Vanuatu	+11		
Venezuela	-4		
Vietnam	+7		
Yemen	+3		
Zambia	+2		
Zimbabwe	+2		

** 1SuA-LSuO (2006 only): 2SuM-1SuN from 2007.*

The listings above refer to a selection of related themes.
For more information, see the Contents (2-5).

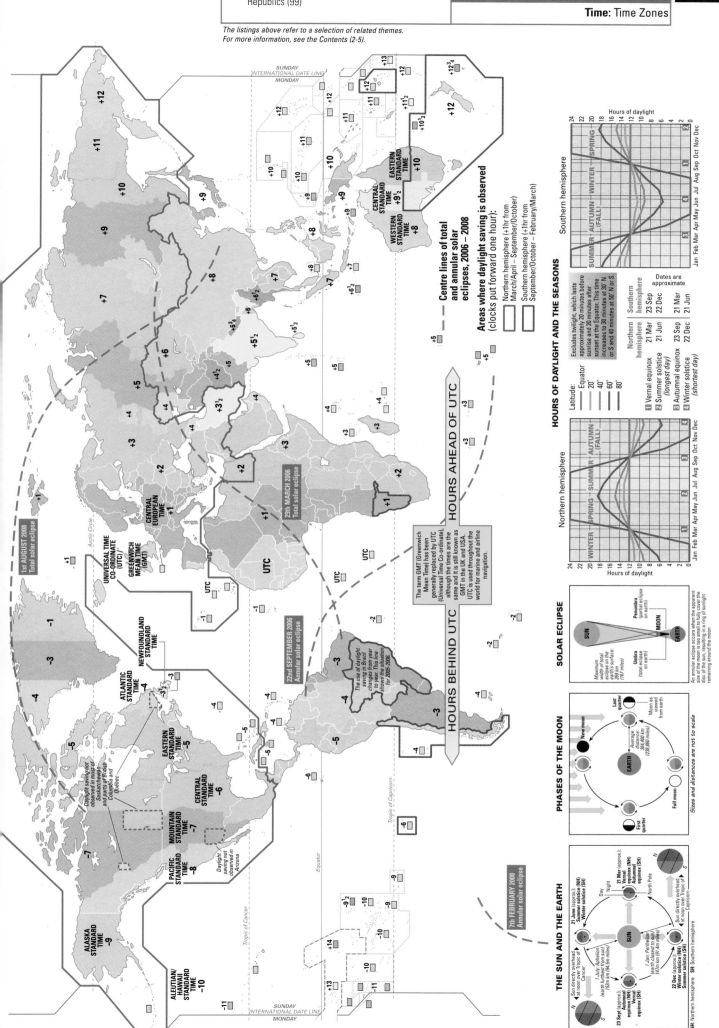

▶ *See also...* World Introduction (22-25); Europe Introduction (42-43); Countries A-Z (108-116)

The listings above refer to a selection of related themes. For more information, see the Contents (2-5).

VISITOR RECEIPTS

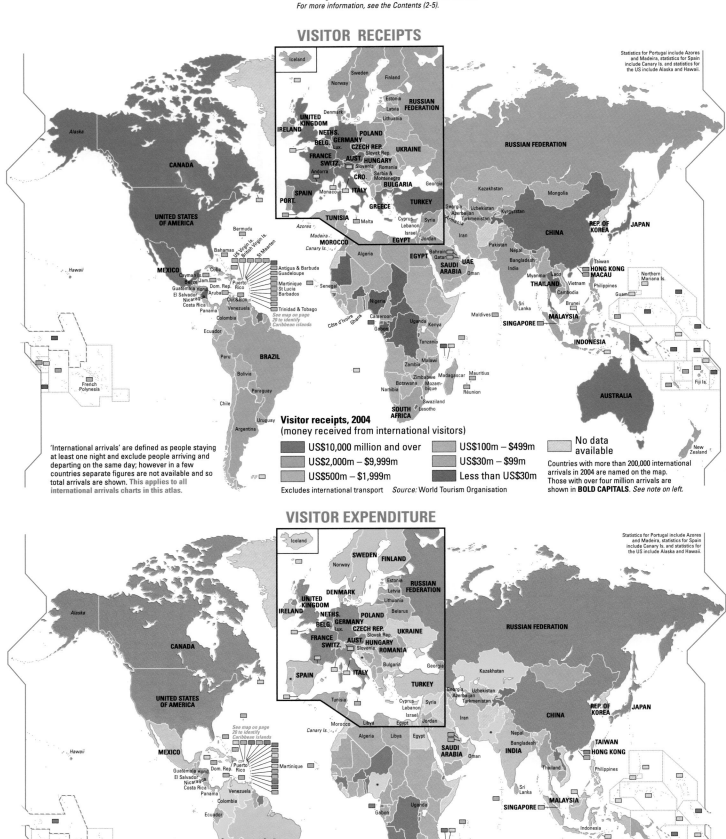

Statistics for Portugal include Azores and Madeira, statistics for Spain include Canary Is. and statistics for the US include Alaska and Hawaii.

'International arrivals' are defined as people staying at least one night and exclude people arriving and departing on the same day; however in a few countries separate figures are not available and so total arrivals are shown. **This applies to all international arrivals charts in this atlas.**

Visitor receipts, 2004
(money received from international visitors)

■ US$10,000 million and over	■ US$100m – $499m
■ US$2,000m – $9,999m	■ US$30m – $99m
■ US$500m – $1,999m	■ Less than US$30m

■ No data available

Excludes international transport   *Source:* World Tourism Organisation

Countries with more than 200,000 international arrivals in 2004 are named on the map. Those with over four million arrivals are shown in **BOLD CAPITALS**. *See note on left.*

VISITOR EXPENDITURE

Statistics for Portugal include Azores and Madeira, statistics for Spain include Canary Is. and statistics for the US include Alaska and Hawaii.

Consistent statistics for outbound travel are unavailable for a number of countries. Countries which indicate significant levels of expenditure but for which departures figures are unavailable, an * is shown. In some instances, departures figures are available but not expenditure.

Visitor expenditure, 2004
(money spent in other countries)

■ US$10,000 million and over	■ US$100m – $499m
■ US$2,000m – $9,999m	■ US$30m – $99m
■ US$500m – $1,999m	■ Less than US$30m

■ No data available

Excludes international transport   *Source:* World Tourism Organisation

Countries with more than 200,000 international departures in 2004 are named on the map. Those with over four million departures are shown in **BOLD CAPITALS**. *See note on left.*

The listings above refer to a selection of related themes.
For more information, see the Contents (2-5).

UNITED STATES TOURISM

UNITED KINGDOM TOURISM

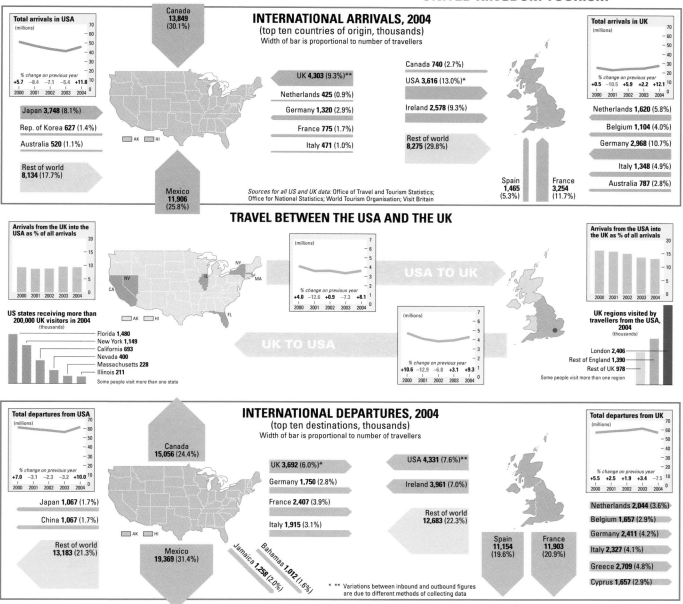

INTERNATIONAL ARRIVALS, 2004
(top ten countries of origin, thousands)
Width of bar is proportional to number of travellers

Total arrivals in USA (millions)
% change on previous year
+5.7 −8.4 −7.1 −5.4 +11.8
2000 2001 2002 2003 2004

Canada 13,849 (30.1%)
Mexico 11,906 (25.8%)

UK 4,303 (9.3%)**
Netherlands 425 (0.9%)
Germany 1,320 (2.9%)
France 775 (1.7%)
Italy 471 (1.0%)

Japan 3,748 (8.1%)
Rep. of Korea 627 (1.4%)
Australia 520 (1.1%)
Rest of world 8,134 (17.7%)

Canada 740 (2.7%)
USA 3,616 (13.0%)*
Ireland 2,578 (9.3%)
Rest of world 8,275 (29.8%)
Spain 1,465 (5.3%)
France 3,254 (11.7%)

Total arrivals in UK (millions)
% change on previous year
+0.5 −10.5 +5.9 +2.2 +12.1
2000 2001 2002 2003 2004

Netherlands 1,620 (5.8%)
Belgium 1,104 (4.0%)
Germany 2,968 (10.7%)
Italy 1,348 (4.9%)
Australia 787 (2.8%)

Sources for all US and UK data: Office of Travel and Tourism Statistics;
Office for National Statistics; World Tourism Organisation; Visit Britain

TRAVEL BETWEEN THE USA AND THE UK

Arrivals from the UK into the USA as % of all arrivals
2000 2001 2002 2003 2004

(millions)
% change on previous year
+4.0 −12.6 +0.9 −7.3 +8.1
2000 2001 2002 2003 2004

USA TO UK

Arrivals from the USA into the UK as % of all arrivals
2000 2001 2002 2003 2004

US states receiving more than 200,000 UK visitors in 2004 (thousands)
Florida 1,480
New York 1,149
California 693
Nevada 400
Massachusetts 228
Illinois 211
Some people visit more than one state

(millions)
% change on previous year
+10.6 −12.9 −6.8 +3.1 +9.3
2000 2001 2002 2003 2004

UK TO USA

UK regions visited by travellers from the USA, 2004 (thousands)
London 2,406
Rest of England 1,390
Rest of UK 978
Some people visit more than one region

INTERNATIONAL DEPARTURES, 2004
(top ten destinations, thousands)
Width of bar is proportional to number of travellers

Total departures from USA (millions)
% change on previous year
+7.0 −3.1 −2.3 −3.2 +10.0
2000 2001 2002 2003 2004

Canada 15,056 (24.4%)
Mexico 19,369 (31.4%)
Jamaica 1,258 (2.0%)
Bahamas 1,012 (1.6%)

UK 3,692 (6.0%)*
Germany 1,750 (2.8%)
France 2,407 (3.9%)
Italy 1,915 (3.1%)

USA 4,331 (7.6%)**
Ireland 3,961 (7.0%)
Rest of world 12,683 (22.3%)

Japan 1,067 (1.7%)
China 1,067 (1.7%)
Rest of world 13,183 (21.3%)

Spain 11,154 (19.6%)
France 11,903 (20.9%)

Total departures from UK (millions)
% change on previous year
+5.5 +2.5 +1.9 +3.4 −7.5
2000 2001 2002 2003 2004

Netherlands 2,044 (3.6%)
Belgium 1,657 (2.9%)
Germany 2,411 (4.2%)
Italy 2,327 (4.1%)
Greece 2,709 (4.8%)
Cyprus 1,657 (2.9%)

* ** Variations between inbound and outbound figures
are due to different methods of collecting data

WORLDWIDE TOURISM

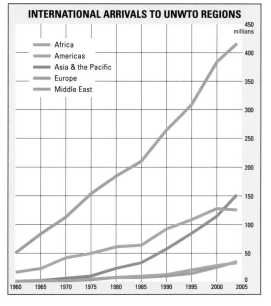

INTERNATIONAL ARRIVALS TO UNWTO REGIONS
450 millions

Africa
Americas
Asia & the Pacific
Europe
Middle East

400
350
300
250
200
150
100
50
0
1960 1965 1970 1975 1980 1985 1990 1995 2000 2005

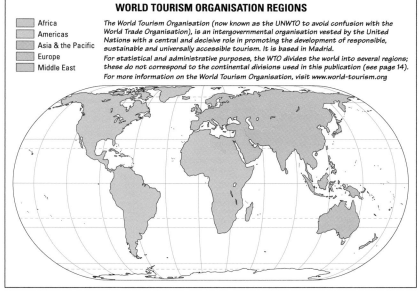

WORLD TOURISM ORGANISATION REGIONS

Africa
Americas
Asia & the Pacific
Europe
Middle East

The World Tourism Organisation (now known as the UNWTO to avoid confusion with the World Trade Organisation), is an intergovernmental organisation vested by the United Nations with a central and decisive role in promoting the development of responsible, sustainable and universally accessible tourism. It is based in Madrid.

For statistical and administrative purposes, the WTO divides the world into several regions; these do not correspond to the continental divisions used in this publication (see page 14).

For more information on the World Tourism Organisation, visit www.world-tourism.org

▶ See also... Time (32-33); Flight Times (39); Cruising (40-41); Europe Transport (50-53); London Airports (63); Berlin Airports (71); Paris Airports (75)

The listings above refer to a selection of related themes.
For more information, see the Contents (2-5).

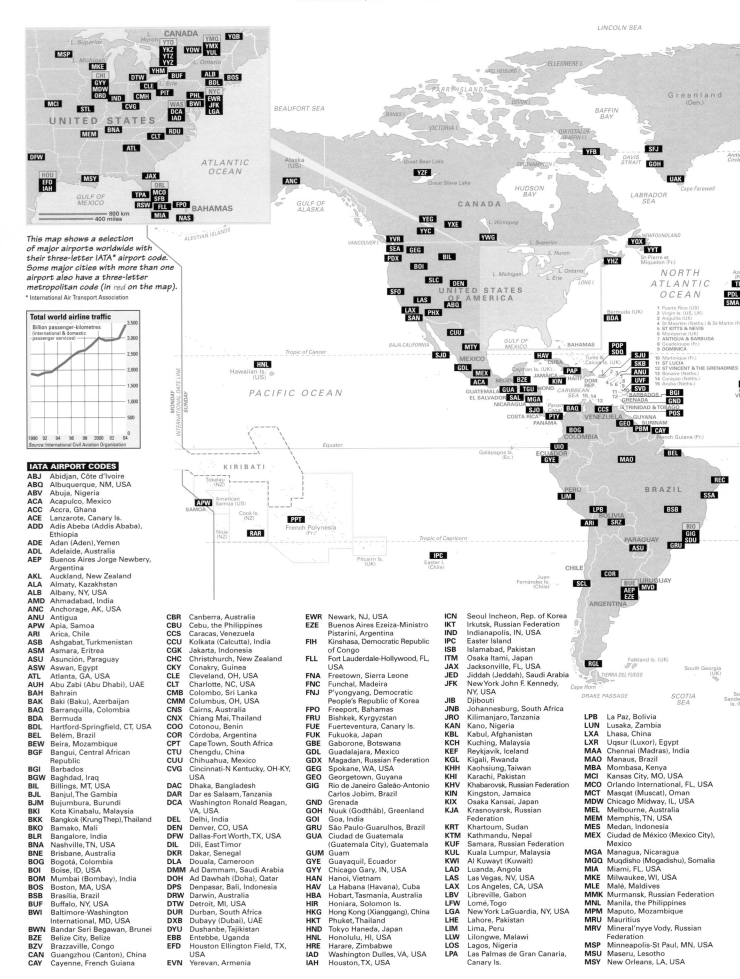

This map shows a selection of major airports worldwide with their three-letter IATA* airport code. Some major cities with more than one airport also have a three-letter metropolitan code (in red on the map).

* International Air Transport Association

Total world airline traffic

Billion passenger-kilometres (international & domestic passenger services)

Source: International Civil Aviation Organisation

IATA AIRPORT CODES

ABJ	Abidjan, Côte d'Ivoire
ABQ	Albuquerque, NM, USA
ABV	Abuja, Nigeria
ACA	Acapulco, Mexico
ACC	Accra, Ghana
ACE	Lanzarote, Canary Is.
ADD	Adis Abeba (Addis Ababa), Ethiopia
ADE	Adan (Aden), Yemen
ADL	Adelaide, Australia
AEP	Buenos Aires Jorge Newbery, Argentina
AKL	Auckland, New Zealand
ALA	Almaty, Kazakhstan
ALB	Albany, NY, USA
AMD	Ahmadabad, India
ANC	Anchorage, AK, USA
ANU	Antigua
APW	Apia, Samoa
ARI	Arica, Chile
ASB	Ashgabat, Turkmenistan
ASM	Asmara, Eritrea
ASU	Asunción, Paraguay
ASW	Aswan, Egypt
ATL	Atlanta, GA, USA
AUH	Abu Zabi (Abu Dhabi), UAE
BAH	Bahrain
BAK	Baki (Baku), Azerbaijan
BAQ	Barranquilla, Colombia
BDA	Bermuda
BDL	Hartford-Springfield, CT, USA
BEL	Belém, Brazil
BEW	Beira, Mozambique
BGF	Bangui, Central African Republic
BGI	Barbados
BGW	Baghdad, Iraq
BIL	Billings, MT, USA
BJL	Banjul, The Gambia
BJM	Bujumbura, Burundi
BKI	Kota Kinabalu, Malaysia
BKK	Bangkok (Krung Thep), Thailand
BKO	Bamako, Mali
BLR	Bangalore, India
BNA	Nashville, TN, USA
BNE	Brisbane, Australia
BOG	Bogotá, Colombia
BOI	Boise, ID, USA
BOM	Mumbai (Bombay), India
BOS	Boston, MA, USA
BSB	Brasília, Brazil
BUF	Buffalo, NY, USA
BWI	Baltimore-Washington International, MD, USA
BWN	Bandar Seri Begawan, Brunei
BZE	Belize City, Belize
BZV	Brazzaville, Congo
CAN	Guangzhou (Canton), China
CAY	Cayenne, French Guiana
CBR	Canberra, Australia
CBU	Cebu, the Philippines
CCS	Caracas, Venezuela
CCU	Kolkata (Calcutta), India
CGK	Jakarta, Indonesia
CHC	Christchurch, New Zealand
CKY	Conakry, Guinea
CLE	Cleveland, OH, USA
CLT	Charlotte, NC, USA
CMB	Colombo, Sri Lanka
CMM	Columbus, OH, USA
CNS	Cairns, Australia
CNX	Chiang Mai, Thailand
COO	Cotonou, Benin
COR	Córdoba, Argentina
CPT	Cape Town, South Africa
CTU	Chengdu, China
CUU	Chihuahua, Mexico
CVG	Cincinnati-N Kentucky, OH-KY, USA
DAC	Dhaka, Bangladesh
DAR	Dar es Salaam, Tanzania
DCA	Washington Ronald Reagan, VA, USA
DEL	Delhi, India
DEN	Denver, CO, USA
DFW	Dallas-Fort Worth, TX, USA
DIL	Dili, East Timor
DKR	Dakar, Senegal
DLA	Douala, Cameroon
DMM	Ad Dammam, Saudi Arabia
DOH	Ad Dawhah (Doha), Qatar
DPS	Denpasar, Bali, Indonesia
DRW	Darwin, Australia
DTW	Detroit, MI, USA
DUR	Durban, South Africa
DXB	Dubayy (Dubai), UAE
DYU	Dushanbe, Tajikistan
EBB	Entebbe, Uganda
EFD	Houston Ellington Field, TX, USA
EVN	Yerevan, Armenia
EWR	Newark, NJ, USA
EZE	Buenos Aires Ezeiza-Ministro Pistarini, Argentina
FIH	Kinshasa, Democratic Republic of Congo
FLL	Fort Lauderdale-Hollywood, FL, USA
FNA	Freetown, Sierra Leone
FNC	Funchal, Madeira
FNJ	P'yongyang, Democratic People's Republic of Korea
FPO	Freeport, Bahamas
FRU	Bishkek, Kyrgyzstan
FUE	Fuerteventura, Canary Is.
FUK	Fukuoka, Japan
GBE	Gaborone, Botswana
GDL	Guadalajara, Mexico
GDX	Magadan, Russian Federation
GEG	Spokane, WA, USA
GEO	Georgetown, Guyana
GIG	Rio de Janeiro Galeão-Antonio Carlos Jobim, Brazil
GND	Grenada
GOH	Nuuk (Godthåb), Greenland
GOI	Goa, India
GRU	São Paulo-Guarulhos, Brazil
GUA	Ciudad de Guatemala (Guatemala City), Guatemala
GUM	Guam
GYE	Guayaquil, Ecuador
GYY	Chicago Gary, IN, USA
HAN	Hanoi, Vietnam
HAV	La Habana (Havana), Cuba
HBA	Hobart, Tasmania, Australia
HIR	Honiara, Solomon Is.
HKG	Hong Kong (Xianggang), China
HKT	Phuket, Thailand
HND	Tokyo Haneda, Japan
HNL	Honolulu, HI, USA
HRE	Harare, Zimbabwe
IAD	Washington Dulles, VA, USA
IAH	Houston, TX, USA
ICN	Seoul Incheon, Rep. of Korea
IKT	Irkutsk, Russian Federation
IND	Indianapolis, IN, USA
IPC	Easter Island
ISB	Islamabad, Pakistan
ITM	Osaka Itami, Japan
JAX	Jacksonville, FL, USA
JED	Jiddah (Jeddah), Saudi Arabia
JFK	New York John F. Kennedy, NY, USA
JIB	Djibouti
JNB	Johannesburg, South Africa
JRO	Kilimanjaro, Tanzania
KAN	Kano, Nigeria
KBL	Kabul, Afghanistan
KCH	Kuching, Malaysia
KEF	Reykjavík, Iceland
KGL	Kigali, Rwanda
KHH	Kaohsiung, Taiwan
KHI	Karachi, Pakistan
KHV	Khabarovsk, Russian Federation
KIN	Kingston, Jamaica
KIX	Osaka Kansai, Japan
KJA	Krasnoyarsk, Russian Federation
KRT	Khartoum, Sudan
KTM	Kathmandu, Nepal
KUF	Samara, Russian Federation
KUL	Kuala Lumpur, Malaysia
KWI	Al Kuwayt (Kuwait)
LAD	Luanda, Angola
LAS	Las Vegas, NV, USA
LAX	Los Angeles, CA, USA
LBV	Libreville, Gabon
LFW	Lomé, Togo
LGA	New York LaGuardia, NY, USA
LHE	Lahore, Pakistan
LIM	Lima, Peru
LLW	Lilongwe, Malawi
LOS	Lagos, Nigeria
LPA	Las Palmas de Gran Canaria, Canary Is.
LPB	La Paz, Bolivia
LUN	Lusaka, Zambia
LXA	Lhasa, China
LXR	Uqsur (Luxor), Egypt
MAA	Chennai (Madras), India
MAO	Manaus, Brazil
MBA	Mombasa, Kenya
MCI	Kansas City, MO, USA
MCO	Orlando International, FL, USA
MCT	Masqat (Muscat), Oman
MDW	Chicago Midway, IL, USA
MEL	Melbourne, Australia
MEM	Memphis, TN, USA
MES	Medan, Indonesia
MEX	Ciudad de México (Mexico City), Mexico
MGA	Managua, Nicaragua
MGQ	Muqdisho (Mogadishu), Somalia
MIA	Miami, FL, USA
MKE	Milwaukee, WI, USA
MLE	Malé, Maldives
MMK	Murmansk, Russian Federation
MNL	Manila, the Philippines
MPM	Maputo, Mozambique
MRU	Mauritius
MRV	Mineral'nyye Vody, Russian Federation
MSP	Minneapolis-St Paul, MN, USA
MSU	Maseru, Lesotho
MSY	New Orleans, LA, USA

1 Puerto Rico (US)
2 Virgin Is. (US, UK)
3 Anguilla (UK)
4 St Maarten (Neths.) & St-Martin (Fr.)
5 ST KITTS & NEVIS
6 Montserrat (UK)
7 ANTIGUA & BARBUDA
8 Guadeloupe (Fr.)
9 DOMINICA
10 Martinique (Fr.)
11 ST LUCIA
12 ST VINCENT & THE GRENADINES
13 Bonaire (Neths.)
14 Curaçao (Neths.)
15 Aruba (Neths.)

See also... Time (32-33); Flight Times (39); Cruising (40-41); Europe Transport (50-53); London Airports (63); Berlin Airports (71); Paris Airports (75)

The listings above refer to a selection of related themes. For more information, see the Contents (2-5).

World **37**

Airports

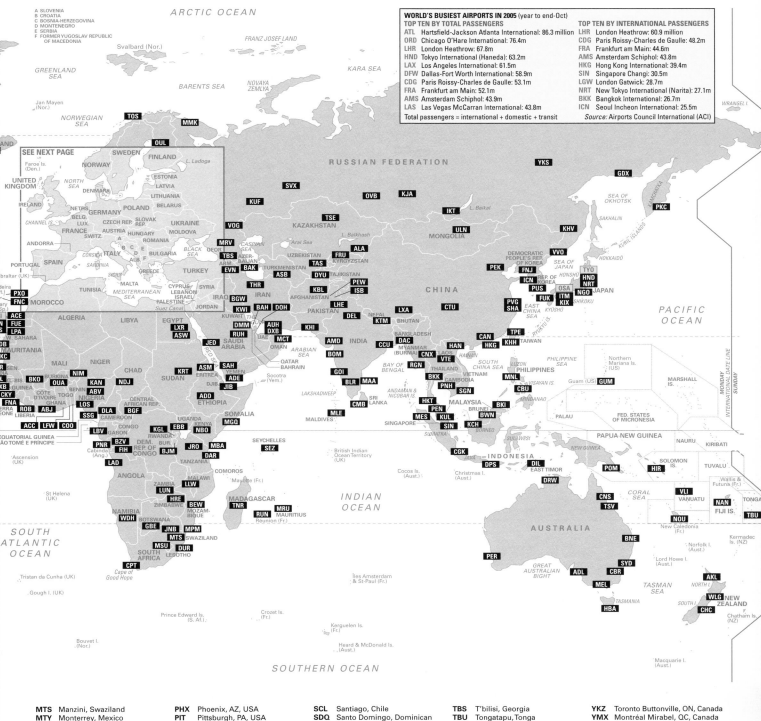

WORLD'S BUSIEST AIRPORTS IN 2005 (year to end-Oct)

TOP TEN BY TOTAL PASSENGERS	
ATL	Hartsfield-Jackson Atlanta International: 86.3 million
ORD	Chicago O'Hare International: 76.4m
LHR	London Heathrow: 67.8m
HND	Tokyo International (Haneda): 63.2m
LAX	Los Angeles International: 61.5m
DFW	Dallas-Fort Worth International: 58.9m
CDG	Paris Roissy-Charles de Gaulle: 53.1m
FRA	Frankfurt am Main: 52.1m
AMS	Amsterdam Schiphol: 43.9m
LAS	Las Vegas McCarran International: 43.8m

Total passengers = international + domestic + transit

TOP TEN BY INTERNATIONAL PASSENGERS	
LHR	London Heathrow: 60.9 million
CDG	Paris Roissy-Charles de Gaulle: 48.2m
FRA	Frankfurt am Main: 44.6m
AMS	Amsterdam Schiphol: 43.8m
HKG	Hong Kong International: 39.4m
SIN	Singapore Changi: 30.5m
LGW	London Gatwick: 28.7m
NRT	New Tokyo International (Narita): 27.1m
BKK	Bangkok International: 26.7m
ICN	Seoul Incheon International: 25.5m

Source: Airports Council International (ACI)

A SLOVENIA
B CROATIA
C BOSNIA-HERZEGOVINA
D MONTENEGRO
E SERBIA
F FORMER YUGOSLAV REPUBLIC OF MACEDONIA

MTS	Manzini, Swaziland	PHX	Phoenix, AZ, USA	SCL	Santiago, Chile	TBS	T'bilisi, Georgia	YKZ Toronto Buttonville, ON, Canada
MTY	Monterrey, Mexico	PIT	Pittsburgh, PA, USA	SDQ	Santo Domingo, Dominican Republic	TBU	Tongatapu, Tonga	YMX Montréal Mirabel, QC, Canada
MVD	Montevideo, Uruguay	PKC	Petropavlovsk-Kamchatskiy, Russian Federation			TER	Terceira, Azores	YOW Ottawa, ON, Canada
NAN	Nadi, Fiji Is.			SDU	Rio de Janeiro Santos Dumont, Brazil	TFN	Tenerife Norte, Canary Is.	YQB Québec, QC, Canada
NAS	Nassau, Bahamas	PNH	Phnom Penh, Cambodia			TFS	Tenerife Sur, Canary Is.	YQX Gander, NL, Canada
NBO	Nairobi, Kenya	POM	Port Moresby, Papua New Guinea	SEA	Seattle-Tacoma, WA, USA	TGU	Tegucigalpa, Honduras	YTZ Toronto City Centre, ON, Canada
NDB	Nouadhibou, Mauritania			SEZ	Mahé, Seychelles	THR	Tehran, Iran	YUL Montréal Dorval, QC, Canada
NDJ	N'djamena, Chad	POP	Puerto Plata, Dominican Rep.	SFB	Orlando Sanford, FL, USA	TNR	Antananarivo, Madagascar	YVR Vancouver, BC, Canada
NGO	Nagoya Centrair, Japan	POS	Port of Spain, Trinidad	SFJ	Kangerlussuaq, Greenland	TOS	Tromsø, Norway	YWG Winnipeg, MB, Canada
NIM	Niamey, Niger	PPT	Papeete, Tahiti, French Polynesia	SFO	San Francisco, CA, USA	TPA	Tampa, FL, USA	YXE Saskatoon, SK, Canada
NKC	Nouakchott, Mauritania	PTY	Ciudad de Panamá (Panama City), Panama	SGN	Ho Chi Minh City (Saigon), Vietnam	TPE	Taipei, Taiwan	YYC Calgary, AB, Canada
NOU	Nouméa, New Caledonia					TSE	Astana, Kazakhstan	YYT St John's, NL, Canada
NRT	Tokyo Narita, Japan	PUS	Busan, Republic of Korea	SHA	Shanghai Hongqiao, China	TSV	Townsville, Australia	YYZ Toronto Lester B. Pearson, ON, Canada
ORD	Chicago O'Hare, IL, USA	PVG	Shanghai Pudong, China	SIN	Singapore	UAK	Narsarsuaq, Greenland	
OUA	Ouagadougou, Burkina	PXO	Porto Santo, Madeira	SJD	San José del Cabo, Mexico	UIO	Quito, Ecuador	YZF Yellowknife, NT, Canada
OUL	Oulu, Finland	RAI	Praia, Cape Verde	SJO	San José, Costa Rica	ULN	Ulaanbaatar (Ulan Bator), Mongolia	
OVB	Novosibirsk, Russian Federation	RAR	Rarotonga, Cook Is.	SJU	San Juan, Puerto Rico			METROPOLITAN CODES
		RDU	Raleigh-Durham, NC, USA	SKB	St Kitts	UVF	Hewanorra, St Lucia	BUE Buenos Aires, Argentina
OXB	Bissau, Guinea-Bissau	REC	Recife, Brazil	SLC	Salt Lake City, UT, USA	VLI	Port-Vila, Vanuatu	CHI Chicago, IL, USA
PAP	Port-au-Prince, Haiti	RGL	Río Gallegos, Argentina	SMA	Santa Maria, Azores	VOG	Volgograd, Russian Federation	HOU Houston, TX, USA
PBM	Paramaribo, Surinam	RGN	Yangon (Rangoon), Myanmar	SRZ	Santa Cruz, Bolivia	VTE	Viangchan (Vientiane), Laos	NYC New York City, NY, USA
PDL	Ponta Delgada, São Miguel, Azores	ROB	Monrovia, Liberia	SSA	Salvador, Brazil	VVO	Vladivostok, Russian Federation	ORL Orlando, FL, USA
		RSW	Southwest Florida, FL, USA	SSG	Malabo, Equatorial Guinea	WDH	Windhoek, Namibia	OSA Osaka, Japan
PDX	Portland, OR, USA	RUH	Ar Riyad (Riyadh), Saudi Arabia	STL	St Louis, MO, USA	WLG	Wellington, New Zealand	RIO Rio de Janeiro, Brazil
PEK	Beijing (Peking), China	RUN	Réunion	SVD	St Vincent	YEG	Edmonton, AB, Canada	TCI Tenerife, Canary Is.
PEN	Pinang (Penang), Malaysia	SAH	Sana'a (Sana), Yemen	SVX	Yekaterinburg, Russian Federation	YFB	Iqaluit, NU, Canada	TYO Tokyo, Japan
PER	Perth, Australia	SAL	San Salvador, El Salvador			YHM	Hamilton, ON, Canada	WAS Washington, DC, USA
PEW	Peshawar, Pakistan	SAN	San Diego, CA, USA	SYD	Sydney, Australia	YHZ	Halifax, NS, Canada	YMQ Montréal, QC, Canada
PHL	Philadelphia, PA, USA			TAS	Toshkent (Tashkent), Uzbekistan	YKX	Yakutsk, Russian Federation	YTO Toronto, ON, Canada

▶ *See also...* Time (32-33); Flight Times (39); Cruising (40-41); Europe Transport (50-53); London Airports (63); Berlin Airports (71); Paris Airports (75)

The listings above refer to a selection of related themes. For more information, see the Contents (2-5).

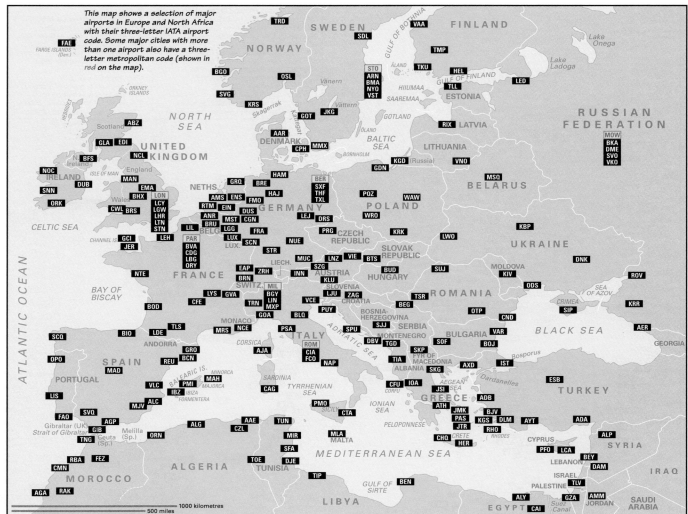

This map shows a selection of major airports in Europe and North Africa with their three-letter IATA airport code. Some major cities with more than one airport also have a three-letter metropolitan code (shown in red on the map).

IATA AIRPORT CODES

AAE	Annaba, Algeria
AAR	Århus, Denmark
ABZ	Aberdeen, Scotland
ADA	Adana, Russian Federation
ADB	Izmir (Smyrna), Turkey
AER	Adler-Sochi, Russian Federation
AGA	Agadir, Morocco
AGP	Málaga, Spain
AJA	Ajaccio, France
ALC	Alacant (Alicante), Spain
ALG	Alger (Algiers), Algeria
ALP	Halab (Aleppo), Syria
ALY	Al Iskandariyah (Alexandria), Egypt
AMM	Amman, Jordan
AMS	Amsterdam, The Netherlands
ANR	Antwerpen (Antwerp), Belgium
ARN	Stockholm Arlanda, Sweden
ATH	Athína (Athens), Greece
AXD	Alexandroúpoli, Greece
AYT	Antalya, Turkey
BCN	Barcelona, Spain
BEG	Beograd (Belgrade), Serbia
BEN	Banghazi (Benghazi), Libya
BEY	Bayrut (Beirut), Lebanon
BFS	Belfast, Northern Ireland
BGO	Bergen, Norway
BGY	Milano (Milan) Bérgamo, Italy
BHX	Birmingham, England
BIO	Bilbao, Spain
BJV	Bodrum-Milas, Turkey
BKA	Moskva (Moscow) Bykovo, Russian Federation
BLQ	Bologna, Italy
BMA	Stockholm Bromma, Sweden
BOD	Bordeaux, France
BOJ	Burgas, Bulgaria
BRE	Bremen, Germany
BRN	Bern (Berne), Switzerland
BRS	Bristol, England
BRU	Bruxelles/Brussel (Brussels), Belgium
BTS	Bratislava, Slovak Republic
BUD	Budapest, Hungary
BVA	Paris Beauvais-Tillé, France
CAG	Cágliari, Italy
CAI	Al Qahirah (Cairo), Egypt
CDG	Paris Roissy-Charles de Gaulle, France

CFE	Clermont-Ferrand, France
CFU	Kérkira (Corfu), Greece
CGN	Köln (Cologne)-Bonn, Germany
CHQ	Haniá (Canea), Greece
CIA	Roma (Rome) Ciampino, Italy
CMN	Casablanca, Morocco
CND	Constanta, Romania
CPH	København (Copenhagen), Denmark
CTA	Catánia, Italy
CWL	Cardiff, Wales
CZL	Constantine, Algeria
DAM	Dimashq (Damascus), Syria
DBV	Dubrovnik, Croatia
DJE	Jerba, Tunisia
DLM	Dalaman, Turkey
DME	Moskva (Moscow) Domodedovo, Russian Federation
DNK	Dnipropetrovs'k, Ukraine
DRS	Dresden, Germany
DUB	Dublin, Ireland
DUS	Düsseldorf, Germany
EAP	EuroAirport [Basel (**BSL**)-Mulhouse (**MLH**)-Freiburg], France/Germany/Switzerland
EDI	Edinburgh, Scotland
EIN	Eindhoven, The Netherlands
EMA	Nottingham East Midlands, England
ENS	Enschede, The Netherlands
ESB	Ankara, Turkey
FAE	Vágar, Faroe Islands
FAO	Faro, Portugal
FCO	Roma (Rome) Fiumicino/Leonardo da Vinci, Italy
FEZ	Fès, Morocco
FMO	Münster-Osnabrück, Germany
FRA	Frankfurt am Main, Germany
GCI	Guernsey
GDN	Gdansk, Poland
GIB	Gibraltar
GLA	Glasgow, Scotland
GOA	Génova (Genoa), Italy
GOT	Göteborg (Gothenburg), Sweden
GRO	Girona, Spain
GRQ	Groningen, The Netherlands
GVA	Genève (Geneva), Switzerland
GZA	Gaza, Palestine Nat. Auth. Region
HAJ	Hannover (Hanover), Germany

HAM	Hamburg, Germany
HEL	Helsinki-Vantaa, Finland
HER	Iráklio (Herakleion), Greece
IBZ	Eivissa (Ibiza), Spain
INN	Innsbruck, Austria
IOA	Ioánina, Greece
IST	Istanbul, Turkey
JER	Jersey
JKG	Jönköping, Sweden
JMK	Míkonos, Greece
JSI	Skíathos, Greece
JTR	Thíra, Greece
KBP	Kyiv (Kiev), Ukraine
KGD	Kaliningrad, Russian Federation
KGS	Kós (Cos), Greece
KIV	Chisinau (Kishinev), Moldova
KLU	Klagenfurt, Austria
KRK	Kraków (Cracow), Poland
KRR	Krasnodar, Russian Federation
KRS	Kristiansand, Norway
LBG	Paris Le Bourget, France
LCA	Larnaca, Cyprus
LCY	London City, England
LDE	Lourdes-Tarbes, France
LED	Sankt-Peterburg (St Petersburg), Russian Federation
LEH	Le Havre, France
LEJ	Leipzig-Halle, Germany
LGG	Liège, Belgium
LGW	London Gatwick, England
LHR	London Heathrow, England
LIL	Lille, France
LIN	Milano (Milan) Linate, Italy
LIS	Lisboa (Lisbon), Portugal
LJU	Ljubljana, Slovenia
LNZ	Linz, Austria
LTN	London Luton, England
LUX	Luxembourg
LWO	L'viv (L'vov), Ukraine
LYS	Lyon (Lyons), France
MAD	Madrid, Spain
MAH	Maó (Mahón), Spain
MAN	Manchester, England
MIR	Monastir, Tunisia
MJV	Murcia, Spain
MLA	Malta
MMX	Malmö, Sweden
MRS	Marseille (Marseilles), France

MSQ	Minsk, Belarus
MST	Maastricht, The Netherlands
MUC	München (Munich), Germany
MXP	Milano (Milan) Malpensa, Italy
NAP	Nápoli (Naples), Italy
NCE	Nice, France
NCL	Newcastle, England
NOC	Horan (Knock), Ireland
NTE	Nantes, France
NUE	Nürnberg (Nuremberg), Germany
NYO	Stockholm Skavsta, Sweden
ODS	Odesa (Odessa), Ukraine
OPO	Porto (Oporto), Portugal
ORK	Cork, Ireland
ORN	Oran, Algeria
ORY	Paris Orly, France
OSL	Oslo, Norway
OTP	Bucuresti (Bucharest), Romania
PAS	Páros, Greece
PFO	Pafos (Paphos), Cyprus
PMI	Palma de Mallorca, Spain
PMO	Palermo, Italy
POZ	Poznan, Poland
PRG	Praha (Prague), Czech Republic
PSA	Pisa, Italy
PUY	Pula, Croatia
RAK	Marrakech, Morocco
RBA	Rabat, Morocco
REU	Reus, Spain
RHO	Ródos (Rhodes), Greece
RIX	Riga, Latvia
ROV	Rostov-na-Donu, Russian Federation
RTM	Rotterdam, The Netherlands
SCN	Saarbrücken, Germany
SCQ	Santiago de Compostela, Spain
SDL	Sundsvall, Sweden
SFA	Sfax, Tunisia
SIP	Simferopol, Ukraine
SJJ	Sarajevo, Bosnia-Herzegovina
SKG	Thessaloníki (Salonika), Greece
SKP	Skopje, Former Yugoslav Republic of Macedonia
SNN	Shannon, Ireland
SOF	Sofiya (Sofia), Bulgaria
SPU	Split, Croatia
STN	London Stansted, England
STR	Stuttgart, Germany

SUJ	Satu Mare, Romania
SVG	Stavanger, Norway
SVO	Moskva (Moscow) Sheremetyevo, Russian Federation
SVQ	Sevilla (Seville), Spain
SXF	Berlin Schönefeld, Germany
SZG	Salzburg, Austria
TGD	Podgorica, Montenegro
THF	Berlin Tempelhof, Germany
TIA	Tiranë (Tirana), Albania
TIP	Tarabulus (Tripoli), Libya
TKU	Turku, Finland
TLL	Tallinn, Estonia
TLS	Toulouse, France
TLV	Tel Aviv-Yafo, Israel
TMP	Tampere, Finland
TNG	Tanger (Tangier), Morocco
TOE	Tozeur, Tunisia
TRD	Trondheim, Norway
TRN	Torino (Turin), Italy
TSR	Timisoara, Romania
TUN	Tunis, Tunisia
TXL	Berlin Tegel, Germany
VAA	Vaasa, Finland
VAR	Varna, Bulgaria
VCE	Venézia (Venice), Italy
VIE	Wien (Vienna), Austria
VKO	Moskva (Moscow) Vnukovo, Russian Federation
VLC	València, Spain
VNO	Vilnius, Lithuania
VST	Stockholm Västerås, Sweden
WAW	Warszawa (Warsaw), Poland
WRO	Wroclaw, Poland
ZAG	Zagreb, Croatia
ZRH	Zürich, Switzerland

METROPOLITAN CODES

BER	Berlin, Germany
LON	London, England
MIL	Milano (Milan), Italy
MOW	Moskva (Moscow), Russian Federation
PAR	Paris, France
ROM	Roma (Rome), Italy
STO	Stockholm, Sweden

► *See also...* Time (32-33); Airports (36-38); Cruising (40-41); Europe Transport (50-53); London Airports (63); Berlin Airports (71); Paris Airports (75)

The listings above refer to a selection of related themes. For more information, see the Contents (2-5).

World **39**

Flight Times

Average flight times from London, New York and Singapore to other major destinations. Hours do not include stopover time, when necessary, from one destination to another.

- Less than 2 hours
- 2 hours – 4 hours 59 mins
- 5 hours – 8 hours 59 mins
- 9 hours – 14 hours 59 mins
- 15 hours – 24 hours 59 mins
- 25 hours and over

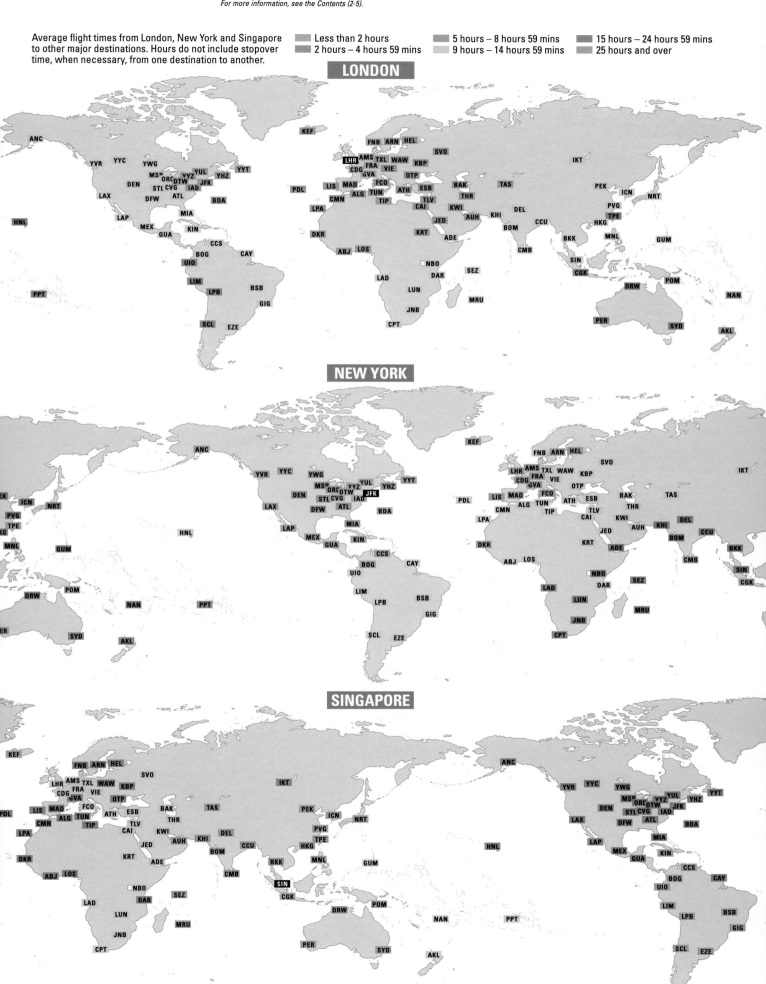

LONDON

NEW YORK

SINGAPORE

The main ocean and river cruise areas are highlighted along with the most visited ports (*red dots*). Follow the *green line* for a typical three-month world cruise route. The Mediterranean and the Caribbean, the two most popular cruising regions, are shown in extra detail below.

Not all ships can dock alongside all ports. On these occasions, ship's launches are used to tender passengers ashore. In some remote regions such as Antarctica, passengers can only travel ashore by Zodiac boats.

Cruises are year-round except in the following regions, where climate or sea conditions limit the season:
Alaska: cruises scheduled between May and September;
US East Coast May – Sep;
Baltic May – Sep;
South Africa Nov – Mar;
Antarctica & South America (Cape Horn) Nov – Feb

PORTS OF CALL: THE BALTIC

400 km
200 miles

Kemi
Luleå
NORWAY
SWEDEN
FINLAND
Vaasa (Vasa)
GULF OF BOTHNIA
ÅLAND
Oslo
Stockholm
Helsinki (Helsingfors)
HIIUMAA
GULF OF FINLAND
Sankt-Peterburg (St Petersburg)
Tallinn
ESTONIA
RUSSIAN FED.
Visby
SAAREMAA
GOTLAND
Rīga
LATVIA
København (Copenhagen)
DENMARK
ÖLAND
BALTIC SEA
Klaipėda
LITHUANIA
Nord-Ostsee (Kiel) Kanal
BORNHOLM
Kaliningrad (Russia)
BELARUS
Kiel
Warnemünde
Gdynia
Travemünde
Gdańsk
Hamburg
GERMANY
POLAND

Cruise passengers (millions)

14
12
10
8
6
4
2
0
1980 1985 1990 1995 2000 2005

Estimated regional breakdown, 2005 (millions)

Caribbean/Florida (incl. Panama Canal) **6.3**
Mediterranean Sea/ Black Sea/Red Sea **2.0**
Alaska/W Canada **0.9**
Norwegian Fjords/ Baltic **0.9**
Mexican Riviera **0.85**
Asia **0.75**
US East Coast/ E Canada **0.7**
Hawaiian Is. **0.6**
South America/ Antarctica **0.4**
Bermuda **0.2**
Other regions **0.8**

BEAUFORT SEA
Barrow
McKINLEY SEA
BERING SEA
Anchorage
Valdez
Skagway & Haines
Seward Whittier
Juneau
Glacier Bay
Sitka
Ketchikan
Misty Fjords
Prince Rupert
Alaska/Canada (Voyage to the Glaciers) cruise area
Vancouver
Victoria
Seattle

NORTH PACIFIC OCEAN

Mexican Riviera cruise area

San Francisco
Los Angeles
Long Beach
San Diego
Ensenada
La Paz
Cabo San Lucas
Mazatlán
Puerto Vallarta
Manzanillo
Acapulco

Tropic of Cancer

Waimea, Lihue & Nawiliwili, Kauai
Honolulu, Oahu
Kahului, Maui
Hilo & Kailua Kona, Hawaii I.

Hawaiian Islands cruise area

MONDAY
INTERNATIONAL DATE LINE
SUNDAY

Polynesia

Pago Pago, Tutuila
Bora Bora
Mooréa
Papeete, Tahiti

South Pacific cruise area

SOUTH PACIFIC OCEAN

Easter I.

Equator

HUDSON BAY
LABRADOR SEA

US East Coast (New England/Canada) cruise area
Québec
Montréal
Saint John
GULF OF ST LAWRENCE
Charlottetown
Halifax
Portland
Boston
Bar Harbor
Cape Cod
Philadelphia
New York
Nantucket
Newport
Martha's Vineyard
Cape Hatteras
Charleston
Natchez
Baton Rouge
Mississippi
New Orleans
Miami
GULF OF MEXICO
BERMUDA TRIANGLE
Hamilton, St George's & Royal Dockyard, Bermuda

NORTH ATLANTIC OCEAN

Europe – New York
Europe – Florida
Transatlantic
Europe – Caribbean
SARGASSO SEA

Uummannaq
Ilulissat
Sisimiut
Nuuk (Godthåb)
Narsarsuaq
Cape Farewell
Arctic Circle

Greater Antilles
CARIBBEAN SEA
Lesser Antilles
Panama Canal

CARIBBEAN & CENTRAL AMERICA INSET

Esmeraldas
Galápagos Is.
Guayaquil
Manaus & Boca de Valeria
Pebas Vendeval
Iquitos
Leticia
Amazon
Santarém & Alter do Chão
Belém
Mouths of the Amazon
Fortaleza
Callao [for Lima]
Recife
Salvador de Bahia

South America cruise area

Rio de Janeiro
Santos [for São Paulo]

Tropic of Capricorn

Valparaíso [for Santiago]
Isla Mocha
Puerto Montt
Montevideo
Buenos Aires
Río de la Plata
Puerto Madryn
Puerto Natáles
Punta Arenas
Strait of Magellan
Ushuaia
TIERRA DEL FUEGO
Cape Horn
DRAKE PASSAGE
SCOTIA SEA

PORTS OF CALL: CARIBBEAN & CENTRAL AMERICA

UNITED STATES
Houston
Galveston
New Orleans
Jacksonville
Mississippi Delta
Tampa
Port Canaveral
Palm Beach
Freeport / Lucaya
GRAND BAHAMA ISLAND
Port Everglades, Fort Lauderdale
Miami
GREAT ABACO
NEW PROVIDENCE
ELEUTHERA
Key West
Nassau
FLORIDA KEYS
ANDROS
CAT I.
SAN SALVADOR
BAHAMAS

GULF OF MEXICO

Tropic of Cancer

Tampico
La Habana (Havana)
CUBA
GREAT EXUMA
LONG I.
CROOKED I.
ACKLINS I.
MAYAGUANA
TURKS & CAICOS IS.
GREAT INAGUA

ATLANTIC OCEAN

Progreso
Playa del Carmen & Calica
Yucatan Channel
ISLA DE LA JUVENTUD
Cozumel
PENINSULA DE YUCATÁN
George Town
CAYMAN IS. (UK)
Guantánamo Bay (US)
Cap-Haïtien
DOMINICAN REPUBLIC
Puerto Plata
ÎLE DE LA GONÂVE
HAITI
HISPANIOLA
Montego Bay
Ocho Rios
JAMAICA
Port-au-Prince
Santo Domingo
PUERTO RICO (US)
San Juan
VIRGIN IS. (US & UK)

Charlotte Amalie, St Thomas
Tortola
Virgin Gorda
Frederiksted & Christiansted, St Croix
Philipsburg, St Maarten
Road Bay
ST MAARTEN (Neths.) & ST-MARTIN (Fr.)
ANGUILLA (UK)
SABA (Neths.)
ST EUSTATIUS (Neths.)

MEXICO
Ixtapa-Zihuatanejo
Acapulco
Huatulco
GOLFO DE TEHUANTEPEC
Santo Tomás de Castilla
GUATEMALA
Belize City
BELIZE
Roatán
GULF OF HONDURAS
Costa Maya
HONDURAS
EL SALVADOR
NICARAGUA
Costa de Mosquitos

CARIBBEAN SEA

Basseterre
ST KITTS & NEVIS
Charlestown
ANTIGUA & BARBUDA
Heritage Quay, St John's
MONTSERRAT (UK)
Plymouth
Volcanic activity currently prevents cruise visits
GUADELOUPE (Fr.)
Pointe-à-Pitre
DOMINICA
Prince Rupert Bay, Portsmouth
Woodbridge Bay, Roseau
MARTINIQUE (Fr.)
Fort-de-France
ST LUCIA
Pte Seraphine, Castries
ST VINCENT
Kingstown
THE GRENADINES
BARBADOS
Bridgetown
GRENADA
St George's
TOBAGO
TRINIDAD & TOBAGO
Port of Spain

Lesser Antilles

PACIFIC OCEAN
Puerto Caldera
Puerto Limón
COSTA RICA
Colón
PANAMA
Balboa
Panama Canal
COLOMBIA

Cartagena
ARUBA (Neths.)
BONAIRE (Neths.)
CURAÇAO (Neths.)
Oranjestad
Willemstad
GOLFO DE VENEZUELA
LAGO DE MARACAIBO
La Guaira [for Caracas]
ISLA MARGARITA
ISLA LA TORTUGA
VENEZUELA
Ciudad Guayana
Orinoco Delta

1000 kilometres
500 miles

PORTS OF CALL: BRITISH ISLES

300 km
150 miles

SHETLAND IS.
Lerwick
FAIR ISLE
ORKNEY IS.
Kirkwall
Invergordon
HEBRIDES
NORTH ATLANTIC OCEAN
Scotland
NORTH SEA
Greenock
Leith [for Edinburgh]
Newcastle upon Tyne
N. Ireland
ISLE OF MAN
ANGLESEY
UNITED KINGDOM
Dublin
IRELAND
Liverpool
England
Wales
Harwich
Waterford
London
Tilbury
Cork
Milford Haven
Bristol
Dover
Southampton
CELTIC SEA
Plymouth
Portland
Falmouth
Fowey
English Channel
Guernsey
ISLES OF SCILLY
CHANNEL IS.
FRANCE

PORTS OF CALL: THE GULF

IRAQ
IRAN
AFGHANISTAN
KUWAIT
THE GULF
QESHM
Bandar-e 'Abbās
Strait of Hormuz
BAHRAIN
Al Manāmah
Al Khaşab
OMAN
QATAR
Sharjah
Dubai
Khawr Fakkan
Ad Dawhah (Doha)
Trucial Coast
Fujairah
GULF OF OMAN
SAUDI ARABIA
UNITED ARAB EMIRATES
Masqaţ (Muscat)
OMAN
JAZĪRAT MAŞĪRAH
ARABIAN SEA

400 km
200 miles

ARCTIC OCEAN

GREENLAND SEA
kjavík
ARK T
Tórshavn
BRITISH ISLES INSET
Eidfjord & Hardangerfjord
Southampton
Dover
Amsterdam

Norwegian Fjords (North Cape/Land of the Midnight Sun) cruise area

Longyearbyen, Spitsbergen
BARENTS SEA
Hammerfest
North Cape
Honningsvåg
Tromsø
NORWEGIAN SEA
Narvik
Ålesund & Geiranger
Molde
Trondheim
Andalsnes
BALTIC INSET
WHITE SEA
Måløy & Olden
Flåm & Gudvangen
Bergen
Stavanger
Oslo
NORTH SEA INSET
Helsinki (Helsingfors)
Baltic (Northern Capitals) cruise area
Stockholm
København (Copenhagen)
Hamburg
Sankt-Peterburg (St Petersburg)
Uglich
Moskva (Moscow)

Black Sea cruise area
CASPIAN SEA
(Western)
Mediterranean cruise area (Eastern)
THE GULF INSET

Funchal, Madeira
Tanger (Tangier)
Valletta
SOUTHERN EUROPE INSET
Casablanca
MEDITERRANEAN SEA
Al Iskandarīyah (Alexandria)
Elat (Eilat)
The Gulf cruise area
Dubai
Strait of Hormuz
GULF OF OMAN

Arrecife
Puerto del Rosario
Las Palmas de Gran Canaria
Santa Cruz de Tenerife
'alma
As Suways (Suez)
Sharm ash Shaykh
Uqşur (Luxor)
Al Aqabah
Bûr Safājah
Isnā (Esna) & Idfū (Edfu)
Aswān & Kawm Umbū
RED SEA
Red Sea cruise area
Atlantic Islands/ West Africa cruise area
Dakar
Banjul
Şalālah
Al Mukallā
ARABIAN SEA
Bab al Mandab
GULF OF ADEN
Djibouti
Mumbai (Bombay)
Goa
Freetown
Monrovia
Grain Coast
Ivory Coast
Gold Coast
Slave Coast
GULF OF GUINEA
Africa-India (Passage to India) cruise area
Kochi (Cochin)
Chennai (Madras)
Colombo
Malé
BAY OF BENGAL
Mombasa
Zanzibar
Victoria, Mahé
Nosy Bé
MOZAMBIQUE CHANNEL
Port Louis, Mauritius
INDIAN OCEAN

Vladivostok
Hakodate
SEA OF JAPAN
Tianjin [for Beijing]
Dalian
Incheon [for Seoul]
Tōkyō
Yokohama
Yantai
Busan
Kōbe
Nagasaki
Chongqing
Nanjing
Wusong
Shanghai
Ningbo
Yangtze
Wuhan
E. CHINA SEA
NORTH PACIFIC OCEAN
Guangzhou (Canton)
Xiamen
Haiphong
Macau
Hong Kong (Xianggang)
Far East cruise area
Yangon (Rangoon)
Da Nang
Manila
Bangkok (Krung Thep)
Nha Trang
Port Blair, S. Andaman
Ho Chi Minh City
Cebu
PHILIPPINE SEA
Pattaya
Phuket
Pinang (Penang)
Kuantan
Kota Kinabalu
Belawan
Malaka (Malacca)
Bandar Seri Begawan
MONDAY INTERNATIONAL DATE LINE SUNDAY
Kuching
Micronesia
Port Kelang [for Kuala Lumpur]
Nias
Padang
Singapore
SOUTH CHINA SEA
Ternate
Pulau Panjang
Jakarta
JAVA SEA
Surabaya
Ujung Pandang
Parepare
Palopo
Ambon
Rabaul
Melanesia
Krakatau
Semarang
Bali
Larantuka, Flores
Honiara
Port Moresby
Christmas I.
Darwin
CORAL SEA
Port Vila, Éfaté
Yasawa
Cairns
GREAT BARRIER REEF
Nouméa
Suva, Viti Levu
Townsville
Nuku'alofa, Tongatapu
Whitsunday Is.
Perth
Australasia/ South Pacific cruise area
Sydney
Bay of Islands
Tauranga [for Rotorua]
GREAT AUSTRALIAN BIGHT
Melbourne
Auckland
TASMAN SEA
Picton
Napier
Wellington
Christchurch
Hobart
Milford Sound
Dunedin
Dusky Sound
Antarctic cruise area
Auckland I.
Campbell I.
Macquarie I.

SOUTH ATLANTIC OCEAN
Durban
Cape Town
Cape of Good Hope
Cape Agulhas
ROUND-THE-WORLD
SOUTHERN OCEAN

Grytviken, Bay of Isles & Elsehul, South Georgia
Port Stanley & West Point, Falkland Is.
Signy & Coronation Is., S. Orkney Is.
SOUTHERN OCEAN
King George I.
Ushuaia
Drake Passage
Hope Bay & Paulet I.
Yankee Harbour & Half Moon I.
Cape Horn
Paradise Harbour & Port Lockroy
WEDDELL SEA
ANTARCTIC PENINSULA
Adelaide & Stonington Is.
Ronne Ice Shelf
South Pole
Marie Byrd Land
Ross Ice Shelf
Wilkes Land
SOUTHERN OCEAN
ANTARCTIC Circle
McMurdo Station & Scott Base
ROSS SEA
Cape Evans
Antarctic cruise area
Cape Hallett
Cape Adare

PORTS OF CALL: SOUTHERN EUROPE

Berching
Regensburg
Dürnstein
GERMANY
Linz
Wien (Vienna)
MOLDOVA
UKRAINE
AUSTRIA
Budapest
HUNGARY
Venézia (Venice)
SLOVENIA
Odesa (Odessa)
BAY OF BISCAY
FRANCE
CROATIA
ROMANIA
SEA OF AZOV
Bordeaux
Savona
Génova (Genoa)
BOSNIA-HERZEGOVINA
Danube Delta
CRIMEA
RUSSIAN FEDERATION
A Coruña
Monte Carlo
Nice
SERBIA
Danube
Constanţa
Sevastopol'
Yalta
Marseille (Marseilles)
Toulon
Livorno (Leghorn)
MONTENEGRO
Varna
BLACK SEA
Sochi
Vigo
Riviera
LIGURIAN SEA
ITALY
Dubrovnik
BULGARIA
Porto (Oporto)
CORSICA
Civitavécchia [for Rome]
Nápoli (Naples)
Bari
ALBANIA
Istanbul
Bat'umi
Barcelona
Ajaccio
FYR OF MACEDONIA
Bosporus
GEORGIA
SPAIN
ANDORRA
Capri
ADRIATIC SEA
Dalmatia
Çanakkale [for Troy]
Trabzon
PORTUGAL
BALEARIC IS.
Sorrento
Kérkira (Corfu)
Dardanelles
TURKEY
Palma de Mallorca
MINORCA
Maó (Mahón)
SARDINIA
Pireás (Piraeus) [for Athens]
Kuşadası
Lisboa (Lisbon)
MAJORCA
Eivissa (Ibiza)
TYRRHENIAN SEA
Catánia
IONIAN SEA
AEGEAN SEA
Praia da Rocha
IBIZA FORMENTERA
Alacant (Alicante)
SICILY
Stretto di Messina
Katákolo
GREECE
Ródos (Rhodes)
Antalya
Cádiz
Málaga
Almería
Githio
PELOPONNESE
RHODES
Tanger (Tangier)
Gibraltar
Ceuta
Melilla (Sp.)
Tunis
Valletta
MALTA
CRETE
Iráklio (Herakleion)
Lemesos (Limassol)
CYPRUS
SYRIA
Casablanca
MEDITERRANEAN SEA
Hefa (Haifa)
Bayrût (Beirut)
LEBANON
Agadir
MOROCCO
ALGERIA
Tarábulus (Tripoli)
GULF OF SIRTE
Banghāzī (Benghazi)
Al Iskandarīyah (Alexandria)
Bûr Sa'īd (Port Said)
ISRAEL
PALESTINE
IRAQ
JORDAN
SAUDI ARABIA
LIBYA
EGYPT
Nile Delta
Suez Canal

1000 kilometres
500 miles

▶ *See also...* World Introduction (22-25); Tourism (34-35); Countries A-Z (108-116)

The listings above refer to a selection of related themes. For more information, see the Contents (2-5).

Key facts	
Number of Countries	48
Area ('000 sq km)	25,926
Population ('000)	799,763
Population Density (per sq km)	31
Gross National Income (US$m)	13,200,398
Visitor Arrivals ('000)	409,570
Visitor Receipts (US$m)	322,678

GNI figures are for 2004. Population figures are taken from the most recent reliable source. Travel figures (UNWTO) are based on overnight stays, not same-day visitors, and are for 2004. For more information see the Countries A-Z section from page 202.

Europe (including the Russian Federation)

EUROPE'S TRAVEL and tourism industry continues to dominate the world and it remains comfortably the world's most visited continent. It has numerous natural and man-made attractions, a generally excellent transport network and a wide range of cities, landscapes and climates. These factors helped draw over 435 million international visitors in 2005, over half the world's total and an increase of some 20 million over 2004. Global recession and the struggle against terrorism depressed the travel industry in 2001 and 2003, but many European travel patterns are well established and impervious to all but the very worst catastrophes. Stability has been vital to this.

That is not to say that Europe has stood still. The political map has altered many times since 1989, as has the membership and influence of the EU (which now rivals the USA as the world's largest economy). Most importantly, these changes have generally been effected peacefully. Given Europe's violent history between 1914 and 1945, this is a considerable achievement.

In general, European states are wealthy, stable, secular, liberal, multi-cultural democracies. Despite linguistic differences, national economies and societies are closely integrated, frontier formalities (for surface travel at any rate) are simple or non-existent and intra-regional trade is high. Apart from some intermittent separatist movements, there is little violent conflict. This inter-dependence, security and stability underpins Europe's vast travel and tourism industry.

Travel overview

Europe's visitor numbers have increased on average by about 2.3% a year since 2000. Although this is below the world average of 3.2%, Europe is a mature market and thus offers less easy opportunities for growth. Intra-regional travel has underpinned Europe's pre-eminence: with so many attractions within easy reach, it is not surprising so many Europeans holiday in their own continent. Nearly nine out of every ten journeys, which start in Europe also finish there. Indeed, trips made by Europeans within Europe account for around half of all international journeys worldwide.

More good news for Europe is that the US market seems to be bouncing back to pre-2001 levels, with an estimated 12.6 million visitors reported in 2005. This is despite the US dollar having lost 6% of its value against the euro in the 12 months up to May 2005, to say nothing of other price increases such as airline fuel and security surcharges.

Whilst the low-cost carriers in Europe continue their seemingly inexorable growth –100 million passengers in 2005 compared to around 50 million in 2003 – the performance of Europe's airlines overall has been encouraging, with a 6% increase in 2005. All of Europe's 25 busiest airports recorded an increase in passenger numbers in year ending October 2005 compared to the previous 12 months (5.25% on average), led by Istanbul with a rise of over 23%. A further 13 airports with one

million-plus passengers saw growth of over 35% in this period. In mature markets, such as the UK, low-cost traffic is expected to continue to grow at around 30% a year, while in newer markets the figure is even higher – 35% in Hungary, for instance. In 2005, low-cost airlines accounted for about 20% of European air travel, as opposed to 5% in 2000. Many observers expect them to account for between a quarter and a third of the continent's market by 2010.

Over 20 European countries now have their own low-cost carriers with more emerging. While not all will survive, the business model has radically changed the face of aviation and has caused major carriers to re-evaluate their pricing, routes and service levels.

Set against this growth is the issue of rising fuel prices which will continue to eat into profitability, particularly for long-haul flights. Fuel surcharges have been imposed by many of the flag-carriers since early 2004 but have so far been resisted by their low-cost rivals. With over half of international journeys in Europe being taken by car, however, the continent's travel industry is much less reliant on air travel than in other parts of the world. With so many countries offering different attractions, history and cultures in such close proximity, touring by rail or road remains popular. Travellers can cover huge swathes of Europe by utilising the continent's integrated transport network.

The seemingly relentless rise of the internet has been another significant feature of the European travel scene. As the preferred booking method for low-cost airlines it has also helped open up many previously under-visited areas of the continent. According to the Centre for Regional and Tourism Research, European online travel sales increased by over 80% between 2003 and 2005 and now accounts for sales of 24 billion euros. This is nearly 10% of the total market: in 1998, online travel was responsible for just 0.1%. The UK, followed by Germany, are the countries with the highest share of internet bookings, although the fastest growth is occurring in the new EU members of Eastern Europe. The internet is increasingly used to research holiday options, even if many may then book through more conventional methods. The continued roll-out of high-speed broadband access across the continent and the increasing willingness of consumers to trust the web for on-line payments are likely to increase this trend. One major hotel chain believes that 50% of all hotel bookings will be online by 2010: at present, the figure is closer to 10%. In the UK, 54% of holidays abroad were pre-paid packages in 2000. By 2004, this had fallen to 45%.

The movement from northern to southern Europe, traditionally in the summer but increasingly at other times, has been happening for decades. Nearly half of all British trips abroad in 2004 were for holidays to the EU15 countries, mainly France and Spain.

Increasingly affordable travel has led to a constant demand for new destinations. Most of the northern Mediterranean coastal region is now seen as a holiday area. To the long-established favourites, one must add Turkey, Croatia, Slovenia and Serbia & Montenegro, all of which saw arrivals increase in 2004 by more than the European average.

Economies

The region's 10 largest economies
Source: World Bank/International Monetary Fund

	GNI US$m 2004	GNI/cap US$ 2004	GDP 2004	growth av p/a '97-'06
Germany	2,488,974	30,194	1.6	1.2
UK	2,016,393	33,361	2.7	2.3
France	1,858,731	30,644	1.4	1.7
Italy	1,503,562	25,878	0.4	1.2
Spain	875,817	21,710	2.5	3.1
Netherlands	515,148	31,397	1.7	2.3
Russia	487,335	3,398	7.2	4.7
Switzerland	356,052	47,541	1.8	1.5
Belgium	322,837	31,149	2.6	2.2
Sweden	321,401	35,704	3.6	2.7

Big spenders

Expenditure on foreign travel (excluding international transport), 2004 – top ten countries (US$ billions) *Source: WTO*

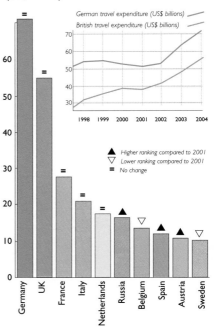

German travel expenditure (US$ billions)
British travel expenditure (US$ billions)

▲ Higher ranking compared to 2001
▽ Lower ranking compared to 2001
= No change

To add to the variety, activities such as camping, city-breaks, skiing and rural holidays are also increasing. Many provide separate holiday options, but sometimes are combined with traditional beach holidays: even skiing, which can be enjoyed in Spain's Sierra Nevada only an hour's drive from the Costa del Sol. Many people take more than one holiday a year to experience more of these ever-increasing alternatives. These factors combined to boost the number of beach holidays taken by Europeans within Europe in 2004 compared to 2003 by 5%, an increase of 3.6 million visits.

According to Eurostat, Europe's economy grew by around 2.2% in 2005. This was below the world average, but – as with visitor arrivals – the continent is generally highly developed and thus offers less opportunity for spectacular increases. Mirroring the performance of the travel industry, the largest growth (in most cases exceeding the world average) is to be found in the east of the continent. Rising fuel costs may have an effect on consumer confidence, but there are few signs that the travel business is going to suffer as a result. Even the spectre of terrorism has not tarnished Europe's appeal. In April 2005, the European Travel Commission commented that 'people are growing more accustomed to living in an unsafe world', and many travellers seem to agree: two weeks after the July 2005 attacks in London, the city's hotel occupancy rates were only slightly down

Heading south

European sunshine destinations ex-UK (000s)
Source: BTA/Visit Britain

	1997	2004
to Spain	8,281	13,833
to France	11,149	11,602
to Greece	1,512	2,709
to Italy	1,801	2,974
to Portugal	1,304	1,804
TOTAL	24,047	32,922
% of all outbound trips	52.3%	51.3%

- Europe occupies 18.9% of the world's land area and is home to 12.4% of the world's population. 65% of the area and 18.0% of the population is provided by Russia.
- Europe accounts for 50.3% of global travel departures and 50.0% of arrivals.
- International travel and tourism contributed over US$320 billion to Europe's economy in 2004.
- 17 countries in Europe received more than US$5 billion from travel and tourism in 2004 and ten received more than US$10 billion.
- Europe has six of the ten most visited countries in the world and seven of the top ten travel earners.
- Germans continue to spend more money on foreign travel than any other nationality.
- 12 European countries received more than 10 million visitors in 2004.
- The most popular destination, France, on its own received about one in eleven of the world's international travellers.
- There were 410 million international tourist arrivals in Europe in 2004, an increase of 100 million since 1997.
- The budget of the EU (approx US$135bn) is only slightly less than the GNI of Argentina.
- The most significant growth in tourist arrivals in 2004 compared to 2003 was in Central and Eastern Europe which showed a rise of 13.8%.
- Europe had over 5.5 million hotel rooms in 2003.
- The Leningrad Metro has the world's longest escalator.
- Russia spans 11 time zones.
- Luxembourg has the highest per capita income of any country in the world.
- Italy is the only country that completely surrounds two other countries (the Vatican City and San Marino).
- The Hermitage in St Petersburg has over 3 million works of art.
- Over 100 tons of tomatoes are thrown during the La Tomatina festival in Buñol in Spain.
- Istanbul is the only city which spans two continents.
- Finland has over 81,000 islands and over 187,000 lakes.
- Andorra is the only country with two heads of state.
- Over 24% of Italians are over 60, the highest percentage in the world.
- Switzerland is the only country with a square flag.
- Lake Baikal in Russia is the deepest lake in the world and holds an estimated 20% of the world's liquid fresh water.

across the continent are now taking steps to respond to this increasingly important aspect of travellers' requirements.

- The sun-migration pattern reverses into a dash to the mountains for winter sports. The central Alps remain ever-popular, but Slovenia, Romania and Bulgaria are fast-emerging destinations.
- The recent opening up of Eastern Europe has led to an increase of travel not only between these countries but also from other parts of Europe. Poland, Hungary and the Czech Republic have been in the forefront.
- The states of the former Yugoslavia, particularly Slovenia, Croatia and – increasingly – Serbia & Montenegro have shown solid growth in recent years and are likely to continue to do so.
- Health and spa holidays are also on the increase: again, Eastern Europe is helping to lead the way.
- Golf holidays in Spain and Portugal, have long been popular, while France's uncrowded courses make it a strengthening force in the market.
- The Mediterranean and the Baltic are, after the Caribbean, the most popular cruise areas in the world.
- No-frills hotels are now competing with deluxe brands for the attention of business and leisure travellers who, having invested little in their air fare, are frequenting higher grade hotels and restaurants than in the past.
- EU enlargement is leading to the ten most recent members being further assimilated into Europe's travel patterns. They are also likely to be offer value for money when compared with many traditional destinations.

Destination overview

- **France** – comfortably Europe's, and the world's, most visited country, accounting for nearly one in five of the continent's international arrivals. Paris is the city-break destination *par excellence* and the Côte d'Azur one of the world's most famous playgrounds. From gastronomy to golf and from adventure breaks to fine art, France's highly varied holiday products cater for virtually all tastes.
- **Spain** – the continent's second most popular destination, and the favourite amongst Europeans (with a 13% market share in 2004 compared to France's 12%). The traditional image of beach holidays on the Mediterranean coast is fast changing, spearheaded by the city-breaks to its many magnificent cities, mainly Madrid, Seville and Barcelona.
- **Italy** – Europe's third most visited country has an enviable blend of climate, culture, natural beauty and urban sophistication. *Benessere* (well-being) and *agriturismi* (farm-stay) holidays are increasingly important niche markets. It is hoped the 2006 Winter Olympics in Turin will boost travel to Piedmont.
- **UK** – with estimates from Visit Britain putting growth in tourist arrivals and receipts at about 4.4%, the UK is expected to break the 30 million visitors mark in 2006. The country has long benefitted from its 'heritage' appeal, particularly in the North American market.
- **Germany** – the country's tourism profile has been raised through an effective series of national and regional marketing campaigns emphasising Germany's diversity. It was one of the first countries to be granted Approved Destination Status by China, which has contributed to a growth of nearly 2 million visitors to bring total arrivals up above the 20 million mark. Germany's vibrant cities have also proved popular.
- **Greece** – with around 1,400 islands, Greece can boast a coastline of some 15,000km, and it is upon this, together with its incomparable heritage sites, that its tourism appeal has largely been founded.
- **Turkey** – one of the consistent star performers of the European travel scene in recent years, Turkey's visitor numbers have risen steadily from 9 million in 1997 to nearly 17 million in 2004. Turkey's appeal has been built on the solid foundations of its beaches and cultural sites, as well as value-for-money.
- **Scandinavia** – a mature market with healthy intra-

■ Big earners

Receipts from foreign travel (excluding international transport), 2004 – top ten countries (US$ billions) *Source: WTO*

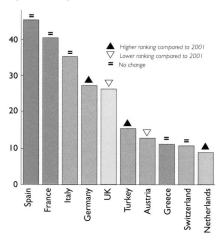

▲ Higher ranking compared to 2001
▽ Lower ranking compared to 2001
= No change

regional trade. Increasing numbers of visitors are drawn by the area's pristine environment and stunning scenery. Short-breaks to the major Scandinavian cities have increased as a result of the rise of the low-cost airlines.

- **Benelux** – these three countries attract around 16 million visitors. Cities such as Amsterdam, Brussels and Bruges are prime short-break destinations.
- **Eastern Europe** – the eight countries in this region that joined the EU in 2004 have benefited from improved air links, reduced border formalities and a favourable rate against the euro. Arrivals to the region grew by 11% in 2004, more than twice the European average. The strong Russian outbound market and well-established patterns of intra-regional travel have also played their part in this increase.

Problem areas

- Further terrorist attacks cannot be ruled out.
- Until the UK adopts the euro (if it does), its imports and exports, including travel, will remain at the mercy of euro/sterling exchange rate fluctuations.
- Although away from the European mainstream, instability is a risk in Russia and some of the former Russian republics. The newly expanded EU's relations with these countries will be of great importance.
- Traffic congestion in some cities has reduced average driving speeds to near walking-pace.
- Air travel has increased more quickly than the investment in air traffic control and airport infrastructure, which can cause delays at peak times, particularly at major hubs: 70% of the air traffic delays in 2004 took place at 30% of Europe's airports.
- Europe's wealth is attracting migrants from poorer parts of the world, which is fuelling social tensions and the growth of right-wing political parties.

on the same period the year before, while Madrid's visitor figures increased in the first nine months of 2004 compared to 2003. In common with other parts of the world, the European travel industry has shown itself to be remarkably resilient. Times are certainly changing; but change is not always for the worse. Certainly, those who value choice, flexibility and value-for-money have never had it so good.

Travel trends

The more extreme tastes in adventure holidays are best satisfied in other continents but, that aside, Europe has something for everyone, from castles to clubs, scuba-diving to ski resorts and golf courses to art galleries. Major patterns or possible future trends, in addition to those discussed above, are as follows.

- In general, people are tending to take more shorter trips rather than one long summer holiday (although this option still remains popular). City breaks are the main examples of this trend, and in 2004 12% more Europeans took city breaks within the continent compared to 2003. Urban fashions come and go, but the main capitals are ever-popular, as are cities such as Bruges, St Petersburg, Istanbul, Tallinn, Dresden, Venice, Barcelona, Munich, Milan, Dubrovnik and Cracow.
- Short breaks to beach destinations such as Majorca, the Côte d'Azur and the Algarve are on the increase.
- Travellers are increasingly looking for holidays that will challenge them and provide new experiences. Adventure holidays fill part of this desire, but educational and foreign-language tourism are growing, as are holidays involving an element of voluntary work.
- The phrases 'responsible tourism' and 'ethical tourism' are in some ways more relevant to other parts of the world than Europe, but numerous resorts

■ Visitors

Visitor arrivals 2004: top ten countries *Source: WTO*

	Visitors (thousands)	Change since 1997
France	75,121	11.4%
Spain	53,599	27.1%
Italy	37,071	6.0%
United Kingdom	27,755	9.1%
Germany	20,137	23.4%
Austria	19,373	14.3%
Turkey	16,826	58.4%
Ukraine	15,629	64.5%
Poland	14,290	-38.1%
Greece	13,787	26.6%

See also... World Physical (26-27); World Political (28-29), World Climate (30)

The listings above refer to a selection of related themes.
For more information, see the Contents (2-5).

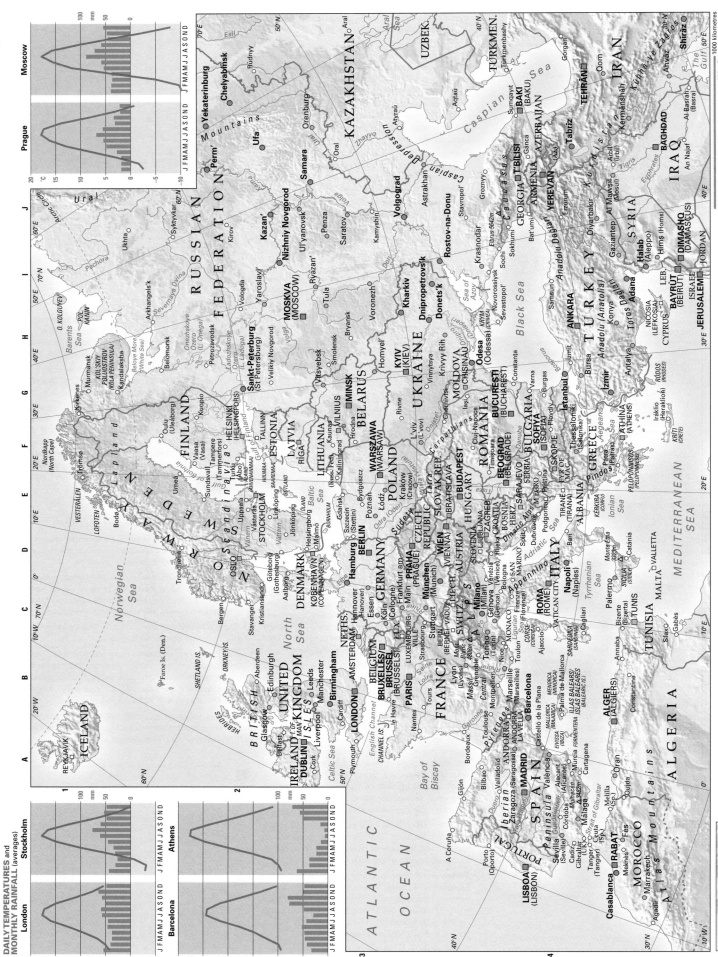

Moscow

Prague

Stockholm

London

Athens

Barcelona

DAILY TEMPERATURES and
MONTHLY RAINFALL (averages)

The listings above refer to a selection of related themes. For more information, see the Contents (2-5).

Columbus Travel Guides' *World Travel Guide* contains detailed climate charts for every country in the world, including temperature, rainfall, sunshine and humidity

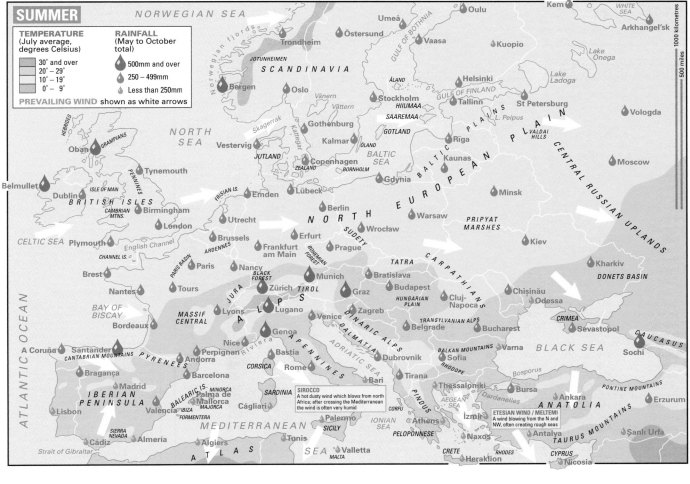

▶ *See also...* Countries A-Z (108-116)

The listings above refer to a selection of related themes. For more information, see the Contents (2-5).

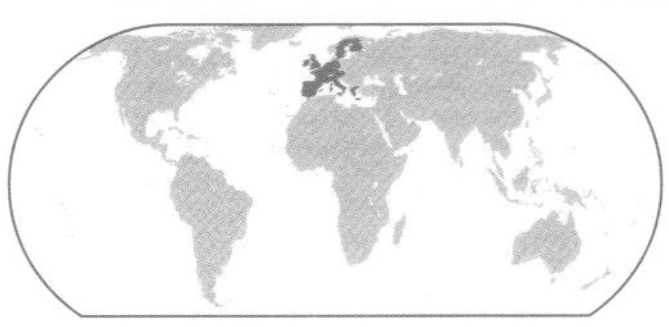

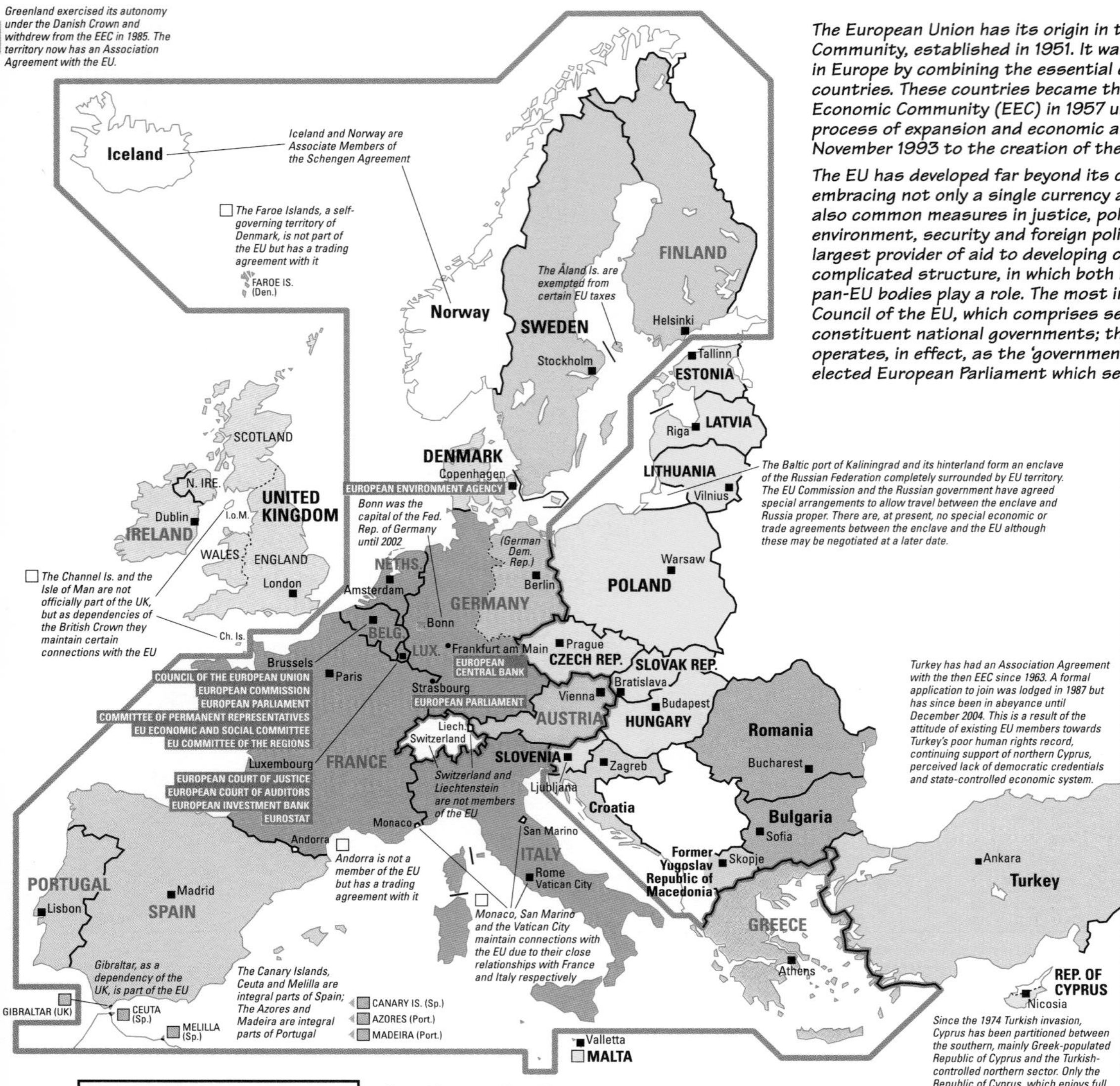

Greenland exercised its autonomy under the Danish Crown and withdrew from the EEC in 1985. The territory now has an Association Agreement with the EU.
Iceland
Iceland and Norway are Associate Members of the Schengen Agreement
The Faroe Islands, a self-governing territory of Denmark, is not part of the EU but has a trading agreement with it
FAROE IS. (Den.)
Norway
SWEDEN
Stockholm
The Åland Is. are exempted from certain EU taxes
FINLAND
Helsinki
Tallinn
ESTONIA
Riga
LATVIA
LITHUANIA
Vilnius
The Baltic port of Kaliningrad and its hinterland form an enclave of the Russian Federation completely surrounded by EU territory. The EU Commission and the Russian government have agreed special arrangements to allow travel between the enclave and Russia proper. There are, at present, no special economic or trade arrangements between the enclave and the EU although these may be negotiated at a later date.
SCOTLAND
N. IRE.
UNITED KINGDOM
I.o.M.
Dublin
IRELAND
WALES
ENGLAND
London
The Channel Is. and the Isle of Man are not officially part of the UK, but as dependencies of the British Crown they maintain certain connections with the EU
Ch. Is.
DENMARK
Copenhagen
EUROPEAN ENVIRONMENT AGENCY
Bonn was the capital of the Fed. Rep. of Germany until 2002
NETHS.
Amsterdam
(German Dem. Rep.)
Berlin
GERMANY
Bonn
POLAND
Warsaw
BELG.
LUX.
Frankfurt am Main
EUROPEAN CENTRAL BANK
Prague
CZECH REP.
SLOVAK REP.
Bratislava
Brussels
COUNCIL OF THE EUROPEAN UNION
EUROPEAN COMMISSION
EUROPEAN PARLIAMENT
COMMITTEE OF PERMANENT REPRESENTATIVES
EU ECONOMIC AND SOCIAL COMMITTEE
EU COMMITTEE OF THE REGIONS
Paris
Strasbourg
EUROPEAN PARLIAMENT
Vienna
AUSTRIA
Budapest
HUNGARY
Liech.
Switzerland
Luxembourg
FRANCE
EUROPEAN COURT OF JUSTICE
EUROPEAN COURT OF AUDITORS
EUROPEAN INVESTMENT BANK
EUROSTAT
SLOVENIA
Ljubljana
Zagreb
Croatia
Switzerland and Liechtenstein are not members of the EU
Romania
Bucharest
Bulgaria
Sofia
Turkey has had an Association Agreement with the then EEC since 1963. A formal application to join was lodged in 1987 but has since been in abeyance until December 2004. This is a result of the attitude of existing EU members towards Turkey's poor human rights record, continuing support of northern Cyprus, perceived lack of democratic credentials and state-controlled economic system.
Monaco
Andorra
Andorra is not a member of the EU but has a trading agreement with it
San Marino
ITALY
Rome
Vatican City
Former Yugoslav Republic of Macedonia
Skopje
Ankara
Turkey
PORTUGAL
Lisbon
Madrid
SPAIN
Monaco, San Marino and the Vatican City maintain connections with the EU due to their close relationships with France and Italy respectively
GREECE
Athens
REP. OF CYPRUS
Nicosia
Gibraltar, as a dependency of the UK, is part of the EU
GIBRALTAR (UK)
CEUTA (Sp.)
MELILLA (Sp.)
The Canary Islands, Ceuta and Melilla are integral parts of Spain; The Azores and Madeira are integral parts of Portugal
CANARY IS. (Sp.)
AZORES (Port.)
MADEIRA (Port.)
Valletta
MALTA
Since the 1974 Turkish invasion, Cyprus has been partitioned between the southern, mainly Greek-populated Republic of Cyprus and the Turkish-controlled northern sector. Only the Republic of Cyprus, which enjoys full international recognition, has been admitted to the EU. The 'Turkish Republic of Northern Cyprus' is not recognised by the EU.

The provisions and conditions of EU membership also apply to the following territories which are integral parts of member states: Canary Is., Ceuta and Melilla (Spain); Azores and Madeira (Portugal) and (both not Schengen) French Guiana, Guadeloupe, Martinique and Réunion (France);

The European Union has its origin in the European Coal and Steel Community, established in 1951. It was originally designed to ensure peace in Europe by combining the essential economic interests of its six member countries. These countries became the founding members of the European Economic Community (EEC) in 1957 under the Treaty of Rome. A gradual process of expansion and economic and political integration led in November 1993 to the creation of the 12-member European Union (EU).

The EU has developed far beyond its original design of a free-trade bloc, embracing not only a single currency and a European Central Bank, but also common measures in justice, policing, immigration, transport, environment, security and foreign policy. The EU is also the world's single largest provider of aid to developing countries. As a result, the EU has a complicated structure, in which both individual national governments and pan-EU bodies play a role. The most important of the latter are: the Council of the EU, which comprises senior representatives of the constituent national governments; the European Commission which operates, in effect, as the 'government' or executive of the EU; and the elected European Parliament which serves as its legislature.

1957 Founder members (6)

Subsequent members:

- **1973** (3)
- **1981** (1)
- **1986** (2)
- **1990** Following the reunification of Germany in 1990, the former German Democratic Republic was automatically admitted to the EEC.
- **1995** (3)
- **2004** (10)

EU-15

EU NEW 10

Accession countries (to join in 2007?)

Candidate countries (to join in 2012/13?)

There are no formal limits on the ultimate boundaries of the EU and other nations may apply to join in future. These include countries which have previously opted out (Norway, Iceland, Switzerland), the Balkan countries yet to be candidates (Bosnia-Herzegovina, Serbia, Montenegro, Albania) and perhaps others beyond Europe in the former Soviet Union, the Levant and North Africa.

The process of joining the EU begins with the signing of an Association Agreement, essentially a free trade accord. The next stage is to become a **Candidate country** by meeting three conditions (The Copenhagen Criteria):
- Democracy, human rights and the rule of law;
- A market economy;
- The adoption of the EU's acquis, which lay down the precepts and standards for all member states and cover almost every aspect of government.

Once a timetable has been agreed for the acquis, the Candidate country is certain to join the EU and becomes an **Accession country**.

EURO ZONE **Members which have adopted monetary union are shown in RED**

The single European currency, the euro, came into being in 1999 along with the European Central Bank which supervises the eurozone and sets interest rates. Since 2002, the euro has been the sole legitimate currency in the 12 (out of 25) EU countries which have adopted it. Eurozone membership requires that a country meets various economic criteria covering inflation, interest and exchange rates, and government finances (although these can be somewhat flexible). The UK and Denmark have derogations under the 1992 Maastricht Treaty while Sweden appears to have no intention to join. Of the 10 countries which joined the EU in 2004, all wish to enter the eurozone and all should be admitted by 2012; at present, they have either pegged their currencies to the euro or allow them to float within a fixed range.

Several countries outside the EU, mostly former colonies and associated territories, have linked their currencies to the euro which is now a major force in international finance.

Schengen countries

The Schengen Agreement allows for the removal of most frontier controls and the harmonisation of procedures governing the movement of people and goods between signatory countries. It also provides for co-operation between law enforcement agencies in specified areas including immigration, terrorism and serious crime. Two non-EU countries, Iceland and Norway, are associate members of the Schengen Agreement.

The United Kingdom and Ireland subscribe only to some parts of the Schengen Agreement.

Most of the Schengen conditions have now been incorporated into the acquis which comprise the basic conditions for entry into the EU. As such, all new EU members will necessarily adopt the Schengen measures in due course.

Principal EU institutions

■ **Capital cities**

SUMMARY TABLE

For more country statistics, including tourism, energy and health, see the Countries A-Z section in the Appendices

Country	Exchange rate, 1st Feb 2006 One euro=	Currency	Central Bank interest rate, 1st Feb 2006 (%)	Standard VAT rate 2005 (%)	Inflation, 2005 average (%)	Unemployment, 2005 average (% of workforce)	Gross National Income (GNI), 2004 (US$ billion)	GDP growth, 2003-2004 (%)	Balance of payments, 2004 (m euros)	Government debt, 2004 (% of GDP)	Gov't expenditure, 2004 (% of GDP)
EUROZONE Central Bank interest rate in the Eurozone is set by the European Central Bank, Frankfurt											
Austria	1		3.25	[1] 20	1.6	5.2	262.2	2.4	+573	64.3	49.9
Belgium	1		3.25	21	2.4	8.4	322.8	2.6	+9,513	96.2	49.5
Finland	1		3.25	[2] 22	1.0	8.3	171.0	3.6	+7,667	45.1	51.1
France	1		3.25	[3] 19.6	1.8	9.2	1,858.7	2.3	–6,760	65.1	53.4
Germany	1		3.25	[4] 16	2.3	9.3	2,489.0	1.6	+83,509	66.4	46.9
Greece	1		3.25	[5] 19	3.4	10.5	183.9	4.7	–8,800	109.3	49.8
Ireland	1		3.25	21	2.2	4.3	137.8	4.5	–1,181	29.8	33.7
Italy	1		3.25	[6] 20	2.4	8.0	1,503.6	1.2	–12,054	106.5	48.6
Luxembourg	1		3.25	15	3.6	5.6	25.3	4.5	+2,851	6.6	45.3
Netherlands	1		3.25	19	1.6	4.7	515.1	1.7	+44,163	53.1	46.6
Portugal	1		3.25	[7] 21	2.5	7.5	149.8	1.2	–8,603	59.4	46.1
Spain	1		3.25	[8] 16	3.4	8.5	875.8	3.1	–44,451	46.9	38.8
NON-EUROZONE											
Cyprus, Rep.of	0.57	*Cyprus Pound*	4.25	15	2.0	7.9	13.6	3.8	–716	72.0	43.6
Czech Republic	28.41	*Koruna*	2.00	[9] 19	2.2	7.9	93.2	4.4	–4,518	36.8	44.3
Denmark	7.46	*Krone*	2.40	[10] 25	1.9	4.5	219.4	2.1	4,493	43.2	55.1
Estonia	15.65	*Kroon*	3.80	18	4.0	6.6	9.4	7.8	–1,148	5.5	36.4
Hungary	252.55	*Forint*	6.00	25	3.3	7.3	83.3	4.6	–7,132	57.4	49.7
Latvia	0.70	*Lats*	4.00	18	7.5	8.6	12.6	9.8	–1,445	14.7	35.8
Lithuania	3.45	*Litas*	3.25	18	2.8	7.0	19.7	7.0	–1,393	19.6	33.2
Malta	0.43	*Maltese Lira*	3.25	18	4.3	7.7	4.9	0.1	–431	75.9	48.8
Poland	3.83	*Zloty*	4.50	22	1.1	17.4	232.4	5.3	–8,406	43.6	43.0
Slovak Republic	37.35	*Koruna*	3.00	19	3.6	16.0	34.9	5.5	–1,156	42.5	40.6
Slovenia	239.51	*Tolar*	6.25	20	2.1	5.9	29.6	4.2	–542	29.8	47.4
Sweden	9.24	*Krona*	1.75	25	1.2	6.4	321.4	3.7	+22,594	51.1	56.7
United Kingdom	0.68	*Sterling*	4.50	[11] 17.5	2.1	4.7	2,016.4	3.2	–34,563	41.5	43.7

[1] 16% in Jungholz & Mittelberg. [2] Excluding Åland Is. [3] 8.5% in Guadeloupe, Martinique & Réunion. [4] Excluding Helgoland & Busingen. [5] 13% on many of the Greek islands. No VAT applies to Mount Athos. [6] Excluding Livigno, the Italian enclave of Campione d'Italia & territorial waters of Lake Lugano. [7] 15% in the Azores & Madeira. [8] Excluding Canary Is., Ceuta & Melilla. [9] Including UK Sovereign Base Areas. [10] Excluding Faroe Is. & Greenland. [11] Excluding Channel Is.

Sources: European System of Central Banks; Eurostat; European Commission; World Bank; oanda.com

The listings above refer to a selection of related themes.
For more information, see the Contents (2-5).

POPULATION DENSITY

Statistics for Denmark include the Faroe Is.

People per square kilometre, 2004

- 400 and over
- 250 – 399
- 150 – 249
- 80 – 149
- 30 – 79
- Less than 30

Source: Eurostat

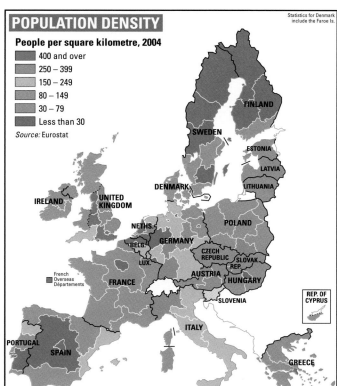

French Overseas Départements

REP. OF CYPRUS

Azores (Port.) | Canary Is. (Sp.)
Madeira (Port.) | Ceuta & Melilla (Sp.)

MALTA

THE EU'S LARGEST URBAN AREAS, 2005

Estimated populations in thousands   *Source:* UN

Paris	9,854	Rome	2,628
London	7,615	Munich	2,318
Rhine-Ruhr North	6,566	Birmingham	2,215
Dortmund-Duisburg-Düsseldorf-Essen		Warsaw	2,204
Madrid	5,145	Manchester	2,193
Barcelona	4,424	Vienna	2,190
Milan	4,007	Lisbon	1,977
Rhine-Main	3,721	Stockholm	1,729
Frankfurt-Darmstadt-Wiesbaden		Budapest	1,670
Berlin	3,328	Rhine-Neckar	1,625
Rhine-Ruhr Middle	3,325	*Mannheim-Ludwigshafen-Heidelberg*	
Düsseldorf-Mönchengladbach-Wuppertal		Lyons	1,408
Athens	3,238	Marseilles - Aix-en-Prov.	1,384
Rhine-Ruhr South	3,084		
Bonn-Cologne-Leverkusen			
Katowice	2,914		
Naples	2,905		
Stuttgart	2,705		
Hamburg	2,686		

THE EU BUDGET

Contributions by member states to the EU, 2006
(Total: 110,160 million euros)

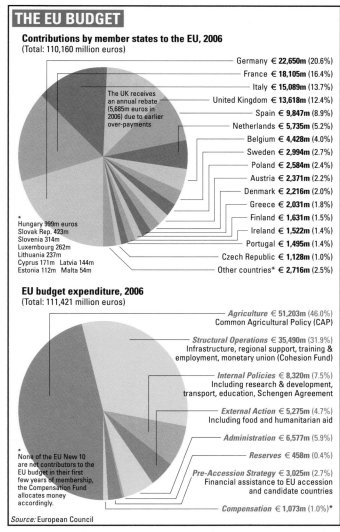

The UK receives an annual rebate (5,685m euros in 2006) due to earlier over-payments

- Germany € **22,650m** (20.6%)
- France € **18,105m** (16.4%)
- Italy € **15,089m** (13.7%)
- United Kingdom € **13,618m** (12.4%)
- Spain € **9,847m** (8.9%)
- Netherlands € **5,735m** (5.2%)
- Belgium € **4,428m** (4.0%)
- Sweden € **2,994m** (2.7%)
- Poland € **2,584m** (2.4%)
- Austria € **2,371m** (2.2%)
- Denmark € **2,216m** (2.0%)
- Greece € **2,031m** (1.8%)
- Finland € **1,631m** (1.5%)
- Ireland € **1,522m** (1.4%)
- Portugal € **1,495m** (1.4%)
- Czech Republic € **1,128m** (1.0%)
- Other countries* € **2,716m** (2.5%)

* Hungary 999m euros
Slovak Rep. 423m
Slovenia 314m
Luxembourg 262m
Lithuania 237m
Cyprus 171m   Latvia 144m
Estonia 112m   Malta 54m

EU budget expenditure, 2006
(Total: 111,421 million euros)

Agriculture € **51,203m** (46.0%)
Common Agricultural Policy (CAP)

Structural Operations € **35,490m** (31.9%)
Infrastructure, regional support, training & employment, monetary union (Cohesion Fund)

Internal Policies € **8,320m** (7.5%)
Including research & development, transport, education, Schengen Agreement

External Action € **5,275m** (4.7%)
Including food and humanitarian aid

Administration € **6,577m** (5.9%)

Reserves € **458m** (0.4%)

Pre-Accession Strategy € **3,025m** (2.7%)
Financial assistance to EU accession and candidate countries

Compensation € **1,073m** (1.0%)*

* None of the EU New 10 are net contributors to the EU budget in their first few years of membership, the Compensation Fund allocates money accordingly.

Source: European Council

INCOME

Statistics for Denmark include the Faroe Is.

Gross domestic product per person, 2004

- 26,000 euros (€) and over
- € 21,000 – 25,999
- € 16,000 – 20,999
- € 13,000 – 15,999
- € 9,000 – 12,999
- € 5,000 – 8,999
- Less than € 5,000

Source: Eurostat

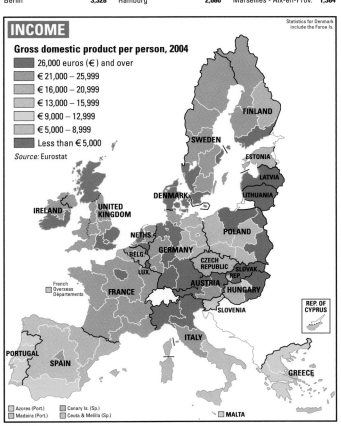

French Overseas Départements

REP. OF CYPRUS

Azores (Port.) | Canary Is. (Sp.)
Madeira (Port.) | Ceuta & Melilla (Sp.)

MALTA

UNEMPLOYMENT

Statistics for Denmark include the Faroe Is.

Unemployed as a percentage of the workforce, 2004

- 20% and over
- 15.0% – 19.9%
- 11.0% – 14.9%
- 8.0% – 10.9%
- 5.0% – 7.9%
- Less than 5.0%

Source: Eurostat

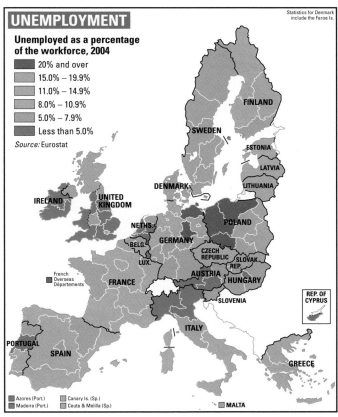

French Overseas Départements

REP. OF CYPRUS

Azores (Port.) | Canary Is. (Sp.)
Madeira (Port.) | Ceuta & Melilla (Sp.)

MALTA

▶ *See also...* Europe National Parks (54); World Monuments Fund (105)

The listings above refer to a selection of related themes. For more information, see the Contents (2-5).

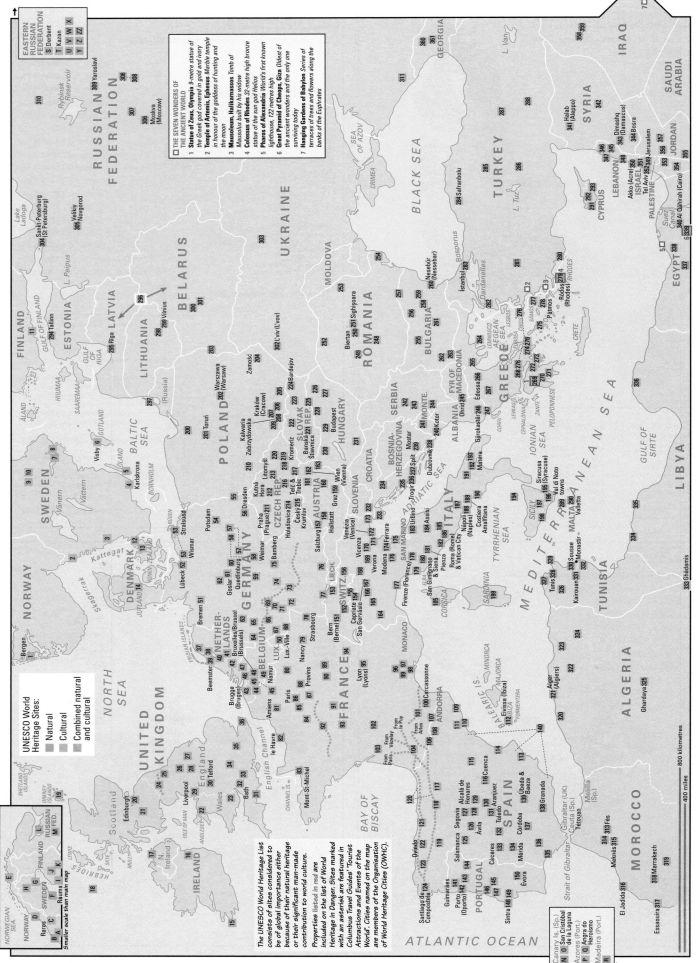

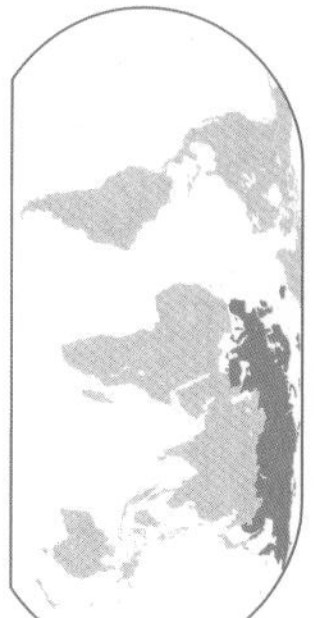

▶ *See also...* Europe National Parks (54); World Monuments Fund (105)

The listings above refer to a selection of related themes. For more information, see the Contents (2-5).

Numbers: main map Letters: insets

EUROPE (including Turkey & Cyprus)

1 Bergen: Bryggen wharf*, Norway
A Urnes: stave church, Norway
B Geirangerfjorden and Nærøyfjorden, Norway
C Røros: mining town, Norway
D Vega Archipelago, Norway
E Alta: rock drawings, Norway
2 Tanum: rock carvings, Sweden
3 Grimeton: Varberg radio station, Sweden
4 Karlskrona: naval city, Sweden
5 Southern Öland: agricultural landscape, Sweden
6 Visby: Hanseatic town and former Viking site, Sweden
7 Birka and Hovgården: archaeological sites, Sweden
8 Stockholm: Skogskyrkogården cemetery, Sweden; Drottningholms Slot (Drottningholm Royal Palace)*, Sweden
9 Falun: mining area of the Great Copper Mountain, Sweden
10 Engelsberg: ironworks, Sweden
F High Coast, Sweden
G Luleå: Gammelstad church village, Sweden
H Lapponian area, Sweden
I Rauma: old town, Finland; Sammallahdenmäki: Bronze Age burial site, Finland
J Petäjävesi: old church, Finland
K Verla: groundwood and board mill, Finland
11 Helsinki (Helsingfors): Suomenlinna Sea Fortress*, Finland
12 Helsingør (Elsinore): Kronborg Slot (Kronborg Castle)*, Denmark
13 Roskilde: cathedral, Denmark
14 Jelling: mounds, runic stones and church, Denmark
15 Skellig Michael: monastic complex, Ireland
16 Brú Na Bóinne: Newgrange, Knowth and Dowth prehistoric sites, Ireland
17 Giant's Causeway* and its coast, Northern Ireland
18 St Kilda, Scotland
19 Orkney: Neolithic monuments, Scotland
20 Edinburgh: old and new towns (incl. Castle*, Palace of Holyroodhouse*, Royal Mus. & Mus. of Scotland*, Scotch Whisky Heritage Centre & Royal Mile* and Scottish Parliament Building*), Scotland
21 New Lanark: industrial village*, Scotland
22 Castles and town walls of King Edward (incl. Caernarfon Castle* and Conwy Castle*), northwest Wales
23 Blaenavon: industrial landscape (incl. Big Pit National Mining Museum of Wales*), Wales
24 Frontiers of the Roman Empire (1): Hadrian's Wall*, England
25 Durham: castle and cathedral*, England
26 Studley Royal Park and Fountains Abbey ruins, England
27 Derwent Valley mills, England
28 Saltaire: industrial village, England
29 Liverpool: maritime mercantile city (incl. Albert Dock*), England
30 Ironbridge Gorge, England
31 Dorset and East Devon coast, England
32 Bath (incl. Roman baths and pumproom*), England
33 Stonehenge*, Avebury and associated Megalithic sites, England
34 Blenheim Palace, England
35 London: Tower of London*, England; London: Westminster Palace*, Westminster Abbey* and St Margaret's Church, England; Kew: Royal Botanic Gardens, England; Maritime Greenwich*, England
36 Canterbury: cathedral*, St Augustine's Abbey and St Martin's Church, England
37 Wouda steam pumping station, The Netherlands
38 Schokland: prehistoric settlements, The Netherlands
39 Droogmakerij de Beemster (Beemster Polder), The Netherlands
40 Amsterdam: defence line, The Netherlands
41 Utrecht: Rietveld Schröderhuis, The Netherlands
42 Kinderdijk-Elshout: mill network, The Netherlands
43 Brugge (Bruges): historic centre, Belgium
44 Tournai: Cathédrale Notre-Dame, Belgium
45 Belfries of Belgium and France (incl. Onze Lieve Vrouwekathedraal, Antwerpen (Antwerp)*), Belgium/France
46 Antwerpen (Antwerp): Plantin-Moretus Museum, Belgium
47 Flemish Begijnhoven (Béguinages), Belgium
48 Bruxelles/Brussel (Brussels): Grand-Place*, Belgium; Bruxelles/Brussel (Brussels): four town houses of architect Victor Horta, Belgium
49 Canal du Centre: four boat-lifts and environs, la Louvière and le Rœulx, Belgium; Mons: Spiennes Neolithic flint mines, Belgium
50 Luxembourg-Ville: old quarters and fortifications
51 Bremen: town hall and statue of Roland, Germany
52 Lübeck: Hanseatic city, Germany
53 Stralsund and Wismar: historic centres, Germany
54 Berlin: Museumsinsel (incl. Pergamonmuseum*), Germany; Potsdam and SW Berlin: palaces and parks (incl. Schloss Sanssouci*), Germany
55 Muskauer Park, Germany, and Park Muzakowski, Poland
56 Dresden Elbe valley: cultural landscape, Germany
57 Eisleben and Wittenberg: Luther memorials, Germany
58 Dessau-Wörlitz: Garden Kingdom, Germany; Dessau and Weimar: Bauhaus buildings, Germany; Weimar: classical city, Germany
59 Schloss Wartburg, Germany
60 Quedlinburg: collegiate church, castle and old town, Germany
61 Goslar: historic town and Rammelsberg mines, Germany
62 Hildesheim: cathedral and St Michaeliskirche, Germany
63 Essen: Zollverein coal mine industrial complex, Germany
64 Aachen (Aix-la-Chapelle): cathedral, Germany
65 **Köln (Cologne): cathedral***, Germany; Brühl: Schloss Augustusburg & Jagdschl. Falkenlust, Germany
66 Upper Middle Rhine Valley, Germany
67 Trier: Roman monuments, cathedral and Liebfrauenkirche, Germany
68 Völklingen: ironworks, Germany
69 Messel Pit fossil site, Germany
70 Lorsch: abbey and Altenmünster, Germany
71 Speyer: cathedral, Germany
72 Maulbronn: Cistercian monastery complex, Germany
73 Frontiers of the Roman Empire (2): Roman Limes, Germany
74 Würzburg: Residenz with gardens and square, Germany
75 Bamberg, Germany
76 Wies: pilgrimage church, Germany
77 Reichenau: monastic island, Germany
78 Strasbourg: Grand Île, France
79 Nancy: Place Stanislas, Pl. de la Carrière and Pl. d'Alliance, France
80 Reims: Cathédrale Notre-Dame, Abbaye St-Remi and Palais du Tau, France
81 Amiens: cathedral, France
82 Le Havre: city rebuilt after Second World War, France
83 Mont-St-Michel* and its bay, France
84 Chartres: cathedral, France
85 Versailles: palace and park*, France
86 Paris: banks of the Seine (incl. Tour Eiffel*, Musée du Louvre*, Musée d'Orsay* and Cathédrale de Notre-Dame*), France
87 Fontainebleau: palace and park, France
88 Provins: fortified medieval town, France
89 Fontenay: Cistercian abbey, France
90 Vézelay: church and hill, France
91 Bourges: cathedral, France
92 Loire Valley between Chalonnes & Sully-sur-Loire, including Château de Chambord, France
93 St-Savin-sur-Gartempe: church, France
94 Arc-et-Senans: royal saltworks, France
95 Lyon (Lyons): historic city, France
96 Orange: Roman theatre and its surroundings and the triumphal arch, France
97 Avignon: historic centre (incl. Palais des Papes*), France
98 Arles: Roman and Romanesque monuments (incl. Roman amphitheatre*), France
99 Remoulins: Pont du Gard Roman aqueduct, France
100 Carcassonne: historic fortified city*, France
101 Canal du Midi, France
102 Vallée du Vézère: Lascaux* and other decorated caves, France
103 St-Émilion: vineyard landscape, France
104 Way of St James pilgrimage route: four routes through France
105 Golfe de Girolata, Golfe de Porto, Piana Calanches and Réserve naturelle Scandola, Corsica, France
106 Mont Perdu/Monte Perdido, France/Spain
107 Madriu-Perafita-Claror valley: cultural landscape, Andorra
108 Vall de Boí: Catalan Romanesque churches, Spain
109 Barcelona: works of Antonio Gaudí (incl. Parque Güell* and Sagrada Familia*), Spain; Barcelona: Palau de la Música Catalaña and the Hospital de Sant Pau: art nouveau buildings, Spain
110 Tarragona: Roman city of Tárraco, Spain
111 Poblet: Cistercian monastery, Spain
112 Eivissa (Ibiza): biodiversity and culture, Spain
113 Elx (Elche): Palmeral (date palm) landscape, Spain
114 València: La Lonja de la Seda (Silk Exchange), Spain
115 Aragón: Mudéjar architecture, Spain
116 Cuenca: historic walled town, Spain
117 San Millán de la Cogolla: Suso and Yuso monasteries, Spain
118 Burgos: cathedral, Spain; Cuevas de Atapuerca: archaeological site, Spain
119 Las Médulas: Roman gold workings, Spain
120 Camino de Santiago: Way of St James pilgrimage route*, Spain
121 Cuevas de Altamira: archaeological site, Spain
122 Oviedo: churches of the Asturias Kingdom and La Foncalada hydraulic structure, Spain
123 Lugo: Roman walls, Spain
124 Santiago de Compostela: old town (incl. cathedral*), Spain
125 Salamanca: old city, Spain
126 Ávila: old town with extra-muros churches, Spain
127 Segovia: old town and Roman aqueduct*, Spain
128 El Escorial: monastery*, Spain
129 Alcalá de Henares: university and historic precinct, Spain
130 Aranjuez: cultural landscape, Spain
131 Toledo: historic city, Spain
132 Guadalupe: Real Monasterio de Santa María, Spain
133 Cáceres: old town, Spain
134 Mérida: archaeological ensemble, Spain
135 Parque Nacional Doñana, Spain
136 Sevilla (Seville): cathedral*, Alcazar and Archivo de Indias, Spain
137 Córdoba: mosque and historic centre, Spain
138 Granada: Alhambra*, Generalife & Albaicín quarter, Spain
139 Úbeda and Baeza: Renaissance monumental ensembles, Spain
140 Mediterranean seaboard prehistoric rock-art sites, Spain
N Parque Nacional de Garajonay, Gomera, Canary Is.
O San Cristóbal de la Laguna, Tenerife, Canary Is.
P Pico: vineyard landscape, Azores
Q Angra do Heroísmo: central area, Terceira, Azores
R Madeira: Laurisilva (laurel forest)
141 Guimarães: historic centre, Portugal
142 Porto (Oporto): historic centre, Portugal
143 Alto Douro wine region, Portugal
144 Vale do Côa: prehistoric rock-art sites, Portugal
145 Tomar: Convent of Christ, Portugal
146 Batalha: Dominican monastery, Portugal
147 Alcobaça: Cistercian monastery, Portugal
148 Sintra: cultural landscape, Portugal
149 Lisboa (Lisbon): Mosteiro dos Jerónimos* and Torre de Belém*, Portugal
150 Évora: historic centre, Portugal
151 Bern (Berne): old city, Switzerland
152 Jungfrau*-Aletsch-Bietschhorn, Switzerland
153 St Gallen (St Gall): convent, Switzerland
154 Monte San Giorgio, Switzerland
155 Bellinzona: group of fortifications, Switzerland
156 Müstair: Benedictine convent of St John, Switzerland
157 Salzburg: historic centre (incl. Mozart's birthplace and residence*), Austria
158 Hallstatt-Dachstein-Salzkammergut: cultural landscape, Austria
159 Graz: historic centre, Austria
160 Semmering Railway, Austria
161 Wachau: cultural landscape, Austria
162 Wien (Vienna): historic centre (incl. Belvedere*), Austria; Wien (Vienna): Schloss Schönbrunn and gardens*, Austria
163 Neusiedlersee, Austria / Fertő, Hungary: cultural landscape
164 Torino (Turin) and surrounding area: Residences of the Royal House of Savoy, Italy
165 Sacri Monti ('Sacred Mountains') of Piedmont and Lombardy, Italy
166 Milano (Milan): church and convent of Santa Maria delle Grazie with 'The Last Supper' by Leonardo da Vinci, Italy
167 Crespi d'Adda: industrial workers' town, Italy
168 Val Camónica: rock drawings, Italy
169 Verona: historic city, Italy
170 Vicenza: city and the Palladian villas of the Veneto, Italy
171 Pádova (Padua): botanical garden, Italy
172 Venézia (Venice) and its lagoon (incl. Basilica di San Marco*, Palazzo Ducale* and Ponte di Rialto*), Italy
173 Aquileia: archaeological site incl. Patriarchal Basilica, Italy
174 Ferrara: Renaissance city and Po delta, Italy
175 Ravenna: early Christian monuments and mosaics, Italy
176 Modena: cathedral, Torre Civica and Piazza Grande, Italy
177 Portovénere, Cinque Terre (Corniglia, Manarola, Monterosso, Riomaggiore, Vernazza) and the islands (Ìsola Palmária, Ì. del Tino and Ì. del Tinetto), Italy
178 Firenze (Florence): historic centre (incl. Duomo Santa Maria del Fiore*, Galleria degli Uffizi*, Ponte Vecchio*), Italy
179 Pisa: Piazza del Duomo (incl. Torre Pendente: The Leaning Tower*), Italy
180 San Gimignano: historic centre, Italy; Siena: historic centre (incl. Piazza del Campo*), Italy
181 Pienza: historic centre, Italy; Val d'Orcia: Renaissance agricultural landscape, Italy
182 Cervéteri and Tarquínia: Etruscan necropolises, Italy
183 Urbino: historic centre, Italy
184 Assisi: Basilica di San Francesco and other Franciscan sites, Italy
185 Tivoli: Villa d'Este, Italy; Tivoli: Villa Adriana (Hadrian's Villa), Italy
186 Vatican City (incl. Basilica di San Pietro*, Musei Vaticani & Capella Sistina*); Roma (Rome): historic centre and extraterritorial properties of the Holy See & San Paolo fuori le Mura (incl. Colosseo*, Fontana di Trevi*, Foro Romano* and Pantheon*), Italy
187 Caserta: Palazzo Reale & gardens, Vanvitelli aqueduct & San Leucio complex, Italy
188 Nápoli (Naples): historic centre, Italy; Herculaneum, Pompeii* and Torre Annunziata: archaeological areas, Italy
189 Costiera Amalfitana, Italy
190 Cilento area: cultural landscape including Parco Nazionale del Cilento e Vallo di Diano, Certosa di San Lorenzo in Padula and the archaeological sites of Paestum and Vélia, Italy
191 Castel del Monte: medieval castle, Italy
192 Matera: I Sassi di Matera troglodyte settlement, Italy
193 Alberobello: Trulli limestone houses, Italy
194 Ìsole Eólie (Lipari Is.), Italy
195 Siracusa (Syracuse) and necropolis of Pantalica, Sicily, Italy
196 Val di Noto: late Baroque towns (Caltagirone, Catánia, Militello in Val di Catánia, Módica, Noto, Palazzolo, Ragusa and Scicli), Sicily, Italy
197 Villa Romana del Casale, Sicily, Italy
198 Agrigento: archaeological area, Sicily, Italy
199 Su Nuraxi di Barúmini, Sardinia, Italy
200 Malbork: Teutonic fortified monastery, Poland
201 Torun: medieval town, Poland
202 Warszawa (Warsaw): historic centre (incl. Warsaw Royal Castle*), Poland
203 Bialowieza Forest, Poland, and Belovezhskaya Puscha, Belarus
204 Zamosc: Renaissance city, Poland
205 Wooden churches of southern Little Poland
206 Wieliczka: salt mines, Poland
207 Kraków (Cracow): historic centre (incl. Market Square* and Wawel Royal Castle*), Poland
208 Kalwaria Zebrzydowska: Mannerist architectural and park landscape complex and pilgrimage park, Poland
209 Oswiecim (Auschwitz): Auschwitz-Birkenau concentration camp*, Poland
210 Jawor and Swidnica: Churches of Peace, Poland
211 Praha (Prague): historic centre (incl. Charles Bridge*, Castle & St Vitus Cathedral* and Old Town Square*), Czech Rep.
212 Kutná Hora*: historical centre, Church of Santa Barbara and Cathedral of Our Lady at Sedlec, Czech Rep.
213 Litomysl Castle, Czech Rep.
214 Holasovice: historical village reservation, Czech Rep.
215 Cesky Krumlov: historic centre, Czech Rep.
216 Telc: historic centre, Czech Rep.; Trebic: Jewish quarter and St Procopius' Basilica, Czech Rep.
217 Lednice-Valtice: cultural landscape, Czech Rep.
218 Brno: Tugendhat Villa, Czech Rep.
219 Zelená Hora: St John of Nepomuk church, Czech Rep.; Kromeríz: castle and gardens, Czech Rep.
220 Olomouc: Holy Trinity column, Czech Rep.
221 Banská Stiavnica: city and mining landscape, Slovak Rep.
222 Vlkolínec: traditional village, Slovak Rep.
223 Spisské Pohradie: Spissky Hrad* and associated monuments, Slovak Rep.
224 Bardejov: fortified medieval town, Slovak Rep.
225 Aggtelek karst caves, Hungary, & Slovak karst caves*, Slovak Rep.
226 Tojaki wine region: cultural landscape, Hungary
227 Hortobágyi National Park, Hungary
228 Hollokö: traditional village, Hungary
229 Budapest: banks of the Danube, Buda Castle* area (incl. Fisherman's Bastion*), Andrássy Avenue and the Millennium Underground, Hungary
230 Pannonhalma: millenary Benedictine monastery and its natural environment, Hungary
231 Pécs: early Christian cemetery of Sopianae, Hungary
232 Skocjan Caves, Slovenia
233 Porec: Episcopal complex, Croatia
234 Plitvice Lakes National Park*, Croatia
235 Sibenik: St James cathedral, Croatia
236 Trogir: historic city, Croatia
237 Split: historic centre with Diocletian's Palace*, Croatia
238 Dubrovnik: old city*, Croatia
239 Mostar: old bridge area, Bosnia-Herzegovina
240 Kotor and its gulf, Montenegro
241 Durmitor National Park, Montenegro
242 Stari Ras: medieval buildings and monuments, Serbia; Sopocani Monastery, Serbia
243 Studenica: monastery, Serbia
244 Decani: monastery*, Serbia
245 Ohrid and its region, FYR of Macedonia
246 Gjirokastër: Ottoman town, Albania
247 **Butrint (Buthrotum): archaeological site**, Albania
248 Horezu: monastery, Romania
249 Orastie Mountains: Dacian fortresses, Romania
250 Southern Transylvania: fortified churches, Romania
251 Sighisoara: historic centre, Romania
252 Maramures: wooden churches, Romania
253 Moldavian churches, Romania
254 Danube Delta, Romania
255 Boyana: church, Bulgaria
256 Sveshtari: Thracian tomb, Bulgaria
257 Srebarna Nature Reserve, Bulgaria
258 Ivanovo: rock-hewn churches, Bulgaria
259 Madara Rider: horseman stone relief, Bulgaria
260 Nesebur (Nessebar): ancient city, Bulgaria
261 Kazanluk: Thracian tomb, Bulgaria
262 Rila: monastery*, Bulgaria
263 Pirin National Park, Bulgaria
264 Athos ('Holy Mountain'), Greece
265 Thessaloníki (Salonika): Palaeochristian and Byzantine monuments, Greece
266 Vergina: archaeological site of Aigai, Greece
267 Metéora: monasteries, Greece
268 Delfí (Delphi): archaeological site*, Greece
269 Olimbía (Olympia): archaeological site*, Greece
270 Bassae: Temple of Apollo Epicurius, Greece
271 Mistrás: medieval ruins, Greece
272 Mycenae* and Tiryns; archaeological sites, Greece
273 Epídavros (Epidaurus): archaeological site*, Greece
274 Athína (Athens): Acropolis*, Greece
275 Delos: archaeological site, Greece
276 Daphni, Hossios Luckas and Néa Moni monasteries, Greece
277 Sámos: Pythagoreion port and Heraion temple remains, Greece
278 Pátmos: historic centre (chorá) with the monastery of St John the Theologian and Cave of the Apocalypse, Greece
279 Ródos (Rhodes): medieval city, Greece
280 Xanthos-Letoon: archaeological site, Turkey
281 Hierapolis-Pamukkale, Turkey
282 Truva (Troy): archaeological site*, Turkey
283 Istanbul: historic areas (incl. Blue Mosque*, Hagia Sophia* and Topkapi Palace*), Turkey
284 Safranbolu: historic city, Turkey
285 Hattusha: Hittite archaeological site, Turkey
286 Göreme National Park* and Cappadocia rock sites, Turkey
287 Divrigi: Great Mosque and hospital, Turkey
288 Nemrut Dag: archaeological site, Turkey
289 Megalithic temples: Ggantija, Hagar Qim*, Mnajdra, Tarxien, Ta'Hagrat and Skorba, Malta
290 Valletta: old city, Malta; Hal Saflieni Hypogeum, Malta
291 Pafos (Paphos): historic city*, Cyprus
292 Troodos region: painted churches, Cyprus
293 Choirokoitia: archaeological site, Cyprus
294 Tallinn: historic centre (incl. Town Hall Square*), Estonia
295 Riga: historic centre*, Latvia
296 Struve Geodetic Arc: a chain of survey triangulations stretching from northern Norway to the Black Sea
297 Curonian Spit, Lithuania/Russian Federation
298 Kernavé Cultural Reserve: archaeological site, Lithuania
299 Vilnius: historic centre, Lithuania
300 Mir: castle complex, Belarus
301 Nyasvizh: architectural, residential and cultural complex of the Radziwill family, Belarus
302 L'viv (L'vov): historic centre, Ukraine
303 Kyiv (Kiev): St Sophia Cathedral*, related monastic buildings and Lavra of Kyiv-Pechersk, Ukraine

RUSSIAN FEDERATION

L Solovetskiye Ostrova: cultural and historic ensemble
M Kizhi Pogost: wooden churches and clock tower
304 Sankt-Peterburg (St Petersburg): historic centre (incl. State Hermitage Museum*)
305 Velikiy Novgorod: historic monuments and surroundings
306 Moskva (Moscow): Kremlin*, Red Square* and St Basil's Cathedral*; Moskva (Moscow): Novodevichy Convent; Kolomenskoye: Church of the Ascension
307 Sergiyev Posad: Trinity Sergius Lavra architectural ensemble
308 Vladimir and Suzdal: White Monuments
309 Yaroslavl: historic centre
310 Ferapontov Monastery
311 Western Caucasus mountain area
S Derbent: citadel, ancient city and fortress
T Kazan: Kremlin
U Komi virgin forests
V Golden Mountains of Altay
W Uvs Nuur basin, Mongolia/Russian Federation
X Lake Baikal
Y Central Sikhote-Alin mountain range
Z Kamchatka volcanoes
ZZ Wrangel Island reserve

AFRICA

312 Tétouan: medina, Morocco
313 Fès: medina*, Morocco
314 Volubilis: archaeological site, Morocco
315 Meknès: historic city, Morocco
316 El Jadida: Portuguese fortified city of Mazagan, Morocco
317 Essaouira: medina, Morocco
318 Marrakech: medina (incl. Djemaa el Fna square* and Saadian Tombs*), Morocco
319 Aït Benhaddou: fortified village, Morocco
320 **Tipasa: archaeological park**, Algeria
321 Alger (Algiers): kasbah, Algeria
322 Benī Hammād: Al Qal'a, Algeria
323 Djemila: Roman ruins, Algeria
324 Timgad: Roman ruins, Algeria
325 M'Zab Valley: fortified towns, Algeria
326 Dougga (Thugga): archaeological site, Tunisia
327 **Ichkeul National Park**, Tunisia
328 Tunis: medina*, Tunisia; Carthage: archaeological site*, Tunisia
329 Kerkouane: Punic town and its necropolis, Tunisia
330 Sousse: medina, Tunisia
331 Kairouan: holy city, Tunisia
332 El Jem: Roman amphitheatre ruins, Tunisia
333 Ghadamis: old town, Libya
334 Sabratha: archaeological site, Libya
335 Leptis Magna: archaeological site, Libya
336 Cyrene: archaeological site, Libya
337 Wadi Al-Hitan (Whale Valley), Egypt
338 **Abu Mina: Christian ruins**, Egypt
339 Memphis: Pyramid fields from Giza to Dahshur and its necropolis*, Egypt
340 Al Qahirah (Cairo): Islamic city, Egypt

ASIA

341 Halab (Aleppo): ancient city of Aleppo*, Syria
342 Tadmur: archaeological site of Palmyra*, Syria
343 Dimashq (Damascus): ancient city, Syria
344 Bosra: ancient city, Syria
345 Anjar: archaeological site, Lebanon; Baalbek: archaeological site of Heliopolis, Lebanon
346 Holy Valley: early Christian monastic settlements, and Forest of the Cedars of God, Lebanon
347 Byblos: archaeological site, Lebanon
348 Soûr (Tyre): archaeological site of Tyre*, Lebanon
349 **Jerusalem: old city and walls** (incl. Temple Mount*, Western (Wailing) Wall*), site proposed by Jordan
350 Akko: old city of Acre, Israel
351 Biblical tels: Megiddo, Hazor and Beer Sheba, Israel
352 Tel Aviv: White City, Israel
353 Masada: fortress and Roman siege works*, Israel
354 The Incense and Spice Route: desert cities in the Negev, Israel
355 Petra: archaeological site*, Jordan
356 Umm ar Rasas (Kastron Mefa'a): archaeological site, Jordan
357 Qasr Amra: desert castle, Jordan
358 Hatra: fortified city remains, Iraq
359 **Ash Sharqat: ancient city of Ashur**, Iraq
360 Upper Svaneti area, Georgia
361 K'ut'aisi: Bagrati Cathedral and Gelati Monastery, Georgia

50 | **Europe**
Airports & High-Speed Rail

▶ **See also...** World Airports (36-38); World Flight
Times (39); Europe Railways & Ferries (52-53);
London Airport Connections (63) • cont >

*The listings above refer to a selection of related themes.
For more information, see the Contents (2-5).*

Faced with stern competition from the ever-expanding high-speed rail services and
the need to utilise precious runway slots for the more lucrative long-haul routes,
several European airlines have been forced into co-operation with rail companies. As
a result, many previously prestigious air routes, such as Air France's Paris–Brussels
and Lufthansa's Stuttgart–Frankfurt, are now run by, or in conjunction with, high-
speed rail operators offering city-centre to city-centre services. As the European
rail network expands, as its standards of safety, speed and comfort improve and
as the continent's airports become more overcrowded, this development is likely to
become more widespread. Increasingly, a consideration of Europe's air routes thus
also requires an appreciation of these complementary high-speed rail services.

Note: the airports shown are selected, on the basic of international passenger
movements, from those which report to Airports Council International (ACI). Some
airports in some countries are therefore not shown.

This map shows only the English version of place
names. This is to avoid excessive repetition and
to keep airport names a reasonable length.

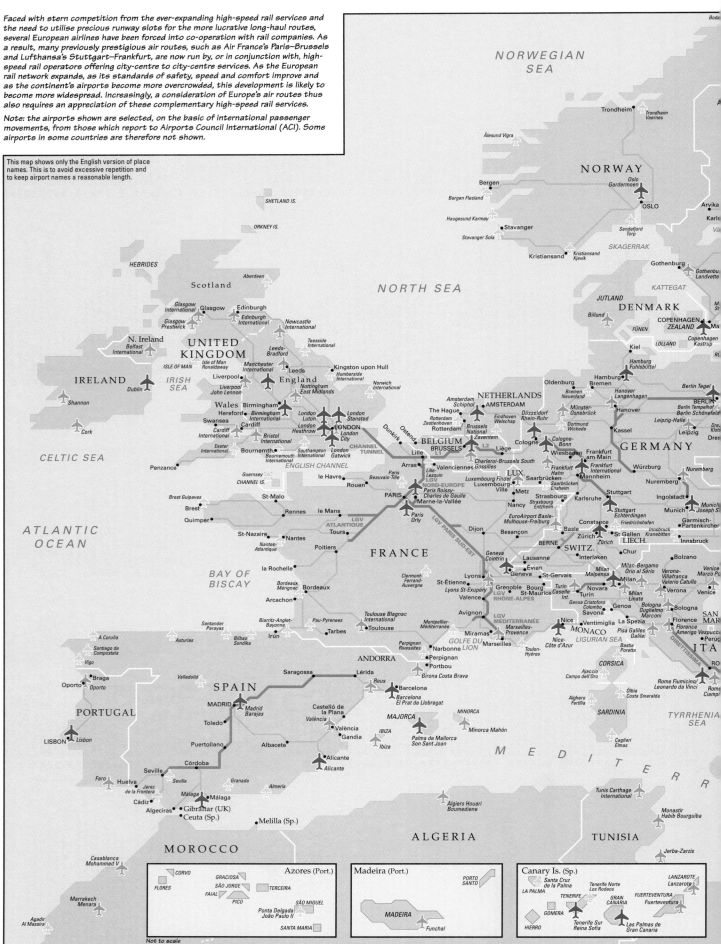

The listings above refer to a selection of related themes.
For more information, see the Contents (2-5).

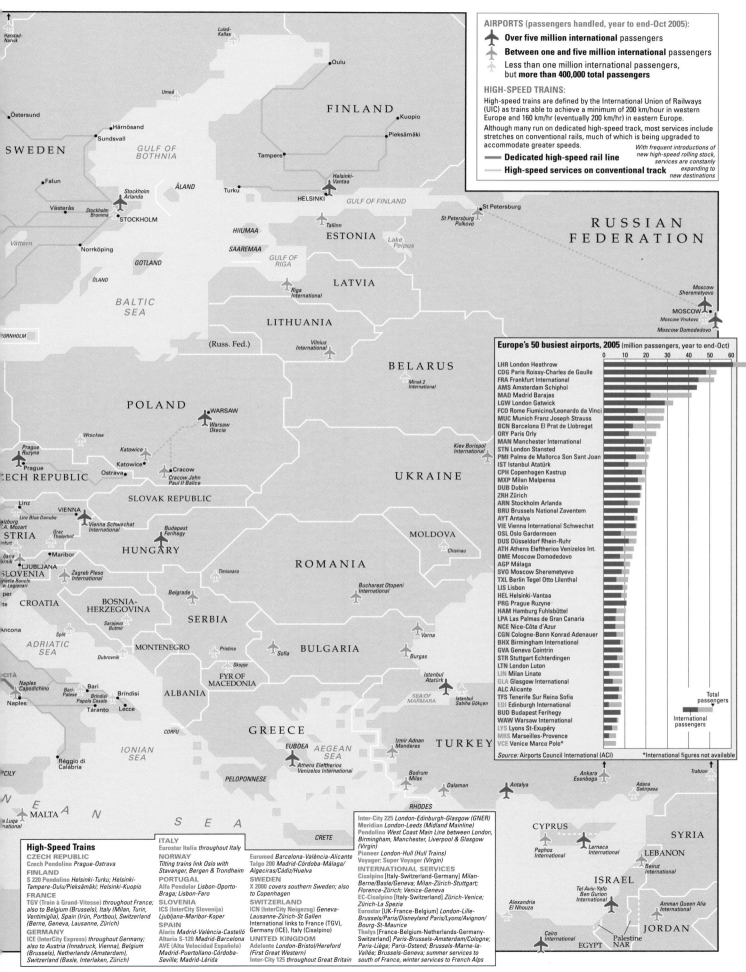

AIRPORTS (passengers handled, year to end-Oct 2005):

✈ **Over five million international** passengers

✈ **Between one and five million international** passengers

✈ Less than one million international passengers,
but **more than 400,000 total passengers**

HIGH-SPEED TRAINS:

High-speed trains are defined by the International Union of Railways (UIC) as trains able to achieve a minimum of 200 km/hour in western Europe and 160 km/hr (eventually 200 km/hr) in eastern Europe.

Although many run on dedicated high-speed track, most services include stretches on conventional rails, much of which is being upgraded to accommodate greater speeds. *With frequent introductions of new high-speed rolling stock, services are constantly expanding to new destinations*

— **Dedicated high-speed rail line**

— **High-speed services on conventional track**

Europe's 50 busiest airports, 2005 (million passengers, year to end-Oct)

Scale: 0 10 20 30 40 50 60

- LHR London Heathrow
- CDG Paris Roissy-Charles de Gaulle
- FRA Frankfurt International
- AMS Amsterdam Schiphol
- MAD Madrid Barajas
- LGW London Gatwick
- FCO Rome Fiumicino/Leonardo da Vinci
- MUC Munich Franz Joseph Strauss
- BCN Barcelona El Prat de Llobregat
- ORY Paris Orly
- MAN Manchester International
- STN London Stansted
- PMI Palma de Mallorca Son Sant Joan
- IST Istanbul Atatürk
- CPH Copenhagen Kastrup
- MXP Milan Malpensa
- DUB Dublin
- ZRH Zürich
- ARN Stockholm Arlanda
- BRU Brussels National Zaventem
- AYT Antalya
- VIE Vienna International Schwechat
- OSL Oslo Gardermoen
- DUS Düsseldorf Rhein-Ruhr
- ATH Athens Eleftherios Venizelos Int.
- DME Moscow Domodedovo
- AGP Málaga
- SVO Moscow Sheremetyevo
- TXL Berlin Tegel Otto Lilenthal
- LIS Lisbon
- HEL Helsinki-Vantaa
- PRG Prague Ruzyne
- HAM Hamburg Fuhlsbüttel
- LPA Las Palmas de Gran Canaria
- NCE Nice-Côte d'Azur
- CGN Cologne-Bonn Konrad Adenauer
- BHX Birmingham International
- GVA Geneva Cointrin
- STR Stuttgart Echterdingen
- LTN London Luton
- LIN Milan Linate
- GLA Glasgow International
- ALC Alicante
- TFS Tenerife Sur Reina Sofia
- EDI Edinburgh International
- BUD Budapest Ferihegy
- WAW Warsaw International
- LYS Lyons St-Exupéry
- MRS Marseilles-Provence
- VCE Venice Marco Polo*

Total passengers

International passengers

Source: Airports Council International (ACI)   *International figures not available

High-Speed Trains

CZECH REPUBLIC
Czech Pendolino *Prague-Ostrava*

FINLAND
S 220 Pendolino *Helsinki-Turku; Helsinki-Tampere-Oulu/Pieksämäki; Helsinki-Kuopio*

FRANCE
TGV (Train à Grand-Vitesse) *throughout France; also to Belgium (Brussels), Italy (Milan, Turin, Ventimiglia), Spain (Irún, Portbou), Switzerland (Berne, Geneva, Lausanne, Zürich)*

GERMANY
ICE (InterCity Express) *throughout Germany; also to Austria (Innsbruck, Vienna), Belgium (Brussels), Netherlands (Amsterdam), Switzerland (Basle, Interlaken, Zürich)*

ITALY
Eurostar Italia *throughout Italy*

NORWAY
Tilting trains link *Oslo with Stavanger, Bergen & Trondheim*

PORTUGAL
Alfa Pendular *Lisbon-Oporto-Braga; Lisbon-Faro*

SLOVENIA
ICS (InterCity Slovenija) *Ljubljana-Maribor-Koper*

SPAIN
Alaris *Madrid-València-Castelló*
Altaria S-120 *Madrid-Barcelona*
AVE (Alta Velocidad Española) *Madrid-Puertollano-Córdoba-Seville; Madrid-Lérida*

Euromed *Barcelona-València-Alicante*
Talgo 200 *Madrid-Córdoba-Málaga; Algeciras/Cádiz/Huelva*

SWEDEN
X 2000 *covers southern Sweden; also to Copenhagen*

SWITZERLAND
ICN (InterCity Neigezug) *Geneva-Lausanne-Zürich-St Gallen*

UNITED KINGDOM
Adelante *London-Bristol/Hereford (First Great Western)*
Inter-City 125 *throughout Great Britain*
Inter-City 225 *London-Edinburgh-Glasgow (GNER)*
Meridian *London-Leeds (Midland Mainline)*
Pendolino *West Coast Main Line between London, Birmingham, Manchester, Liverpool & Glasgow (Virgin)*
Pioneer *London-Hull (Hull Trains)*
Voyager; Super Voyager *(Virgin)*

INTERNATIONAL SERVICES
Cisalpino [Italy-Switzerland-Germany] *Milan-Berne/Basle/Geneva; Milan-Zürich-Stuttgart; Florence-Zürich; Venice-Geneva*
EC-Cisalpino [Italy-Switzerland] *Zürich-Venice; Zürich-La Spezia*
Eurostar [UK-France-Belgium] *London-Lille-Brussels/Paris/Disneyland Paris/Lyons/Avignon/Bourg-St-Maurice*
Thalys [France-Belgium-Netherlands-Germany-Switzerland] *Paris-Brussels-Amsterdam/Cologne; Paris-Liège; Paris-Ostend; Brussels-Marne-la-Vallée; Brussels-Geneva; summer services to south of France, winter services to French Alps*

▶ See also... Cruising (40-41); Europe Airports &
High-Speed Rail (50-51); UK Airports, Motorways &
Ferries (62)

The listings above refer to a selection of related themes.
For more information, see the Contents (2-5).

This map shows principal passenger rail and shipping routes in Europe. Some of the railways marked have limited services but are included because of their significance (such as connection to resort or international crossing).

A number of European rail passes are available, offering free travel on many rail and ferry services.

The Eurailpass is valid for first-class rail travel in the countries shown on the map. For those under 26, the Eurailpass Youth is valid in the same countries for second-class rail travel. The pass is not available to European residents or to visitors from Algeria, Morocco, Tunisia, Turkey or the Russian Federation.

European residents are eligible for the Inter-Rail pass, offering train travel in the area shown on the map, excluding the country of purchase.

Passes are available for one or more zones within the validity area.

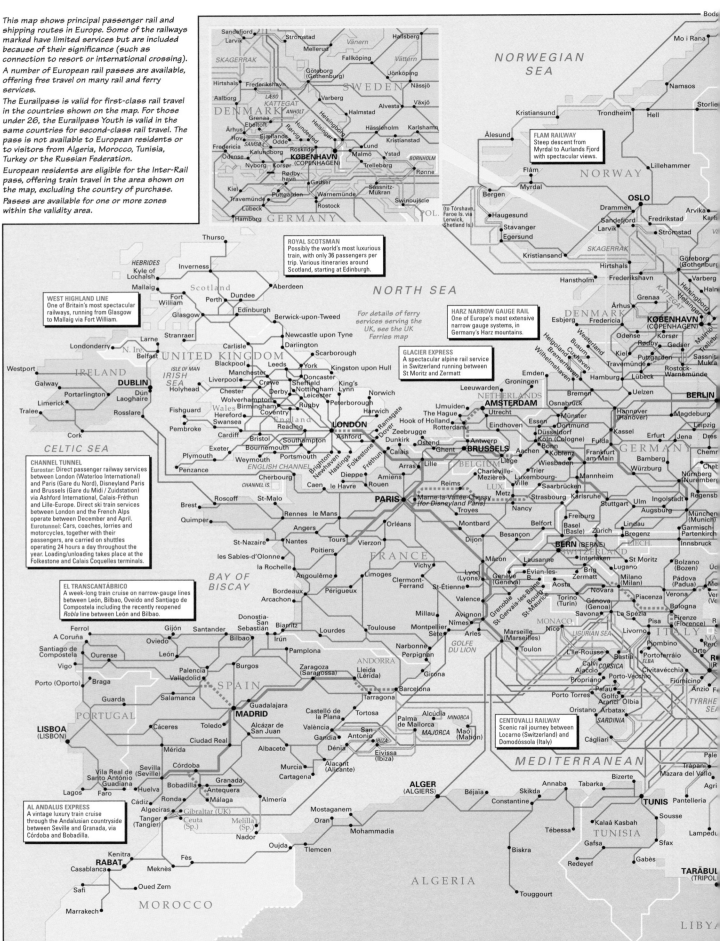

▶ *See also...* Cruising (40-41); Europe Airports & High-Speed Rail (50-51); UK Airports, Motorways & Ferries (62)

The listings above refer to a selection of related themes. For more information, see the Contents (2-5).

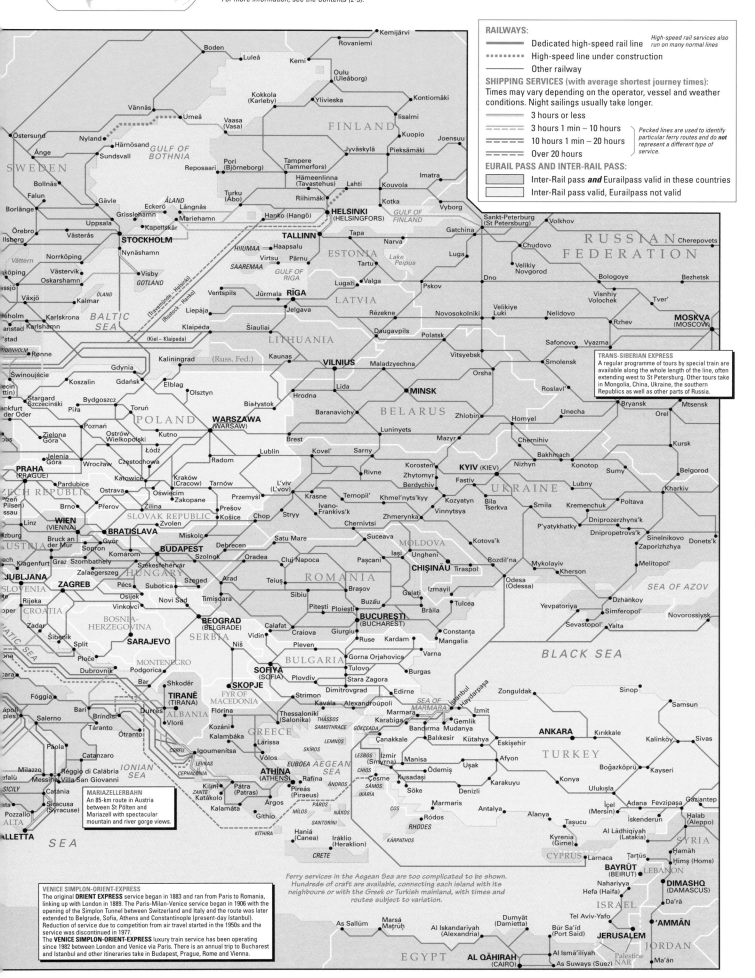

▶ See also... UNESCO Heritage (48-49);

The listings above refer to a selection of related themes.
For more information, see the Contents (2-5).

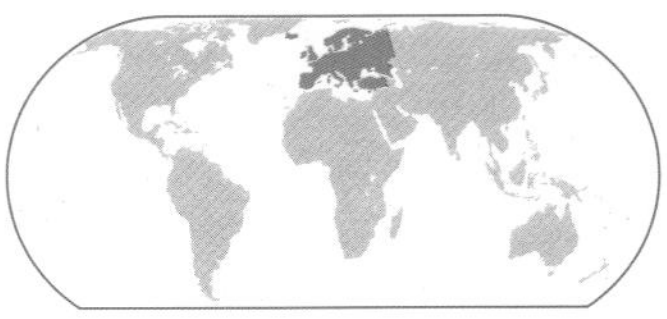

This map shows the most important areas that have been designated as National Parks throughout Western and Central Europe.

Sites marked with an asterisk (*) are featured in Columbus Travel Guides' *Tourist Attractions and Events of the World*

Iceland
1 **Jökulsárgljúfur** Spectacular glacial canyon landscape
2 **Skaftafell** Example of active glacial landscape
3 **Thingvellir** Broad forested plain, home of historic Iceland parliam't

Norway
4 **Øvre Pasvik** Forest & tundra
5 **Stabbursdalen** Arctic landscape: tundra, lakes, gravel plains & forest
6 **Øvre Anarjokka** Undulating tundra with woodland & lakes
7 **Reisa** Mixed mountain country
8 **Øvre Dividal** Mountainous country with tundra & woodland
9 **Ånderdalen** Mixed mountain country
10 **Saltfjellet-Svartisen** Varied landscape; fjords, mountains & glacier
11 **Børgefjell** Remote mountain area with varied habitats
12 **Gressåmoen** Mountainous country & spruce forest
13 **Dovrefjell** Mountainous tundra & snowfields; famous for its flora
14 **Rondane** Mixed mountain country
15 **Jostedalsbreen** Europe's largest mainland glacier
16 **Jotunheimen** Mountainous area with tundra, bogs & forest
17 **Hardangervidda** Large mountain plateau, a popular walking area

Sweden
18 **Vadvetjåkka** Wild terrain with karst caves
19 **Abisko** Mountain & forest with tundra, lakes & rivers
20 **Muddus** Forest, tundra & bog
21 **Padjelanta, Sarek and Stora Sjöfallet** 3 parks protect Europe's largest wilderness area; mixed landscape
22 **Pieljekaise** Wooded mountain country with tundra, open water & bogs
23 **Skuleskogen** Coastal forest landscape
24 **Töfsingdalen** Woodland, tundra & bog
25 **Sånfjället** Woodland, tundra & bog
26 **Hamra** Woodland, tundra & bog, noted for its insects
27 **Garphyttan** Forest & meadows
28 **Tiveden** Hilly forest, lakes & bogs
29 **Store Mosse** Predominantly boggy, with lakes & forest
30 **Gotska Sandön** Sand & gravel island

Finland
31 **Pallas-ja-Ounastunturin** Upland plateau & taiga, with lakes, tundra, gorges & forest
32 **Lemmenjoen** Wilderness mountain area; gold rush in 1940's
33 **Urho Kekkosen** Large wilderness area with fells, forest & peatlands
34 **Pyhätunturin** Mountainous area with tundra, bogs & forest
35 **Oulangen** Varied tundra landscape
36 **Petkeljärven** Typical Finnish lakeland scenery
37 **Linnansaaren** Lake & islands
38 **Pyhä-Häkin** Mainly forest & bog
39 **Seitsemisen** Typical S Finland landscape with forest & bog
40 **Liesjärven** Lakes, previously cultivated land & forest
41 **Saaristomeren** Extensive island group with mixed habitats

Denmark
42 **Rebild Bakker** Glacial valleys, hills & woodland; home to largest 4th July celebrations outside US

Ireland
43 **Glenveagh** Mixed upland area
44 **Connemara** Typical W Ireland mountain area
45 **Killarney*** Ancient woodland with moorland, lakes, bogs, wetland & mountains
46 **Wicklow Mountains** Partly wooded mountains with upland moorland & grassland

United Kingdom
47 **Cairngorms** Mountain region with ski resorts
48 **Loch Lomond & The Trossachs** Lakes & wooded valley with literary associations
49 **Northumberland** Mainly upland grassy moorland; Hadrian's Wall in S
50 **Lake District** Mountain & lakeland; very popular all year
51 **Yorkshire Dales** Varied upland country
52 **North York Moors** Hilly uplands with heather moorland
53 **Peak District** Limestone in the south, with many caves; high peat moors in the north
54 **Snowdonia*** Mountain country with lakes, moorland, grassland & woodland
55 **Pembrokeshire Coast** Scenic coastline; varied seabird habitats
56 **Brecon Beacons*** Mainly grass-covered mountain area
57 **Exmoor** High heather moorland & wooded valleys, with dramatic coastline
58 **Dartmoor** Granite uplands with heather & grassland
59 **New Forest** Woodland & heath; famous for wild ponies

Netherlands
60 **Dwingelderveld** Heathland, fen & woodland with lakes
61 **De Hoge Veluwe** Variety of habitats: heathland, dunes, fens, wet heath & woodland
Veluwezoom Heath & mixed woodland
62 **De Biesbosch** Confluence of Maas & Waal

Germany
63 **Niedersächsisches Wattenmeer** East Frisian Islands; mudflats & saltmarsh
64 **Hamburgisches W'meer & Schleswig-Holsteinisches W'meer** Mudflats & saltmarsh
65 **Vorpommersche Boddenlandschaft** Mudflats & saltmarsh with dunes, lagoons, lakes & woodland
66 **Jasmund** Varied landscape with cliffs, lakes & woodland
67 **Müritz** Woodland & lakes with heath, marsh & pasture
68 **Unteres Odertal** Floodplain of the Oder; park shared with Poland
69 **Sächsische Schweiz** Numerous rock towers; lower slopes wooded; deep valleys
70 **Hoch Harz** Wooded mountains with moorland, bogs & lakes
71 **Bayerischer Wald** Wooded mountain area
72 **Berchtesgaden** Mountain landscape with Alpine pastures, small glaciers, cliffs, lakes & varied woodland

France
73 **Vanoise** & **Écrins** High mountain scenery
74 **Mercantour** Some of the best parts of the Maritime Alps
75 **Port-Cros** Small wooded island
76 **Cévennes** Varied mountain & forest
77 **Pyrénées-Occidentales** Diverse mountain landscape; snowfields, pastures & woodland

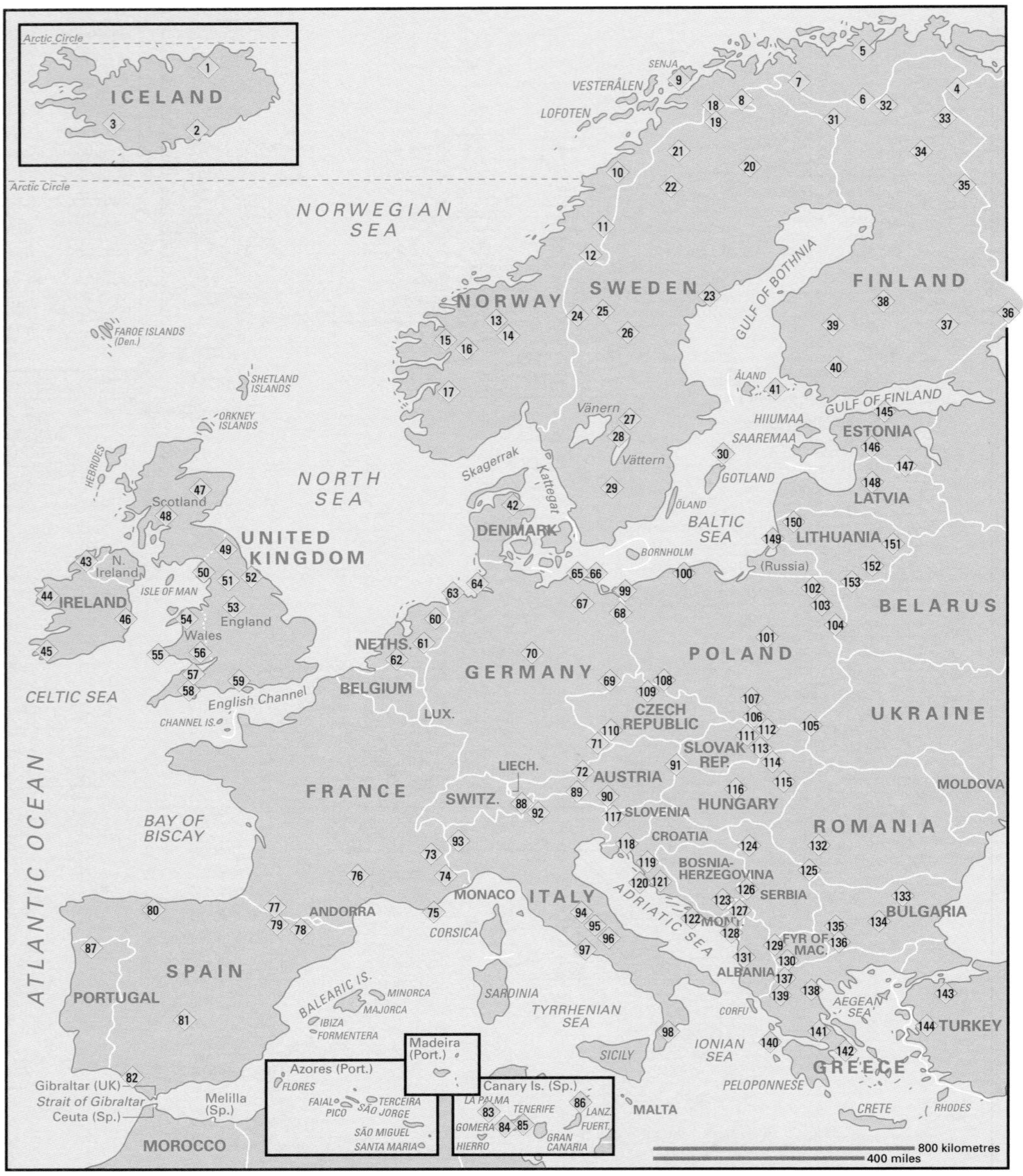
Arctic Circle
ICELAND
NORWEGIAN SEA
NORTH SEA
SENJA
VESTERÅLEN
LOFOTEN
NORWAY
SWEDEN
FINLAND
GULF OF BOTHNIA
ÅLAND
GULF OF FINLAND
HIIUMAA
SAAREMAA
ESTONIA
LATVIA
LITHUANIA
(Russia)
BELARUS
FAROE ISLANDS (Den.)
SHETLAND ISLANDS
ORKNEY ISLANDS
HEBRIDES
Scotland
UNITED KINGDOM
N. Ireland
IRELAND
ISLE OF MAN
England
Wales
Skagerrak
Kattegat
Vänern
Vättern
GOTLAND
ÖLAND
BALTIC SEA
BORNHOLM
DENMARK
CELTIC SEA
English Channel
CHANNEL IS.
NETHS.
BELGIUM
LUX.
GERMANY
POLAND
CZECH REPUBLIC
SLOVAK REP.
UKRAINE
MOLDOVA
LIECH.
AUSTRIA
SWITZ.
HUNGARY
SLOVENIA
CROATIA
ROMANIA
FRANCE
BAY OF BISCAY
ATLANTIC OCEAN
BOSNIA-HERZEGOVINA
SERBIA
MONT.
MONACO
ITALY
ADRIATIC SEA
BULGARIA
ANDORRA
CORSICA
FYR OF MAC.
ALBANIA
SPAIN
PORTUGAL
BALEARIC IS.
MINORCA
MAJORCA
IBIZA
FORMENTERA
SARDINIA
TYRRHENIAN SEA
CORFU
AEGEAN SEA
TURKEY
IONIAN SEA
SICILY
GREECE
PELOPONNESE
CRETE
RHODES
MALTA
Gibraltar (UK)
Strait of Gibraltar
Ceuta (Sp.)
Melilla (Sp.)
MOROCCO
Madeira (Port.)
Azores (Port.)
FLORES
FAIAL
PICO
SÃO JORGE
TERCEIRA
SÃO MIGUEL
SANTA MARIA
Canary Is. (Sp.)
LA PALMA
GOMERA
HIERRO
TENERIFE
GRAN CANARIA
LANZ.
FUERT.
800 kilometres
400 miles

Spain
78 **Aigües Tortes-Sant Maurici** Characteristic glacial landscape of high Pyrenees
79 **Ordesa** Spectacular mountain & gorge scenery; forests & Alpine pastures
80 **Covadonga** Mountain area with mixed woodlands, pasture & glacial lakes
81 **Tablas de Daimiel** Small wetland
82 **Doñana** Guadalquivir delta; important wildlife site
83 **Caldera de Taburiente** Volcanic landscape
84 **Garajonay** Sub-tropical forests
85 **Cañadas del Teide** Volcanic landscapes
86 **Timanfaya** Volcanic landscapes

Portugal
87 **Peneda-Gerês** Mountain & forest area; cliffs & rock formations

Switzerland
88 **The Swiss National Park** Strictly controlled mountainous area; forests, pastures, lakes, cliffs & snowfields

Austria
89 **Hohe Tauern** High Alpine scenery; forests in lower areas
90 **Nockberge** Forested mountain area with bogs & moors
91 **Donau-auen** Danube flood plain E of Vienna
Neusiedler See Europe's largest steppe lake, over half is thick reedbeds

Italy
92 **Stelvio** Typical Alpine scenery & large glacier
93 **Gran Paradiso** High Alpine country; famous for the Ibex
94 **Monti Sibillini** Upspoilt mountain area with folklore connections
95 **Gran Sasso e Monti della Laga** Varied landscape of mountains, rivers & lakes
96 **Abruzzo** Wooded mountainous area
Maiella Group of high peaks with karst plains
97 **Circeo** Coastal marsh & rocky promontory
98 **Calábria** Three areas of wooded mountainous landscape

Poland
99 **Wolinski** Woodland, lakes and sea cliffs; white-tailed sea eagle the main attraction
100 **Slowinski** Coastal landscape with shifting sand dunes
101 **Kampinoski** Varied landscape nr. Warsaw
102 **Mazurski & Wigierski** Numerous lakes and extensive forests
103 **Biebrzanski** Central Europe's largest area of natural peat bogs
104 **Bialowieski** Europe's largest original lowland forest; principal attraction the European bison
105 **Bieszczadzki** Remote wooded mountain area in E Carpathians
106 **Babiogórski, Tatrzanski, Gorczanski & Pieninski** Four parks in the spectacular High Tatra mountains
107 **Ojcówski** Hilly landscape with many rock pinnacles
108 **Gory Stolowe & Karkonoski** Dramatic mountain scenery of the Sudety Mountains

Czech Republic
109 **Krkonose** Wooded mountain area with Alpine pastures, meadows, bogs & lakes
110 **Sumava** Forested slopes, ancient mountains & peat bogs

Slovak Republic
111 **Vysoké Tatry*** (High Tatras) **Nízke Tatry*** (Low Tatras) Spectacular mtn area: forests, lakes, grassland & bogs
112 **Pieninsky** Limestone mountains with mixed forests
113 **Slovenská raj** Karst plateau with extensive caves

Hungary
114 **Aggtelek** Important karst scenery
Bukk Hilly forested region
115 **Hortobágyi** Varied steppe landscape with rich birdlife
116 **Kiskunság** Wide range of lowland habitats

Slovenia
117 **Triglav** Limestone mountain scenery & mixed forest

Croatia
118 **Risnjak** Limestone mountain scenery & mixed forest
119 **Plitvice Lakes*** Scenic lakes linked by waterfalls formed by limestone deposition
Paklenica Limestone peaks, gorges & mixed forest
120 **Kornati** Limestone islands, karst scenery
121 **Krka** Park follows the route of the Krka river; lakes, dams, gorges, falls & woodland
122 **Mljet** Western part of island

Bosnia-Herzegovina
123 **Sutjeska** Wooded mountainous area; mixed landscape & reserve of virgin forest

Serbia
124 **Fruska Gora** Wooded hilly valley
125 **Djerdap** Gorge of the Danube; dam has created a long thin lake
126 **Tara** Mixed upland

Montenegro
127 **Durmitor** Mountain area in the west, Tara Gorge in east; mixed landscape & karst
Biogradska Gora Mountain area with high grasslands & five lakes
128 **Lovcen** Wooded limestone mountains
Skadarsko jezero Montenegran part of Lake Scutari

Former Yugoslav Rep. of Macedonia
129 **Mavrovo** Mountain area, partly wooded
130 **Galicica** S end of Dinaric Alps; mostly natural forest
Pelister Wooded mountain area with Alpine pastures

Albania
131 **Divjaka** Dunes & coastal woodland with rich birdlife on neighbouring lagoon

Romania
132 **Retezat** Mountain country with extensive forests

Bulgaria
133 **Rusenski Lom** Deciduous woodland
134 **Central Balkan** Widely varied landscape; thick forests
135 **Vitosa** Varied mountain area
136 **Pirin** High mountains; forest & mixed landscape
Rila Alpine peaks & many small lakes: the 'Eyes of the Rila'

Greece
137 **Préspa** Shallow lakes with reed- & sedge-beds
138 **Olimbos (Olympus)** Mountain area with maquis & forest; home of the gods in ancient Greek mythology
139 **Píndos** Wooded mountain area
Vikos-Aóos Wooded mountain area; Vikos & Aóos gorges
140 **Aínos** Area around Mt Aínos
141 **Iti Óros** Wooded mountain area
Parnassós Wilderness mountain area; mixed habitats
142 **Párnitha** Limestone area; maquis
Soúnion Typical Greek coastline

Turkey
143 **Manyas-Kuscenneti** Bird reserve, part of large lake
144 **Sipil Dagi** Home of the famous 'crying rock' of Niobe

Estonia
145 **Lahemaa** Wooded area & scenic coast
146 **Soomaa** Marsh & forest, severe annual flooding
147 **Karula** Forested area with glacial debris

Latvia
148 **Gauja** River & gorge scenery; the 'Switzerland of Latvia'

Lithuania
149 **Kursiv Nerija** Long sand spit with popular beaches; ice fishing in winter
150 **Zemaitija** Forest with popular Lake Plateliai
151 **Aukstaitija (Ignalina)** Forest & lakes; great diversity of wildlife
152 **Trakai** 5 lakes; Trakai Castle as centrepiece
153 **Dzukija** Confluence of Nemunas & Merkys rivers

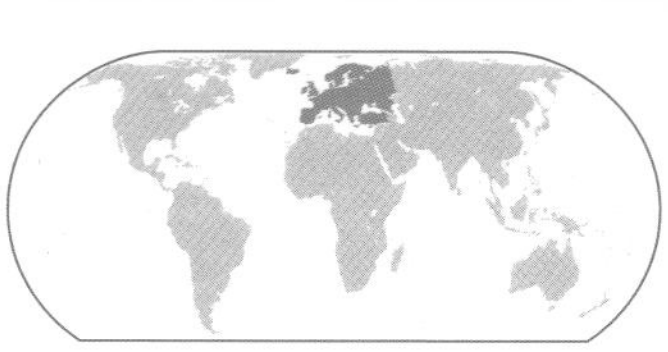

▶ *See also...* Attractions in UK (64), Belgium (67), Netherlands (69), Germany (73), France (77), Iberia (79) and Italy (86)

The listings above refer to a selection of related themes.
For more information, see the Contents (2-5).

This map shows a selection of theme and amusement parks in Europe. Most of these are members of either the International Association of Amusement Parks and Attractions (IAAPA) or the various national associations of amusement parks.
For more information see
www.ticketforfun.com

Parks marked with an asterisk (*) are featured in Columbus Travel Guides' *Tourist Attractions and Events of the World.*
Thanks to Jeff Bertus Leisure for help in compiling this section.

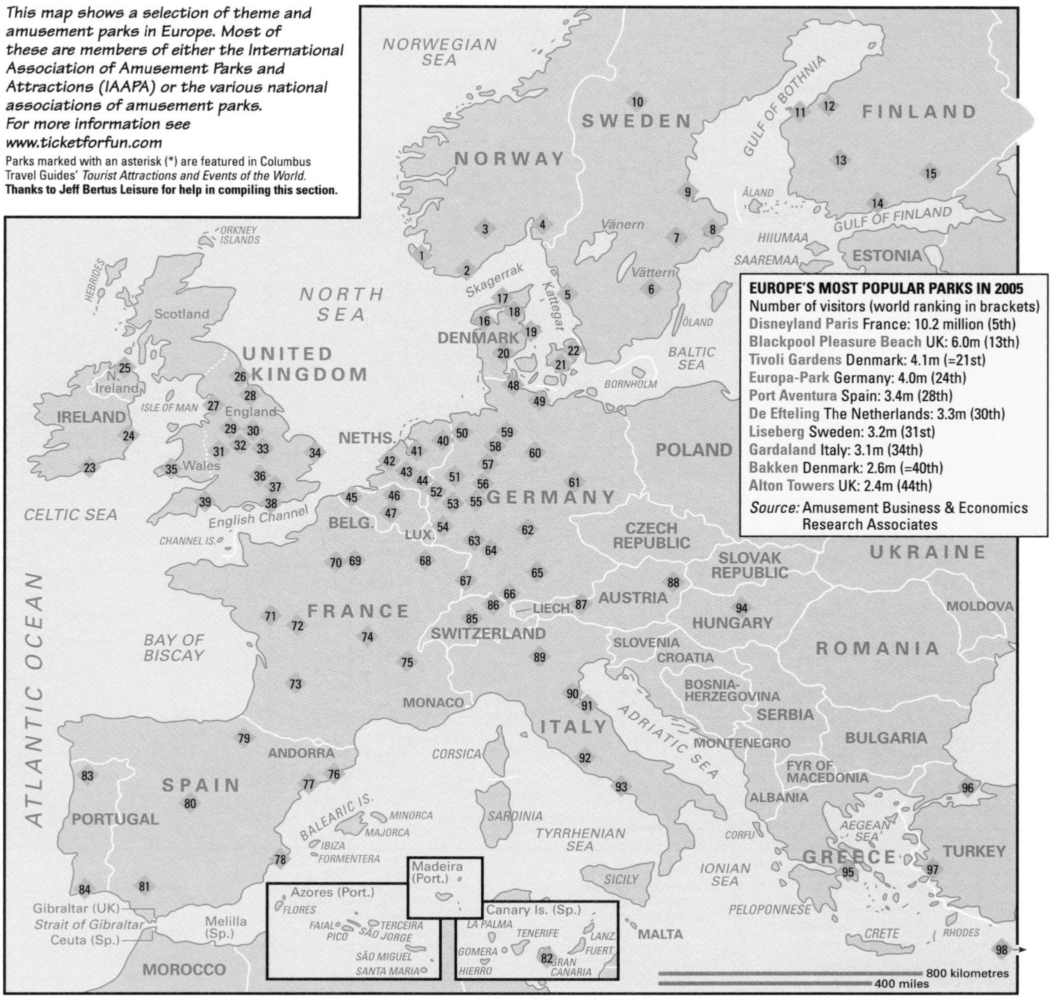

EUROPE'S MOST POPULAR PARKS IN 2005
Number of visitors (world ranking in brackets)
Disneyland Paris France: 10.2 million (5th)
Blackpool Pleasure Beach UK: 6.0m (13th)
Tivoli Gardens Denmark: 4.1m (=21st)
Europa-Park Germany: 4.0m (24th)
Port Aventura Spain: 3.4m (28th)
De Efteling The Netherlands: 3.3m (30th)
Liseberg Sweden: 3.2m (31st)
Gardaland Italy: 3.1m (34th)
Bakken Denmark: 2.6m (=40th)
Alton Towers UK: 2.4m (44th)
Source: Amusement Business & Economics Research Associates

Norway
1 Lunds Tivoli, Ålgård
Amusement park
2 Kristiansand Dyrepark
Norway's largest zoo and amusement park
3 Bo Sommarland, Bø
Combined waterpark and theme park
4 TusenFryd & VikingLandet, Vinterbro
Theme park and a small water park; VikingLandet is a re-enactment of the Viking Age

Sweden
5 Liseberg, Gothenburg
Large theme park with convention facilities and harbour
6 Astrid Lindgren's World, Vimmerby
Park dedicated to the world-famous childrens' author
7 Parken Zoo i Eskilstuna
Zoo, amusement park and waterpark
8 Gröna Lunds Tivoli, Stockholm
Amusement park in the centre of Stockholm, founded 1883
9 Furuviksparken, Gavle
Amusement park and zoo
10 Jamtli Historieland, Östersund
Combined indoor and outdoor museum

Finland
11 Wasalandia, Vaasa
Family theme park with Tropical Spa Tropiclandia
12 Lillbacka Powerpark, Alahärmä
Large amusement park with karting circuit, hotel & conference centre
13 Tampereen Sarkanniemi Oy, Tampere
City-centre amusement park and entertainment centre; includes an art museum, dolphinarium and planetarium
14 Linnanmäki*, Helsinki
Finland's most popular amusement park with live stage shows and a Sea Life Centre
15 Tykkimäki, Kouvola
Large amusement park with reptile zoo and dance pavilion

Denmark
16 Jesperhus Blomstherpark, Nykøbing, Mors
Animal and flower parks; family entertainment centre
17 Fårup Aquapark & Sommerland, Saltum
Amusement park with more than 30 activities and Scandinavia's largest waterpark
18 Tivoliland, Aalborg
Large amusement park
19 Djurs Sommerland, Nimtofte
Amusement park with more than 60 activities and shows and a waterpark
20 LEGOLAND Billund*
Theme park based on LEGO toy products; interactive attractions, building challenges, *Driving School* & *Miniland*
21 BonBon-Land, Holme-Olstrup
Fourth-largest amusement park in Denmark with over 60 attractions and activities
22 Dyrehavsbakken ('Bakken'), Klampenborg
The world's oldest amusement park, over 100 attractions
Tivoli Gardens*, Copenhagen
Large amusement park in the centre of Copenhagen, opened in 1843; a mixture of new and old rides; the famous Copenhagen Christmas Market is held here in Nov & Dec

Ireland
23 Perks Pleasure Park, Youghal
Seaside amusement park with neighbouring wildlife park
24 Clara Lara Fun Park, Wicklow
Park and amusement centre plus a junior playground

United Kingdom
25 Barry's Amusement Park, Portrush
Family amusement park with rides for all ages
26 The New Metroland, Gateshead
Europe's largest indoor funfair with many rides
27 Blackpool Pleasure Beach*
Opened in 1896, over 145 attractions and rides classified according to their 'terror factor'; one of the biggest collections of white-knuckle rides in the world, plus spectacular shows & Ripley's Believe It or Not! Odditorium
Camelot Theme Park, Chorley, Lancashire
A medieval world with over 100 attractions and rides
28 Flamingo Land and Holiday Village*, Malton
Amusement park and zoo with eight coaster rides and many extreme rides in White Knuckle Valley
Lightwater Valley, Ripon
Theme park with unique attractions including the world's first suspended hang-glider ride
29 Alton Towers*, near Stoke-on-Trent
One of the UK's most popular theme parks with 125 rides and attractions in a number of different kingdoms: *Ugland, Forbidden Valley, Towers Street* and *Cred Street*
Gullivers Kingdom, Matlock Bath
Theme park with over 35 rides and hot-air balloon flights
30 American Adventure World, Ilkeston
Adventure park with a American theme
31 West Midland Safari Park, Bewdley
Drive-around safari park; leisure area with over 25 rides
32 Drayton Manor Park*, Tamworth
Theme park with over 100 rides and attractions, plus a zoo, parkland, lakes and walks
33 Wicksteed Park, Kettering
UK's oldest theme park, opened in 1921
34 Pleasurewood Hills, Lowestoft
50 rides, sea lion and parrot shows, a castle and theatre
35 Oakwood*, Narberth
Theme park with over 40 attractions including stage shows
36 LEGOLAND Windsor*
Over 50 interactive rides, building workshops and driving schools in beautiful parkland
37 Chessington World of Adventures*
Amusement park and zoo with gorillas and large cats
Thorpe Park, Chertsey
The UK's fastest changing thrill park with many white-knuckle rides
38 Harbour Park, Littlehampton
Seaside amusement park with extensive undercover facilities and arcades
39 Crealy Adventure Park, Exeter
A re-creation of a country childhood; with six different realms combining magic, adventure, action, animals, farming and nature

The Netherlands
40 Attractiepark Slagharen, Slagharen
Theme park with Wild West shows and over 40 rides
Avonturenpark Hellendoorn
Amusement park with many rides and animal attractions
41 Dolfinarium Harderwijk
Europe's largest marine theme park featuring six different shows with animals plus a dolphin rehabilitation centre, an open-air dolphin lagoon and a research centre
Walibi World, Dronten
Family amusement park famous for its rollercoasters
42 Drievliet, Rijswijk
Family park with over 30 major attractions, shows and playgrounds
Duinrell, Wassenaar
Family park with educational exhibitions; over 50 rides and water attractions
43 De Efteling, Kaatsheuvel
One of Europe's leading family leisure parks; a full range of attractions includes spectacular shows and PandaVision, an educational 3D journey through the world of nature
44 BillyBird Park Hemelrijk, Volkel
Artificial lake with nature area, beaches, restaurants, pools and interactive playground
Toverland, Sevenum
Large indoor and outdoor amusement park

Belgium
45 Bellewaerde Park, Ypres
Mix of attractions and exotic animals in a natural setting
Boudewijn Seapark, Bruges
Family park, famous for its dolphinarium; with rides, skating, boating, Seal Island and other animals
Plopsaland, De Panne
Theme park for families with children up to 12 years old
46 Bobbejaanland, Lichtaart
Amusement and theme park with 45 major rides, including *The Revolution* and *Arcade 2000*; also includes *Kinderland*, a covered children's play area with 20 rides
47 Bruparck, Brussels
Includes Mini-Europe, cinemas and IMAX, tropical swimming pool and saunaland
Walibi Belgium, Wavre
Over 50 attractions and shows; includes Aqualibi, a tropical waterpark

Germany
48 Familien-Freizeitpark Tolk-Schau, Tolk
Amusement park situated in a scenic landscape
49 Hansapark, Sierksdorf
Theme park with many rides and attractions including water circus and 3,000-seat Hansapark Theatre
50 Ferienzentrum Schloss Dankern, Haren
Family entertainment centre with many water facilities
51 Movie Park Germany, Bottrop
Movie theme park with over 40 attractions and shows including stunt shows and a free-fall tower
52 Kernwasser Wunderland, Kalkar
Unique amusement park for children up to 12 years old on the site of a former nuclear power station
53 Phantasialand, Brühl
Theme park divided into six areas: *China Town, Old Berlin, Fantasy, Mystery, Mexico* and *Silver City*; attractions include shows and culinary delicacies
54 Eifelpark, Gondorf bei Bitburg
Wild animal park and amusement park with open-air theatre
55 Panoramapark Sauerland, Kirchhundem
Wild animal park and amusement park with its own 500-kilowatt windpower station
56 Fort Fun Abenteuerland, Bestwig
Indoor and outdoor children's amusement park; offers facilities for corporate events
57 Safari & Hollywood-Park, Schloss Holte-Stukenbrock
Combined safari park and amusement park
58 Dinosaurier Park Münchehagen, Rehburg-Loccum
Dinosaur park
59 Heide-Park, Soltau
Amusement park with shows and 40 major rides
Serengeti Safaripark, Hodenhagen
Animal park with over 1,000 animals and three themed areas: *Monkey Land, Leisure Land* and *Water Land*
60 Autostadt, Wolfsburg
Theme park of the automobile: Volkswagen distribution centre combined with car museum, displays, go-kart track and rides
61 BELANTIS, Leipzig
Attractions and live shows in six BELANTIS Worlds: *Castle BELANTIS, Beach of the Gods, Valley of the Pharoahs, Country of the Counts, Island of the Knights* and *Coast of the Discoverers*
62 Freizeit-Land, Geiselwind
Theme park and zoo, including four rollercoasters
63 Holiday-Park, Hassloch
Theme park with many attractions and rides including a 180-degree cinema and a live show parade
64 Erlebnispark Tripsdrill, Cleebronn
Germany's oldest amusement park with rides and animals
65 LEGOLAND Deutschland, Günzburg
Unique blend of entertainment and learning by play for families with children up to 13 years old
66 Ravensberger Spieleland, Meckenbeuren
Largest playground in the world with over 40 attractions
67 Europa-Park, Rust
One of Europe's major parks, close to France & Switzerland

France
68 Walibi Lorraine, Maizières-les-Metz
Amusement park with over 30 attractions and shows
69 Disneyland Resort Paris*, Marne-la-Vallée
Disneyland Paris is divided into five areas: *Main Street USA, Frontierland, Adventure-land, Fantasyland* and *Discoveryland. Walt Disney Studios Park*, opened in 2002, takes visitors back to the golden age of Hollywood and also behind the scenes of movie-making. *Disney Village* is Europe's largest entertainment complex.
La Mer de Sable, Ermenonville
Amusement park developed into themed areas: *China, Wild West* and *Morocco*; includes *Babagattau Village*
Parc Astérix*, Plailly
Theme park offering visitors a 3D trip into comic strip Asterix's universe, spread out over six neighbourhoods
70 Le Jardin d'Acclimatation, Paris
Amusement park with family rides and a zoo
71 Grand Parc du Puy du Fou, Les Espesses
Historical park with live shows and other attractions
72 Futuroscope, Jaunay-Clan, near Poitiers
Space-age park with advanced visual-image technology including an IMAX screen, virtual reality and Cyberspace
73 Walibi Aquitaine, Roquefort
With an 18th century castle and 20 attractions and shows
74 Le Pal, Dompierre sur Besbre
Animal and amusement park; shows feature sea lions, parrots and birds
75 Walibi Rhône-Alpes, Les Avenières
Regional amusement park with more than 30 rides and a waterpark area

Spain
76 Parc d'Atraccions Tibidabo, Barcelona
Urban amusement park, founded 1899, renovated 1988
77 Port Aventura*, Salou
Includes Costa Caribe waterpark and Zona de Playa beach
78 Terra Mítica*, Benidorm
Five areas: *Egypt, Iberia, Greece, Rome* and *The Islands*, illustrate the past, present and future of Mediterranean culture
79 Txiki Park, Pamplona
Family entertainment centre designed for children
80 Parque de Atracciones Casa de Campo, Madrid
Urban amusement park, Madrid's main entertainment centre
Warner Brothers Movie World, Madrid
Movie theme park with live shows and numerous attractions including Superman and Batman rides
81 Parque Isla Mágica, Seville
Theme park based upon exploration of the New World by 16th century Spanish adventurers
82 Sioux City, San Agustín, Gran Canaria
Western-themed park with stage shows and concerts

Portugal
83 Bracalândia, Braga
Theme park with various themed areas and attractions
84 Zoomarine, Albufeira
Zoo and marine park taking its theme from the Algarve's links with the sea

Switzerland
85 Mystery Park, Interlaken
Theme parks presenting unexplained mysteries of the world
86 Conny-Land, Lipperswil
Amusement park with underwater and animal shows

Austria
87 Freizeitpark Familienland, St Jakob in Haus
Amusement park with over 40 attractions
88 Wiener Prater, Vienna
Amusement park for over 100 years

Italy
89 Gardaland, Castelnuovo del Garda
Huge multifunctional amusement park with many attractions; four themed villages; profusion of plants and flowers
90 Mirabilandia, Ravenna
Amusement park with rides, stage shows and concerts
91 Fiabilandia, Rímini
Amusement park and funfair
92 Luneur, Rome
Traditional amusement park and funfair, 30 years old
93 Edenlandia, Naples
One of Italy's largest amusement parks

Hungary
94 Budapesti Vidam Park, Budapest
Amusement park with 33 games and rides; more than one million visitors per year

Greece
95 Luna Park 'Ta Aidonakia', Athens
20 family and children's rides

Turkey
96 Tatilya Turizm, Avcilar, Istanbul
Largest indoor entertainment centre in Europe and the Middle East, Tatilya is a holiday and amusement republic with its own president, citizens and constitution
97 Aqua Fantasy, Selçuk
Turkey's largest water park

Cyprus
98 WaterWorld, Ayia Napa
Cyprus' largest waterpark and most popular attraction

▶ *See also...* UNESCO Heritage (48-49)

The listings above refer to a selection of related themes.
For more information, see the Contents (2-5).

Principal museums and art galleries in the Russian Federation east of Moscow are included on the Asian map, p.129

EUROPEAN CAPITALS/CITIES OF CULTURE

1985	Athens	1999	Weimar
1986	Florence	2000	Avignon, Bergen,
1987	Amsterdam		Bologna, Brussels,
1988	Berlin		Cracow, Helsinki,
1989	Paris		Prague, Reykjavík,
1990	Glasgow		Santiago de Compostela
1991	Dublin	2001	Oporto, Rotterdam
1992	Madrid	2002	Bruges, Salamanca
1993	Antwerp	2003	Graz
1994	Lisbon	2004	Genoa, Lille
1995	Luxembourg	2005	Cork
1996	Copenhagen	2006	Patras
1997	Thessaloniki	2007	Luxembourg-Ville, Sibiu
1998	Stockholm	2008	Liverpool, Stavanger

Europe's most important museums and art galleries are listed here. Selection is based on importance and depth of the collection and its cultural diversity within a geographic spread.

Most cities named will also offer the visitor a number of smaller museums of specialist interest. Many single great works of art may also be housed in local cathedrals and churches.

Compiled by Jon A. Gillaspie
email: let@sarastro.com

Principal contents of institution:
- **AA** Applied & decorative art
- **AR** Archaeology / ancient art
- **FA** Fine art (paintings, sculpture)
- **FO** Folk art & culture / ethnography
- **H** History / historical site / reconstruction
- **NH** Natural history
- **ST** Science / technology
- **W** Wide range of subjects

Amsterdam THE NETHERLANDS
- **AA FA** Hermitage ann de Amstel
- **W** Rijksmuseum
- **FA** Stedelijk Museum; Van Gogh Museum

Ankara TURKEY
- **AR** Museum of Anatolian Civilizations

Antalya TURKEY
- **AR** Archaeological Museum

Antibes FRANCE
- **FA** Musée Picasso

Athína (Athens) GREECE
- **AR** Acropolis Museum; National Archaeological Museum
- **W** Benáki Museum
- **AR** Museum of Cycladic and Ancient Greek Art

Barcelona SPAIN
- **AR** Museu Arqueològic
- **FA** Museu d'Art Contemporani; Museu Nacional d'Art de Catalunya; Museu Picasso

Bath ENGLAND
- **AA** Museum of Costume
- **AR** Roman Baths and Museum

Bayeux FRANCE
- **AA** Bayeux Tapestry

Bérgamo ITALY
- **FA** Accademia Carrara

Berlin GERMANY
- **AR** Ägyptisches Museum; Antiken Museum
- **W** Dahlem museums

- **ST** Deutsches Teknikmuseum
- **W** Kulturforum includes:
- **FA** Gemäldegalerie
- **AA** Kunstgewerbemuseum
- **NH** Museum für Naturkunde
- **W** Museumsinsel includes:
- **FA** Alte Nationalgalerie
- **AR** Bodemuseum; Pergamonmuseum

Bern (Berne) SWITZERLAND
- **FA** Kunstmuseum

Bilbao SPAIN
- **FA** Museo de Bellas Arte; Museo Guggenheim

Bologna ITALY
- **AR** Museo Civico Archeologico

Bonn GERMANY
- **NH** Alexander-Koenig-Museum
- **FA** Kunstmuseum

Bradford UNITED KINGDOM
- **ST** National Museum of Photography, Film & TV

Bratislava SLOVAK REPUBLIC
- **FA** National Gallery
- **W** National Museum

Brugge (Bruges) BELGIUM
- **FA** Groeningemuseum

Bruxelles/Brussel (Brussels) BELGIUM
- **FA** Musées Royaux des Beaux-Arts

Bucharest ROMANIA
- **FA** National Art Museum
- **AR H** National History Museum

Budapest HUNGARY
- **H** Holocaust Museum
- **FA** Museum of Fine Arts; National Gallery
- **AA** National Jewish Museum
- **W** National Museum

Cágliari SARDINIA, ITALY
- **AR** Museo Nazionale Archeologico

Cambridge ENGLAND
- **W** Fitzwilliam Museum

Cardiff WALES
- **FO** Museum of Welsh Life [St Fagans]
- **W** National Museum and Gallery of Wales

Cork IRELAND
- **AA** Crawford Municipal Art Gallery

Den Haag (The Hague) THE NETHERLANDS
- **W** Gemeentemuseum
- **FA** Mauritshuis

Dresden GERMANY
- **AA** Gemäldegalerie Alte Meister

Dublin IRELAND
- **FA** National Gallery
- **W** National Museum

Düsseldorf GERMANY
- **W** Kunstmuseum
- **FA** Kunstsammlung Nordrhein-Westfalen

Edinburgh SCOTLAND
- **W** Royal Museum and Museum of Scotland
- **FA** Scottish National Portrait Gallery

El Escorial SPAIN
- **FA** Monasterio de El Escorial

Les Eyzies-de-Tayac FRANCE
- **AR** Musée national de Préhistoire

Figueres SPAIN
- **FA** Teatre-Museu Dalí

Firenze (Florence) ITALY
- **FA** Bargello; Uffizi

- **AR** Museo Archeologico

Frankfurt am Main GERMANY
- **FA** National Gallery
- **FA** Museum für Moderne Kunst
- **W** Museumsufer includes:
- **AA FA** Städel; Museum für Kunsthandwerk

Gdansk POLAND
- **W** National Art Museum

Génova (Genoa) ITALY
- **FA** Galleria Nazionale di Palazzo Spinola; Palazzo Bianco; Palazzo Rosso

Gent (Ghent) BELGIUM
- **FA** Museum voor Schone Kunsten

Glasgow SCOTLAND
- **W** Burrell Collection
- **FA** Gallery of Modern Art (GOMA); Hunterian Art Gallery and Museum

Göteborg (Gothenburg) SWEDEN
- **W** Konstmuseet
- **AA** Röhsska Konstlöjdmuseet

Graz AUSTRIA
- **FA** Alte Galerie; Kunsthaus
- **W** Landesmuseum Joanneum

Guimarães PORTUGAL
- **AA** Museu Alberto Sampaio
- **AR** Museu Martins Sarmiento
- **AA** Sé (Cathedral museum) [Braga]

Hamburg GERMANY
- **FA** Kunsthalle
- **AA** Museum für Kunst und Gewerbe

Hannover (Hanover) GERMANY
- **FA** Sprengel Museum

Helsinki (Helsingfors) FINLAND
- **FA** Helsinki kaupingin museo
- **FA** Kansallismuseo; Kiasma

Hildesheim GERMANY
- **AR** Roemer-Pelizaeus Museum

Iasi ROMANIA
- **H** Palace of Culture

Iráklio (Heraklion) CRETE, GREECE
- **AR** Archaeological Museum

Istanbul TURKEY
- **W** Museum of Turkish and Islamic Art

København (Copenhagen) DENMARK
- **AR** Nationalmuseet
- **W** Ny Carlsberg Glyptotek
- **FA** Statens Museum for Kunst

Köln (Cologne) GERMANY
- **FA** Ludwig Museum; Wallraf-Richartz Museum
- **AR** Römisch-Germanisches Museum

Kraków (Cracow) POLAND
- **W** Czartoryski Museum
- **FA** National Museum
- **FO** Museum of Ethnography

Kyiv (Kiev) UKRAINE
- **H** Historical Treasures Museum
- **FA** Russian Art Museum

Lausanne SWITZERLAND
- **H** Musée Olympique

Lille FRANCE
- **FA** Musée des Beaux-Arts

Lisboa (Lisbon) PORTUGAL
- **FA** Museu Nacional de Arte Antiga
- **W** Museu Calouste Gulbenkian

Liverpool ENGLAND
- **FA** Walker Art Gallery
- **W** World Museum

Ljubljana SLOVENIA
- **FA** National Gallery
- **W** National Museum

London ENGLAND
- **W** British Museum; Museum of London
- **FA** National Gallery; National Portrait Gallery; Tate Britain; Tate Modern
- **NH** Natural History Museum
- **ST** Science Museum
- **AA** Victoria and Albert Museum

Luxembourg-Ville LUXEMBOURG
- **W** Musée national d'Histoire et d'Art
- **NH** Musée national d'Histoire naturelle

Madrid SPAIN
- **FA** Centro de Arte Reina Sofía; Museo del Prado; Museo Thyssen-Bornemisza
- **AR** Museo Arqueológico Nacional
- **W** Museo de América

Málaga SPAIN
- **FA** Museo Picasso

Milano (Milan) ITALY
- **FA** Civico Museo di Arte Contemporanea; Pinacoteca Ambrosiana; Pinacoteca di Brera
- **AR** Museo Civico di Archeologia

Minsk BELARUS
- **FA** Belarusian State Art Museum
- **W** National Museum of History and Culture

Monaco
- **NH ST** Musée Océanographique

Moskva (Moscow) RUSSIAN FEDERATION
- **AA** Kremlin
- **FA** Mus. of Private Collections; Tretyakov Gallery
- **W** Pushkin Museum of Fine Arts

München (Munich) GERMANY
- **FA** Alte Pinakothek; Neue Pinakothek; Pinakothek der Moderne
- **AA** Bayerisches Nationalmuseum
- **ST** Deutsches Museum
- **AR** Glyptothek und Antikensammlungen

Nápoli (Naples) ITALY
- **AR** Museo Archeologico Nazionale

Nice FRANCE
- **FA** Fondation Maeght [St-Paul-de-Vence]
- **FA** Musée Marc-Chagall; Musée Matisse

Novgorod RUSSIAN FEDERATION
- **AA** Museum of History, Architecture and Art

Nuoro SARDINIA, ITALY
- **FO** Museo Etnografico

Oslo NORWAY
- **FA** Nasjonalgalleriet
- **FO** Norsk Folkemuseum
- **AR** Vikingskiphuset

Oxford ENGLAND
- **W** Ashmolean Museum
- **FA** Museum of Modern Art (MOMA)

Palermo SICILY, ITALY
- **AR** Museo Archeologico Regionale
- **FO** Museo Etnografico Pitrè

Paris FRANCE
- **ST** Cité des Sciences et de l'Industrie
- **W** Institut du Monde Arabe; Louvre
- **FA** Musée d'Orsay; Musée Marmottan; Musée national d'art moderne (Centre Georges Pompidou); Musée national du Moyen-Âge; Musée national Picasso; Musée Rodin

Pátra (Patras) GREECE
- **AR** Archaeological Museum of Patras

Perúgia ITALY
- **AR** Museu Archeologico Nazionale dell'Umbria

Porto (Oporto) PORTUGAL
- **AA** Museu Nacional Soares dos Reis

Praha (Prague) CZECH REPUBLIC
- **AA** Jewish Museum; Museum of Decorative Arts (UPM)
- **FA** Museum of Modern and Contemporary Czech Art; Mucha Museum; Museum of Modern Czech Sculpture (Zbraslav); National Gallery of Old Bohemian Art (St George Convent)
- **NH** National Museum
- **ST** National Museum of Technology

Preston ENGLAND
- **H** National Football Museum

Quinson FRANCE
- **AR** Musée de Préhistoire

Reykjavík ICELAND
- **W** Thjódminjasafn Íslands (National Museum)

Riga LATVIA
- **AA** Museum of Decorative and Applied Arts

Roma (Rome) ITALY & Vatican City
- **W** Capitoline museums includes:
- **AR** Museo Capitolino
- **W** Museo del Palazzo dei Conservatori
- **AR** Museo Nazionale di Villa Giulia; Museo Naz. Romano
- **FA** Galleria Borghese; Gall. Doria Pamphilj; Pal. Barberini
- **W** Musei Vaticani

Rotterdam THE NETHERLANDS
- **FA** Museum Boymans-van Beuningen

Salamanca SPAIN
- **AA** Museum Art Nouveau y Art Deco

Sankt-Peterburg (St Petersburg) RUSSIAN FED.
- **W** State Hermitage Museum
- **FO** Museum of Anthropology and Ethnography
- **W** Russian Museum

Selçuk TURKEY
- **AR** Archaeological Museum

Sibiu ROMANIA
- **FO** ASTRA museums
- **AA FA** The Brukenthal Museum

Siena ITALY
- **W** Ospedale di Santa Maria della Scala

Sofia BULGARIA
- **FO** Ethnographic Museum
- **FA** National Art Gallery
- **AR H** National Historical Museum

Stavanger NORWAY
- **AR** Arkeologist Museum
- **W** Stavanger Museum and Maritime Museum

Stockholm SWEDEN
- **FA** Modernamuseet
- **AA** Nationalmuseum
- **H** Statens Historiska Museet
- **AR** Vasamuseet

Stuttgart GERMANY
- **FA** Staatsgalerie

Tallinn ESTONIA
- **FA** National Art Museum

Thessaloníki (Salonika) GREECE
- **AR** Archaeological Museum
- **FO** Folklore Museum

Tiranë (Tirana) ALBANIA
- **AR** National Archaeology Museum
- **FA** National Art Gallery
- **W** National Historical Museum

Toledo SPAIN
- **AR** Museo de Arte Visigótico
- **FA** Museo de Santa Cruz

València SPAIN
- **ST** Ciutat de les Arts i les Ciències
- **FA** Museo de Bellas Artes San Pio V

Venézia (Venice) ITALY
- **FA** Collezione Guggenheim; Galleria dell'Accademia
- **W** Museo Correr
- **AA** Museo Vitrario di Murano

Vilnius LITHUANIA
- **FA** Lithuanian History and Ethnographic Museum

Warszawa (Warsaw) POLAND
- **W** National Museum

Weimar GERMANY
- **FA** Schlossmuseum

Wien (Vienna) AUSTRIA
- **AA FA** Kunsthistorisches Museum; Österreichische Galerie, Belvedere
- **W** MuseumsQuartier includes:
- **FA** MUMOK (Museum moderner Kunst); Leopold Mus.

Zürich SWITZERLAND
- **W** Kunsthaus
- **W** Schweizerisches Landesmuseum

The listings above refer to a selection of related themes.
For more information, see the Contents (2-5).

A symbol next to a resort's name in the listing below indicates that it is an outstanding example in that category. This is the publisher's selection, and is by its nature subjective. The lack of a symbol does not necessarily mean that the resort does not possess this quality or facility.

▲ **THE MOST BEAUTIFUL RESORTS**
Ski areas with spectacular scenery

❄ **SNOWSURE**
The best reputations for season-long snow cover

▲ **SUMMER SKIING DESTINATIONS**
Resorts where lifts stay open for skiing or boarding during the summer

◆ **EXPERT**
Best of the black diamond destinations

■ **BEGINNER SKI AREAS**
Best choices for first timers

★ **FAMILY FRIENDLY**
Ideal choices for family ski holidays

● **PARTY TOWNS**
Après ski centres

▼ **SNOWBOARDER HEAVEN**
Best bets for boarders

★ **NOT JUST SKIING**
Plenty to do if you don't want to slide

✔ **ECO-FRIENDLY REPUTATION**
(not all resorts have been graded in this category)

Information supplied by Snow24 plc
www.snow24.com

THE LARGEST LINKED RESORT AREAS △

Portes du Soleil (650 km of ski piste) *France/*
9 Châtel   *Switz.*
10 Avoriaz
11 les Gets
11 Morzine
54 Torgon
55 Champéry-Planachaux / Val-d'Illiez / Les Crosets
Grand Massif (265 km) *France*
12 Morillon les Essert
13 Samoëns
14 Sixt
15 Flaine
Paradiski (425 km) *France*
23 les Arcs
24 Peisey / Nancroix-Vallandry
27 la Plagne / les Coches / Montchavin / Plagne Montalbert
28 Champagny-en-Vanoise
Espace Killy (300 km) *France*
25 Tignes
26 Val d'Isère
Trois Vallées (600 km) *France*
29 Courchevel
29 la Tania
30 Méribel
31 Val Thorens
32 les Menuires
33 St-Martin-de-Belleville
Les Sybelles (350 km) *France*
35 le Corbier
35 la Toussuire
36 St-Jean d'Arves

Grand Serre-Chevalier (250 km) *France*
45 Briançon
45 Serre-Chevalier
Milky Way (400 km) *France/Italy*
46 Montgenèvre
117 Clavière
117 San Sicário / Cesana
118 Sestriere
119 Sàuze d'Oulx
4 Valleys (412 km) *Switzerland*
56 Verbier
57 la Tzoumas (Mayens-de-Riddes)
International (350 km) *Italy/Switzerland*
65 Zermatt
123 Breuil-Cervinia
124 Valtournenche
TopCard (308 km) *Switzerland*
79 Davos
80 Klosters / Fideris
KiWest (400 km) *Austria*
99 Hopfgarten im Brixental
99 Westendorf
100 Söll
101 Kitzbühel
Sella Ronda (510 km) *Italy*
142 Arabba
143 Campitello di Fassa
143 Canazei
144 Santa Cristina / Pranauron
144 Selva Gardena (Wolkenstein)
145 Ortisei (St Ulrich)
146 Alta Badia [Colfosco / Corvara / La Villa (Stern) / San Cassiano (St Kassian) / Pedráces / San Leonardo (St Leonard)]

Germany
1 Feldberg ■★
2 Oberstdorf ▲★■●
3 Garmisch-Partenkirchen ▲❄▲◆●★✔
4 Bayrischzell ■
5 Reit im Winkl ▲■★

France
6 la Bresse-Hohneck ■▼
7 Métabief / le Mont d'Or ★★
8 Abondance / la Chapelle d'Abondance ▲■★
9 Châtel ▲■★
10 Avoriaz ❄◆■●▼
11 les Gets ▲■★✔
11 Morzine ▲◆■●▼
12 Morillon les Essert ▲■
13 Samoëns ▲■★
15 Flaine ❄■▲▼✔
16 les Carroz ▼
17 la Clusaz ▲◆
18 Notre-Dame-de-Bellecombe ■
19 Praz-sur-Arly ★
20 Megève ❄■◆★
21 Chamonix-Mont-Blanc ▲❄◆●▼
22 les Contamines-Montjoie ▲❄★
22 St-Nicolas-de-Véroce ★
23 les Arcs ❄■◆●▼
25 Tignes ❄▲▲◆●▼
26 Val d'Isère ❄▲◆●▼✔
27 la Plagne / les Coches / Montchavin / Plagne Montalbert ■▼★
28 Champagny-en-Vanoise ▲▼
29 Courchevel ❄■◆●▼
29 la Tania ■✔
30 Méribel / Brides-les-Bains ▲◆●▼★
31 Val Thorens ❄▲■◆▼
32 les Menuires ◆■●▼
33 St-Martin-de-Belleville ▲■
34 Valmorel ■★▼
35 le Corbier ■▼
35 la Toussuire ▼
36 St-Jean d'Arves ▲
37 Villard-de-Lans / Cote 2000 ■▼
38 Correncon-en-Vercors ■
39 les Sept Laux (le Pleiney / Prapoutel) ▲■
40 Vaujany / Oz-en-Oisans ▲◆
41 Alpe d'Huez / Auris-en-Oisans / Villard-Reculas ❄❄◆■●✔
42 les Deux-Alpes ❄▲■◆●▼✔
43 la Grave ▲❄▲◆

44 Valloire ❄☆★
45 Briançon ▲★
   Serre-Chevalier ▲■▲▼◆★✔
46 Montgenèvre ❄■●▼
47 Risoul ■▲▼
48 Vars ❄
49 les Orres ■▲▼
50 Pra-Loup ■▲▼
51 Val d'Allos-la-Foux ❄
52 Auron / St-Étienne-de-Tinée ▲●
53 Beuil-les-Launes ▲
   Valberg ■

Switzerland
55 Champéry-Planachaux / Val-d'Illiez / Les Crosets ▲■▲
56 Verbier ❄■◆●▲▼★
57 la Tzoumas (Mayens-de-Riddes) ❄★
58 Villars-sur-Ollon / Gryon ❄▲▲■▼
59 les Diablerets ▲▲▲●✔
60 Château-d'Oex ▲■▲▼
61 Gstaad-Saanenland ▲▲❄●▼★✔
62 Adelboden ▲■▲▼
63 Lenk ▲■●▼
64 Crans-Montana ❄▲▲◆●▼★✔
65 Zermatt ▲❄▲◆●▼★✔
66 Saas-Fee ▲❄▲■●▼★✔
67 Bettmeralp ▲❄
   Fiesch ★
   Mörel-Breiten ✔
68 Sörenberg ▲
69 Mürren / Stechelberg ▲◆■★✔
   Wengen ▲❄❄●★
70 Riederalp ▲
71 Interlaken / Wilderswil bei Interlaken ▲■▲★
72 Grindelwald ▲❄◆■★✔
73 Engelberg ▲▲◆●▼✔
74 Laax ▲❄◆★▼
75 Flims ❄▲◆●▼
76 Flumserberg ▲▼
77 Lenzerheide-Valbella ▲◆■●▼
   Parpan ▲★
78 Arosa ▲❄★★
79 Davos ❄▲◆●▼★✔
80 Klosters / Fideris ▲▲◆■▼
81 Celerina ❄
   Samedan ❄
82 St Moritz ❄◆●▼★✔
83 Sils-Maria ▲❄
84 Maloja ❄
85 Pontresina ❄❄★
86 Samnaun ●★

Austria
87 St Gallenkirch ▲▼
88 Kleinwalsertal [Hirschegg /Mittelberg / Riezlern] ▲❄
89 Lech / Oberlech ❄❄■●▼✔
   Zürs ◆
90 St Anton am Arlberg / St Jakob am Arlberg ❄▲◆●▼✔
   St Christoph am Arlberg ❄◆
91 Ischgl / Silvretta ❄❄●▼✔
92 Ehrwald ▲■
   Lermoos ▲■
93 Obergurgl / Hochgurgl ▲❄❄

94 Sölden ❄▲◆●★✔
95 Hintertux ▲▲✔
96 Mayrhofen ▲■▲●▼★✔
97 Zell am Ziller ▲■●
98 Alpbach ▲◆✔
99 Hopfgarten im Brixental ■▲▼
   Westendorf ▲■▲●▼
100 Söll ■●
101 Kitzbühel ▲◆■●▼★
102 Fieberbrunn ◆●▼
   St Johann im Tirol ▲■●▼
103 Saalbach Hinterglemm ◆■●▼✔
104 Leogang ▲■▲
105 Kaprun ▲▲▲■▼✔
106 Zell am See ■▲◆★▼
107 Badgastein ❄❄
108 Bad Hofgastein ■▲●★
109 Grossarl ▼
110 Flachau ●▼
111 Altenmarkt-Zauchensee ★
112 Annaberg im Lammertal ■
113 Ramsau am Dachstein ▲❄▲▼
   Schladming ▲▲■●▼★✔
114 St Michael im Lungau ▲❄
115 Bad Kleinkirchheim ▲▲▼★

Italy
116 Limone Piemonte ■●
117 Clavière ■■
118 Sestriere ❄◆●▼
119 Sàuze d'Oulx ■●
120 Bardonécchia ■■●
121 la Thuile ❄■
122 Courmayeur ◆●★
123 Breuil-Cervinia ▲▲●
124 Valtournenche ❄
125 Champoluc / Antagnod ❄■
126 Gressoney-la-Trinité / Gressoney-St Jean ❄■
127 Alaga-Valsésia ❄◆
128 Livigno ❄■●▼
129 Bormio ●▲★
130 Folgárida ▼
131 Passo Tonale ❄▲■★★
132 Madonna di Campíglio ▲●▼✔
133 Andalo ●
134 Folgária ▼
135 Lavarone / Luserna ▲
136 Asiago / Canove ★
137 Cavalese ❄★
138 Obereggen ■
139 Bellamonte ■
140 San Martino di Castrozza ▲●▼★
141 Alleghe ■
142 Arabba ❄▲◆■▼
143 Campitello di Fassa ■▼
   Canazei ●■
144 Santa Cristina / Pranauron ▲■■
   Selva Gardena (Wolkenstein) ▲▲●■
146 **Alta Badia** [Colfosco / Corvara / La Villa (Stern) / San Cassiano (St Kassian) / Pedráces / San Leonardo (St Leonard)] ▲■●★
147 Cortina ❄▲■●★
148 San Vigilio di Marebbe ❄
149 Versciaco (Vierschach) ❄★

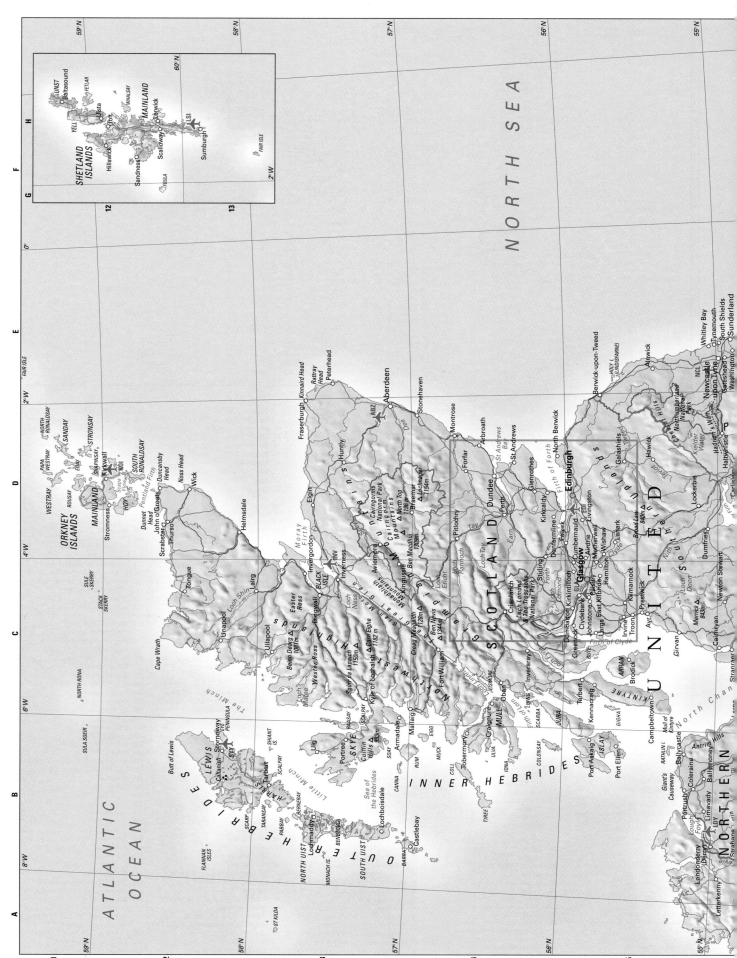

ATLANTIC OCEAN

NORTH SEA

SHETLAND ISLANDS
YELL
UNST
Baltasound
FETLAR
Uyea
WHALSAY
MAINLAND
Toft
Berwick
LSI
Hillswick
Sandness
Scalloway
FOULA
Sumburgh
FAIR ISLE

ORKNEY ISLANDS
NORTH RONALDSAY
SANDAY
PAPA WESTRAY
WESTRAY
STRONSAY
ROUSAY
SHAPINSAY
EDAY
Kirkwall
MAINLAND
HOY
SOUTH RONALDSAY
Scapa Flow
Pentland Firth
Stromness
Dunnet Head
John o'Groats
Duncansby Head

SULE SKERRY
STACK SKERRY
SULA SGEIR
NORTH RONA
FLANNAN ISLES
ST KILDA
SULE SKERRY

Cape Wrath
Thurso
Scrabster
Wick
Noss Head
Helmsdale
Tongue
Durness
Unapool
Lairg
Ullapool
Loch Shin

Butt of Lewis
LEWIS
Stornoway
EYE PENINSULA
Callanish
Tarbert
HARRIS
SCALPAY
TARANSAY
SCARP
PABBAY
BERNERAY
NORTH UIST
Lochmaddy
MONACH IS.
BENBECULA
SOUTH UIST
Lochboisdale
BARRA
Castlebay

SHIANT IS.
SCALPAY
RAASAY
Portree
SKYE
Uig
SOAY
CANNA
RUM
EIGG
MUCK
COLL
TIREE
Armadale
Mallaig
Tobermory
COLONSAY
ULVA
IONA
MULL
Craignure
Oban
SCARBA
JURA
Port Askaig
ISLAY
Port Ellen
GIGHA
Tarbert
Kennacraig
Campbeltown
Mull of Kintyre
KINTYRE

INNER HEBRIDES

The Minch
Little Minch
Sea of the Hebrides
Loch Maree
Wester Ross
Loch Torridon
Kyle of Lochalsh

Fraserburgh
Kinnaird Head
Rattray Head
Peterhead
Aberdeen
ABZ
Stonehaven
Montrose
Arbroath
St Andrews Bay
St Andrews
Forfar
Dundee
Perth
Glenrothes
Kirkcaldy
Dunfermline
Firth of Forth
Edinburgh
North Berwick

Huntly
Elgin
Invergordon
Inverness
Black Isle
NW
Aviemore
Cairngorms National Park
Moor Top
Ben Macdhui 1309m
Braemar
Lochnagar 1154m
Pitlochry
Loch Rannoch
Loch Tay
Loch Earn
Stirling
Cumbernauld
Falkirk
Livingston
Airdrie
Motherwell
Wishaw
Hamilton
Lanark

SCOTLAND

NORTHWEST HIGHLANDS
Beinn Dearg 1081m
Easter Ross
Dingwall
Strathspey
Sgurr na Lapaich 1150m
Beinn Eighe 1182m
Loch Ness
Great Glen
Monadhliath Mountains
Kingussie
Loch Ericht
Creag Meagaidh 1128m
Fort William
Ben Nevis 1344m
Glen Coe
GRAMPIAN MOUNTAINS
Loch Lomond & The Trossachs National Park
Loch Lomond
Crianlarich
Inveraray
Loch Fyne
Dumbarton
Greenock
Clydebank
Paisley
Glasgow
Johnstone
GLA
East Kilbride
Kilmarnock
Prestwick
Troon
Ayr

ARRAN
Brodick
Largs
Firth of Clyde
Irvine
North Channel
RATHLIN I.
Giant's Causeway
Portrush
Coleraine
Ballymoney
Ballycastle
Antrim Hills
Limavady
Ballymena
Londonderry

NORTHERN

UNITED
Merrick 843m
Loch Doon
Newton Stewart
Dumfries
Girvan
Stranraer
Cairnryan
Loch Ryan

SOUTHERN UPLANDS
Nith
Dumfries
Lockerbie

Berwick-upon-Tweed
Galashiels
Tweed
HOLY I. (LINDISFARNE)
Hawick
Teviot
Alnwick
Northumberland National Park
Cheviot Hills
Kielder Water
Hadrian's Wall
Haltwhistle
Carlisle
NCL
Newcastle upon Tyne
Gateshead
Washington
South Shields
Tynemouth
Whitley Bay
Sunderland

60° N 59° N 58° N 57° N 56° N 55° N
8° W 6° W 4° W 2° W 0° 2° W

For more information, see the Contents (2-5).

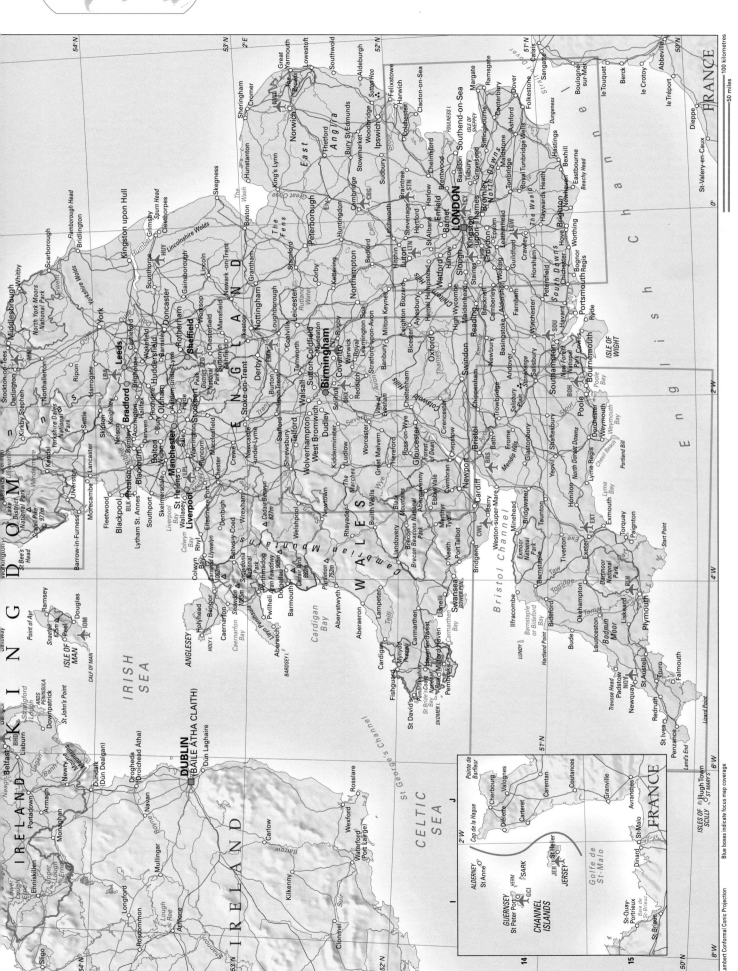

See also... Europe National Parks (54); UK Attractions (64)

The listings above refer to a selection of related themes. For more information, see the Contents (2-5).

The European Blue Flag Campaign is an environmental awareness raising activity by the Foundation for Environmental Education in Europe (FEEE).

To qualify for a Blue Flag, a beach has to fulfil a number of strict criteria regarding water quality (compliance with the EU Bathing Water Directive), environmental education and information, environmental management and safety and services. The Blue Flag is awarded annually and is valid for one year. The map shows beaches awarded the Blue Flag in 2005. For more information visit: www.seasideawards.org.uk

The UK maps show geographical counties, and not the administrative counties and unitary authorities which have, for administrative purposes, replaced them. Geographical counties give a more familiar picture of the divisions of the UK: they are also of a more consistent size, as they do not reflect the growth of urban populations over the last 200 years. For more information on geographical countries, visit: www.abcounties.co.uk

Scotland
1 Montrose Seafront
2 Broughty Ferry
3 St Andrews: East Sands
  St Andrews: West Sands
4 Elie Harbour
5 Burntisland
6 Aberdour: Silver Sands
Northumbria
7 Whitley Bay South
  Tynemouth: King Edward's Bay
  Tynemouth: Longsands South
8 South Shields: Sandhaven
  Whitburn North: Seaburn
Yorkshire
9 Whitby
10 Scarborough: North Bay
11 Bridlington North
12 Hornsea
13 Cleethorpes Central
Heart of England
14 Mablethorpe Central
  Sutton on Sea Central

15 Skegness: Tower Esplanade
East of England
16 Sheringham
17 Cromer
18 Mundesley
19 Sea Palling
20 Great Yarmouth: Gorleston on Sea
21 Lowestoft North
  Lowestoft South
22 Southwold Pier
23 Felixstowe South
24 Dovercourt
25 Brightlingsea
26 Shoeburyness East
  Shoebury Common
  Southend-on-Sea: Jubilee Beach
South East England
27 Birchington: Minnis Bay
  Westgate-on-Sea: West Bay
28 Margate: Westbrook Bay
29 Eastbourne: Pier to Wish Tower
30 Littlehampton: Coastguards
31 Bognor Regis: East of Pier
32 West Wittering
Southern England
33 Hayling Island: Beachlands Central
  Hayling Island: Beachlands West
34 Bournemouth: Alum Chine
  Bournemouth: Durley Chine
  Bournemouth: Fisherman's Walk
  Bournemouth: Southbourne

35 Poole: Branksome Chine
  Poole: Canford Cliffs Chine
  Poole: Sandbanks
  Poole: Shore Road
36 Swanage Central
Isle of Wight
37 Ryde East
38 Sandown
  Shanklin
South West
39 Dawlish Warren
40 Torquay: Oddicombe
  Torquay: Meadfoot
41 Brixham: Shoalstone Breakwater
42 Blackpool Sands
43 Bigbury-on-Sea North
  Challaborough
44 Falmouth: Gyllyngvase
45 Sennen Cove
46 St Ives: Porthmeor
  St Ives: Porthminster
47 Porthtowan
48 Polzeath
49 Westward Ho!
50 Croyde Bay
  Woolacombe
51 Ilfracombe: Tunnels Beaches
Wales
52 Southerndown
  Porthcawl: Rest Bay
53 Swansea: Bracelet Bay
  Swansea: Caswell Bay
  Swansea: Langland Bay
54 Port-Eynon
55 Pembrey Country Park: Cefn Sidan
56 Amroth
  Saundersfoot
57 Tenby Castle
  Tenby North
  Tenby South
58 Lydstep
59 Dale
60 Broad Haven North
61 Newgale
62 St David's: Whitesands
63 Cardigan: Poppit Sands
64 Aberporth
65 New Quay: Traeth y Harbwr
66 Aberystwyth North
67 Borth
68 Tywyn
69 Fairbourne: Ffriog
70 Barmouth: Abermaw
71 Criccieth
72 Pwllheli: Marian y De
73 Abersoch
74 Dinas Dinlle
75 Penmaenmawr
76 Rhos-on-Sea
77 Prestatyn Central
Anglesey
78 Newborough: Llanddwyn
79 Holy Island: Porth Dafarch
  Holy Island: Trearddur Bay
80 Benllech
81 Llanddona
Northern Ireland
82 Magilligan: Benone Strand
  Downhill Strand
83 Portstewart Strand
  Portrush: East Strand
  Portrush: West Strand
  Portrush: White Rocks
84 Tyrella
85 Cranfield West

International arrivals (millions)

Source: World Tourism Organisation

Blue Flag beach 2005
Geographical county boundary
English Tourist Board boundary
National Park

100 kilometres
50 miles

Same scale as main map

West Country

Blue boxes indicate focus map coverage

Same scale as main map

► **See also...** Contents (2-5) – this country features in many thematic and regional maps throughout the *BTEC First Travel Atlas*.

Europe **61**

United Kingdom

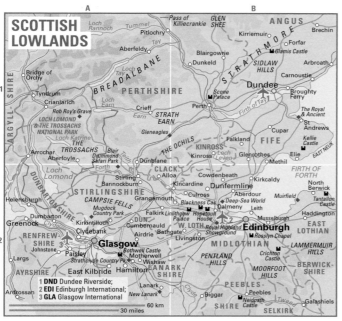

SCOTTISH LOWLANDS

1 DND Dundee Riverside;
2 EDI Edinburgh International;
3 GLA Glasgow International

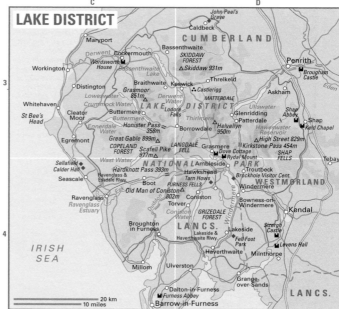

LAKE DISTRICT

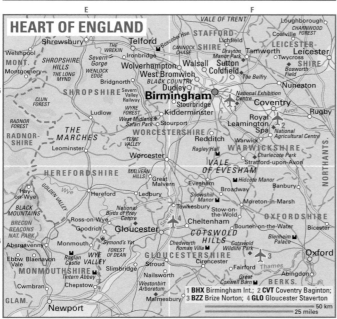

HEART OF ENGLAND

1 BHX Birmingham Int.; 2 CVT Coventry Baginton;
3 BZZ Brize Norton; 4 GLO Gloucester Staverton

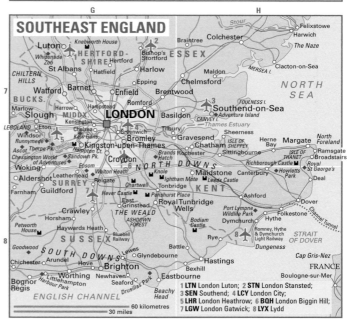

SOUTHEAST ENGLAND

1 LTN London Luton; 2 STN London Stansted;
3 SEN Southend; 4 LCY London City;
5 LHR London Heathrow; 6 BGH London Biggin Hill;
7 LGW London Gatwick; 8 LYX Lydd

WEST COUNTRY

1 NQY Newquay St Mawgan; 2 PLH Plymouth;
3 EXT Exeter; 4 BOH Bournemouth International;
5 BRS Bristol International; 6 CWL Cardiff International

NEW YEAR Hogmanay (**Edinburgh**)
JAN 1st New Year's Day Parade (**London**)
JAN Celtic Connections (**Glasgow**)
JAN 25th Burns Night (**Scotland**)
late JAN Up Helly Aa (**Lerwick, Shetland**)
MAR-APR Ideal Home Show (**London**)
APR **London** Marathon
APR Oxford-Cambridge Boat Race (**London**)
APR **Edinburgh** International Science Festival
APR 30th Beltane: Celtic Fire Festival
MAY 1st Hobby Horse (**Minehead & Padstow**)
MAY Furry Dance (**Helston**) MAY Mayfest (**Glasgow**)
end MAY Chelsea Flower Show (**London**)
MAY-JUN **Bath** International Festival
MAY-AUG Glyndebourne Opera Festival
early JUN Queen's Birthday parade: Trooping The Colour (**London**)
JUN Royal Highland Show (**Ingliston**)
JUN Aldeburgh Festival   late JUN Glastonbury Festival
JUN-JUL **York** Mystery Plays; 2004 and every four years
JUN-JUL Lawn Tennis Championships (**Wimbledon**)
JUN-AUG Riding of the Marches (**England-Scotland borders**)
JUN-AUG **Cardiff** Festival   JUL Henley Royal Regatta
JUL Llangollen International Music Eisteddfod
JUL/AUG WOMAD World Music Festival (**Reading**)
JUL/AUG Highland Games (various places in **Scotland**)
JUL-SEP Promenade Concerts 'Proms' (**London**)
early AUG Royal National Eisteddfod (**Wales**: venue changes)
AUG Three Choirs Festival (**Gloucester/Hereford/Worcester**)
AUG **Edinburgh** International Festival & Fringe; Military Tattoo
AUG **Brecon** Jazz Festival
AUG Great British Beer Festival (**London**)
AUG Bank Holiday Notting Hill Carnival (**London**)
SEP Royal Highland Gathering (**Braemar**)
SEP-NOV Blackpool Illuminations
NOV 5th Guy Fawkes Night
early NOV **London-Brighton** Veteran Car Rally
NOV **London** Film Festival; **London** Jazz Festival
NOV **Cardiff** Screen Festival
NOV State Opening of Parliament (**London**)
NOV Lord Mayor's Procession and Show (**London**)

600 metres
300 metres
Sea level

62 **Europe**

UK: Airports, Motorways & Ferries

▶ **See also...** Flight Times (39); Europe Airports &
High-Speed Rail (50-51); Europe Railways & Ferries
(52-53); London Airport Connections (63)

The listings above refer to a selection of related themes.
For more information, see the Contents (2-5).

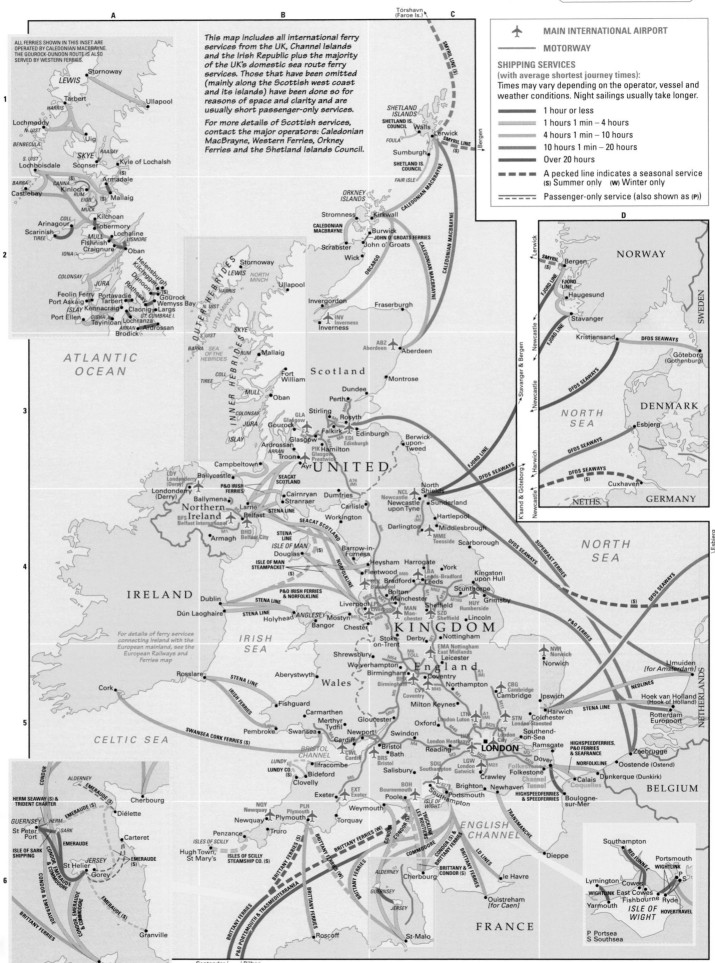

See also... Flight Times (39); Europe Airports &
High-Speed Rail (50-51); Europe Railways & Ferries
(52-53); UK Airports, Motorways & Ferries (62)

The listings above refer to a selection of related themes.
For more information, see the Contents (2-5).

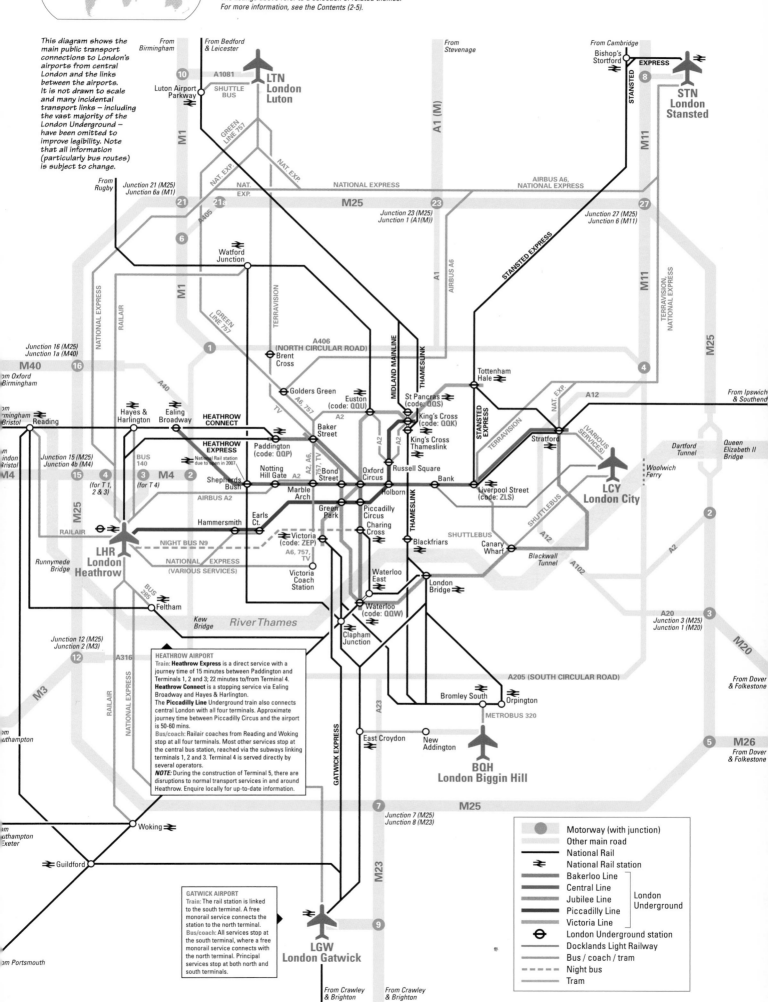

This diagram shows the main public transport connections to London's airports from central London and the links between the airports. It is not drawn to scale and many incidental transport links – including the vast majority of the London Underground – have been omitted to improve legibility. Note that all information (particularly bus routes) is subject to change.

HEATHROW AIRPORT
Train: Heathrow Express is a direct service with a journey time of 15 minutes between Paddington and Terminals 1, 2 and 3; 22 minutes to/from Terminal 4.
Heathrow Connect is a stopping service via Ealing Broadway and Hayes & Harlington.
The Piccadilly Line Underground train also connects central London with all four terminals. Approximate journey time between Piccadilly Circus and the airport is 50-60 mins.
Bus/coach: Railair coaches from Reading and Woking stop at all four terminals. Most other services stop at the central bus station, reached via the subways linking terminals 1, 2 and 3. Terminal 4 is served directly by several operators.
NOTE: During the construction of Terminal 5, there are disruptions to normal transport services in and around Heathrow. Enquire locally for up-to-date information.

GATWICK AIRPORT
Train: The rail station is linked to the south terminal. A free monorail service connects the station to the north terminal.
Bus/coach: All services stop at the south terminal, where a free monorail service connects with the north terminal. Principal services stop at both north and south terminals.

Legend:
- ● Motorway (with junction)
- Other main road
- National Rail
- ≠ National Rail station
- Bakerloo Line
- Central Line
- Jubilee Line } London Underground
- Piccadilly Line
- Victoria Line
- ⊕ London Underground station
- Docklands Light Railway
- Bus / coach / tram
- Night bus (dashed)
- Tram

▶ **See also...** Attractions in Belgium (67), Netherlands (69), Germany (73), France (77), Iberia (79) and Italy (86)

The listings above refer to a selection of related themes. For more information, see the Contents (2-5). See also the Columbus Tourist Attractions & Events of the World.

Legend:
- Theme park, leisure park
- Museum, gallery
- Religious building
- Park, reserve, zoo, etc.
- Historic/notable building
- Water-related attraction
- Other place of interest

Attractions in cities marked in **red** are listed around the edge of the map

100 kilometres
50 miles

Edinburgh
National Gallery of Scotland
Royal Museum & Museum of Scotland
Royal Scottish Academy
Scottish National Portrait Gallery
Our Dynamic Earth
St Giles' Cathedral
Edinburgh Zoo
Holyrood House & Arthur's Seat
Royal Botanic Gardens
Edinburgh Castle
Palace of Holyroodhouse
Scottish Parliament
Royal Yacht Britannia, *Leith*
Calton Hill
Charlotte Square
Royal Mile

London
British Museum
Courtauld Institute Galleries
Imperial War Museum
London Dungeon
London Planetarium
Madame Tussaud's
Museum of London
National Gallery
National Portrait Gallery
Natural History Museum
Royal Academy of Arts
Science Museum
Somerset House
Tate Britain
Tate Modern
Victoria & Albert Museum
Wallace Collection
Neasden Temple
St Paul's Cathedral
Westminster Abbey
London Zoo
Hampstead Heath
Buckingham Palace
Harrods
Palace of Westminster & Big Ben
Tower of London
Keats House
Kensington Palace
Kenwood House
London Aquarium
British Airways London Eye
Camden Market
Whitehall & Downing Street
Lords Cricket Ground & Museum
Piccadilly Circus

Glasgow
Burrell Collection
Clydebuilt
Gallery of Modern Art (GOMA)
Glasgow Science Centre
Hunterian Art Gallery & Museum
Kelvingrove Art Gallery & Museum
Museum of Transport
Cathedral
Glasgow School of Art
Waverley Historic Paddle Steamer
Celtic Park (Parkhead)
Ibrox Stadium

Liverpool
The Beatles Story
Merseyside Maritime Museum
Tate Liverpool
Walker Art Gallery
World Museum
Liverpool Anglican Cathedral
Metropolitan Cathedral
St George's Hall
Speke Hall
Albert Dock
Port Sunlight

Newcastle upon Tyne
New Metroland, Gateshead
Baltic Centre for Contemporary Art
Discovery Museum
Laing Art Gallery
Life Science Centre
Sage Gateshead
Tyne bridges
Angel of the North

York
Jorvik Viking Centre
National Railway Museum
York Castle Museum
Clifford's Tower
Merchant Adventurers' Hall
Minster
City walls
The Shambles

Manchester
Granada Studios
Imperial War Museum North
John Rylands Library
Lowry Centre
Manchester Art Gallery
Museum of Science & Industry
Urbis
Heaton Park, Prestwich
Salford Quays
Castlefield Urban Heritage Park
Old Trafford

Birmingham
Barber Institute of Fine Arts
Birmingham Museum & Art Gallery
Museum of the Jewellery Quarter
Aston Hall
National Sealife Centre

Cardiff
Museum of Welsh Life, *St Fagans*
National Museum & Gallery of Wales
Techniquest
Llandaff Cathedral
Cardiff Castle
National Assembly Building (Senedd)
Wales Millennium Centre
Cardiff Bay
Millennium Stadium

Oxford
Ashmolean Museum
Modern Art Oxford
University & Pitt Rivers Museums
University

Bristol
At-Bristol
British Empire & Commonwealth Museum
Industrial Museum
Cathedral of St Peter & St Paul
St Mary Redcliffe Church
Bristol Zoological Gardens
Georgian House
Clifton Suspension Bridge
SS Great Britain

Bath
Museum of Costume
Roman Baths & Pumproom
The King's Circus
Royal Crescent

Channel Islands (inset)
Fort Grey Shipwreck Mus.
Oatlands Craft Centre
Occupation Museum
German Underground Hosp.
Victor Hugo's House

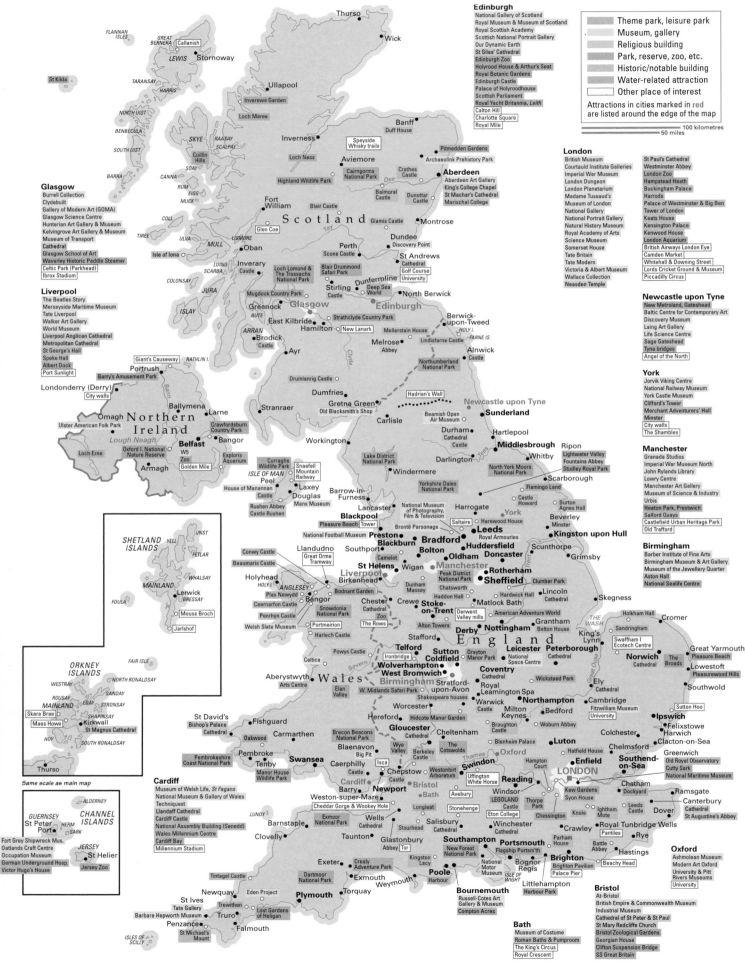

▶ **See also...** Contents (2-5) – this country features in many thematic and regional maps throughout the *BTEC First Travel Atlas*.

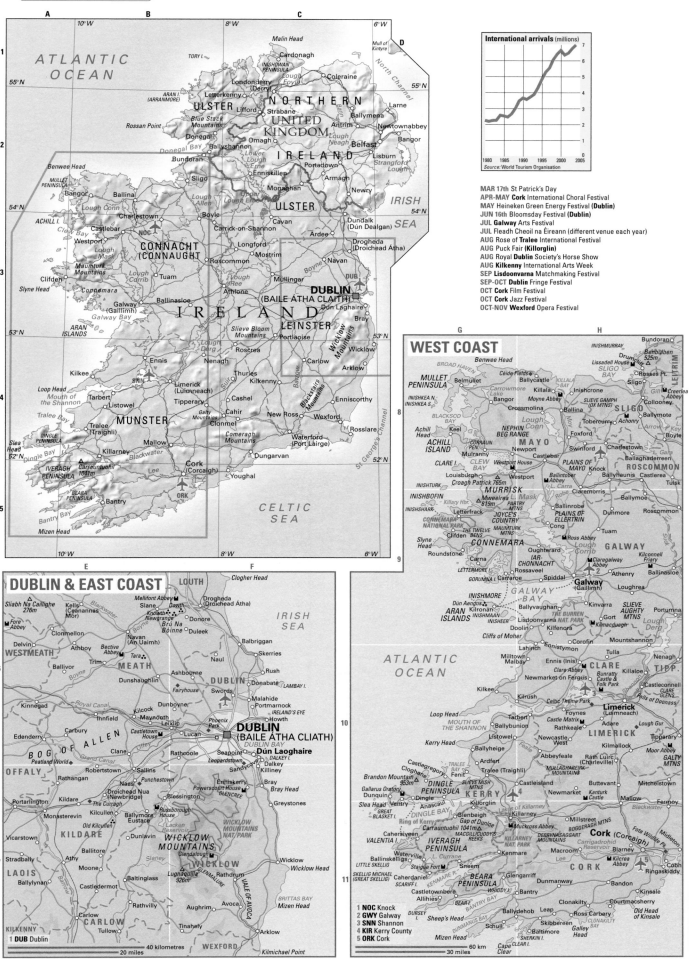

International arrivals (millions)

Source: World Tourism Organisation

MAR 17th **St Patrick's Day**
APR-MAY **Cork** International Choral Festival
MAY Heineken Green Energy Festival (**Dublin**)
JUN 16th Bloomsday Festival (**Dublin**)
JUL **Galway** Arts Festival
JUL Fleadh Cheoil na Éireann (different venue each year)
AUG Rose of **Tralee** International Festival
AUG Puck Fair (**Killorglin**)
AUG Royal **Dublin** Society's Horse Show
AUG **Kilkenny** International Arts Week
SEP **Lisdoonvarna** Matchmaking Festival
SEP-OCT **Dublin** Fringe Festival
OCT **Cork** Film Festival
OCT **Cork** Jazz Festival
OCT-NOV **Wexford** Opera Festival

The listings above refer to a selection of related themes.
For more information, see the Contents (2-5).

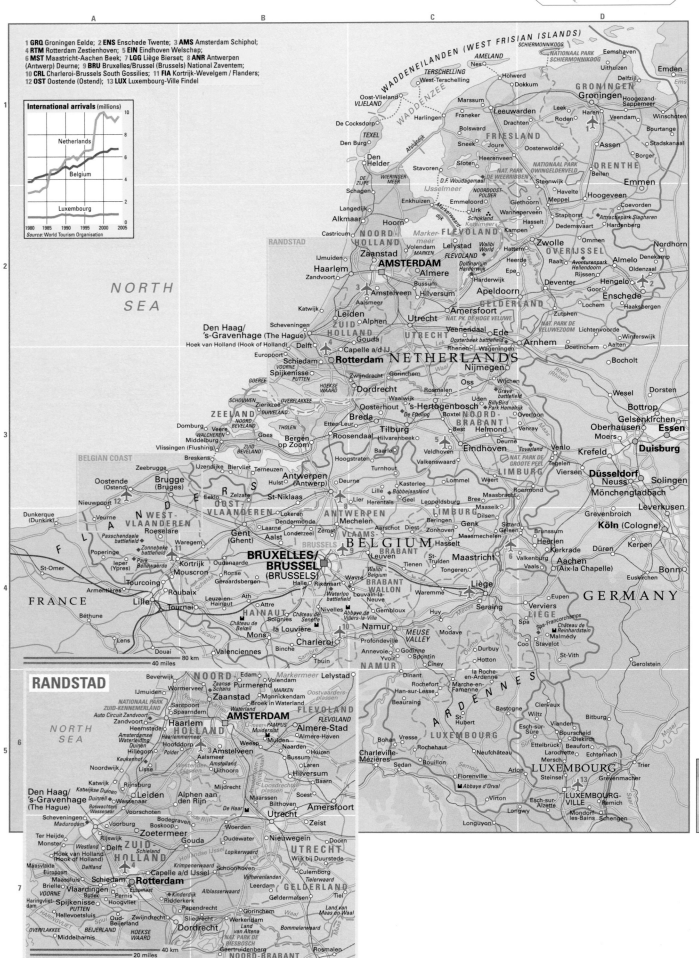

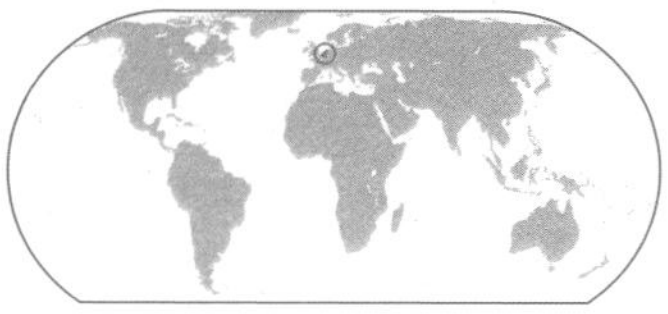

The listings above refer to a selection of related themes. For more information, see the Contents (2-5). See also the Columbus Tourist Attractions & Events of the World.

BELGIAN COAST

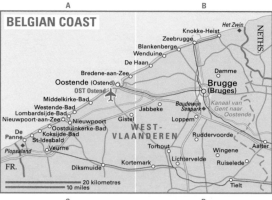

BRUSSELS

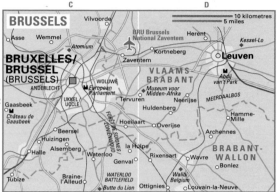

FEB Bruges Festival Musica Antiqua
MAR Bal des Rats Morts: Dead Rats Ball **(Ostend)**
before LENT Carnival **(Binche, Eupen, Malmédy,** and **countrywide)**
LENT Laetare: street parade **(Stavelot)**
APR Festival van Vlaanderen **(Flanders)**
MAY Kattenfestival: cat festival **(Ypres),** with a parade of giant cats every 3 years
MAY KunstenFESTIVALdesArts: international cultural festival **(Brussels)**
MAY Brussels Jazz Marathon
MAY Hanswijkprocessie: Procession of Our Lady **(Mechelin)**
MAY Heilig-Bloedprocessie: Holy Blood Procession **(Bruges)**
TRINITY SUNDAY Ducasse: Chariot of Gold procession; and Combat de Lumeçon: St George killing the dragon **(Mons)**
JUN-OCT Festival de Wallonie **(Wallonia)**
JUN Couleur Café: world music event **(Brussels)**

JUN/JUL Ommegang: medieval-style procession **(Brussels)**
JUL Rock Werchter: rock festival **(Leuven)**
JUL De Gentse Feesten: multicultural festival **(Ghent)**
JUL Kroningsfeesten: Virgin Mary procession **(Tongeren)**; 2009 and every seven years
JUL 21st Belgian National Day
JUL Boetprocessie: penitents' procession **(Veurne)**
AUG Tapis des Fleurs: floral carpet (Grand Place, **Brussels**); even years
AUG Ducasse: parade of giants **(Ath)**
AUG Breugel Festival **(Wingene)**
SEP Belgian Beer Weekend **(Brussels)**
SEP Combat de l'Échasse d'Or: Fight for the Golden Stilt **(Namur)**
OCT Hasseltse Jeneverfeesten **(Hasselt)**
DEC Marché de Noël: Christmas market (Grand Place, **Brussels)**

Brugge (Bruges)
Boudewijn Seapark
Groeningemuseum
Memlingmuseum
Onze Lieve Vrouwekerk
Begijnhof
Belfort
Canals
Markt

Gent (Ghent)
Museum voor Schone Kunsten
Stedelijk Museum voor Actuele Kunst Gent (SMAK)
St-Baafskathedraal
Belfort & Lakenhalle
Gravensteen
Graslei
St-Michielsbrug

Liège
Musée Curtius
Musée de la Vie Wallonne
Cathédrale St-Paul
Église St-Barthélemy
Église St-Jacques
Palais des Princes-Évêques

Legend (theme park map):
Theme park, leisure park
Museum, gallery
Religious building
Park, reserve, zoo, etc.
Historic/notable building
Water-related attraction
Other place of interest
Attractions in cities marked in red are listed around the map

THE WESTERN FRONT
A selection of important sites relating to the First World War in SW Belgium and NE France

Front Line, Feb 1915 – Mar 1918
† Cemetery
Memorial
M Museum
★ Preserved battlefield
War remains and fortifications

Map produced with the help of Battlefield Tours, tel +44 (0)121 430 5348, www.battlefieldtours.co.uk

Antwerpen (Antwerp)
Etnografisch Museum
Koninklijk Museum voor Schone Kunsten
Modemuseum (MOMU)
Museum Mayer van den Bergh
Museum Plantin-Moretus
Rubenshuis
Onze Lieve Vrouwkathedraal
St-Pauluskerk
Dierentuin van Antwerpen
Stadhuis
Grote Markt
Wijk Zurenborg

Mechelen
Speelgoedmuseum
Technopolis
St-Romboutskathedraal
Parc Zoologique de Planckendael
Stadhuis

Bruxelles/Brussel (Brussels)
Bruparck
Autoworld
Centre Belge de la Bande Dessinée
Musées Bellevue
Musée David et Alice van Buuren
Musée Horta
Musée des Instruments de Musique (MIM)
Musée Magritte
Musées Royaux des Beaux-Arts
Musées Royaux d'Art et d'Histoire
Musée des Sciences Naturelles

Abbaye Notre-Dame-de-la-Cambre
Basilique nationale du Sacré-Cœur
Cathédrale des Sts-Michel-et-Gudule
Palais Royale
Stadhuis
Serres royales de Laeken
Atomium
Grand Place
Mannekin Pis

The listings above refer to a selection of related themes.
For more information, see the Contents (2-5).

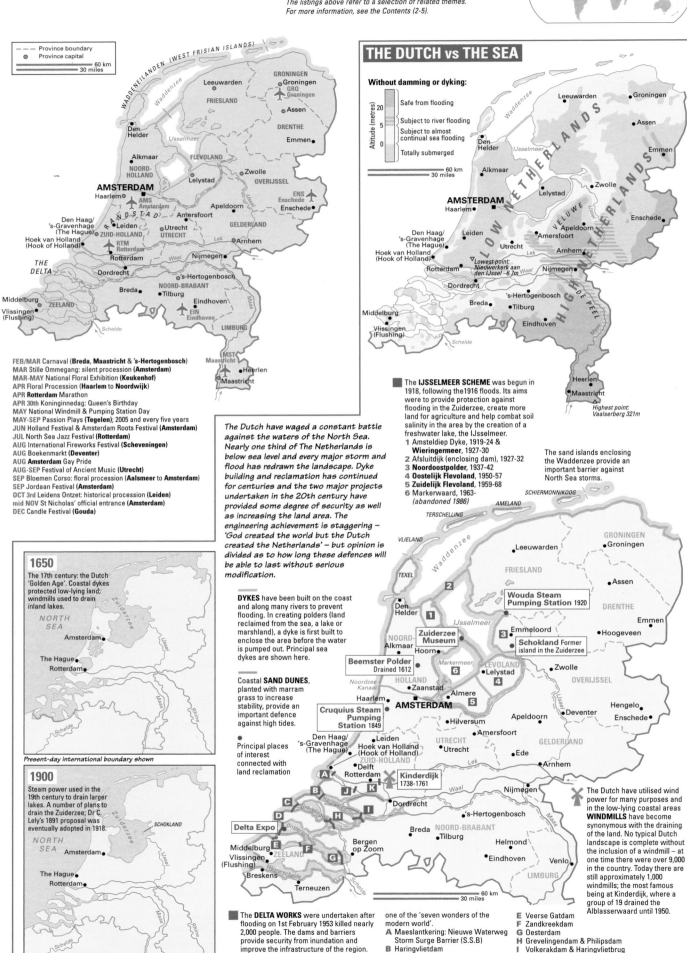

--- Province boundary
● Province capital

60 km
30 miles

WADDENEILANDEN (WEST FRISIAN ISLANDS)

Waddenzee

Leeuwarden
FRIESLAND

GRONINGEN
Groningen
GRQ
Groningen

Den Helder

IJsselmeer

Assen
DRENTHE

Emmen

Alkmaar

FLEVOLAND

NOORD-HOLLAND

Lelystad
Zwolle
OVERIJSSEL

ENS
Enschede

AMSTERDAM
Haarlem
AMS
Amsterdam

Apeldoorn
Enschede

RANDSTAD

Amersfoort

Den Haag/
's-Gravenhage
(The Hague)

Leiden
ZUID-HOLLAND

Utrecht
UTRECHT

GELDERLAND

Hoek van Holland
(Hook of Holland)

RTM
Rotterdam

Arnhem

Rotterdam

Nijmegen

THE DELTA

Dordrecht

Waal

's-Hertogenbosch

Maas

NOORD-BRABANT

Breda

Tilburg

Middelburg

ZEELAND

Eindhoven

EIN
Eindhoven

Vlissingen
(Flushing)

Schelde

LIMBURG

MST
Maastricht

Heerlen

Maastricht

FEB/MAR Carnaval (**Breda, Maastricht** & **'s-Hertogenbosch**)
MAR Stille Ommegang: silent procession (**Amsterdam**)
MAR-MAY National Floral Exhibition (**Keukenhof**)
APR Floral Procession (**Haarlem** to **Noordwijk**)
APR **Rotterdam** Marathon
APR 30th Koninginnedag: Queen's Birthday
MAY National Windmill & Pumping Station Day
MAY-SEP Passion Plays (**Tegelen**); 2005 and every five years
JUN Holland Festival & Amsterdam Roots Festival (**Amsterdam**)
JUL North Sea Jazz Festival (**Rotterdam**)
AUG International Fireworks Festival (**Scheveningen**)
AUG Boekenmarkt (**Deventer**)
AUG **Amsterdam** Gay Pride
AUG-SEP Festival of Ancient Music (**Utrecht**)
SEP Bloemen Corso: floral procession (**Aalsmeer** to **Amsterdam**)
SEP Jordaan Festival (**Amsterdam**)
OCT 3rd Leidens Ontzet: historical procession (**Leiden**)
mid NOV St Nicholas' official entrance (**Amsterdam**)
DEC Candle Festival (**Gouda**)

1650

The 17th century: the Dutch 'Golden Age'. Coastal dykes protected low-lying land; windmills used to drain inland lakes.

NORTH SEA

Zuiderzee

Amsterdam

The Hague
Rotterdam

IJssel

Maas

Schelde

Rhine

Present-day international boundary shown

1900

Steam power used in the 19th century to drain larger lakes. A number of plans to drain the Zuiderzee; Dr C. Lely's 1891 proposal was eventually adopted in 1918.

NORTH SEA

Zuiderzee

SCHOKLAND

Amsterdam

The Hague
Rotterdam

IJssel

Maas

Schelde

Rhine

THE DUTCH vs THE SEA

Without damming or dyking:

Altitude (metres)

20
5
0

Safe from flooding
Subject to river flooding
Subject to almost continual sea flooding
Totally submerged

60 km
30 miles

Waddenzee

Leeuwarden
Groningen

Assen

Den Helder
IJssel

Alkmaar

Lelystad
Zwolle

Emmen

LOW NETHERLANDS

VELUWE
Apeldoorn
Amersfoort

Enschede

AMSTERDAM
Haarlem

HIGH NETHERLANDS

Leiden

Utrecht

Arnhem

Den Haag/
's-Gravenhage
(The Hague)

Hoek van Holland
(Hook of Holland)

∇ *Lowest point:*
Nieuwerkerk aan
den IJssel −6.7m

Lek

Rotterdam

Waal

Nijmegen

Dordrecht

's-Hertogenbosch

DE PEEL

Breda

Tilburg

Middelburg

Eindhoven

Vlissingen
(Flushing)

Schelde

Heerlen

Maastricht

Highest point:
Vaalserberg 321m

The Dutch have waged a constant battle against the waters of the North Sea. Nearly one third of The Netherlands is below sea level and every major storm and flood has redrawn the landscape. Dyke building and reclamation has continued for centuries and the two major projects undertaken in the 20th century have provided some degree of security as well as increasing the land area. The engineering achievement is staggering – 'God created the world but the Dutch created the Netherlands' – but opinion is divided as to how long these defences will be able to last without serious modification.

DYKES have been built on the coast and along many rivers to prevent flooding. In creating polders (land reclaimed from the sea, a lake or marshland), a dyke is first built to enclose the area before the water is pumped out. Principal sea dykes are shown here.

Coastal **SAND DUNES**, planted with marram grass to increase stability, provide an important defence against high tides.

● Principal places of interest connected with land reclamation

■ The **IJSSELMEER SCHEME** was begun in 1918, following the 1916 floods. Its aims were to provide protection against flooding in the Zuiderzee, create more land for agriculture and help combat soil salinity in the area by the creation of a freshwater lake, the IJsselmeer.
1 Amsteldiep Dyke, 1919-24 & **Wieringermeer**, 1927-30
2 **Afsluitdijk (enclosing dam)**, 1927-32
3 **Noordoostpolder**, 1937-42
4 **Oostelijk Flevoland**, 1950-57
5 **Zuidelijk Flevoland**, 1959-68
6 Markerwaard, 1963-(abandoned 1986)

The sand islands enclosing the Waddenzee provide an important defence against North Sea storms.

SCHIERMONNIKOOG
AMELAND
TERSCHELLING
VLIELAND
TEXEL

Waddenzee

GRONINGEN
Leeuwarden
Groningen

FRIESLAND

Assen

2

Wouda Steam Pumping Station 1920

DRENTHE

1

IJsselmeer

3
Emmeloord

Emmen

Hoogeveen

Den Helder

NOORD-
Alkmaar

Hoorn

Zuiderzee Museum

Schokland Former island in the Zuiderzee

Markermeer

6

FLEVOLAND

Zwolle

Beemster Polder Drained 1612

Lelystad

OVERIJSSEL

Noordzee Kanaal

Zaanstad

4

HOLLAND

Almere

5

Hengelo

Haarlem

Deventer

Enschede

Cruquius Steam Pumping Station 1849

AMSTERDAM

Hilversum

Apeldoorn

Den Haag/
's-Gravenhage
(The Hague)

Leiden

UTRECHT

Amersfoort

GELDERLAND

Hoek van Holland
(Hook of Holland)

Delft

Utrecht

Ede

ZUID-HOLLAND

Rotterdam

Kinderdijk 1738-1761

Lek

Arnhem

A

Waal

Nijmegen

B

J

K

Dordrecht

C

Haringvliet

H

I

D

's-Hertogenbosch

Delta Expo

Oosterschelde

NOORD-BRABANT

Breda

Tilburg

Helmond

Middelburg

E

F

Bergen op Zoom

Vlissingen
(Flushing)

ZEELAND

G

Eindhoven

Venlo

Breskens

Terneuzen

Westerschelde

Schelde

LIMBURG

60 km
30 miles

The Dutch have utilised wind power for many purposes and in the low-lying coastal areas **WINDMILLS** have become synonymous with the draining of the land. No typical Dutch landscape is complete without the inclusion of a windmill – at one time there were over 9,000 in the country. Today there are still approximately 1,000 windmills; the most famous being at Kinderdijk, where a group of 19 drained the Alblasserwaard until 1950.

■ The **DELTA WORKS** were undertaken after flooding on 1st February 1953 killed nearly 2,000 people. The dams and barriers provide security from inundation and improve the infrastructure of the region. The Delta Works and Afsluitdijk (IJsselmeer dam) together are considered one of the 'seven wonders of the modern world'.
A Maeslantkering: Nieuwe Waterweg Storm Surge Barrier (S.S.B.)
B Haringvlietdam
C Brouwersdam
D Oosterschelde S.S.B.
E Veerse Gatdam
F Zandkreekdam
G Oesterdam
H Grevelingendam & Philipsdam
I Volkerakdam & Haringvlietbrug
J Hartelkering
K Hollandse IJssel S.S.B.

The listings above refer to a selection of related themes.
For more information, see the Contents (2-5). See also the Columbus
Tourist Attractions and Events of the World.

Legend:
- Theme park, leisure park
- Museum, gallery
- Religious building
- Park, reserve, zoo, etc.
- Historic/notable building
- Water-related attraction
- Other place of interest

Attractions in cities marked in red are listed on the left of the map

Amsterdam
Museum Amstelkring
Amsterdams Historisch Museum
Anne Frankhuis
Hermitage aan de Amstel
Joods Historisch Museum
Madame Tussaud Scenerama
Museum Het Rembrandthuis
Nederlands Scheepvaart Museum
NeMo (New Metropolis)
Rijksmuseum
Stedelijk Museum
Tropenmuseum
Van Gogh Museum
Esnoga Synagogue
Nieuwe Kerk
Westerkerk
Artis
Bloemenmarkt
Begijnhof
Koninklijk Paleis
Amsterdam canals (grachten)

Haarlem
Frans Halsmuseum
Teylers Museum
St Bavokerk
Vleeshal
Grote Markt

Leiden
Museum Boerhaave
Molenmuseum De Valk
Naturalis
Stedelijk Museum De Lakenhal
Rijksmuseum van Oudheden
Rijksmuseum voor Volkenkunde
De Burcht

Den Haag (The Hague)
Madurodam
Museum voor Communicatie
Gemeentemuseum
Mauritshuis
Museum Mesdag; Panorama Mesdag
Museon
Schilderijengalerij Prins Willem V
Binnenhof
Paleis Noordeinde

Delft
Koninklijk Nederlands
Leger- en Wapenmuseum
Prinsenhof
Nieuwe Kerk
Oude Kerk

Rotterdam
Kunsthal
Historisch Museum
Het Schielandshuis
Museum Boymans-Van Beuningen
Museum De Dubbelde Palmboom
Nederlands Architectuurinstituut
Diergaarde Blijdorp
Boat trips to the port
Erasmusbrug
Maritiem Museum
Euromast

Gouda
Stedelijk Museum Het Catharina Gasthuis
Sint Jan
Stadhuis

Utrecht
Centraal Museum
Museum Het Catharijneconvent
Nationaal Museum van Speelklok Tot Pierement
Nederlands Spoorwegmuseum
Domkirk; Domtoren
Pieterskerk
Rietveld Schröderhuis

A   B   C   D   E   F

North Sea

DENMARK

JYLLAND (JUTLAND)   *FYN (FÜNEN)*   *SJÆLLAND (ZEALAND)*

BORNHOLM (Den.)   Rønne

Baltic Sea

Deutsche Bucht

NORDFRIESISCHE INSELN   Westerland   *SYLT*   *FÖHR*

Flensburg   Kappeln   *Kieler Bucht*   *MØN*   *FALSTER*

Husum   Schleswig   Eckernförde   Puttgarden   *FEMRAN*   *Femer Belt*   *LOLLAND*   Rødbyhavn   *Darsser Ort*   *ZINGST*   Kap Arkona   Sassnitz

St Peter-Ording   Rendsburg   Kiel   Plön   *RÜGEN*

HELGOLAND   Heide   Neumünster   Oldenburg in Holstein   *Mecklenburger Bucht*   Stralsund   *Pomeranian Bay*

Helgoländer Bucht   SCHLESWIG-HOLSTEIN   Neustadt in Holstein   Warnemünde   Greifswald

Brunsbüttel   Itzehoe   Bad Döberan   Rostock   Anklam   *USEDOM*   *WOLIN*

FRISIAN ISLANDS   *OSTFRIESISCHE INSELN*   Cuxhaven   Elmshorn   Lübeck   Travemünde   Wismar   *RLG*   *Oderhaff*

WADDENEILANDEN   Norden   Wilhelmshaven   Stade   Norderstedt   Mölln   Schwerin   *Schweriner See*   MECKLENBURG-VORPOMMERN   Neubrandenburg   Pasewalk

Emden   Bremerhaven   Wedel   *HAM*   HAMBURG   Güstrow   Teterow   *Plauer See*

Leeuwarden   Groningen   Leer   Bremervörde   Hamburg   Lauenburg   Ludwigslust   *Müritz*   Neustrelitz   Prenzlau   Szczecin (Stettin)

Oldenburg   Zeven   Winsen   *Elbe*   *Elde*   Wittstock   Gransee   Templin

NETHERLANDS   Papenburg   BREMEN   Rotenburg   Lüneburg   Dannenberg   Perleberg   Schwedt an der Oder   POLAND

Emmen   Cloppenburg   Delmenhorst   Bremen   Verden   Soltau   Wittenberge   Neuruppin   Eberswalde-Finow

Löningen   *BRE*   Bassum   Uelzen   Salzwedel   *Havel*   Oranienburg   Gorzów Wielkopolski

Nordhorn   Meppen   Diepholz   NIEDERSACHSEN (LOWER SAXONY)   *TXL*   BERLIN   Frankfurt an der Oder

Apeldoorn   Lingen   Nienburg   *Aller*   Celle   Gifhorn   Gardelegen   Stendal   Brandenburg   Potsdam   *THF*   BERLIN

Arnhem   Rheine   Osnabrück   Wunstorf   *HAJ*   Hannover (Hanover)   Wolfsburg   *SKF*   Fürstenwalde

Enschede   Stadtlohn   *FMO*   Minden   Rinteln   Peine   Braunschweig   Magdeburg   BRANDENBURG   Eisenhüttenstadt

Nijmegen   Münster   Herford   Hildesheim   Salzgitter   SACHSEN-ANHALT

Bocholt   Coesfeld   Bielefeld   Hameln   Goslar   Halberstadt   Dessau   Lutherstadt Wittenberg   Lübben   *Spreewald*

Recklinghausen   Gütersloh   Detmold   Höxter   *Harz*   Quedlinburg   Lübbenau   Cottbus

Gelsenkirchen   Hamm   Beckum   Paderborn   Warburg   Göttingen   Nordhausen   Hettstedt   Herzberg   *Neisse*

Oberhausen   NORDRHEIN-WESTFALEN   Dortmund   *DTM*   *Lippe*   Arnsberg   Brilon   Kassel   Heiligenstadt   Halle-Neustadt   Halle   *LEJ*   Torgau   Senftenberg

Duisburg   Bochum   Hagen   (NORTH RHINE-WESTPHALIA)   Schmallenberg   Eschwege   Mühlhausen   Wurzen   Hoyerswerda

Essen   *DUS*   Wuppertal   Leipzig   Meissen   Görlitz

Krefeld   Düsseldorf   Remscheid   Homberg   Eisenach   Gotha   Erfurt   Weimar   SACHSEN (SAXONY)   *DRS*   Dresden

Mönchengladbach   Neuss   Solingen   Leverkusen   G E R M A N Y

Maastricht   Köln (Cologne)   Siegen   Marburg   Bad Hersfeld   THÜRINGEN   Arnstadt   Jena   Gera   Altenburg   Freiberg   Liberec

Aachen (Aix-la-Chapelle)   *CGN*   Bonn   Kreuztal   Giessen   *Thüringer Wald*   Rudolstadt   Zwickau   Chemnitz

Euskirchen   HESSEN (HESSE)   Wetzlar   Schlüchtern   Fulda   Suhl   Saalfeld   (THURINGIA)   Plauen   Hof   *Erzgebirge*

Andernach   Koblenz   *Eifel*   *Mosel*   Bad Homburg vor der Höhe   *Rhön*   Meiningen   Sonneburg   *Frankenwald*

RHEINLAND-PFALZ (RHINELAND-PALATINATE)   Wiesbaden   Frankfurt am Main   Bad Kissingen   Coburg   *PRAHA (PRAGUE)*

LUX.   Trier   *Hunsrück*   Mainz   Offenbach am Main   Schweinfurt   Kulmbach   Marktredwitz   *Labe*

LUXEMBOURG-VILLE   Idar-Oberstein   *FRA*   Darmstadt   Bamberg   Bayreuth   Pegnitz   *Vltava*

Worms   Bensheim   Würzburg   Weiden in der Oberpfalz   Plzeň   CZECH REPUBLIC

SAARLAND   Kaiserslautern   Bad Windsheim   Erlangen   Sulzbach-Rosenberg   Amberg   *Bohemian Forest*

Metz   Homburg   Ludwigshafen am Rhein   Mannheim   Rothenburg ob der Tauber   Fürth   *NUE*   Nürnberg (Nuremberg)   Schwandorf   Cham   České Budějovice

Neustadt an der Weinstrasse   Heidelberg   Bad Mergentheim   Ansbach   Schwabach   Regensburg   Deggendorf   Linz

Saarbrücken   Karlsruhe   Heilbronn   Gunzenhausen   *Frankische Alb*   Straubing   *Danube*   *Donau*

FRANCE   Nancy   Pforzheim   Maulbronn   Ludwigsburg   Treuchtlingen   *Isar*   Passau

Leonberg   Aalen   BAYERN (BAVARIA)   Ingolstadt   Landshut   Eggenfelden

Strasbourg   Baden-Baden   Stuttgart   Göppingen   Nördlingen   Donauwörth   Freising   Dorfen   Altötting

Offenburg   BADEN-WÜRTTEMBERG   Tübingen   Reutlingen   *Schwäbische Alb*   Neu-Ulm   Ulm   Augsburg   Dachau   *MUC*

Lahr   Balingen   *Donau (Danube)*   Biberach   Memmingen   München (Munich)   Rosenheim   Traunstein

Freiburg im Breisgau   Tuttlingen   Sigmaringen   *Allgäu*   Marktoberdorf   *Chiemsee*   *Enns*

Mulhouse   Donaueschingen   Singen   *Bodensee Lake Constance*   Bad Waldsee   Kempten   Salzburg

Belfort   *Schwarzwald (Black Forest)*   Konstanz (Constance)   Friedrichshafen   Lindau   Garmisch-Partenkirchen   *Bayerische Alpen*   Berchtesgaden   *Watzmann 2713m*

Basel (Basle)   Zürich   *Mädelegabel 2645m*   *Zugspitze 2963m*   Innsbruck   *Saalach*

SWITZERLAND   Lucerne   *VADUZ*   *LIECH.*   A L P S   AUSTRIA

BERN (BERNE)

6°E   8°E   10°E   12°E   14°E

54°N   52°N   50°N   48°N

Lambert Equal Area Projection   Blue boxes indicate focus map coverage

200 kilometres   100 miles

See also... Europe Airports & High-Speed Rail (50-51); Europe Railways & Ferries (52-53)

The listings above refer to a selection of related themes. For more information, see the Contents (2-5).

JAN-FEB Fasching: Carnival (**Munich**)
FEB Berliner Filmfestspiele: **Berlin** International Film Festival
APR Walpurgisnacht: witches' sabbath festival (**Harz** region)
MAY-SEP Rattenfängerspiele: Ratcatcher's Play (**Hameln**)
MAY-SEP Passionsspiele: Passion Play (**Oberammergau**); 2010 and every ten years
JUN Karneval der Kulturen: Carnival of the Cultures (**Berlin**)
JUN 14th City Foundation Day (**Munich**)
JUN Christopher Street Day (**Berlin**)
JUN Corpus Christi Procession (**Hüfingen; Cologne** & **Munich**)
JUN Kieler Woche: regatta (**Kiel**)
JUL-JUL Fürstenhochzeit: royal marriage (**Landshut**); 2005 and every four years
JUN-AUG Meistertrunk: 'Long Drink' history play (**Rothenburg ob der Tauber**)
JUL Love Parade (**Berlin**)
JUL-AUG Bayreuther Festspiele: Wagner opera festival (**Bayreuth**)
AUG Der Rhein in Flammen: The Rhine in Flames (**Braubach to Koblenz**)
AUG Schlossfest: castle festival (**Heidelberg**)
SEP Dürkheimer Wurstmarkt: sausage & wine festival (**Bad Dürkheim**)
SEP **Berlin** Marathon
SEP-OCT Oktoberfest (**Munich**); Cannstatter Volksfest (**Stuttgart**)
OCT Weinlesefest: wine fair & Queen of Wine (**Neustadt an der Weinstrasse**)
OCT **Frankfurt** Book Fair
NOV Hamburger Dom: festival (**Hamburg**)
NOV-DEC Weihnachtsmarkt: Christmas markets (**Munich, Nuremberg** & countrywide)

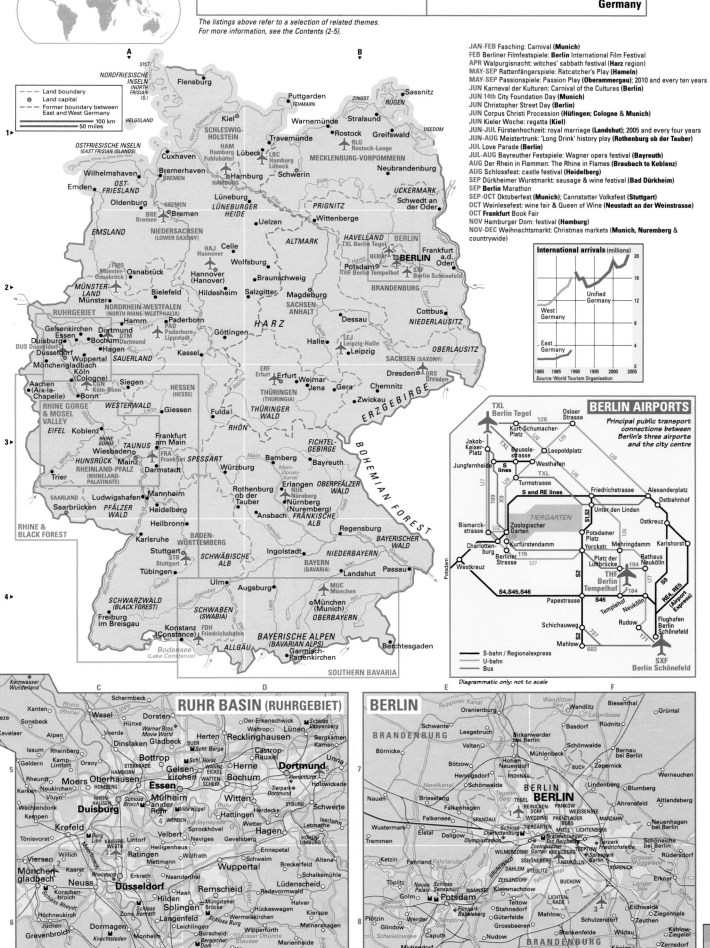

International arrivals (millions)

Source: World Tourism Organisation

BERLIN AIRPORTS

Principal public transport connections between Berlin's three airports and the city centre

Diagrammatic only: not to scale

RUHR BASIN (RUHRGEBIET)

1 NRN Niederrhein; 2 MGL Düsseldorf Mönchengladbach 3 DUS Düsseldorf Rhein-Ruhr; 4 ESS Essen; 5 DTM Dortmund Wickede

BERLIN

1 TXL Berlin Tegel; 2 THF Berlin Tempelhof; 3 SXF Berlin Schönefeld

▶ **See also...** Contents (2-5) – this country features in many thematic and regional maps throughout the *BTEC First Travel Atlas.*

The listings above refer to a selection of related themes. For more information, see the Contents (2-5).

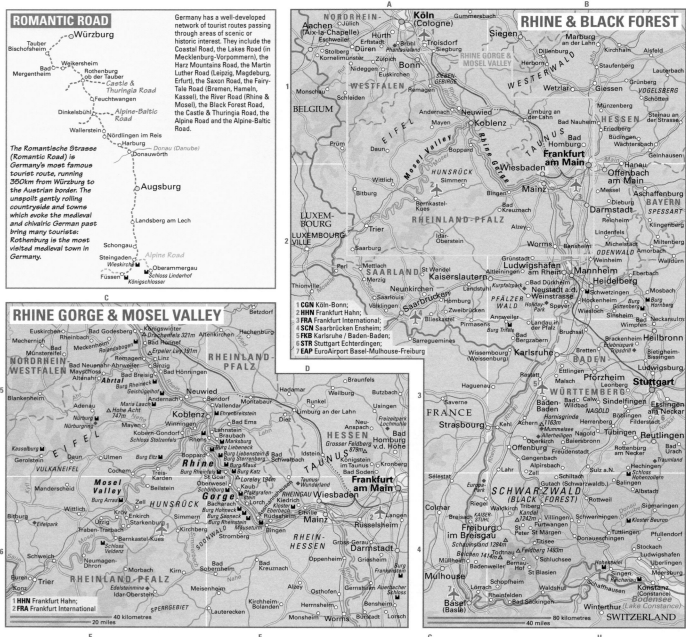

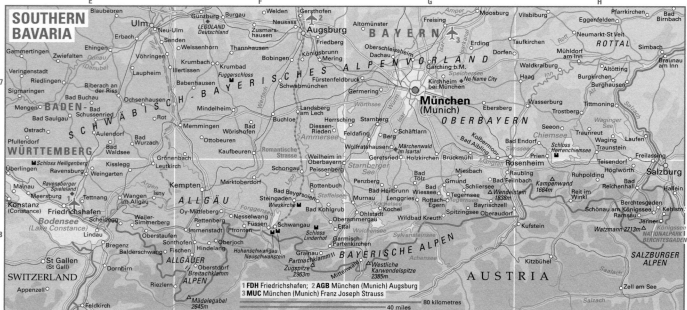

The listings above refer to a selection of related themes. For more information, see the Contents (2-5). See also the Columbus Tourist Attractions and Events of the World.

Legend

- Theme park, leisure park
- Museum, gallery
- Religious building
- Park, reserve, zoo, etc.
- Historic/notable building
- Water-related attraction
- Other place of interest

Attractions in cities marked in red are listed around the edge of the map

100 kilometres
50 miles

Map labels

SYLT · NORDFREISISCHE INSELN · Westerland · Flensburg · Familien-Freizeitpark Tolk-Schau · Husum · Schleswig · St Petri-Dom · Schloss Gottorf · Kiel · Freilichtmuseum · Hindenburgufer · Kieler Förde · Puttgarden · FEHMARN · Nationalpark Vorpommersche Boddenlandschaft · ZINGST · Nationalpark Jasmund · Sassnitz · RÜGEN · Stralsund · Altstadt · USEDOM

Helgoland · Nationalpark Schleswig-Holsteinisches Wattenmeer · Itzehoe · Lübeck · Buddenbrookhaus · Altstadt · Travemünde · Holsteinische Schweiz · Hansapark · Warnemünde · Wismar · Rostock · Greifswald · Schwerin · Schloss · Schweriner See · MECKLENBURG-VORPOMMERN · Neubrandenburg · Town fortifications

Nationalpark Niedersächsisches Wattenmeer · Cuxhaven · Nationalpark Hamburgisches Wattenmeer · Hamburg · HAMBURG · Ludwigslust · Schloss · Elde · Müritz-Nationalpark · Neustrelitz

Norden · Wilhelmshaven · BREMEN · Bremerhaven · Deutsches Schiffahrtsmuseum · Lüneburg · Rathaus · Wittstock · Wittenberge · Schwedt an der Oder · Nationalpark Unteres Odertal

Emden · Oldenburg · Delmenhorst · Bremen · Focke Museum · Neues Museum Weserburg · St Petri-Dom · Marktplatz · Heide-Park · Uelzen · Stendal · Schloss Rheinsberg · Eberswalde-Finow

Lingen · Nordhorn · Diepholz · NIEDERSACHSEN (LOWER SAXONY) · Ferienzentrum Schloss Dankern · Serengeti Safaripark · Celle · Kloster Wienhausen · Altstadt · BRANDENBURG · Grunewald · BERLIN · Frankfurt an der Oder

Recklinghausen · Ikonenmuseum · Bochum · Deutsches Bergbau Museum · Gelsenkirchen · Schloss Horst · Essen · Museum Folkwang · Villa Hügel · Osnabrück · Minden · Schachtschleuse · Dinosaurier Park Münchehagen · Hannover (Hanover) · Kestner Museum · Sprengel Museum · Herrenhäuser Gärten · Wolfsburg · Autostadt · SACHSEN-ANHALT · Magdeburg · Dom · Brandenburg · Potsdam · Filmpark Babelsberg · Nikolaikirche · Schloss Sanssouci · Neues Palais · Spree

Kernwasser Wunderland · Münster · Westfälisches Landesmuseum · Dom · Herford · Bielefeld · Hameln · Hildesheim · Römer- und Pelizaeus Museum · St Michaeliskirche & Dom · Braunschweig · Dom · Kloster unser Lieben Frauen · Halberstadt · Dom St Stephanus · Domschatz · Lutherstadt Wittenberg · Lutherhalle · Wörlitz · Schlosspark · Dessau · Lübben · Lübbenau · Spreewald · Cottbus

Schloss Vischering · Schloss Nordkirchen · Safari & Hollywood-Park · Paderborn · Bad Gandersheim · Alte Lateinschule · Goslar · Altstadt · Einbeck · Marktplatz · Tiedexerstrasse · Nationalpark Hochharz · Quedlinburg · Stiftskirche St Servatius · Schloss · Altstadt · Wernigerode · Rathaus · Breite Strasse · Torgau · Hoyerswerda

Movie Park Germany · Oberhausen · Duisburg · Dortmund · Krefeld · Wuppertal · Hagen · Westfälisches Freilichtmuseum · Arnsberg · NORDRHEIN-WESTFALEN (NORTH RHINE-WESTPHALIA) · Schloss Wilhelmsthal · Göttingen · Altstadt · Nordhausen · Halle · Staatliche Galerie Moritzburg · Merseburg · Dom · Naumburg · Dom · Leipzig · Meissen · Staatliche Porzellanmanufaktur Albrechtsburg · Schloss Moritzburg · Dresden · Görlitz · Nationalpark Sächsische Schweiz

Düsseldorf · Mönchengladbach · Neuss · Remscheid · Solingen · Leverkusen · Köln (Cologne) · Phantasialand · Schloss Augustusburg & Jagdschloss Falkenlust · Siegen · Fort Fun Abenteuerland · Panorama Sauerland · Marburg · Elisabethkirche · Schloss · Oberstadt · Kassel · Gemäldegalerie Alte Meister · Hessisches Landesmuseum · Wilhelmshöhe · Erfurt · Dom · Krämerbrücke · Anger · Weimar · Schlossmuseum · Park an der Ilm · Goethehaus · Schillerhaus · Jena · Gotha · THÜRINGEN (THURINGIA) · Gera · Altenburg · Lindenau-Museum · SACHSEN (SAXONY) · Chemnitz · Annaberg-Buchholz · St Annenkirche · Zwickau

Aachen (Aix-la-Chapelle) · Ludwig Forum · Dom · Monschau · Fachwerkhäuser · Bonn · Giessen · Wetzlar · Fulda · Schloss Wartburg · Suhl · Thüringer Wald · Werra · Plauen · Freizeitpark-Plohn · Hof

Koblenz · Ehrenbreitstein · Marksburg · Burg Eltz · Burg Münzenberg · RHEINLAND-PFALZ (RHINELAND-PALATINATE) · Eifelpark · Burg Rheinfels · Loreley · Rheintal · Moseltal · Bad Homburg vor der Höhe · Burg Kaiserpfalz · Wallfahrtskirche Vierzehnheiligen · Schweinfurt · Plassenburg · Bamberg · Dom · Altes Rathaus · Bayreuth · Markgräfliches Opernhaus

Trier · Dom · Liebfrauenkirche · Amphitheater · Porta Nigra · Hauptmarkt · Mosel · Burg Rheinstein · Rüdesheim · Kloster Eberbach · Mainz · Gutenberg Mus. · Wiesbaden · Frankfurt am Main · Offenbach am Main · Aschaffenburg · Main · Würzburg · Residenz · Schloss Weissenstein · Erlangen · Fürth · Nürnberg (Nuremberg) · Germanisches Nationalmuseum · Sebalduskirche · Luitpoldhain · Cham

Lorsch · Kloster · Darmstadt · Worms · Dom · HESSEN (HESSE) · Lahn · Freizeit-Land · Main-Donau-Kanal · Rothenburg ob der Tauber · Altstadt · Playmobil · Ansbach

Ludwigshafen am Rhein · Mannheim · Städtische Kunsthalle · Heidelberg · Schloss · Universität · Philosophenweg · Schloss Schwetzingen · Schloss Weikersheim · Schwäbisch Hall · Marktplatz · Regensburg · Dom · Nationalpark Bayerischer Wald

Kaiserslautern · SAARLAND · Speyer · Dom · Holiday-Park · Bad Wimpfen · Bad Wimpfen am Berg · Heilbronn · Eichstätt · Bischöflicher Residenzbezirk · Deggendorf

Alte Völklinger Hütte · Saarbrücken · Altstadt · Burg Trifels · Schloss Bruchsal · Maulbronn · Kloster · Erlebnispark Tripsdrill · Ludwigsburg · Märchengarten · Schloss · Romantische Strasse · Ingolstadt · Passau · Glasmuseum · Veste Oberhaus

Rastatt · Karlsruhe · Schloss Favorite · Pforzheim · Baden-Baden · Lichtentaler Allee · Göppingen · Eichstätt · BAYERN (BAVARIA) · Landshut · Eggenfelden · Burghausen · Burg

Offenburg · Tübingen · Schloss · Platanenallee · Reutlingen · Ulm · Münster · LEGOLAND Deutschland · Augsburg · Fuggerei · Konzentrationslager Dachau · Oberschleissheim · Neues Schloss · Stuttgart · BADEN-WÜRTTEMBERG · Schwäbisch Hall · Rhein (Rhin)

Freiburg im Breisgau · Augustinermuseum · Münster · Donaueschingen · Schwarzwald (Black Forest) · Schloss Hohenzollern · Zweifaltenkirche · Memmingen · Ottobeuren · Klosterkirche · Starnberger See · Rosenheim · Schloss Herrenchiemsee · Chiemsee · Berchtesgaden · Kehlstein · Nationalpark Berchtesgaden

Badenweiler · St Blasien · Dom · Reichenau · Mainau · Kurpark · Konstanz (Constance) · Bodensee (Lake Constance) · Lindau · Ravensburger Spieleland · Kempten · Wieskirche · Oberammergau · Schloss Linderhof · Königsschlösser von Hohenschwangau & Neuschwanstein · Garmisch-Partenkirchen · Partnachklamm · Wank · Zugspitze · Breitachklamm · Nebelhorn · Oberstdorf · München (Munich) · Europa-Park · Donau (Danube) · Iller · Lech · Isar · Inn · Ammersee

City attraction lists

Berlin
Ägyptisches Museum · Antiken Museum · Bauhaus Archiv · Dahlem Museums · Deutsches Teknikmuseum · Dokumentationzentrum der Berliner Mauer · Hamburger Bahnhof-Museum für Gegenwart · Haus am Checkpoint Charlie · Jüdisches Museum · Kulturforum · Kunstgewerbemuseum · Museum für Naturkunde · Museumsinsel · Berliner Dom · Botanischer Garten · Zoologischer Garten · Brandenburger Tor · Bundestag (Reichstag) · Philharmonie · Schloss Charlottenburg · Sony Center · AquaDom & Sea Life Centre · Fernsehturm · Gendarmenmarkt · Kurfürstendamm · Nikolaiviertel · Potsdamer Platz · Unter den Linden

Hamburg
Altonaer Museum · Kunsthalle · Museum für Kunst & Gewerbe · Hauptkirche St Michaelis · Planten un Blomen · Tierpark Hagenpark (zoo) · Aussenalster · Hafen (port) · Altstadt · Fernsehturm · Reeperbahn

Düsseldorf
Hetjens Museum · Kunstmuseum · Kunstsammlung Nordrhein-Westfalen · EKŌ-House · Schloss Jägerhof · Altstadt · Königsallee (Kö)

Köln (Cologne)
Agfa Foto-Historama · Ludwig Museum · Museum für Ostasiatische Kunst · Römisch-Germanisches Museum · Schnütgen Museum · Wallraf-Richartz Museum · Dom · St Gereonskirche · Fernsehturm

Bonn
Haus der Geschichte · Kunstmuseum Bonn · Museum Alexander Koenig · Rheinisches Landesmuseum · Münster · Beethovenhaus

Frankfurt am Main
Goethe-Haus · Jüdisches Museum · Museum für Moderne Kunst · Museumsufer · Palmengarten · Zoo · Römerberg

Stuttgart
Linden Museum · Mercedes-Benz Museum · Staatsgalerie · Württembergischer Landesmuseum · Schlossgarten

München (Munich)
Alte & Neue Pinakothek · Antikensammlungen · Bayerisches Nationalmuseum · Deutsches Museum · Glyptothek · Pinakothek der Moderne · Dom · Englischer Garten · Residenz · Schloss Nymphenburg · Marienplatz · Olympiaturm

Dresden
Albertinum · Zwinger Museums · Dom · Frauenkirche · Dresdner Schloss · Japanisches Palais · Semperoper · Schloss Pillnitz · Zwinger · Blaues Wunder

Leipzig
BELANTIS · Grassimuseum · Museum der Bildenden Kunst · Museum in der "Runden Ecke" · Nikolaikirche · Altes Rathaus · Völkerschlachtdenkmal

For more information, see the Contents (2-5).

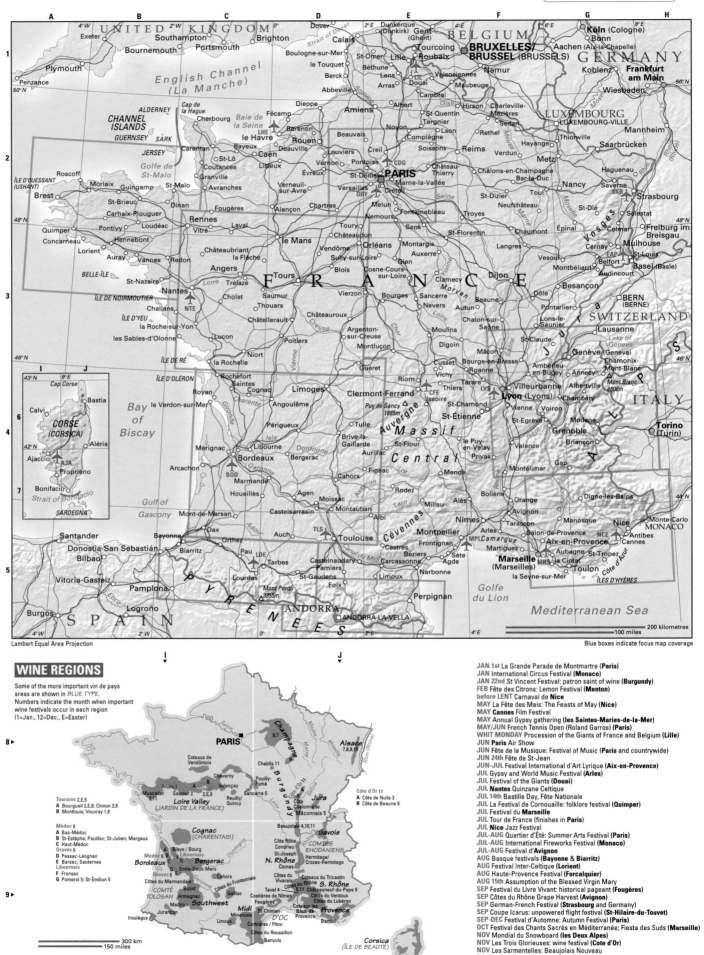

Lambert Equal Area Projection

200 kilometres
100 miles

Blue boxes indicate focus map coverage

WINE REGIONS

Some of the more important vin de pays areas are shown in *BLUE TYPE*. Numbers indicate the month when important wine festivals occur in each region (1=Jan., 12=Dec., E=Easter)

300 km
150 miles

JAN 1st La Grande Parade de Montmartre (**Paris**)
JAN International Circus Festival (**Monaco**)
JAN 22nd St Vincent Festival: patron saint of wine (**Burgundy**)
FEB Fête des Citrons: Lemon Festival (**Menton**)
before LENT Carnaval de **Nice**
MAY La Fête de Mais: The Feasts of May (**Nice**)
MAY **Cannes** Film Festival
MAY Annual Gypsy gathering (**les Saintes-Maries-de-la-Mer**)
MAY/JUN French Tennis Open (Roland Garros) (**Paris**)
WHIT MONDAY Procession of the Giants of France and Belgium (**Lille**)
JUN **Paris** Air Show
JUN Fête de la Musique: Festival of Music (**Paris** and countrywide)
JUN 24th Fête de St-Jean
JUN–JUL Festival International d'Art Lyrique (**Aix-en-Provence**)
JUL Gypsy and World Music Festival (**Arles**)
JUL Festival of the Giants (**Douai**)
JUL **Nantes** Quinzane Celtique
JUL 14th Bastille Day, Fête Nationale
JUL La Festival de Cornouaille: folklore festival (**Quimper**)
JUL Festival du **Marseille**
JUL Tour de France (finishes in **Paris**)
JUL **Nice** Jazz Festival
JUL-AUG Quartier d'Été: Summer Arts Festival (**Paris**)
JUL-AUG International Fireworks Festival (**Monaco**)
JUL-AUG Festival d'**Avignon**
AUG Basque festivals (**Bayonne** & **Biarritz**)
AUG Festival Inter-Celtique (**Lorient**)
AUG Haute-Provence Festival (**Forcalquier**)
AUG 15th Assumption of the Blessed Virgin Mary
SEP Festival du Livre Vivant: historical pageant (**Fougères**)
SEP Côtes du Rhône Grape Harvest (**Avignon**)
SEP German-French Festival (**Strasbourg** and Germany)
SEP Coupe Icarus: unpowered flight festival (**St-Hilaire-du-Touvet**)
SEP-DEC Festival d'Automne: Autumn Festival (**Paris**)
OCT Festival des Chants Sacrés en Méditerranée; Fiesta des Suds (**Marseille**)
NOV Mondial du Snowboard (**les Deux Alpes**)
NOV Les Trois Glorieuses: wine festival (**Cote d'Or**)
NOV Les Sarmentelles: Beaujolais Nouveau
DEC Festival of Lights (**Lyons**)
DEC Marché de Noël: Christmas market (**Strasbourg**)

The listings above refer to a selection of related themes.
For more information, see the Contents (2-5).

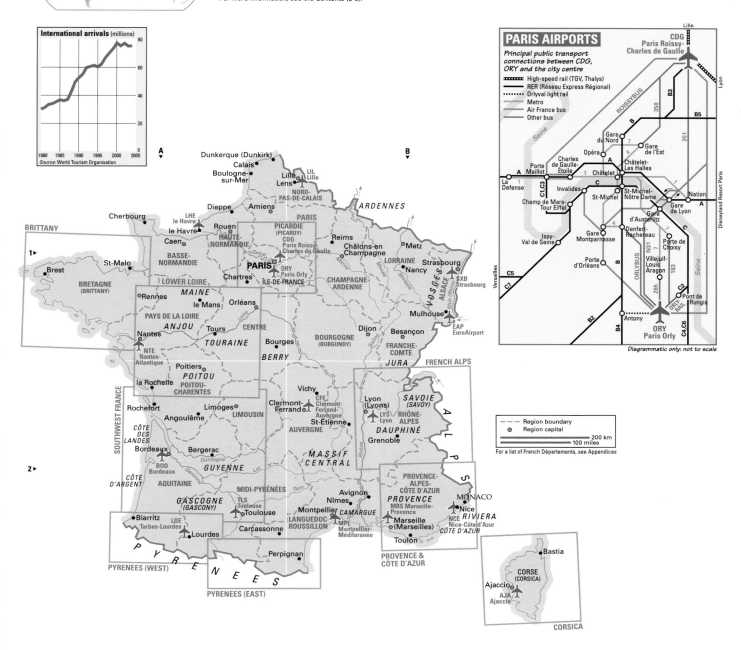

International arrivals (millions)

Source: World Tourism Organisation

PARIS AIRPORTS

Principal public transport connections between CDG, ORY and the city centre

- High-speed rail (TGV, Thalys)
- RER (Réseau Express Régional)
- Orlyval light rail
- Metro
- Air France bus
- Other bus

CDG — Paris Roissy-Charles de Gaulle
ORY — Paris Orly

Diagrammatic only: not to scale

Region boundary
Region capital

200 km
100 miles

For a list of French Départements, see Appendices

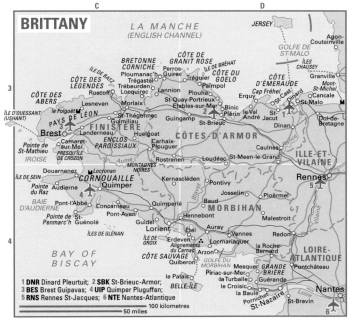

BRITTANY

LA MANCHE (ENGLISH CHANNEL)

BAY OF BISCAY

1 **DNR** Dinard Pleurtuit; 2 **SBK** St-Brieuc-Armor;
3 **BES** Brest Guipavas; 4 **UIP** Quimper Pluguffan;
5 **RNS** Rennes St-Jacques; 6 **NTE** Nantes-Atlantique

100 kilometres
50 miles

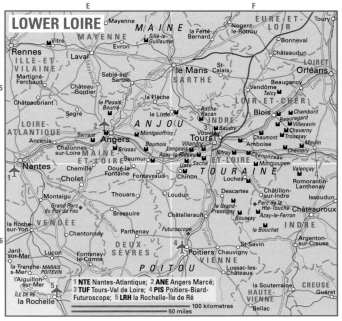

LOWER LOIRE

1 **NTE** Nantes-Atlantique; 2 **ANE** Angers Marcé;
3 **TUF** Tours-Val de Loire; 4 **PIS** Poitiers-Biard-
Futuroscope; 5 **LRH** la Rochelle-Île de Ré

100 kilometres
50 miles

2000 metres
1000 metres
Sea level

▶ See also... Winter Sports (57); The Alps (88-89); The Mediterranean (94)

The listings above refer to a selection of related themes.
For more information, see the Contents (2-5).

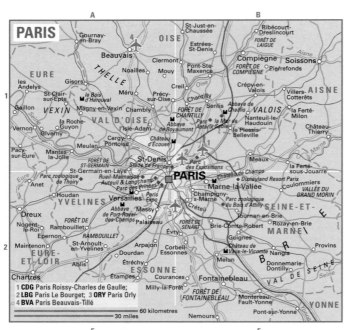

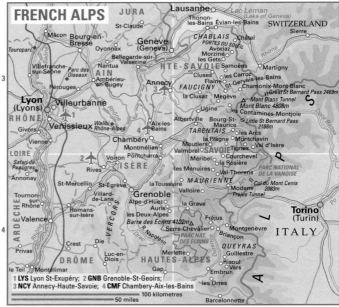

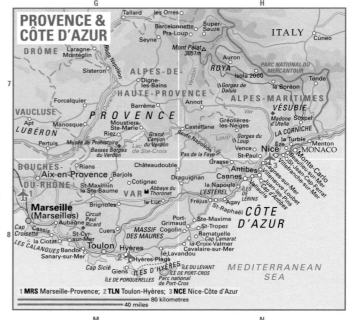

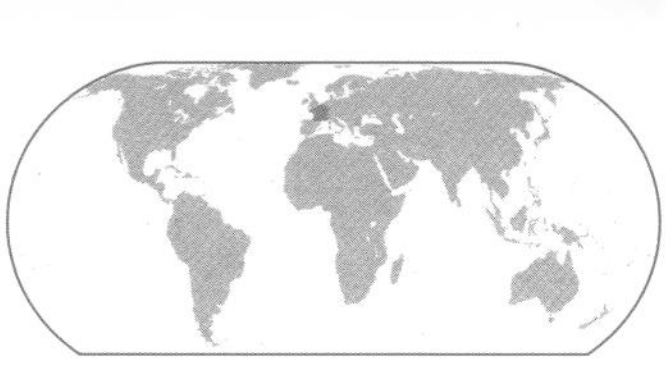

See also... Attractions in UK (64), Belgium (67), Netherlands (69), Germany (73), Iberia (79) and Italy (86)

The listings above refer to a selection of related themes. For more information, see the Contents (2-5). See also the Columbus Tourist Attractions & Events of the World.

Legend:
- Theme park, leisure park
- Museum, gallery
- Religious building
- Park, reserve, zoo, etc.
- Historic/notable building
- Water-related attraction
- Other place of interest

Attractions in cities marked in red are listed above and below the map

200 kilometres / 100 miles

Paris
Le Jardin d'Acclimatation, Centre Georges-Pompidou, Cité des Sciences et de l'Industrie, Institut du Monde Arabe, Louvre, Musée d'Orsay, Musée Marmottan Monet, Musée national du Jeu de Paume, Musée national du Moyen-Âge, Musée national de l'Orangerie, Musée national Picasso, Musée Rodin, Basilique Royale de St-Denis, Cathédrale de Notre-Dame, Église du Dôme, Panthéon, Sacré-Cœur, Ste-Chapelle, Jardin de Luxembourg, La Grande Arche de la Défense, Hôtel des Invalides, Opéra Garnier, Palais de Chaillot, Arc de Triomphe de l'Étoile, Champs-Élysées, Cimetière de Montmartre, Cimetière du Père-Lachaise, Le Marais, Montmartre, Place de la Concorde, Place des Vosges, Tour Eiffel

Orange: Théâtre Antique, Arc de Triomphe

Avignon: Musée Calvet, Musée du Petit Palais, Palais des Papes, Pont St-Bénézet

Nîmes: Jardin de la Fontaine, Les Arènes, Maison Carrée

Lyon (Lyons): Musée d'Art contemporain, Musée des Beaux-Arts, Musée de la Civilisation Gallo-Romaine, Musée Henri-Malartre, Centre d'histoire de la Résistance, Musée historique des Tissus, Basilique du Fourvière, Maison des Canuts, Quartier St-Jean

Nice: Fondation Maeght St-Paul-de-Vence, Musée d'Art moderne et d'Art contemporain, Musée Marc Chagall, Musée Matisse, Promenade des Anglais, Riviera Corniche roads

[Map of France with numerous city and attraction labels including regions: NORD-PAS-DE-CALAIS, PICARDIE, NORMANDIE, BRETAGNE, PAYS DE LA LOIRE, CENTRE, ÎLE-DE-FRANCE, CHAMPAGNE-ARDENNE, LORRAINE, ALSACE, BOURGOGNE, FRANCHE-COMTÉ, POITOU-CHARENTES, LIMOUSIN, AUVERGNE, RHÔNE-ALPES, AQUITAINE, MIDI-PYRÉNÉES, LANGUEDOC-ROUSSILLON, PROVENCE-ALPES-CÔTE D'AZUR, CORSE, and MONACO]

SPAIN

JAN 5th Cabalgata de los Reyes Magos: Three Kings Parade (**Barcelona**)
JAN Festividad de **San Sebastián**: drum parades
before Lent Carnaval (**Cádiz**, **Madrid** and countrywide)
MAR Las Fallas de **València**
EASTER Semana Santa: Holy Week (**Seville** and countrywide)
APR La Feria de **Sevilla**
APR Moros y Cristanos mock battle: St George's Festival (**Alcoy**)
APR 23rd La Diada de Sant Jordi: Day of St George 'Day of Lovers' (**Barcelona**)
MAY Cruces de Mayo and national flamenco competition (**Córdoba**)
MAY Feria del Caballo: horse fair (**Jeréz de la Frontera**)
MAY Festimad Alternative Music Festival (**Madrid**)
MAY-JUN Fiestas de San Isidro (**Madrid**)
WHIT SUNDAY Romería del Rocío: pilgrimage (near **Huelva**)
JUN Sonar: electronic music festival (**Barcelona**)
JUN Haro: Wine war (**La Rioja**)
JUN 23-24th Festes de Sant Joan (**Barcelona** and Catalonia)
JUN 24th Xiquets de Valls: human towers (**Valls**)
JUN-JUL GREC: **Barcelona** Summer Festival
JUN-JUL International Festival of Music and Dance (**Granada**)
JUL Los Sanfermines: running of the bulls (**Pamplona**)
JUL Jazzaldia: Festival de Jazz de **San Sebastián**
JUL Santa Marta de Ribarteme: 'near-death' pilgrimage (**Las Nieves**, **Pontevadra**)
JUL 22nd Cuesta de los Danzadores: stilt dancers (**Anguiano**, La Rioja)
JUL 25th Feast of St James (**Santiago de Compostela**)
AUG Semana Grande, includes Basque Herri Kilorak: traditional sports (**Bilbao**)
AUG Moros y Cristanos mock battle and mystery play (**Elx**)
AUG La Tomatina: Tomato Battle (**Buñol**)
SEP **San Sebastián** International Film Festival
SEP 19th Americas Day (**Oviedo**)
SEP 24th Festa de la Mercè: Our Lady of Mercy Festival (**Barcelona**)
OCT-NOV **Madrid** Autumn Festival
PORTUGAL
before Lent Lisbon Carnival   APR **Lisbon** Half Marathon
MAY 13th Pilgrimage to the Shrine of Our Lady of **Fátima**
MAY Queimade Fitas: academic celebrations (**Coimbra**)
JUN Festas de Lisboa: festivities in honour of three saints (**Lisbon**)
JUL Festa do Colete Encarnado: Festival of the Red Waistcoat (**Vila Franca de Xira**)
AUG Romaria de Nossa Senhora de Agonia: fair & pilgrimage (**Viana do Castelo**)
OCT Fiera de Outabro: October Festival (**Vila Franca de Xira**)
OCT 13th Pilgrimage to the Shrine of Our Lady of **Fátima**
NOV Feira Nacional de Cavalo: National Horse Fair (**Golegã**)
NEW YEAR'S EVE Noite Mágica: Magic Night (**Lisbon**)

The listings above refer to a selection of related themes. For more information, see the Contents (2-5). See also the Columbus Tourist Attractions & Events of the World.

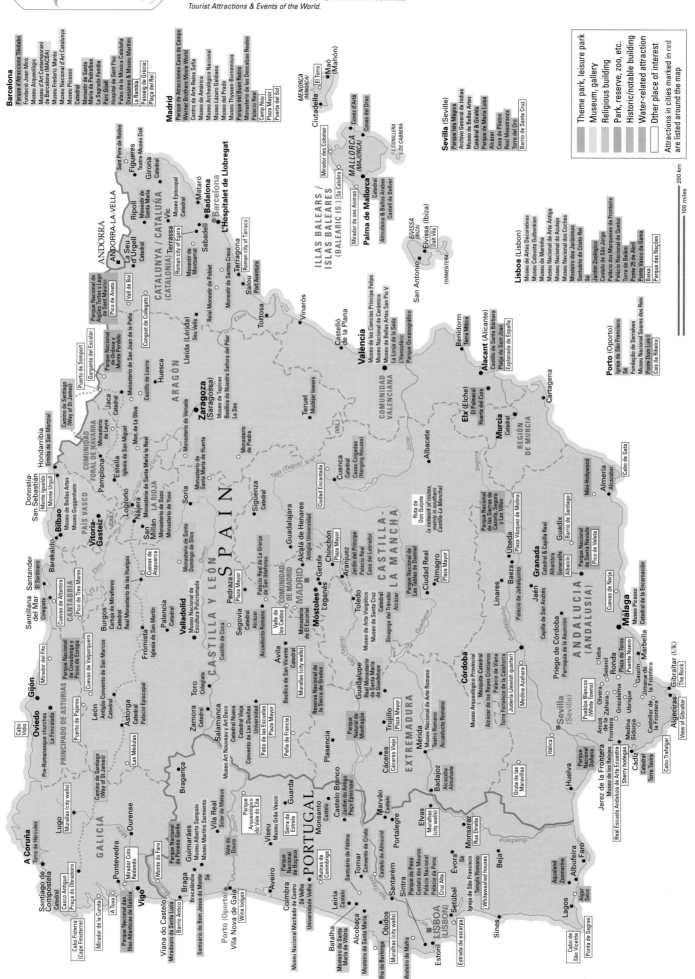

See also... The Mediterranean (94)

The listings above refer to a selection of related themes.
For more information, see the Contents (2-5).

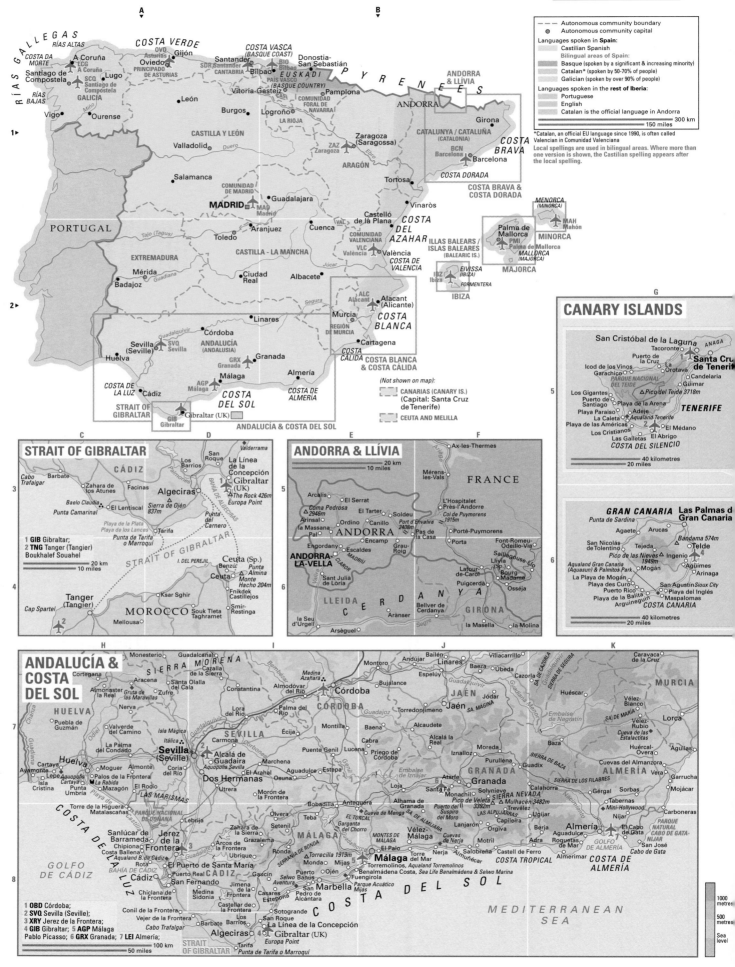

The listings above refer to a selection of related themes.
For more information, see the Contents (2–5).

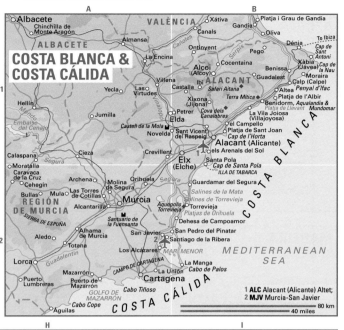

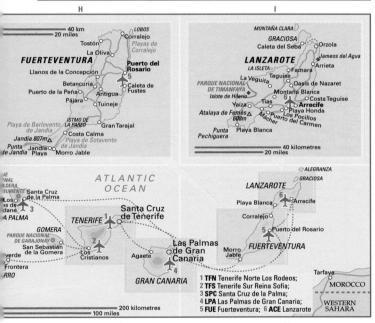

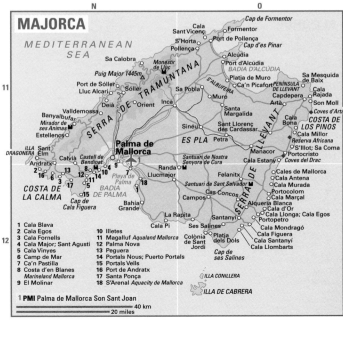

82 **Europe**

Portugal

See also... Contents (2-5) – this country features in many thematic and regional maps throughout the *BTEC First Travel Atlas*.

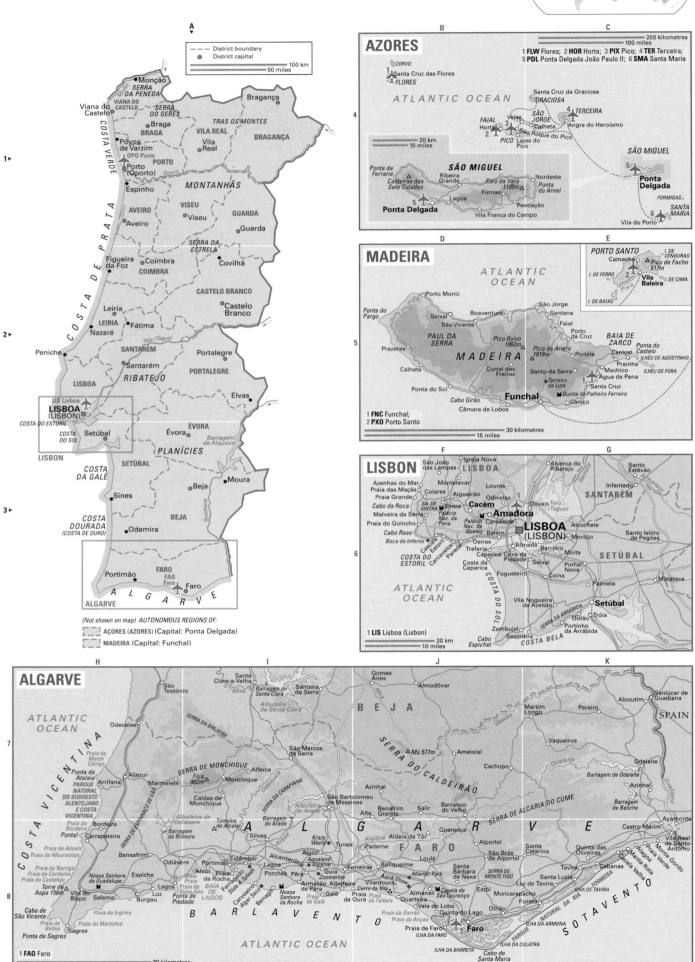

See also... Attractions in UK (64), Belgium (67), Netherlands (69), Germany (73), France (77) and Iberia (79)

The listings above refer to a selection of related themes. For more information, see the Contents (2-5). See also the Columbus Tourist Attractions and Events of the World.

Milano (Milan)
Il Cenacolo (Last Supper)
Civico Museo di Arte Contemporanea
Museo Civico di Archeologico
Museo Nazionale della Scienza e Tecnica Leonardo da Vinci
Museo Poldi-Pezzoli
Pinacoteca Ambrosiana
Pinacoteca di Brera
Duomo
Santa Maria presso San Satiro
Giardini Pubblici
Castello Sforzesco
Galleria Vittorio Emanuele II
Teatro alla Scala
Quadrilatero d'Oro
Stadio Meazza (San Siro)

Torino (Turin)
Galleria Civica d'Arte Moderna e Contemporanea
Galleria Sabauda
Museo dell'Automobile
Museo Egizio
Museo Nazionale del Cinema
Pinacoteca Giovanni e Marella Agnelli
Palazzo Reale
Basilica di Superga
Duomo di San Giovanni
Piazza San Carlo

Verona
Arche Scagliari
Basilica di San Zeno Maggiore
Chiesa di Sant'Anastasia
Arena
Casa di Giulietta
Castelvecchio
Piazza delle Erbe
Piazza dei Signori

Bologna
Museo Civico Archeologico
Museo Civico Medievale e del Rinascimento
Pinacoteca Nazionale
Basilica di San Petronio
Piazzale Maggiore e del Nettuno
Torre Pendenti

Venézia (Venice)
Ca d'Oro
Collezione Peggy Guggenheim
Galleria dell'Accademia
Museo Correr
Museo Diocesano
Museo Vitrario di Murano
Basilica di San Marco
Chiesa di Santa Maria della Salute
Chiesa di Santa Maria Gloriosa dei Frari
Chiesa di San Zaccaria
Palazzo Ducale
Scuola di San Giorgio degli Schiavoni
Scuola di San Rocco
Villa Fóscari (at Malcontenta)
Canal Grande
Museo Storico Navale
Ponte di Rialto
Ponte dei Sospiri (Bridge of Sighs)
Arsenale
Burano
Ghetto
Murano
Piazza San Marco

Firenze (Florence)
Galleria degli Uffizi
Galleria dell'Accademia
Museo Archeologico
Museo dell'Opera del Duomo
Museo di San Marco
Museo di Storia della Scienza
Palazzo e Museo Nazionale del Bargello
Palazzo Medici-Riccardi
Palazzo Pitti
Chiesa di San Lorenzo
Chiesa di Santa Croce
Chiesa di Santa Maria del Carmine
Chiesa di Santa Maria Novella
Chiesa di Santo Spirito
Piazza del Duomo
Giardino di Boboli
Orsanmichele
Palazzo Vecchio
Ponte Vecchio

Pádova (Padua)
Basilica di Sant'Antonio
Capella degli Scrovegni
Chiesa degli Eremitani
Villa Pisani, Strà
Orto Botanico

Ravenna
Basilica di Sant'Apollinare in Classe
Basilica di San Vitale
Mausoleo di Galla Placídia
Domus dei Tappeti di Pietra

Génova (Genoa)
Galleria Nazionale di Palazzo Spinola
Museo di Arte Orientale
Palazzo Bianco
Palazzo Rosso
Cattedrale di San Lorenzo
Casa Mazzini
Acquario di Génova
Centro Storico
Gran Bigo
Lanterna

Roma (Rome) & Vatican City
Luneur
Galleria Borghese
Galleria Doria Pamphili
Museo Capitolino
Museo del Palazzo dei Conservatori
Museo Nazionale di Villa Giulia
Museo Nazionale Romano
Musei Vaticani e Cappella Sistina
Palazzo Barberini
Basilica di San Giovanni in Laterano
Basilica di San Paolo Fuori le Mura
Basilica di San Pietro
Chiesa del Gesù
Chiesa di Santa Maria Maggiore
Chiesa di Santa Maria della Vittoria
Giardini Vaticani
Castel Sant'Angelo
Colosseo
Keats-Shelley Memorial House
Pantheon
Fontana di Trevi
Campidoglio
Catacombe
Fori Imperiali
Foro Romano
Palatino
Piazza Navona
Piazza del Popolo
Piazza di San Pietro
Piazza del Spagna & Spanish Steps
Terme di Caracalla

Nápoli (Naples)
Edenlandia
Museo Archeologico Nazionale
Palazzo e Galleria Nazionale di Capodimonte
Certosa di San Martino
Castel Nuovo
Catacombe di San Gennaro
Porto di Santa Lucia

Palermo
Museo Archeologico Regionale
Museo Etnografico Pitrè
La Martorana
Palazzo dei Normanni

Legend:
Theme park, leisure park
Museum, gallery
Religious building
Park, reserve, zoo, etc.
Historic/notable building
Water-related attraction
Other place of interest
Attractions in cities marked in red are listed around the map

200 km
100 miles

▶ *See also...* Contents (2-5) – these countries feature in many thematic and regional maps throughout the *BTEC First Travel Atlas*.

▶ *See also...* Winter Sports (57); Germany (70-73);
France (74-77); Italy (83-86); Central Europe: South (90)

The listings above refer to a selection of related themes.
For more information, see the Contents (2-5).

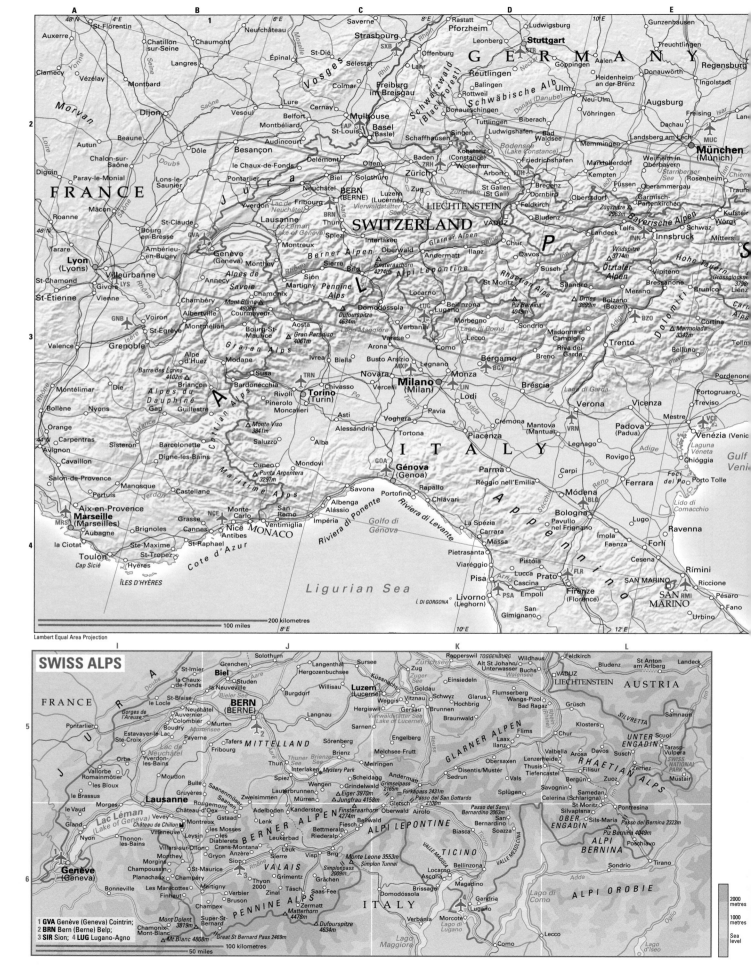

See also... Winter Sports (57); Germany (70-73); France (74-77); Italy (83-86); Central Europe: South (90)

The listings above refer to a selection of related themes.
For more information, see the Contents (2-5).

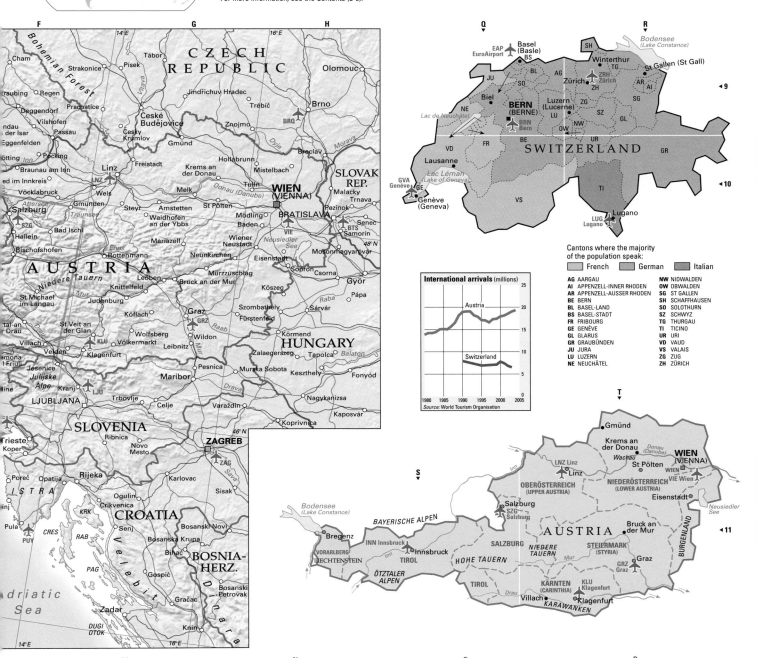

Cantons where the majority of the population speak:

French — German — Italian

AG	AARGAU	NW NIDWALDEN
AI	APPENZELL-INNER RHODEN	OW OBWALDEN
AR	APPENZELL-AUSSER RHODEN	SG ST GALLEN
BE	BERN	SH SCHAFFHAUSEN
BL	BASEL-LAND	SO SOLOTHURN
BS	BASEL-STADT	SZ SCHWYZ
FR	FRIBOURG	TG THURGAU
GE	GENÈVE	TI TICINO
GL	GLARUS	UR URI
GR	GRAUBÜNDEN	VD VAUD
JU	JURA	VS VALAIS
LU	LUZERN	ZG ZUG
NE	NEUCHÂTEL	ZH ZÜRICH

International arrivals (millions)

Austria

Switzerland

1980 1985 1990 1995 2000 2005

Source: World Tourism Organisation

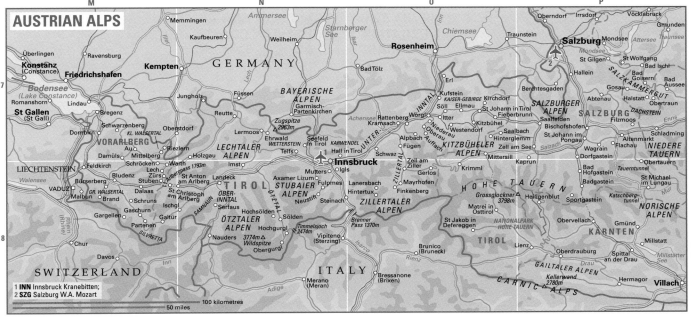

AUSTRIAN ALPS

1 INN Innsbruck Kranebitten;
2 SZG Salzburg W.A. Mozart

100 kilometres
50 miles

2000 metres
1000 metres
Sea level

▶ *See also...* Contents (2–5) – these countries feature in many thematic and regional maps throughout the *BTEC First Travel Atlas.*

Lambert Equal Area Projection

SLOVENIA AND THE CROATIAN COAST

1 **LJU** Ljubljana Brnik; 2 **ZAG** Zagreb Pleso;
3 **PUY** Pula; 4 **ZAD** Zadar; 5 **SPU** Split;
6 **DBV** Dubrovnik; 7 **SJJ** Sarajevo Butmir.

ROMANIAN AND BULGARIAN COAST

1 **OTP** Bucharest Otopeni;
2 **BBU** Bucharest Baneasa;
3 **CND** Constanta Mihail Kogalniceanu;
4 **VAR** Varna; 5 **BOJ** Burgas

1000 metres
500 metres
Sea level

For more information, see the Contents (2-5).

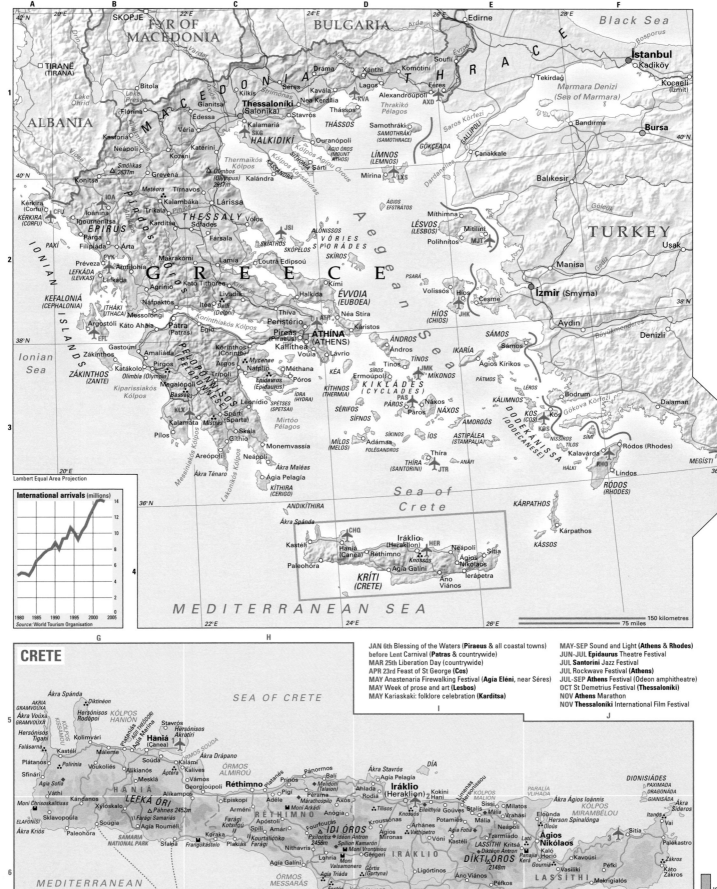

The listings above refer to a selection of related themes.
For more information, see the Contents (2-5).

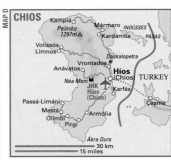

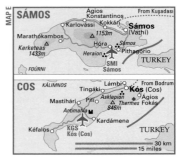

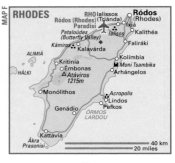

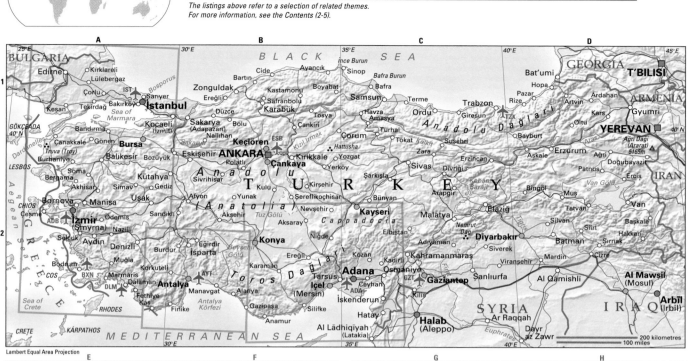

▶ *See also...* The Mediterranean (94)

Europe **93**

Turkey

The listings above refer to a selection of related themes.
For more information, see the Contents (2-5).

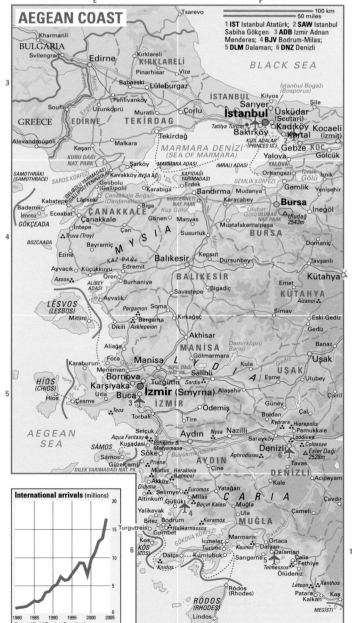

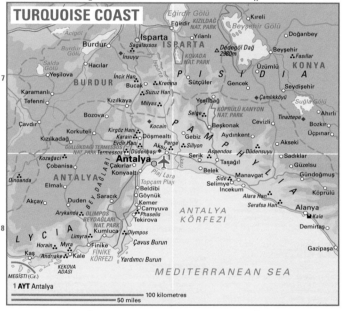

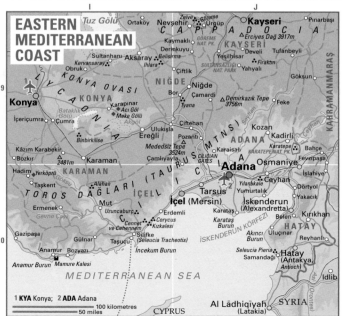

The listings above refer to a selection of related themes.
For more information, see the Contents (2-5).

This map shows the principal diving destinations in the Mediterranean Sea and the main underwater attractions including the existence of soft corals or sea fans, cliffs and caves and shipwrecks (including submerged aircraft). The diver may encounter turtle and dolphin at any time, shark and rays less often, but only those places where regular sightings occur are indicated here. Whales are now exceedingly rare.

Diving facilities for each destination, including availability of scuba diving equipment and related support services, are graded as limited, good or excellent. It must be emphasised that these grades are a general reflection on the overall availability of everything required by the visiting scuba diver and are not an interpretation of the standards found within any one facility or organisation.

Each diving destination provides every level of depth from the very shallow to the extremely deep.

FRANCE: SOUTH COAST
`1 2 3 4 D S T W` ★
Dive sites all along the coast; main facilities in Marseilles, Nice and Toulon
Shipwreck 'Liban' off Cap Croisette and submarine 'Rubis' off Cap Camarat are outstanding; the diving infrastructure on mainland France is rather limited, largely because French divers favour the club system for diving; PADI is, however, opening up new shops and facilities all the time and it is worth requesting a PADI Centre List before departure

FRANCE: CORSICA
`1 2 3 4 D S T W` ★
Dive sites all around the island; main facilities in Ajaccio, Calvi and Sagone
British Vickers Viking, Canadian CL215 and US B17 bomber provide three very unusual aircraft wrecks off the west coast

ITALY: MAINLAND
`1 2 3 4 D S T W` ★★★
Dive sites all around the coast; facilities in all major towns, especially Genoa and Portofino
Diving is very popular in Italy; there are numerous shipwrecks, both ancient and modern, although many lie in very deep waters; cave systems on the Adriatic coast and steep underwater cliffs everywhere; away from the busy industrial ports, water clarity is very good

ITALY: SARDINIA
`1 2 3 4 D S T W` ★✓
Dive sites all around the island; facilities centred on Bosa, Cágliari, Orosei and Palau
Several shipwrecks including 'Romagna'; at least one aircraft plus several cave systems including the Nereo Caves off Cape Caccia

ITALY: WESTERN ISLANDS
(Capráia, Elba, Giannutri, Gíglio, Montecristo)
`1 2 3 4 D S T W` ★
Dive sites all around the islands; some facilities on Elba but generally very limited on the islands – best nearby mainland facilities at Portofino
Spectacular vertical cliffs with outstanding seafans, red coral and large shoals of tuna; a few very exciting shipwrecks, such as the vehicle ferry 'Nasim II' off Giannutri

ITALY: SICILY
`1 2 3 4 D S T W` ★★
Dive sites all around the island; facilities centred on Catánia, Messina and Palermo
Shipwreck 'Amerique' on the northern tip of the island; Sicily attracts large pelagics and large shoals of tuna at certain times of the year

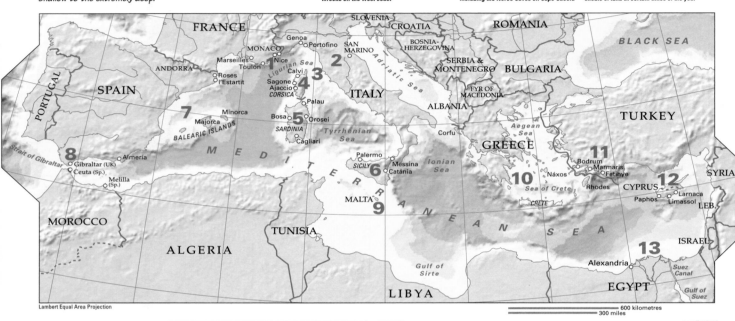

Lambert Equal Area Projection

600 kilometres
300 miles

Sea level
-200 metres
-1000 metres
-2000 metres

SPAIN
`1 2 3 4 D S T W` ★★★✓
Main dive areas Balearic Islands and Costa Brava; best facilities at l'Estartit and Roses (Costa Brava), Almería, Majorca, Minorca
Submarine cave system 'Pont en Gill' holds outstanding examples of submerged stalactites and stalagmites; the Medes Islands (off l'Estartit) are a protected marine reserve where the flora and fauna is quite prolific

GIBRALTAR
`1 2 3 4 D S T W` ★★★
Main dive sites off the western and southern coastlines; facilities in Gibraltar town
Shipwrecks 'Excellent' and 'Rosslyn' just outside Gibraltar Harbour are outstanding; there is also ongoing artificial reef programme which involves the sinking of small vessels near Rosia Bay

MALTA
`1 2 3 4 D S T W` ★★★
Dive sites all around the islands; facilities in all resort towns
Diving is very popular here although a valid medical certificate and proof of diving experience/qualifications are required; outstanding submarine arches, walls, reefs, tunnels and caves plus some new and very exciting shipwrecks deliberately sunk for divers

Dive sites:
1 Soft corals / sea fans
2 Steep underwater cliffs
3 Cave diving
4 Shipwrecks
White square: not present

Regular sightings of:
D Dolphins
S Sharks / rays / pelagics
T Turtles
W Whales
White square: not regularly seen

Facilities for the diver:
★ Limited ★★ Good ★★★ Excellent

GREECE
`1 2 3 4 D S T W` ★★
Main dive areas Corfu, Crete, Náxos and Rhodes; best facilities on Crete
Until recently, Greece frowned upon scuba divers; today, however, new centres are opening all the time and there are several sites of ancient amphora where the diver is allowed to look but not touch; there are also spectacular submarine cave systems

CYPRUS
`1 2 3 4 D S T W` ★★★
Main dive sites off the southern and western coastlines; facilities centred on Larnaca, Limassol and Paphos
12,000 tonne ro-ro ferry 'Zenobia' sank off Larnaca in 1980 and is the largest shipwreck in the Mediterranean; the seas are very warm but Cyprus suffers from severe over-fishing
The Turkish Republic of Northern Cyprus has less opportunities for divers and limited facilities

TURKEY
`1 2 3 4 D S T W` ★★★✓
Dive sites all along the coast; facilities centred on the southwest coast, in particular at Bodrum, Fetihye and Marmaris
Many ancient amphora wrecks available for inspection and new diving areas are being explored all the time before being opened to visitors

EGYPT: NORTH COAST
`1 2 3 4 D S T W` ★
Main dive sites and facilities at Alexandria
Not as popular as Egypt's Red Sea coast and often overlooked; the remains of Cleopatra's Palace were recently found in Alexandria Harbour
For Egypt's Red Sea dive sites, see page 109

Data compiled by Ned Middleton, all rights reserved
email: ned@nedmiddleton.demon.co.uk

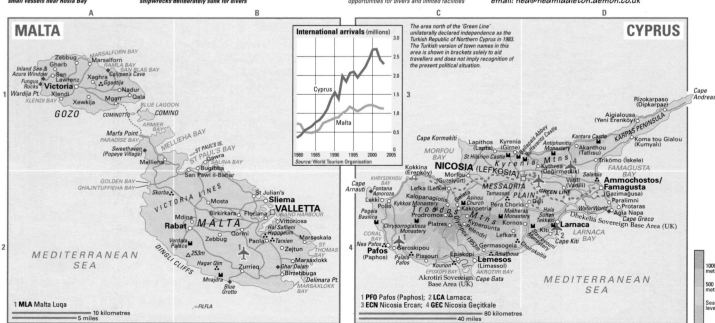

MALTA

CYPRUS

International arrivals (millions)
Cyprus
Malta
1980 1985 1990 1995 2000 2005
Source: World Tourism Organisation

The area north of the 'Green Line' unilaterally declared independence as the Turkish Republic of Northern Cyprus in 1983. The Turkish version of town names in this area is shown in brackets solely to aid travellers and does not imply recognition of the present political situation.

MARSALFORN BAY
Zebbug Marsalforn RAMLA BAY SAN BLAS BAY
Gharb San Calypso's Cave
Inland Sea & Lawrenz Xaghra Ggantija
Azure Window Victoria Xlendi Nadur Qala
Fungus Rocks GOZO Xewkija Mgarr
Wardija Pt. XLENDI BAY BLUE LAGOON
COMINOTTO COMINO
Marfa Point ARMIER BAY
PARADISE BAY MELLIEHA BAY
Sweethaven ST PAUL'S IS.
(Popeye Village) Mellieha ST PAUL'S BAY
Gawra SALINA BAY
Bugibba
San Pawl il-Bahar
GOLDEN BAY Skorba VICTORIA LINES
GHAJNTUFFIEHA BAY Mosta St Julian's
Mdina Birkirkara Sliema
Rabat MALTA Floriana VALLETTA
Mtarfa GRAND HARBOUR
Zebbug Qormi Vittoriosa
Verdala Palace Paola Tarxien
253m Hal Saflieni Hypogeum
Hagar Qim Zurrieq Marsaskala
Mnajdra Ghar Dalam ST THOMAS BAY
MEDITERRANEAN SEA Birzebbuga Marsaxlokk
DINGLI CLIFFS Delimara Pt.
MARSAXLOKK BAY
Blue Grotto
FILFLA

1 **MLA** Malta Luqa
10 kilometres
5 miles

Cape Kormakiti Lapithos (Lapta) Kyrenia (Girne) Bellapais Abbey St Hilarion Castle Buffavento Castle Antiphonitis Monastery Kantara Castle Akanthou (Tatlisu)
MORFOU BAY Kokkina (Erenköy) Morfou (Güzelyurt) NICOSIA (LEFKOSIA) Kythrea (Değirmenlik) Trikomo (Iskele) Koma tou Gialou (Kumyali)
Cape Arnauti KHRYSOKHOU BAY Lefka (Lefke) Fontana Amorosa Asinou Church Pera Chorio Dali Salamis FAMAGUSTA BAY
Lakki Polis Kalopanagiotis Kykkos Monastery Kakopetria Makheras Monastery Kornos Sultan Tekkesi Ammochostos/Famagusta (Gazimagusa) WaterWorld Paralimni
Pegeia Basilica Chrysorrogiatissa Monastery Prodromos Platres Troodos Mts Olympos 1953m Kyperounta Kiti WaterWorld Agia Napa
Nea Paphos Geroskipou Kourion MESSARIA PLAIN GREEN LINE Larnaca Protaras Cape Greco
Pafos (Paphos) Palaia Pafos Pissouri Episkopi Amathous Dhekelia Sovereign Base Area (UK) Cape Kiti
EPISKOPI BAY Kourion Lemesos (Limassol) AKROTIRI BAY Akrotiri Sovereign Base Area (UK) Cape Gata
CORAL BAY Germasogeia Choirokoitia
RIZOKARPASO (Dipkarpaz) Aigialousa (Yeni Erenköy) KARPAS PENINSULA Cape Andreas
Lefkara Kiti

1 **PFO** Pafos (Paphos) 2 **LCA** Larnaca
3 **ECN** Nicosia Ercan 4 **GEC** Nicosia Geçitkale

80 kilometres
40 miles

1000 metres
500 metres
Sea level

MEDITERRANEAN SEA

The listings above refer to a selection of related themes.
For more information, see the Contents (2-5).

Modified Lambert Equal Area Projection

▶ **See also...** Contents (2–5) – these countries feature in many thematic and regional maps throughout the *BTEC First Travel Atlas*.

NORWAY
FEB **Holmenkollen** Ski Festival
MAY-JUN **Bergen** International Festival
MAY-JUN **Bergen** Night Jazz Festival ('Nattjazz')
JUN Midsummer Eve
JUL **Forde** Folk Music Festival
JUL **Molde** International Jazz Festival
JUL Riddu Riddu Festival (**Kåfjord, nr Alta**)
JUL-AUG **Notodden** International Blues Festival
AUG Elvefestivalen (**Vormsund**)
AUG **Oslo** Jazz Festival
AUG International Chamber Music Festival (**Stavanger**)
AUG Norwegian International Film Festival (**Haugesund**)

DENMARK
MAY 21st **Aalborg** Carnival
JUN **Skagen** Festival
JUN Midsummer Eve
JUN-JUL Viking Festival (**Frederikssund**)
JUN-JUL **Roskilde** Festival
JUL **Copenhagen** Jazz Festival
JUL 4th US Independence Festival (**Rebild**)
AUG Fire Festival Regatta (**Silkeborg**)
AUG Denmark Tattoo (**Varde**, every 3 years)
AUG **Copenhagen** International Ballet Festival
AUG Baltic Sail (**Helsingør**)
AUG **Esbjerg** International Chamber Music Festival
AUG European Medieval Festival (**Horsens**)
AUG-SEP **Århus** Festival

SWEDEN
JAN-FEB **Kiruna** Snow Festival
APR 30th Walpurgis Night (countrywide)
MAY **Drottningholm** Court Theatre
JUN 6th Swedish National Day (**Stockholm** & countrywide)
JUN Midsummer Eve
JUN-JUL Musik van Siljan (**Lake Siljan**)
JUN-JUL **Östhammar** Music Week
JUL **Falun** Folkmusik Festival ('Ethno')
JUL Trästock Festival ('Woodstock') (**Skellefteå**)
AUG **Stockholm** Water Festival
AUG Göteborgskalaseti: **Gothenburg** Party
AUG Medieval Week (**Gotland**)
SEP **Stockholm** Beer & Whisky Festival
NOV **Stockholm** International Film Festival
DEC 10th Nobel Prize ceremony (**Stockholm**)
Peace Prize awarded in Oslo
DEC 13th St Lucia Day (countrywide)

FINLAND
MAR Tar Skiing Race (**Oulu**)
JUN Midsummer Eve
JUN Midnight Sun Film Festival (**Sodankylä**)
JUN-JUL **Kuopio** Dance & Music Festival
JUL **Savonlinna** Opera Festival
JUL **Pori** Jazz Festival
JUL Tammerfest (**Tampere**)
JUL **Kotka** Maritime Festival
AUG-SEP **Helsinki** Festival
DEC 6th Finland Independence Day

▶ *See also...* Contents (2–5) – these countries feature in many thematic and regional maps throughout the *BTEC First Travel Atlas*.

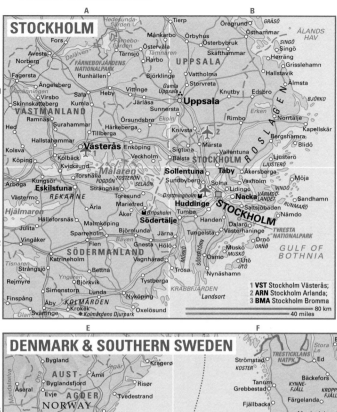

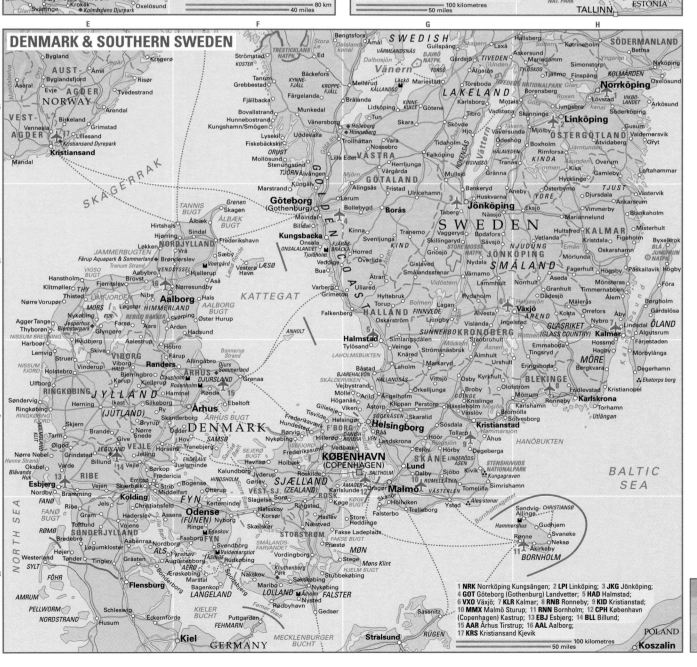

▶ *See also...* Contents (2-5) – these countries feature in many thematic and regional maps throughout the *BTEC First Travel Atlas*.

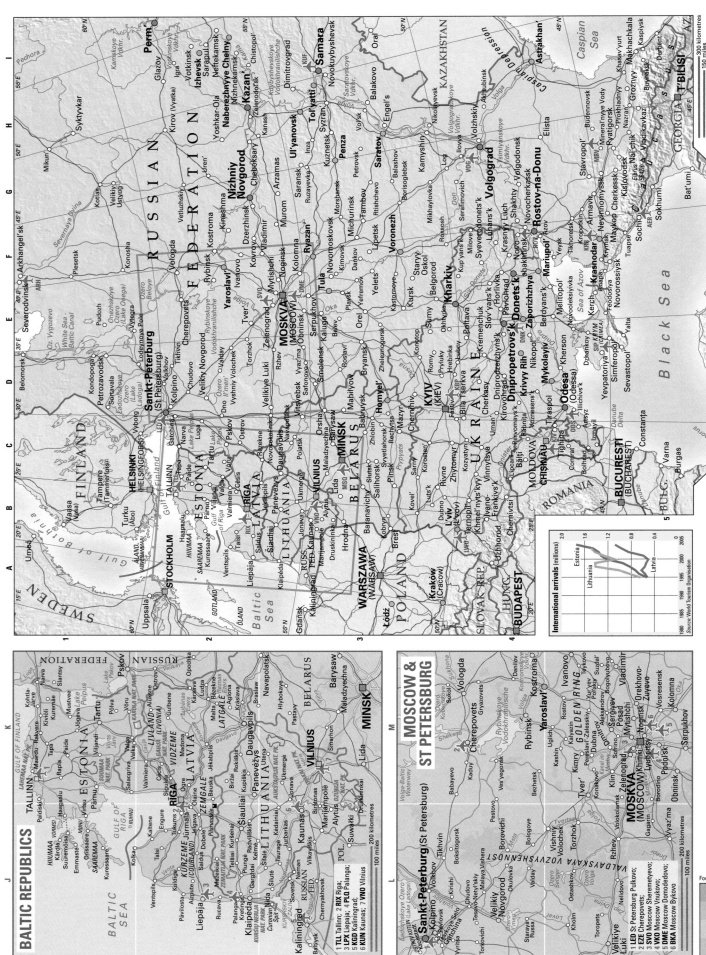

BALTIC REPUBLICS

1 TLL Tallinn; 2 RIX Riga;
3 LPX Liepaja; 4 PLQ Palanga;
5 KGD Kaliningrad;
6 KUN Kaunas; 7 VNO Vilnius

MOSCOW & ST PETERSBURG

1 LED St Petersburg Pulkovo;
2 EZE Cherepovets;
3 SVO Moscow Sheremetyevo;
4 VKO Moscow Vnukovo;
5 DME Moscow Domodedovo;
6 BKA Moscow Bykovo

International arrivals (millions)

Source: World Tourism Organisation

Focus map

500 metres
200 metres
Sea level

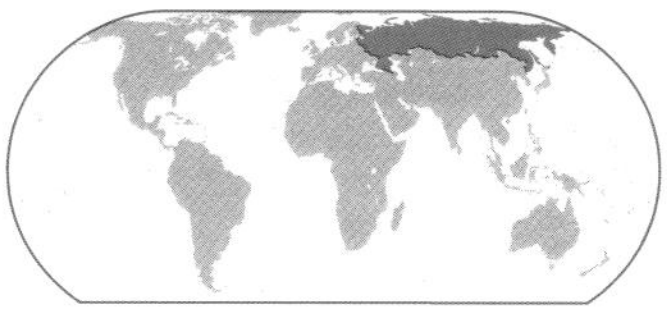

The listings above refer to a selection of related themes.
For more information, see the Contents (2-5).

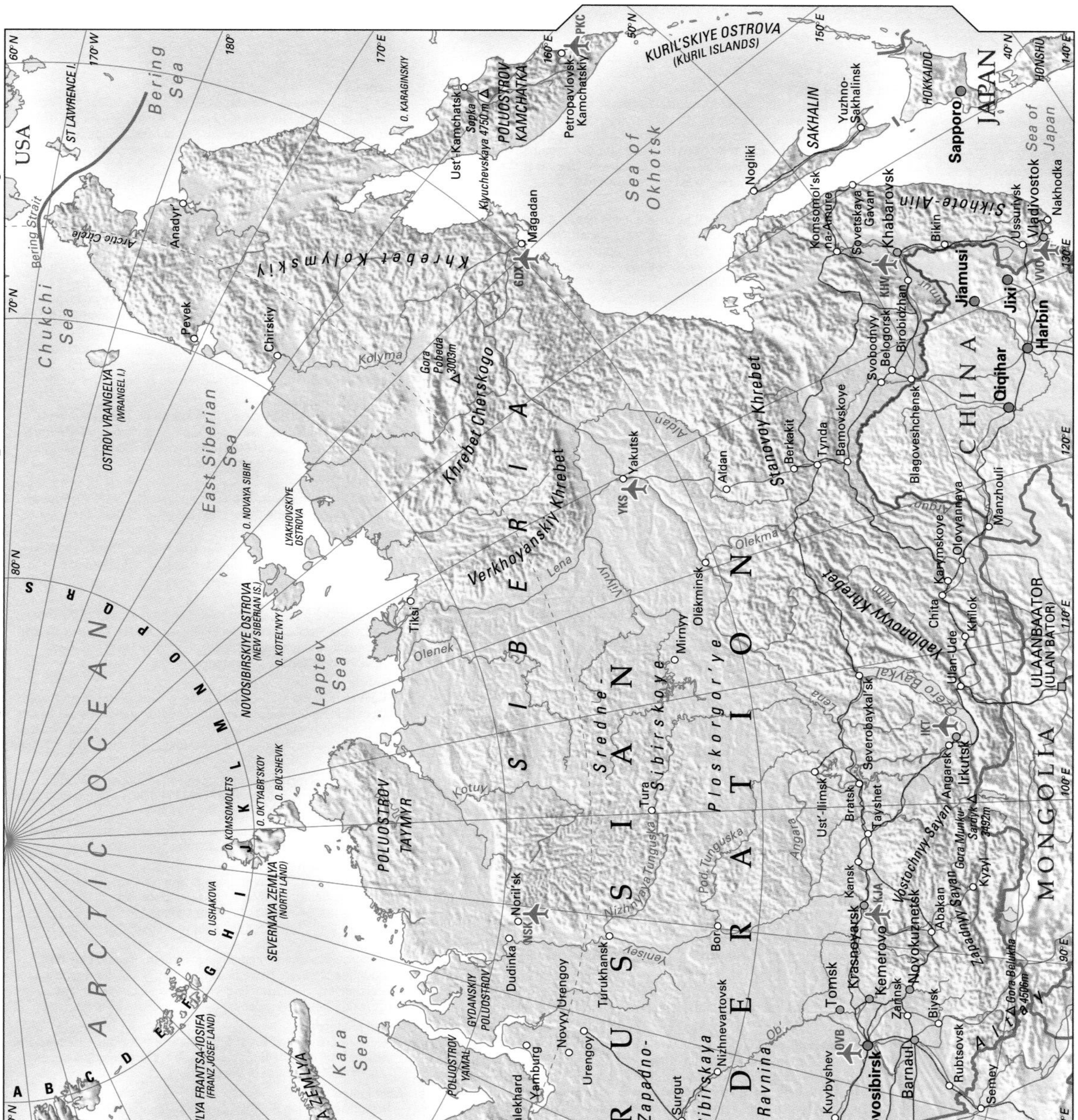

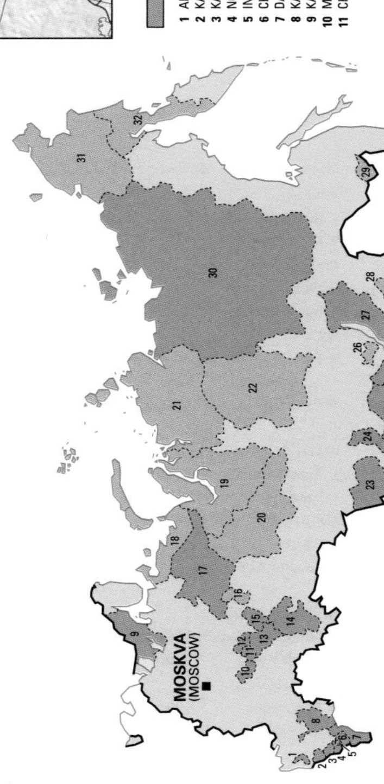

TRANS-SIBERIAN RAILWAY

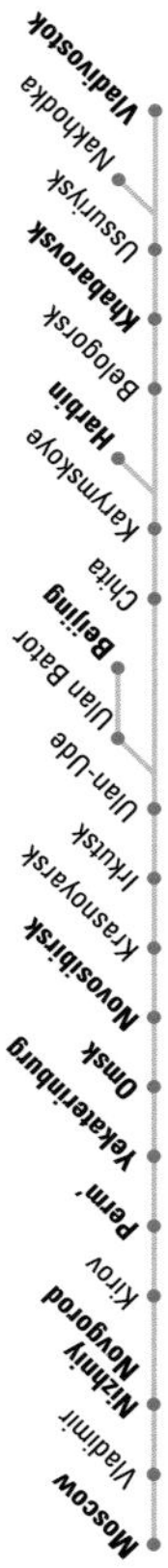

	Moscow	Vladimir	Nizhniy Novgorod	Kirov	Perm'	Yekaterinburg	Omsk	Novosibirsk	Krasnoyarsk	Irkutsk	Ulan-Ude	Chita	Karymskoye	Belogorsk	Khabarovsk	Ussuriysk	Nakhodka	Vladivostok
Km	210	461	917	1,397	1,778	2,676	3,303	4,065	5,152	5,608	6,165	6,261	7,613	7,834	8,492	9,146	9,402	9,258
Miles	130	286	570	868	1,105	1,663	2,052	2,526	3,201	3,485	3,894	4,730	4,736	4,868	5,277	5,683	5,842	5,753

Distances from Moscow ▲

Lambert Equal Area Projection

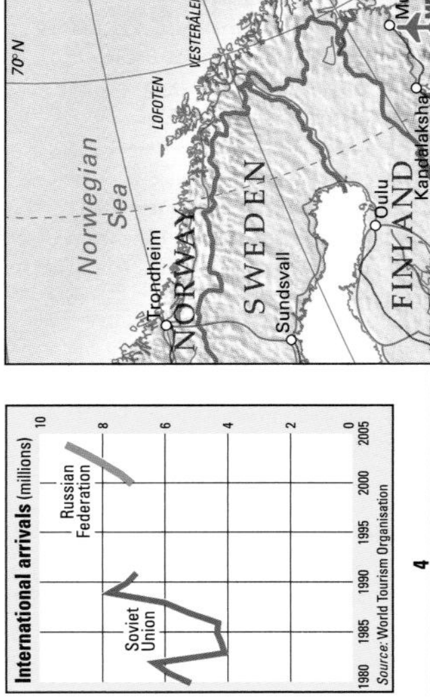

1000 kilometres
500 miles

Legend

REPUBLIC		Autonomous Area or Region	
1 ADYGEYA		12 MARI-EL	
2 KARACHAY-CHERKESSIA		13 TATARSTAN	
3 KABARDINO-BALKARIA		14 BASHKORTOSTAN	
4 NORTH OSSETIA (ALANIA)		15 UDMURTIA	
5 INGUSHETIA		16 Komi-Permyak	
6 CHECHNYA		17 KOMI	
7 DAGESTAN		18 Nenets	
8 KALMYKIA		19 Yamalo-Nenets	
9 KARELIA		20 Khanty-Mansi	
10 MORDOVIA		21 Taymyr	
11 CHUVASHIA		22 Evenki	
		23 ALTAY	
		24 KHAKASSIA	
		25 TUVA	
		26 Ust'-Ordyn-Buryat	
		27 BURYATIA	
		28 Agin-Buryat	
		29 Jewish Autonomous Region	
		30 SAKHA (YAKUTIA)	
		31 Chukot	
		32 Koryak	

International arrivals (millions)

Russian Federation

Soviet Union

1980 1985 1990 1995 2000 2005

Source: World Tourism Organisation

▶ *See also...* World Physical (26-27)

The listings above refer to a selection of related themes. For more information, see the Contents (2-5).

1: Geographical Definitions

The following list covers a number of the main geographical terms which are used to describe areas of the world. In many cases there is no officially adopted definition. Different industries, cultures and international bodies will use their own definitions which are, if consistently applied, as valid of those used by any other. The definitions of the continents, for example, are often not those which have been used in this atlas. Some of these ambiguities are referred to here.

Arabian Peninsula
Geographical region comprising: Bahrain, Kuwait, Oman, Qatar, Saudi Arabia, United Arab Emirates, Yemen.

Australasia
Geographical region comprising: Australia, New Caledonia, New Zealand, Solomon Islands, Vanuatu and the island of New Guinea including all of Papua New Guinea. Often described as equivalent to all of Oceania between the Equator and 47°S. The term is not commonly used in Australia and New Zealand because of confusion with Australia itself.

Bahama Islands
Group of islands in the Atlantic Ocean comprising the Commonwealth of The Bahamas and the Turks and Caicos Islands.

Balkans, The
The Balkan Peninsula, which is bordered by the Adriatic and Ionian Seas to the west, the Aegean and Black Seas to the east and the Mediterranean Sea to the south. The countries occupying this peninsula are described as Balkan states: Albania, Bosnia-Herzegovina, Bulgaria, Croatia, Greece, Former Yugoslav Republic of Macedonia, Romania, Slovenia, Serbia, Montenegro and the European part of Turkey.

Borneo
Island in the Malay Archipelago (qv) divided between Brunei, Indonesia (the provinces of Central, East, South and West Kalimantan) and Malaysia (the states of Sabah and Sarawak).

British Isles
Geographical region comprising: United Kingdom (qv), Republic of Ireland, Isle of Man, Channel Islands.

Caribbean
General tourist destination term used to describe the West Indies (qv) and sometimes the countries with coastlines on the Caribbean Sea (such as Venezuela and Eastern Mexico).

Caroline Islands
Archipelago in the west Pacific Ocean. Islands comprise the Federated States of Micronesia and Palau.

Celebes
Island in the Malay Archipelago (qv), Sulawesi in Indonesian.

Central America
Geographical region comprising: Belize, Costa Rica, El Salvador, Guatemala, Honduras, Nicaragua, Panama. Sometimes considered part of the North American (qv) continent.

Ceylon
Island off the southeast coast of India, officially Sri Lanka.

Channel Islands
Group of islands comprising Jersey, Guernsey, Alderney, Sark and Herm, situated off the northwest coast of France. They are possessions of the British Crown and not officially part of the United Kingdom (qv).

East Indies
General geographical term sometimes applied loosely to India, Indochina and the Malay Archipelago (qv). Often used as alternative to the Malay Archipelago or the Republic of Indonesia itself. The term is now rarely used.

Europe
Continent. Northern boundary formed by Arctic Ocean. Eastern boundary formed by Ural Mountains, Ural River and Caspian Sea. Southern boundary formed by Caucasus Mountains, Black Sea, Bosporus, Aegean Sea and Mediterranean Sea. Western boundary formed by Atlantic Ocean. Includes Iceland, Svalbard and area of Turkey west of the Bosporus.

Far East
General geographical term describing east and South-East Asia: Brunei, Cambodia, China, Indonesia, Japan, Democratic People's Republic of Korea (North Korea), Republic of Korea (South Korea), Laos, Malaysia, Myanmar (Burma), the Philippines, Singapore, Taiwan, Thailand, Vietnam. Sometimes extended to include Mongolia and eastern Siberian region of the Russian Federation.

Formosa
Island off the southeast coast of the People's Republic of China, known variously as Taiwan, the Republic of China, Taiwan (RoC) or China (Taiwan) .

Great Britain
Geographical region comprising: England, Scotland, Wales.

Greater Antilles
Group of Caribbean islands comprising: Cayman Islands, Cuba, Hispaniola, Jamaica, Puerto Rico.

Hispaniola
Island in the Greater Antilles (qv) divided between the Dominican Republic and Haiti.

Iberia
Peninsula in southwest Europe occupied by Spain, Portugal, Andorra and Gibraltar.

Indochina
Geographical region comprising: Cambodia, Laos, Peninsular Malaysia, Myanmar, Singapore, Thailand, Vietnam.

Isle of Man
An island in the Irish Sea between Great Britain (qv) and Ireland. It is a possession of the British Crown and not officially part of the United Kingdom (qv).

Latin America
Defined either as: the Spanish- and Portuguese-speaking countries of the Americas (sometimes also including French-speaking Haiti); or all of the Americas south of the United States. This latter, more general, definition is the one used in this atlas.

Lesser Antilles
Group of Caribbean islands comprising: Leeward Islands (qv), Windward Islands (qv), Aruba, Barbados, Bonaire, Curaçao, Trinidad and Tobago. Also includes the chain of small Venezuelan islands east of Bonaire.

Leeward Islands
Group of Caribbean islands comprising: Anguilla, Antigua and Barbuda, Dominica, Guadeloupe, Montserrat, Saba, St Eustatius, St Kitts and Nevis, St Maarten/St Martin, Virgin Islands.

Low Countries
Geographical region comprising: Belgium, Luxembourg, The Netherlands.

Maghreb
Arabic name for northwest Africa and, in the Moorish period, Spain. Algeria, Morocco and Tunisia are described as Maghreb countries.

Malay Archipelago
The largest island group in the world, off the southeast coast of Asia and between the Indian and Pacific Oceans. Major islands include Borneo (qv), Sulawesi (Celebes, qv), Jawa (Java), New Guinea and Sumatera (Sumatra). Countries within this archipelago: Brunei, Indonesia, East Malaysia, Papua New Guinea, the Philippines.

Mediterranean
General tourist destination term used to describe the islands of the Mediterranean Sea and the countries bordering it.

Melanesia
Collective name for the islands in the southwest Pacific Ocean, south of the Equator and northeast of Australia. Includes: Fiji Islands, Nauru, New Caledonia, Papua New Guinea (excluding New Guinea mainland), Solomon Islands, Vanuatu.

Micronesia
Collective name for the islands in the west Pacific Ocean, north of the Equator and east of the Philippines. Includes: Guam, Kiribati (west), Marshall Islands, Federated States of Micronesia, Northern Mariana Islands, Palau.

Middle East
General geographical term describing a loosely defined area comprising: countries of the Arabian Peninsula (qv), Egypt, Iran, Iraq, Israel, Jordan, Lebanon, Syria. Sometimes extended to include Algeria, Cyprus, Libya, Morocco, Sudan, Tunisia and Turkey

Near East
Rarely used general geographical term describing an area of SW Asia: the Arabian Peninsula, Cyprus, Israel, Jordan, Lebanon, Syria, Turkey. Often extended to Egypt and Sudan.

Netherlands Antilles
Islands of the West Indies administered by The Netherlands, comprising: Bonaire, Curaçao, Saba, St Eustatius, St Maarten. Aruba, formerly part of the Netherlands Antilles, is a separate part of the Kingdom of the Netherlands.

New Guinea
Island in the Malay Archipelago (qv) divided between Papua New Guinea and the Indonesian province of Irian Jaya.

North America
Continent comprising: USA, Canada, Mexico, Bermuda, West Indies (qv). Usually considered to also include Greenland and (less commonly) Central America.

Oceania
General geographical term describing the islands of the central and south Pacific Ocean, including Melanesia, Micronesia and Polynesia. Sometimes extended to include Australia, New Zealand and the Malay Archipelago (qv).

Polynesia
Collective name for the islands of the central and south Pacific Ocean. Includes: American Samoa, Cook Islands, Easter Island, French Polynesia, Hawaii, Kiribati (east), New Zealand, Niue, Pitcairn Islands, Samoa, Tokelau, Tonga, Tuvalu, Wallis & Futuna.

Scandinavia
Geographical region comprising: Denmark, Norway, Sweden. Generally extended to include Finland and (less commonly) Iceland.

South America
Continent comprising: countries on mainland south of Panama, Falkland Islands, Galapagos Islands.

South-East Asia
Geographic region comprising Maynmar, Laos, Thailand, Vietnam, Cambodia, Malaysia, Singapore, Brunei and the Philippines. Sometimes taken to include Indonesia, Taiwan, Macau, Hong Kong and the southern coastal areas of China.

Ulster
Geographical region comprising Northern Ireland plus the counties of Cavan, Donegal and Monaghan in the Republic of Ireland. It is often used (incorrectly) as an unofficial term to describe Northern Ireland.

United Kingdom
Country comprising Great Britain (qv) and Northern Ireland. The Isle of Man and the Channel Islands are Crown dependencies and not officially part of the UK.

West Indies
Islands enclosing the Caribbean Sea, comprising: Bahama Islands (qv), Greater Antilles (qv), Lesser Antilles (qv).

Windward Islands
Group of Caribbean islands comprising: Grenada, Martinique, St Lucia, St Vincent and The Grenadines.

2: Highest & Lowest

Name	*Metres*	*Feet*	*Country*
AFRICA			
▲ **Kilimanjaro (Kibo)**	5,895	19,340	Tanzania
▼ **Lake Assal**	–155	–509	Djibouti
ANTARCTICA			
▲ **Vinson Massif**	4,897	16,066	Antarctica
▼ **(ice covered)**	–2,538	–8,327	Antarctica
ASIA			
▲ **Everest (Qomolangma Feng/ Sagarmatha)**	8,850	29,035	China-Nepal
▼ **Dead Sea**	–411	–1,349	Israel-Jordan-Palestine
AUSTRALASIA & OCEANIA			
▲ **Aoraki (Cook)**	3,754	12,315	New Zealand
▼ **Lake Eyre**	–16	–52	Australia
EUROPE & RUSSIAN FEDERATION			
▲ **Elbrus**	5,642	18,510	Russian Fed.
▼ **Caspian Sea**	–28	–92	Russia-C. Asia-Caucasus
NORTH AMERICA			
▲ **McKinley (Denali)**	6,194	20,321	Alaska, USA
▼ **Death Valley**	–86	–282	California, USA
SOUTH AMERICA			
▲ **Aconcagua**	6,960	22,834	Argentina
▼ **G. Bajo de S. Julián**	–105	–344	Argentina

Name	*Metres*	*Feet*	*Country*
SOME OTHER NOTABLE MOUNTAINS			
K2 (Chogori/ Qogir Feng)	8,611	28,250	China-Kashmir
Kangchenjunga	8,586	28,170	India-Nepal
Makalu	8,463	27,766	China-Nepal
Dhaulagiri	8,167	26,795	Nepal
Nanga Parbat	8,126	26,660	Kashmir
Annapurna	8,091	26,545	Nepal
Gosainthan (Xixabangma Feng)	8,013	26,289	China
Qullai Garmo	7,495	24,590	Tajikistan
Ojos del Salado	6,908	22,664	Argentina-Chile
Huascarán	6,768	22,205	Peru
Logan	5,959	19,550	Yukon, Canada
Damavand	5,681	18,638	Iran
Citlaltépetl (Orizaba)	5,610	18,405	Mexico
Kenya (Kirinyaga)	5,199	17,057	Kenya
Ararat	5,165	16,946	Turkey
Mont Blanc	4,808	15,774	France-Italy
Ras Dashen	4,533	14,872	Ethiopia
Whitney	4,418	14,495	California, USA
Kinabalu	4,094	13,432	Malaysia
Fuji	3,776	12,388	Japan

3: The World's Longest Rivers

Local names are shown in square brackets.

River	*Length: (km)*	*(miles)*	*Source(s) and outflow*
Nile Luvironza-Ruvuvu-Kagera-White Nile	6,825	4,240	Lake Victoria region – Mediterranean Sea
Amazon Apurimac-Ene-Tambo-Ucayali	6,516	4,049	Peruvian Andes – Atlantic Ocean
Chang Jiang (Yangtze) [Tuotuo-Tongtian-Jinsha]	6,380	3,964	Tanggula Shan, China – East China Sea
Mississippi-Missouri Red Rock-Beaverhead	5,969	3,709	SW Montana – Gulf of Mexico
Ob-Irtysh [Ertix]	5,568	3,459	Altay Mountains, China – Kara Sea
Yenisey Selenga-Angara	5,550	3,448	Western Mongolia – Kara Sea
Huang He (Yellow)	5,464	3,395	Bayan Har Shan, China – Yellow Sea
Congo Lualaba	4,667	2,900	Katanga Plateau, Congo D.R. – Atlantic Ocean
Paraná Río de la Plata	4,500	2,796	Serra da Mantiquera, Brazil – Atlantic Ocean
Mekong [Za-Lancang]	4,425	2,749	Tanggula Shan, China – South China Sea
Amur Kerulen-Argun	4,416	2,744	Eastern Mongolia – Sea of Japan
Lena Kirenga	4,400	2,734	Baikal Mtns, Russian Fed., – Laptev Sea
Mackenzie Finlay-Peace-Slave	4,241	2,635	Omineca Mtns, BC, Canada – Beaufort Sea
Niger [Joliba/Kworra]	4,184	2,599	Guinea/Sierra Leone border – Gulf of Guinea
Murray-Darling	3,750	2,330	Gt. Dividing Range, Australia – Southern Ocean

4: Conversions (Kilometres/ Miles; Metres/Feet; Centimetres/Inches; Centigrade/Fahrenheit)

Kms	**10**	**20**	**30**	**40**	**50**	**60**	**70**	**80**	**90**	**100**
Mi	6.2	12.4	18.6	24.9	31.1	37.3	43.5	49.7	55.9	62.1
M	**10**	**20**	**30**	**40**	**50**	**60**	**70**	**80**	**90**	**100**
Ft	33	66	98	131	164	197	230	262	295	328

Cms	**10**	**20**	**30**	**40**	**50**	**60**	**70**	**80**	**90**	**100**
Ins	3.9	7.9	11.8	15.7	19.7	23.6	27.6	31.5	35.4	39.4
°C	**-10**	**-5**	**0**	**5**	**10**	**15**	**20**	**25**	**30**	**35**
°F	14	23	32	41	50	59	68	77	86	95

The listings above refer to a selection of related themes.
For more information, see the Contents (2-5).

5: Glossary of Foreign Geographical Terms

The following list provides the English equivalents for some of the most common foreign geographical terms used in this and other international atlases.

Term	Language	English
Å, -å	Danish, Norwegian	Stream
Abar, Abyar	Arabic	Wells
Açude	Portuguese	Reservoir
Adalar	Turkish	Islands
Adasi	Turkish	Island
Agia, Ágios	Greek	Saint
Aiguille(s)	French	Peak(s)
Ain, Aïn	Arabic	Spring, well
-air	Indonesian	Stream
Ákra, Akrotírion	Greek	Cape, point
Ala-	Finnish	Lower
A'lá	Arabic	Upper
Alt-	German	Old
Alta, Alto	Italian, Portug., Spanish	Upper
Altiplanicie	Spain	High plain, mesa
Älv, -älven	Swedish	River
am, an	German	On, upon
Áno	Greek	Upper
Anse	French	Bay
Ao	Chinese, Thai	Bay
'Aqabat	Arabic	Pass
Arrecife	Spanish	Reef
Arroio/Arroyo	Portuguese/Spanish	Watercourse
Archipiélago	Spanish	Archipelago
Aust-	Norwegian	East, eastern
Austral	Spanish	Southern
'Ayn	Arabic	Spring, well
Baai	Afrikaans	Bay
Bab	Arabic	Strait
Bach	German	Stream
Bad	German	Spa
Badiyat	Arabic	Desert
Bælt	Danish	Strait
Baharu	Malay	New
Bahía	Spanish	Bay
Bahiret	Arabic	Lagoon
Bahr	Arabic	Bay, canal, lake
Bahra/Bahrat	Arabic	Lagoon/Lake
Baía/Baie	Portuguese/French	Bay
Baixo	Portuguese	Lower
Baja, Bajo	Spanish	Lower
Bala	Persian	Upper
Ban	Cambodian, Laotian, Thai	Village
-bana	Japanese	Cape, point
Bañado	Spanish	Marshy land
Banc/Banco	French/Spanish	Sandbank
Bandao	Chinese	Peninsula
Bandar	Arabian, Malay, Persian	Inlet, port
-bando	Korean	Peninsula
Baraj, Baraji	Turkish	Dam
Barat	Indonesian, Malay	West, western
Barqa	Arabic	Hill
Barra	Portuguese	Sandbank
Barracão	Portuguese	Dam, weir
Barragem	Portuguese	Reservoir
Baruun	Mongolian	Western
Bas, Basse	French	Lower
Bassin	French	Basin
Batin, Batn	Arabic	Depression
Becken	German	Basin
Beek	Flemish	Stream
bei	German	At, near
Bei	Chinese	North, northern
Beinn, Ben	Gaelic	Mountain
Belogor'ye	Russian	Mountain
Bereg	Russian	Bank, shore
-berg	Norwegian, Swedish	Mountain
Berg(e)	German	Mountain(s)
Besar	Indonesian, Malay	Big, great
Bir, Bîr/Bi'ar	Arabic	Well/Wells
Birkat, Birket	Arabic	Pool, well
-bjerg	Danish	Hill
Boca	Portuguese, Spanish	Mouth
Bocche	Italian	Estuary, mouths
Bodden	German	Bay, gulf
Bogazi	Turkish	Strait
Bogen	Norwegian	Bay
Bois	French	Woods
Boloto	Russian	Bog, marsh
Bol'sh-aya, -iye, -oy, -oye	Russian	Big
-bong	Korean	Mountain
Boquerón	Spanish	Pass
Bor	Polish	Forest
-botn/-botten	Norwegian/Swedish	Valley floor
Bouche	French	Estuary, mouth
-bre, -breen	Norwegian	Glacier
Bredning	Danish	Bay
Bron	Afrikaans	Spring, well
-brønn	Norwegian	Spring, well
Bucht/Bugt	German/Danish	Bay
Buhayrat, Buheirat	Arabic	Lake
Bukhta	Russian	Bay
Bukit	Malay	Hill

Term	Language	English
Bukt, Bukten	Norwegian, Swedish	Bay
Bulag	Mongolian	Spring
Bulak	Russian, Uighur	Spring
Burg	German	Castle
Burun, Burnu	Turkish	Cape, point
Büyük	Turkish	Big
Cabeço	Portuguese	Summit
Cabeza	Spanish	Summit
Cabo	Portuguese, Spanish	Cape, headland
Cachoeira	Portuguese	Waterfall
Cala/Caleta	Catalan/Spanish	Inlet
Cañada	Spanish	Ravine
Cañadón	Spanish	Gorge
Canal	Portuguese, Spanish	Channel
Cañe	Spanish	Stream
Cañon	Spanish	Canyon
Cap/Capo	Catalan, French/Italian	Cape, headland
Catarata	Spanish	Waterfall
Cayo(s)	Spanish	Islet(s), rock(s)
Cerro	Spanish	Hill, peak
Chaco	Spanish	Plain
Chaîne	French	Mountain chain
Chalb	Arabic	Watercourse
Chapada	Portuguese	Hills, uplands
Chebka	Arabic	Hill
-chedo	Korean	Archipelago
Chenal	French	Channel
Chiang	Thai	Town
-ch'on	Korean	River
Chong	Thai	Bay
Chott	Arabic	Marsh, salt lake
Chuluu	Mongolian	Mountain
Chute	French	Waterfall
Ci	Indonesian	Stream
Ciénaga	Spanish	Marshy lake
Cima/Cime	Italian/French	Summit
Città/Ciudad	Italian/Spanish	City, town
Co	Tibetan	Lake
Col	French	High pass
Collado	Spanish	Hill, saddle
Colle	Italian	Pass
Collina	Italian	Hill
Colline(s)	French	Hill(s)
Combe	French	Valley
Conca	Italian	Hollow
Cordillera	Spanish	Mountain chain
Corne/Corno	French/Italian	Peak
Costa	Italian, Portug., Spanish	Coast, shore
Côte	French	Coast, slope
Coteau(x)	French	Hill(s)
Cove	Catalan	Cave
Cuchilla	Spanish	Mountain chain
Cuenca	Spanish	River basin
Cueva	Spanish	Cave
Cun	Chinese	Village
Da	Chinese	Big
Dag/Dagh	Turkish/Persian	Mountain
Daglar	Turkish	Mountain
-dake	Japanese	Peak
-dal	Afrikaans, Danish, Norwegian, Swedish	Valley
Danau	Indonesian	Lake
Dao	Chinese	Island
Darreh	Persian	Valley
Daryacheh	Persian	Lake
Dasht	Persian, Urdu	Desert
Davaa	Mongolian	Pass
Denizi	Turkish	Sea
Dhar	Arabic	Hills, mountain
-diep	Flemish	Channel
Djebel/Djibâl	Arabic	Mountain/Mtns.
-do	Korean	Island
Dolina	Russian	Valley
Dolna/Dolní	Bulgarian/Czech	Lower
Dolny	Polish	Lower
Dong	Chinese	East, eastern
Dong	Thai	Mountain
-dong	Korean	Village
Donja, Donji	Serbo-Croat	Lower
Dorf	German	Village
-dorp	Afrikaans	Village
Dûr	Arabic	Mountains
Dzüün	Mongolian	East, eastern
Eiland(en)	Afrikaans, Flemish	Island(s)
-elv, -elva	Norwegian	River
Embalse	Spanish	Reservoir
Embouchure	French	Estuary
Ensenada	Spanish	Bay
Erg	Arabian	Desert & dunes
Eski	Turkish	Old
Estero	Spanish	Inlet, estuary, swamp
Estrecho	Spanish	Strait
Estreito	Portuguese	Strait
Étang	French	Lake, lagoon
Fajj	Arabic	Watercourse
Fels	German	Rock

Term	Language	English
Feng	Chinese	Peak
Fiume	Italian	River
-fjäll, -fjället	Swedish	Mountain
-fjärden	Swedish	Fjord
-fjell, -fjellet	Norwegian	Mountain
-fjord, -fjorden	Danish, Norwegian	Fjord, lagoon
Fleuve	French	River
Foce	Italian	River-mouth
-fonn	Norwegian	Glacier
Förde	German	Inlet
Forêt/Forst	French/German	Forest
-foss	Norwegian	Waterfall
Fuente	Spanish	Source, well
-gan	Japanese	Rock
Gang	Chinese	Harbour
Garet	Arabic	Hill
Gardaneh	Persian	Pass
Gat	Flemish	Channel
-gata	Japanese	Inlet, lagoon
Gau	German	District
Gave	French	Torrent
-gawa	Japanese	River
Gebel	Arabic	Mountain
Gebergte	Afrikaans	Mountain range
Gebiet	German	District, region
Gebirge	German	Mountains
Gedigi	Turkish	Pass
Gezîret/Gezâir	Arabic	Island/Islands
Ghadfat	Arabic	Watercourse
Ghadir	Arabic	Well
Ghard	Arabic	Sand dunes
Ghubbat	Arabic	Bay
Gipfel	German	Peak
Gletscher	German	Glacier
Gobi	Mongolian	Desert
Gol	Mongolian	River
Göl, Gölü	Turkish	Lake
Golfe	French	Bay, gulf
Golfete	Spanish	Bay
Golfo	Italian, Spanish	Bay, gulf
Gora	Bulgarian	Forest
Gora/Góra	Russian, Serbo-Croat/Polish	Mountain
Górka	Polish	Hill
Gornja, Gornji	Serbo-Croat	Upper
Gory/Góry	Russian/Polish	Mountains
Goulet	French	Narrow entrance
Grabean	German	Ditch, trench
-grad	Bulgarian, Russian, Serbo-Croat	Town, castle
Grand, Grands	French	Big
Grat	German	Crest, ridge
Greben'	Russian	Ridge
-gród	Polish	Town, castle
Groot	Afrikaans	Big
Gross, -e, -en, -er	German	Big
Grotta/Grotte	Italian/French	Cave, grotto
Grund	German	Ground, valley
Gryada	Russian	Ridge
Guan	Chinese	Pass
Guba	Russian	Bay
Guelta	Arabic	Well
-gunto	Japanese	Island group
Gunung	Indonesian, Malay	Mountain
Hadabat	Arabic	Plain
Hadh, Hadhat	Arabic	Sand dunes
-haehyop	Korean	Strait
Hafar	Arabic	Wells
Hafen	German	Harbour, port
Haff	German	Bay
Hai	Chinese	Sea
Halbinsel	German	Peninsula
-halvøya	Norwegian	Peninsula
Hamad-a, -et	Arabic	Plateau
Hammad-ah, -at	Arabic	Plain, rocky plateau
-hamn	Norwegian, Swedish	Harbour
Hamun	Persian	Marsh
-hanto	Japanese	Peninsula
Hardt	German	Wooded hills
Harrat	Arabic	Lava fields
Hassi, Hasy	Arabic	Well
-haug	Norwegian	Hill
Haut, -e	French	Upper
Hawr	Arabic	Lake
-havn	Danish, Norwegian	Harbour
Hazm	Arabic	Plateau
He	Chinese	River
-hede	Danish, Norwegian	Heath
-hegység	Hungarian	Mountains
-hei/Heide	Norwegian/German	Heath, moor
Hersónisos	Greek	Peninsula
Higashi-	Japanese	East, eastern
-hisar	Turkish	Castle
Hisn	Arabic	Fort
-hø	Norwegian	Peak
Hoch/Hoë	German/Afrikaans	High
Hoek	Flemish	Cape, point
Hög/-høg(d)	Swedish/Norwegian	High, height
Höhe, Hohen-	German	Height

The listings above refer to a selection of related themes.
For more information, see the Contents (2-5).

Term	Language	Meaning
Hoog	Flemish	High
-høoj	Danish	Hill
Hora/Hory	Czech	Mountain/Mtns
Horn	German	Peak, summit
Horní	Czech	Upper
Hot	Mongolian	Town
-høy	Norwegian	Height
-hrad	Czech	Castle
Hu	Chinese	Lake
Hügel	German	Hill
Idd	Arabic	Well
Idhan	Arabic	Sand dunes
'Idwet	Arabic	Mountain
Île(s)/Ilha(s)	French/Portuguese	Island(s)
Illa, Illes	Catalan	Island, islands
im, in	German	In
Inférieur, -e	French	Lower
Insel(n)	German	Island(s)
Irmak	Turkish	Large river
'Irq	Arabic	Sand dunes
Isla(s)/Isle	Spanish/French	Island(s)
Islote	Spanish	Small island
Iso	Finnish	Big
Ísola, Isole	Italian	Island, islands
Istmo	Spanish	Isthmus
Jabal	Arabic	Mountain
-järvi	Finnish	Lake
-jaure, -javrre	Lappish	Lake
Jazirat/Jaza'ir	Arabic	Island/Islands
Jbel, Jebel	Arabic	Mountain
-jima	Japanese	Island
-joki/-jokka	Finnish/Lappish	River
-jøkulen	Norwegian	Glacier
-jökull	Icelandic	Glacier
Jun	Arabic	Bay
Kaap	Afrikaans	Cape
-kai	Japanese	Sea, bay, inlet
Kali	Indonesian	River
Kamm	German	Crest, ridge
Kampung	Indonesian, Malay	Village
Kanaal/Kanal	Flemish/German, Russian	Canal
-kapp	Norwegian	Cape
Karif	Arabic	Well
Kathib	Arabic	Sand dunes
Káto	Greek	Lower
-kawa	Japanese	River
Kecil	Indonesian, Malay	Small
Kepulauan	Indonesian	Archipelago
Kereb	Arabic	Hill, ridge
Keski-	Finnish	Central, middle
Khalîg, Khalij	Arabic	Bay, gulf
Khao	Thai	Peak
Khashm	Arabic	Mountain
Khawr, Khor/Khowr	Arabic/Persian	Inlet
Khrebet	Russian	Mountain range
Kis-	Hungarian	Small
Kita-	Japanese	North, northern
Klamm	German	Ravine
Klein	Afrikaans, German	Small
Klint/Klit	Danish	Cliff/Dunes
Klong	Thai	Canal, creek
Kloof	Afrikaans	Gorge
Ko/Koh	Thai/Cambodian	Island
-ko	Japanese	Lake, inlet
Kólpos	Greek	Gulf
Koog	German	Polder
Kop/Kopf	Afrikaans/German	Hill
Körfezi	Turkish	Bay, gulf
Kotlina	Czech, Polish	Basin, depression
Kotlovina	Russian	Depression
-köy	Turkish	Village
Kraj	Czech, Polish, Serbo-Croat	Region
Kray	Russian	Region
Kreis	German	District
Kryazh	Russian	Ridge
Kuala	Malay	Estuary
Küçük	Turkish	Small
Kuduk	Russian	Spring, well
Kuh	Persian	Mountain
Kul'	Russian	Lake
Kület	Arabic	Hill
Kum	Russian	Sandy desert
-kundo	Korean	Island group
-kylä	Finnish	Village
Lac	French	Lake
Laem	Thai	Point
Lago	Italian, Portug., Spanish	Lake
Lagoa	Portuguese	Lagoon
Laguna	Spanish	Lagoon, lake
Lam	Thai	Stream
Län	Swedish	Province
Land	German	Province, area
Lande	French	Heath, sandy moor
Las/Les	Polish/Czech, Russian	Forest, wood
Laut	Indonesia	Sea
Lednik	Russian	Glacier
lès, lez	French	Beside, near
Liedao	Chinese	Island group
Lille	Danish, Norwegian	Small
Liman	Russian	Bay, gulf
Liman, Limani	Turkish	Harbour, port
Límni	Greek	Lake, lagoon
Ling	Chinese	Mountain range
Llano	Spanish	Plain, prairie
Loma	Spanish	Hill
-luoto	Finnish	Rocky island
-lyng	Danish	Heath
Macizo	Spanish	Massif
Madinat	Arabic	City, town
Mae Nam	Thai	River
Mala/Malé	Serbo-Croat/Czech	Small
Malaya, -oye, -yy	Russian	Small
-man	Korean	Bay
Manâqîr	Arabic	Hills
Mar	Portuguese, Spanish	Sea
Marais	French	Marsh, swamp
Mare	Italian/Romanian	Sea/Big
Marsá	Arabic	Anchorage, inlet
Marsch	German	Fen, marsh
Masabb	Arabic	Estuary
Mashâsh	Arabic	Well
Massif	French	Mountains, upland
Mayor	Spanish	Higher, larger
Meer	Afrikaans, Flemish, German	Lake, sea
Méga, Megál-a, -i, -o	Greek	Big
Menor	Portuguese, Spanish	Lesser, smaller
Mer	French	Sea
Mersa	Arabic	Anchorage, inlet
Mesa, Meseta	Spanish	Tableland
Mesto	Czech, Serbo-Croat	Town
Mezzo	Italian	Middle, mid-
Miasto	Polish	Town
Mic/Mikr-í, ón	Romanian/Greek	Small
Mina'	Arabic	Harbour, port
Minami-	Japanese	South, southern
Minqâr	Arabic	Hill
-misaki	Japanese	Cape, point
Mishâsh, Mushâsh	Arabic	Well
Miti	Greek	Cape
Mittel-, Mitten-	German	Central, middle
Mjesto	Serbo-Croat	Town
Monasterio/Moni	Spanish/Greek	Monastery
Mont/Monte	French/Italian, Portuguese, Spanish	Mountain
Montagne(s)	French	Mountain(s)
Monti	Italian	Mountains
Moor	German	Bog, moor, swamp
Moos	German	Bog, moss
More	Russian	Sea
Mörön	Mongolian	River
Morro	Portuguese	Hill, mountain
-mose	Danish	Bog, moor
Moyen, -ne	French	Middle, mid-
Muara	Indonesian	Estuary
Mudiriyat	Arabic	Province
Muntii	Romanian	Mountains
-myr	Norwegian, Swedish	Moor, swamp
Mys	Russian	Cape
na	Bulgarian, Russian, Serbo-Croat	On
nad	Czech, Polish, Russian	Above, over
-nada	Japanese	Gulf, sea
Nádrz	Czech	Reservoir
-naes	Danish	Cape, point
Nafud	Arabic	Desert, dune
Nagor'ye	Russian	Highland, uplands
Nagy-	Hungarian	Big, great
Nahr	Arabic	River
Nakhon	Thai	Town
Nam	Korean, Vietnamese	South, southern
Nam	Burmese, Thai, Vietnamese	River
Nan	Chinese	South, southern
Naqb	Arabic	Pass
Nasb	Arabic	Hill, mountain
Né-a, -on, -os	Greek	New
Neder-	Flemish	Lower
Nehri	Turkish	River
Nei	Chinese	Inner
-nes	Icelandic, Norwegian	Cape, point
Neu-/Neuf, Neuve	German/French	New
Nevado	Spanish	Peak
-ni	Korean	Village
Nieder-	German	Lower
Nieu	Afrikaans	New
Nieuw, -e, -en, -er	Flemish	New
Nishi	Japanese	West, western
-nísi	Greek	Island
Nizhn-eye, -iy,	Russian	Lower
Nízina/Nízni	Czech	Lowland/Lower
Nizmennost'	Russian	Lowland
Noord-	Flemish	North, northern
Nord	Danish, French, German	North, northern
Nordre, Nørre	Danish	Northern
Norra	Swedish	Northern
Norte	Portuguese, Spanish	North
Nos	Bulgarian, Russian	Point, spit
Nótios	Greek	Southern
Nou	Romanian	New
Nouv-eau, -elle	French	New
Nova	Italian	New
Nova, Novi	Bulgarian, Serbo-Croat	New
Nova, Novo	Portuguese	New
Nová, Nové, Novy	Czech	New
Nov-aya, -o, -oye, -yy, -yye	Russian	New
Nowa, Nowe, Nowy	Polish	New
Nudo	Spanish	Mountain
Nueva, Nuevo	Spanish	New
Nuruu	Mongolian	Mountains
Nusa	Indonesian	Island
Nuur	Mongolian	Lake
Ny-	Danish, Norwegian, Swedish	New
-ö, -ön/-ø	Swedish/Danish	Island
-oaivi, -oaivve	Lappish	Hill, mountain
Ober-	German	Upper
Oblast'	Russian	Province
Occidental	Spanish	Western
-odde	Danish, Norwegian	Cape, point
Ogla, Oglet	Arabic	Well
Okrug	Russian	District
Ömnö-	Mongolian	South, southern
Onder	Flemish	Lower
Öndör-	Mongolian	Upper
-oog	German	Island
Oost, -er, -elijk	Flemish	East, eastern
Orasu	Romanian	Town
Oriental, -e	French, Romanian, Spanish	Eastern
Ormani	Turkish	Forest
Órmos	Greek	Bay
Óros/Óri	Greek	Mountain/Mtns.
Ost-/Øster-	German/Danish, Norweg.	East, eastern
Ostan	Persian	Province
Östra-	Swedish	East, eastern
Ostrov(a)	Russian	Island(s)
Otok/Otoci	Serbo-Croat	Island/Islands
Oud, -e, -en, -er	Flemish	Old
Oued	Arabic	Dry river-bed
Ovasi	Turkish	Plain
Over-	Danish, Flemish	Upper
Över-, Övre-	Norwegian, Swedish	Upper
-øy, -a	Norwegian	Island
Ozero, Ozera	Russian	Lake, lakes
-pää	Finnish	Hill
Palai-á, -ó, Palió	Greek	Old
Parbat	Urdu	Mountain
Parc	French	Park
Pas	French	Low pass, strait
Paso	Spanish	Pass, strait
Pass/Passo	Spanish/Italian	Pass
Pays	French	Region
Pegunungan	Indonesian	Mountain range
Pélagos	Greek	Sea
Peña(s)	Spanish	Cliff(s), rocks(s)
Pendi	Chinese	Basin
Penisola	Italian	Peninsula
Peñon	Spanish	Cliff
Pereval	Russian	Pass
Perv-o, -yy	Russian	First
Peski	Russian	Sands, desert
Petit, -e, -es	French	Little
Pic	French, Spanish	Peak, summit
Pico/Picacho	Portuguese, Spanish	Peak, summit
Pik	Russian	Peak, summit
Pingyuan	Chinese	Plain
Pizzo	Italian	Peak, summit
-plaat	Dutch	Sandbank, shoal
Plage	French	Beach
Plaine/Planicie	French/Spanish	Plain
Plaj(i)	Turkish	Beach(es)
Planalto	Portuguese	Plateau
Planina	Bulgarian, Serbo-Croat	Mountains
Platja/Playa	Catalan/Spanish	Beach
Plato	Afrikaans, Bulg., Russian	Plateau
Platte	German	Plateau, plain
Plosina	Czech	Tableland
Ploskogor'ye	Russian	Plateau
pod	Czech, Russian	Under
Pohor-í, -ie	Czech	Mountain range
Pointe	French	Cape, point
Poluostrov	Russian	Peninsula
Pólwysep	Polish	Peninsula
Pongo	Spanish	Water gap
Ponta, Pontal	Portuguese	Point
Portile	Romanian	Gate
Portillo	Spanish	Gap, pass
Porto	Catalan, Italian, Portug.	Harbour, port
Pradesh	Hindi	State
Praia	Portuguese	Beach, shore
près	French	Near
Presqu'île	French	Peninsula
Pri-	Russian	Near
Proliv	Russian	Strait

The listings above refer to a selection of related themes.
For more information, see the Contents (2-5).

Term	Language	Meaning
Protoka	Russian	Channel
Prusmyk	Czech	Pass
Przelecz	Polish	Pass
Pubu	Chinese	Waterfall
Pueblo	Spanish	Village
Puente	Spanish	Bridge
Puerta	Spanish	Narrow pass
Puerto	Spanish	Harbour, port
Puk-	Korean	North, northern
Pulau	Indonesian, Malay	Island
Puna	Spanish	Desert plateau
Punta	Catalan, Italian, Spanish	Cape, point
Puntjak	Indonesian	Mountain
Puy	French	Peak
Qa	Arabic	Depression
Qalamat, Qalib	Arabic	Well
Qanat	Arabic, Persian	U'ground conduit
Qararat	Arabic	Depression
Qâret	Arabic	Hill
Qiao	Chinese	Bridge
Qiuling	Chinese	Hills
Qoz	Arabic	Hill
Qu	Tibetan	Stream
Quan	Chinese	Spring
Quedas	Portuguese	Rapids
Qulban	Arabic	Wells
Qum	Persian	Sand
Qundao	Chinese	Archipelago
Qûr, Qurrayat	Arabic	Hills
Qurnat	Arabic	Peak
Quwayrat/Qurûn	Arabic	Hill/Hills
Ramlat	Arabic	Sands
Râs/Ra's	Arabic/Arabic, Persian	Cape, point
Raso	Portuguese	Upland
Ravnina/Razlivy	Russian	Plain
Região	Portuguese	Region
Reprêsa	Portuguese	Dam
Reshteh	Persian	Mountain range
-retto	Japanese	Island chain
-rev	Norwegian	Cliff, reef
Ri	Tibetan	Mountain
-ri	Korean	Village
Ria/Ría	Portuguese/Spanish	River-mouth
Ribeirão	Portuguese	River
Ribeiro	Portuguese	Stream
Rio/Río	Portuguese/Spanish	River
Rivier/Rivière	Afrikaans/French	River
Rocher	French	Cliff, rock
Rocque	French	Rock
Rt	Serbo-Croat	Cape, point
Rücken	German	Ridge
Rud, Rudkhaneh	Persian	River
Rudohorie	Czech	Mountains
-saari	Finnish	Island
Sabkhat	Arabic	Salt-flat
Sagar, Sagara	Hindi	Lake
Sahl	Arabic	Plain
Sahra	Arabic	Desert
-saki	Japanese	Cape, point
Salada/Salar, Salina	Spanish	Salt lake/Salt pan
Salto	Portuguese, Spanish	Waterfall
-san	Japanese, Korean	Mountain
-sanchi	Japanese	Mountainous area
Saniyat	Arabic	Well
Sanmaek	Korean	Mountain range
-sanmyaku	Japanese	Mountain range
San	Italian, Portug., Spanish	Saint
Sankt/Sant	German/Catalan	Saint
Santa, Santo	Italian, Portug., Spanish	Saint
São	Portuguese	Saint
Satu	Romanian	Village
Schloss	German	Castle, mansion
Schutzgebiet	German	Reserve
Sebkra	Arabic	Salt-flat
See	German	Lake
-sehir	Turkish	Town
Selat	Indonesian	Channel, strait
Selatan	Indonesian, Malay	South, southern
-selkä	Finnish	Open water, ridge
Selo	Russian, Serbo-Croat	Village
Selva	Spanish	Forest, wood
-sen	Japanese	Mountain
Serra/Serrania	Catalan, Portug. /Span.	Mountain range
-seto	Japanese	Channel, strait
Sever-naya, -noye, -nyy, -o	Russian	North, northern
Sfintu	Romanian	Saint
Shahr	Persian	Town
Sha'ib, -an	Arabic	Watercourse
Shamo	Chinese	Desert
Shan	Chinese	Mountain(s)
Shandi	Chinese	Mountainous area
Shang	Chinese	Upper
Shankou	Chinese	Pass
Shanmai	Chinese	Mountain range
Sharm	Arabic	Cove, inlet
Shatt	Arabic	River, river-mouth
-shima/-shoto	Japanese	Island/Island group
Shuiku	Chinese	Reservoir
Sierra	Spanish	Mountain range
Silsilesi	Turkish	Mountain range
Sint	Afrikaans, Flemish	Saint
-sjø/sjön	Norwegian/Swedish	Lake
Skala, Skaly	Czech	Cliff, rock
-skog	Norwegian	Woods
-slette	Norwegian	Plain
Sliabh, Slieve	Gaelic	Mountain, upland
Sloboda	Russian	Suburb, large village
Sø	Danish, Norwegian	Lake
Söder-, Södra	Swedish	Southern
Solonchak	Russian	Salt lake
Sommet	French	Peak, summit
Sønder-	Danish	Southern
Søndre	Danish, Norwegian	Southern
Sopka	Russian	Hill
Sør	Norwegian	Southern
sous	French	Under
Spitze	German	Peak
Sredn-a, -i	Bulgarian	Central, middle
Sredn-e, -eye, -iy, -yaya	Russian	Central, middle
-stad	Afrikaans, Norwegian, Swedish	Town
-stadt	German	Town
Stara, Stari	Serbo-Croat	Old
Stará, Staré	Czech	Old
Star-aya, oye, -yy, -yye	Russian	Old
Stausee	German	Reservoir
Stenó	Greek	Pass, strait
Step'	Russian	Steppe
Stít	Czech	Peak
Stor-, Stora/Store	Swedish/Danish	Big
Strand	Gaelic, German	Beach
-strand	Danish, Norwegian, Swedish	Beach
Strasse	German	Road
-strede	Norwegian	Passage, strait
Strelka	Russian	Spit
Stretto	Italian	Strait
Sud	French	South
Süd(er)	German	South (southern)
Suhul	Arabic	Plain
Suid	Afrikaans	South
-suido	Japanese	Channel, strait
Sul	Portuguese	South
sul, sull'	Italian	On
Sund	Swedish	Sound, strait
Sungai	Indonesian, Malay	River
-suo	Finnish	Marsh, swamp
Supérieur/Superior	French/Spanish	Upper
Sur	Spanish	South
sur	French	On
Sveti	Serbo-Croat	Saint
Szent-	Hungarian	Saint
-take	Japanese	Peak
Tal	German	Valley
Tall(ât)	Arabic	Hill(s)
Tang	Persian	Pass, strait
Tanjung	Indonesian, Malay	Cape, point
Taraq	Arabic	Hills
Tasek	Malay	Lake
Tau	Russian	Mountain(s)
Tekojärvi	Finnish	Reservoir
Tell	Arabic	Hill
Teluk	Indonesian	Bay
Tengah	Indonesian	Middle
Teniet	Arabic	Pass
Tepe, Tepesi	Turkish	Hill, peak
Tepeler, Tepeleri	Turkish	Hills, peaks
Terre/Tierra	French/Spanish	Land
Thale	Thai	Lake
Tilat	Arabic	Hill
Timur	Indonesian	East, eastern
-tind, -tinderne	Norwegain	Peak, peaks
Tir'at	Arabic	Canal
-tji	Indonesian	Stream
-to	Japanese	Island
-toge	Japanese	Pass
-tong	Korean	Village
Tonle	Cambodian	Lake
-topp	Norwegian	Peak
Torrente	Spanish	Rapids
Travesía	Spanish	Desert
Tulul	Arabic	Hills
Túnel	Spanish	Tunnel
über	German	Above
-udden	Swedish	Cape, point
Új-	Hungarian	New
Ujung	Indonesian	Cape, point
-umi	Japanese	Inlet
Unter-	German	Lower
'Uqlat	Arabic	Well
-ura	Japanese	Inlet
'Urayq	Arabic	Sand ridge
'Uruq	Arabic	Area of dunes
Ust'ye	Russian	Estuary
Utara	Indonesian	North, northern
Uttar	Hindi	Northern
Uul	Mongolian	Mountains
Uval	Russian	Hill
'Uyun	Arabic	Springs
-vaara(t)	Finnish	Hill(s)
-vaart	Flemish	Canal
-våg	Norwegian	Bay
Val, Vall	Italian, Spanish	Valley
Vale	Portuguese, Romanian	Valley
Valle/Vallée	Italian, Spanish/French	Valley
Vallon	French	Small valley
-vann	Norwegian	Lake
-város	Hungarian	Town
-varre	Norwegian	Mountain
Väster, Västra	Swedish	Western
-vatn	Icelandic, Norwegian	Lake
-vatnet	Norwegian	Lake
-vatten, vattnet	Swedish	Lake
Vaux	French	Valleys
Vecchio	Italian	Old
Vechi	Romanian	Old
Velha, Velho	Portuguese	Old
Velik-a, -i	Serbo-Croat	Big
Velik-aya, -iy, -iye	Russian	Big
Vel'k-á, -é, -y	Czech	Big
Verkhn-e, -eye, -iy, -yaya	Russian	Upper
-vesi	Finnish	Lake, water
Vester	Danish	Western
Vest, Vestre	Norwegian	West, western
-vidda	Norwegian	Plateau
Vieja, Viejo/ Vieux	Spanish/French	Old
Vig/-vik	Danish/Norwegian	Bay
Vila	Portuguese	Small town
Ville	French	Town
Víztároló	Hungarian	Reservoir
Vodokhranilishche	Russian	Reservoir
Volcán	Spanish	Volcano
Vorota	Russian	Channel, strait
Vostochn-aya, -oye, -yy	Russian	Eastern
Vozvyshennost'	Russian	Uplands
Vpadina	Russian	Depression
Vrch(y)	Czech	Mountain(s)
Vrchovina	Czech	Mountainous area
Vysocina	Czech	Upland
Vysok-aya, -oye	Russian	Upper
Wad	Flemish	Sand-flat
Wâdi, Wadi	Arabic	Watercourse
Wahat	Arabic	Oasis
Wai	Chinese	Outer
Wald	German	Forest
Wan/-wan	Chinese/Japanese	Bay
Wand	German	Cliff
Wasser	German	Lake, water
Wes-	Afrikaans	West
West, Wester	Flemish, German	West
Wielk-a, -i, -ie, -o	Polish	Big
Wysok-a, -i, -ie	Polish	Upper
Xi	Chinese	Stream, west
Xia	Chinese	Gorge, lower
Xian	Chinese	County
Xiao	Chinese	Small
Xu	Chinese	Islet
-yama	Japanese	Mountain(s)
Yang	Chinese	Ocean
Yarimadasi	Turkish	Peninsula
Yeni	Turkish	New
Yli-	Finnish	Upper
Ytre-	Norwegian	Outer
Ytter-	Norwegian, Swedish	Outer
Yuan	Chinese	Spring
Yugo-	Russian	Southern
Yunhe	Chinese	Canal
Yuzhn-aya, -o, -oye, -yy	Russian	South, southern
-zaki	Japanese	Cape, point
Zalew	Polish	Bay, inlet, lagoon
Zaliv	Russian	Bay
-zan	Japanese	Mountain
Zapadn-aya, -o, -oye, -yy	Russian	West, western
Zatoka	Polish	Gulf
-zee	Flemish	Sea
Zemlya	Russian	Land
-zhen	Chinese	Town
Zhong	Chinese	Middle
Zhou	Chinese	Islet
Zui	Chinese	Point, spit
Zuid	Flemish	South
Zuid-elijk, er	Flemish	Southern

▶ See also... Climate maps (30,45); Appendix 5: Glossary of Foreign Geographical Terms (101-103)

The listings above refer to a selection of related themes. For more information, see the Contents (2-5).

6: Glossary of Regional Climate Terms

An alphabetical list of the main climate terms used in various parts of the world.

Benguela Current *Africa*
A cold current flowing north along the west coast of South Africa, cooling the coastal region.

Berg Wind *Africa*
A hot dry wind which blows from the interior to the coastal regions of Namibia and South Africa.

Bora *Europe*
A cold dry wind which blows from the N and NE, affecting the Adriatic coastlines of Croatia, Italy and Slovenia.

California Current *North America*
A cold current which flows south along the west coast of California and Mexico, cooling the coastal region, and responsible for the frequent sea fogs particularly during the summer.

Canary Current *Africa*
An extension of the North Atlantic Drift (qv), flowing south along the NW Africa coast and moderating temperatures in the coastal region.

Chinook *North America*
A warm dry wind which blows down the eastern slopes of the Rockies, rapidly melting lying snow.

Crachin *Asia*
Light rain in the northern mountains and coastal regions of Vietnam.

Cyclone *Asia*
Tropical cyclones (qv) in the SW Indian Ocean are simply called cyclones. The season lasts from November to May.

El Niño *South America*
A change in the ocean-atmosphere system in the Pacific, increasing water temperatures in the central and eastern equatorial Pacific Ocean and bringing rain to the NW coast of South America. A periodic phenomenon, it often affects the western coast of America as far north as California. In some years the weather pattern of the whole American continent can be disrupted, and in exceptional years its effects can be experienced worldwide.

Etesian Wind / Meltemi *Europe*
A wind blowing from the N and NW in the eastern Mediterranean and the Aegean, often creating rough seas.

Föhn *Europe*
A wind which blows down Alpine valleys, warming as it descends, and melts snow rapidly.

Garúa *South America*
A heavy mist on the Pacific slope of the Andes in a normally very dry part of the coast.

Ghibli *Africa*
Local name for the Sirocco (qv) in Libya.

Guinea Monsoon *Africa*
Warm humid winds blowing from the SW in West Africa between April and September, associated with the rainy season.

Gulf Stream *North America*
A warm current which flows NE from the Gulf of Mexico. After passing Newfoundland, it divides and follows three separate routes: 1. northwest towards Europe (the North Atlantic Drift (qv)); 2. southeast; 3. recirculating around an area north of Bermuda.

Harmattan *Africa*
A dry and dusty NE wind in West Africa blowing from the Sahara, associated with the dry season; cool at night and warm in the day. Opposite of the Guinea Monsoon (qv).

Hurricane *North America*
The name used for a tropical cyclone (qv) in the N Atlantic and NE Pacific Oceans. The Atlantic hurricane season lasts from June to November, the peak period being August to October. The NE Pacific season is from June to October. For more information on N Atlantic hurricanes, see the N America climate page. (The term is also used in the Beaufort Scale of wind speed: force 12 and above).

Kharif *Asia*
The rainy season in northern India and Arab countries.

Khamsin / Sharav *Africa*
A hot dry wind blowing from the S and SE in the eastern Mediterranean, warming the coastal region and helping to create dust storms and a hazy atmosphere.

Labrador Current *North America*
A cold current flowing south along the east coast of Canada, carrying icebergs and keeping the coastal region relatively cool druing the summer; fogs are caused off the Newfoundland coast where the current meets the warmer Gulf Stream flowing NE from the Gulf of Mexico.

La Niña *South America*
The opposite phenomenon to El Niño. Warm surface water flows towards Asia and colder water from the ocean depths moves to the surface in the eastern equatorial Pacific. Evaporation decreases and rainfall in the region is reduced. Often La Niña occurs the year after El Niño, with drought affecting the areas which experienced flooding the year before.

Leveche *Europe*
A hot, dry and dusty wind in southern Spain which blows from the Sahara.

Mistral *Europe*
A strong cold dry wind blowing from the north in southern France; known as Cers in Aude département.

Monsoon Winds *Asia*
Seasonal winds which change direction during the year; during the dry season in India the NE monsoon blows dry air from the land and during the wet season the SW monsoon blows humid air from the ocean, bringing heavy rain (**Monsoon Rains**). The term is also used in Africa and Australasia.

Mozambique Current / Agulhas Current *Africa*
A warm current flowing south and west along the coast of Mozambique and eastern South Africa, warming the coastal region.

North Atlantic Drift *Europe*
An extension of the Gulf Stream (qv) which helps to maintain relatively mild winters in the British Isles and along the Norwegian coast.

Peru Current / Humboldt Current *South America*
A cold current flowing north along the west coast of South America and cooling the coastal region as far as the Equator.

Severe Cyclonic Storm *Asia*
The name used for a tropical cyclone (qv) in the N Indian Ocean, most likely to occur in May-June & Oct-Nov (Arabian Sea) and Apr-May & Oct-Dec (Bay of Bengal).

Severe Tropical Cyclone *Asia*
The name used for a tropical cyclone (qv) in the SW Pacific Ocean, peak period December to March and the SE Indian Ocean, where it is also known as a Willy-Willy (qv), peak period January-March.

Shamal *Africa*
A hot dry wind which blows from the NW in Iraq and The Gulf.

Sirocco *Europe*
A hot dusty wind blowing towards Europe from north Africa. Known as the Ghibli (qv) in Libya and Leveche (qv) in Spain. Its origins are the same as the Khamsin (qv) or Sharav (qv). On the northern Mediterranean coast, particularly in southern Italy, the wind is moist after crossing the Mediterranean.

Tropical Cyclone *Asia and North America*
A storm with low atmospheric pressure at the centre and strong winds blowing around it, accompanied by a great deal of precipitation. It rotates anticlockwise in the northern hemisphere and clockwise in the southern. The central area has light winds and higher temperatures (the 'eye'), feeling oppresive after the strong winds preceding it, but is soon followed by even stronger winds in the opposite direction. Temperate cyclones are much less violent and are usually called depressions or lows. Tropical cyclones which reach winds of at least 17 metres/second (39mph) they are called tropical storms and assigned a name. If winds reach 33 metres/second (74mph) they are called in different parts of the world: hurricane, typhoon, severe tropical cyclone, severe cyclonic storm, willy-willy or simply cyclone.

Typhoon *Asia*
The term for a tropical cyclone (qv) in the NW Pacific and the China Seas. The typhoon season lasts from May to January but most occur between July and October.

Willy-Willy *Asia*
The name used for a tropical cyclone (qv) affecting the coasts of northern Australia. Likely to occur between December to April, the peak period is January to March.

7: The World's Major Urban Areas

The list shows the world's largest urban agglomerations, with UN estimates of their population in 2005. The UN defines the term 'urban agglomeration' as a contiguous area inhabited at a density regarded as urban, ignoring administrative boundaries.

The ten largest cities in 1900 and in 1800 are listed at the foot of the page.

Urban area & country	Pop. ('000)
Tokyo-Kawasaki-Yokohama, Japan	35,327
Mexico City, Mexico	19,013
New York-Newark, NY, USA	18,498
Mumbai (Bombay), India	18,336
São Paulo, Brazil	18,333
Delhi, India	15,334
Kolkata (Calcutta), India	14,299
Buenos Aires, Argentina	13,349
Jakarta, Indonesia	13,194
Shanghai, China	12,665
Dhaka, Bangladesh	12,560
Los Angeles-Long Beach-Santa Ana, CA, USA	12,146
Karachi, Pakistan	11,819
Rio de Janeiro, Brazil	11,469
Osaka-Kobe, Japan	11,286
Cairo, Egypt	11,146
Lagos, Nigeria	11,135
Beijing, China	10,849
Metro Manila, the Philippines	10,677
Moscow, Russian Fed.	10,672
Paris, France	9,854
Istanbul, Turkey	9,760
Seoul, Rep. of Korea	9,592
Tianjin, China	9,346
Chicago, IL, USA	8,711
Lima, Peru	8,180
London, United Kingdom	7,615
Bogotá, Colombia	7,594
Tehran, Iran	7,352
Hong Kong, China	7,182
Chennai (Madras), India	6,915
Bangkok, Thailand	6,604
Rhine-Ruhr North, Germany	6,559
Bochum-Dortmund-Duisburg-Essen	
Bangalore, India	6,532
Lahore, Pakistan	6,373
Hyderabad, India	6,145
Wuhan, China	6,003
Baghdad, Iraq	5,910
Kinshasa, Dem. Rep. of Congo	5,717
Santiago, Chile	5,623
Riyadh, Saudi Arabia	5,514
Miami, FL, USA	5,380
Philadelphia, PA, USA	5,325
St Petersburg, Russian Fed	5,315
Belo Horizonte, Brazil	5,304
Ahmadabad, India	5,171
Madrid, Spain	5,145
Toronto, OT, Canada	5,060
Ho Chi Minh City, Vietnam	5,030
Chongqing, China	4,975
Shenyang, China	4,916
Dallas-Fort Worth, TX, USA	4,612
Khartoum, Sudan	4,495
Pune (Poona), India	4,485
Barcelona, Spain	4,424
Sydney, NS, Australia	4,388
Singapore	4,372
Boston, MA, USA	4,313
Atlanta, GA, USA	4,284
Houston, TX, USA	4,283
Washington, DC, USA	4,190
Chittagong, Bangladesh	4,171
Hanoi, Vietnam	4,147
Yangon (Rangoon), Myanmar	4,082
Bandung, Indonesia	4,020
Milan, Italy	4,007

Urban area & country	Pop. ('000)
Detroit, MI, USA	3,980
Ankara, Turkey	3,953
Guadalajara, Mexico	3,905
Guangzhou, China	3,881
Jeddah, Saudi Arabia	3,807
Pôrto Alegre, Brazil	3,795
Alexandria, Egypt	3,760
Casablanca, Morocco	3,743
Rhine-Main, Germany	3,700
Frankfurt-Darmstadt-Wiesbaden	
Surat, India	3,671
Melbourne, VI, Australia	3,663
Busan, Rep. of Korea	3,527
Recife, Brazil	3,527
Monterrey, Mexico	3,517
Abidjan, Côte d'Ivoire	3,516
Montréal, QU, Canada	3,511
Chengdu, China	3,478
Phoenix-Mesa, AZ, USA	3,393
San Francisco-Oakland, CA, USA	3,342
Brasília, Brazil	3,341
Salvador, Brazil	3,331
Berlin, Germany	3,328
Rhine-Ruhr Middle, Germany	3,325
Düsseldorf-Mönchenglad.-Wuppertal	
Johannesburg, South Africa	3,288
Kabul, Afghanistan	3,288
Pyongyang, DPR of Korea	3,284
Caracas, Venezuela	3,276
Fortaleza, Brazil	3,261
Algiers, Algeria	3,260
Xi'an, China	3,256
Athens, Greece	3,238
Medellín, Colombia	3,236
Nagoya, Japan	3,189
Cape Town, South Africa	3,103
Changchun, China	3,092
Rhine-Ruhr South, Germany	3,084
Bonn-Cologne-Leverkusen	
East Rand (Ekurhuleni), S. Africa	3,043
Kanpur, India	3,040
Tel Aviv-Yafo, Israel	3,025
Seattle, WA, USA	2,959
Katowice, Poland	2,914
Naples, Italy	2,905
Addis Ababa, Ethiopia	2,899
Harbin, China	2,898
Kano, Nigeria	2,884
Curitiba, Brazil	2,871
Luanda, Angola	2,839
San Diego, CA, USA	2,818
Fukuoka-Kitakyushu, Japan	2,815
Nanjing, China	2,806
Jaipur, India	2,796
Zibo, China	2,775
Surabaya, Indonesia	2,735
Dalian, China	2,709
Stuttgart, Germany	2,705
Hamburg, Germany	2,686
Dar es Salaam, Tanzania	2,683
Jinan, China	2,654
Durban, South Africa	2,643
Incheon, Rep. of Korea	2,642
Campinas, Brazil	2,640
Rome, Italy	2,628
Kiev, Ukraine	2,623
Lucknow, India	2,589
Cali, Colombia	2,583
Faisalabad, Pakistan	2,533

1900:

London, United Kingdom	6,500
New York, USA	4,200
Paris, France	3,300
Berlin, Germany	2,700
Chicago, USA	1,700
Vienna, Austro-Hungarian Empire	1,700
Tokyo, Japan	1,500
St Petersburg, Russia	1,400
Manchester, United Kingdom	1,400
Philadelphia, USA	1,400

1800:

Peking, China	1,100
London, Great Britain	900
Canton, China	800
Tokyo (Edo), Japan	700
Constantinople, Ottoman Empire	600
Paris, France	550
Naples, Kingdom of Naples	450
Hangchow, China	400
Osaka, Japan	380
Kyoto, Japan	380

► *See also...* UNESCO Heritage (48-49)

The listings above refer to a selection of related themes.
For more information, see the Contents (2-5).

Appendices **105**

8-11

8: The World's Tallest Buildings

Height is measured from the street level of the main entrance to the structural or architectural top of the building, including spires but excluding antennae and flag poles. The list shows the world's tallest traditional buildings (structures intended primarily for human habitation with the great majority of their height divided into occupiable levels). Buildings under construction, TV-tower hybrids and other structures not recognised as traditional buildings are excluded. The world's tallest freestanding structure is Toronto's CN Tower (553m).

Name & location	Height (m)	Date
Taipei 101, Taipei, Taiwan	509	2004
Petronas Tower 1, Kuala Lumpur, Malaysia	452	1998
Petronas Tower 2, Kuala Lumpur, Malaysia	452	1998
Sears Tower, Chicago, IL, USA	442	1974
Jin Mao Tower, Shanghai, China	421	1998
Two International Finance Cent., Hong Kong, China	415	2003
CITIC Plaza, Guangzhou, China	391	1997
Shun Hing Square, Shenzhen, China	384	1996
Empire State Building, New York, NY, USA	381	1931
Central Plaza, Hong Kong, China	374	1992
Bank of China Tower, Hong Kong, China	367	1990
Emirates Office Tower, Dubai, UAE	355	2000

Name & location	Height (m)	Date
Tuntex Sky Tower, Kaohsiung, Taiwan	348	1997
Aon Center, Chicago, IL, USA	346	1973
The Centre, Hong Kong, China	346	1998
John Hancock Center, Chicago, IL, USA	344	1969
Shimao International Plaza, Shanghai, China	333	2005
Wuhan International Securities Bldg, Wuhan, China	331	2005
Ryugyong Hotel, Pyongyang, DPR of Korea	330	1992
Q1 Tower, Surfers Paradise, QL, Australia	323	2005
Burj al Arab, Dubai, UAE	321	1999
Chrysler Building, New York, NY, USA	319	1930
Nina Tower I, Hong Kong, China	319	2005
Bank of America Plaza, Atlanta, GA, USA	312	1992
US Bank Tower, Los Angeles, CA, USA	310	1989
Menara Telekom, Kuala Lumpur, Malaysia	310	2001
Jumeirah Emirates Towers Hotel, Dubai, UAE	309	2000
AT&T Corporate Center, Chicago, IL, USA	307	1989
JPMorganChase Tower, Houston, TX, USA	305	1982
Baiyoke Tower II, Bangkok, Thailand	304	1997
Two Prudential Plaza, Chicago, IL, USA	303	1990
Kingdom Centre, Riyadh, Saudi Arabia	302	2002
First Canadian Place, Toronto, ON, Canada	298	1976
Yokohama Landmark Tower, Yokohama, Japan	296	1993
Wells Fargo Plaza, Houston, TX, USA	296	1983
311 South Wacker Drive, Chicago, IL, USA	293	1990

Name & location	Height (m)	Date
SEG Plaza, Shenzhen, China	292	2000
American International, New York, NY, USA	290	1932
Key Tower, Cleveland, OH, USA	289	1991
Plaza 66, Shanghai, China	288	2001
One Liberty Place, Philadelphia, PA, USA	288	1987
Bank of America Tower, Seattle, WA, USA	285	1985
Tomorrow Square, Shanghai, China	285	2003
Chongqing World Trade Centre, Chongqing, China	283	2005
Cheung Kong Centre, Hong Kong, China	283	1999
The Trump Building, New York, NY, USA	283	1930
Bank of America Plaza, Dallas, TX, USA	281	1985
OUB Centre, Singapore	280	1986
Republic Plaza, Singapore	280	1995
UOB (United Overseas Bank) Plaza One, Singapore	280	1992
Citicorp Center, New York, NY, USA	279	1977
Hong Kong New World Tower, Shanghai, China	278	2002
Scotia Plaza, Toronto, ON, Canada	275	1988
Williams Tower, Houston, TX, USA	275	1983
Wuhan World Trade Tower, Wuhan, China	273	1998
Renaissance Tower, Dallas, TX, USA	270	1974
Dapeng International Plaza, Guangzhou, China	269	2004
21st Century Tower, Dubai, UAE	269	2003
Al Faisaliyah Center, Riyadh, Saudi Arabia	267	2000
900 North Michigan Avenue, Chicago, IL, USA	265	1989

9: The World's Longest Bridge Spans

Name & location	Type	Length (m)	Date
Akashi Kaikyo, Kobe–Akashi Island, Japan	Suspension	1,991	1998
Storebælt East, Fyn (Fünen)–Sjælland (Zealand), Denmark	Suspension	1,624	1998
Runyang South, Yangtze River, Zhenjiang, Jiangsu, China	Suspension	1,490	2005
Humber, Kingston upon Hull, England, UK	Suspension	1,410	1981
Jiangyin, Yangtze River, Jiangsu, China	Suspension	1,385	1999
Tsing Ma, Lantau Island–Tsing Yi Island, Hong Kong, China	Suspension	1,377	1997
Verrazano Narrows, Brooklyn–Staten Island, NY, USA	Suspension	1,298	1964
Golden Gate, San Francisco Bay, CA, USA	Suspension	1,280	1937
Höga Kusten (High Coast), Ångermanälven R., Kramfors, Sweden	Suspension	1,210	1997
Mackinac Straits, Mackinaw City–St Ignace, MI, USA	Suspension	1,158	1957
Minami Bisan-Seto, Kojima–Sakaide [Honshu–Shikoku], Japan	Suspension	1,100	1988
Bosporus II (Fatih Sultan Mehmet), Turkey	Suspension	1,090	1988
Bosporus I (Atatürk), Turkey	Suspension	1,074	1973
George Washington, Hudson River, NJ-NY, USA	Suspension	1,067	1931
Kurushima Kaikyo 3;2, Onomichi–Imabari [Honshu–Shikoku], Japan	Suspension	1,030;1,020	1999
Ponte 25 de Abril, Tagus River, Lisbon, Portugal	Suspension	1,013	1966
Forth Road, Edinburgh, Scotland, UK	Suspension	1,006	1964
• *LONGEST BRIDGE SPANS OF OTHER TYPES:*			
Tatara, Onomichi – Imabari [Honshu – Shikoku], Japan	Cable-stayed	890	1999
Pont de Normandie, Seine River, Le Havre, France	Cable-stayed	856	1995
Pont de Québec, St Lawrence River, QC, Canada	Cantilever Truss	549	1917
Forth Rail, Edinburgh, Scotland, UK	Cantilever Truss	521	1890
Lupu, Huangpu River, Shanghai, China	Steel Arch	550	2003
New River Gorge, Fayetteville, WV, USA	Steel Arch	518	1977

10: The World's Longest Tunnels

Name & location (excludes metro tunnels)	Type	Length (km)	Date
Seikan, Tsugaru Strait [Honshu–Hokkaido], Japan	Rail	53.9	1988
Channel Tunnel, Strait of Dover [England–France]	Rail	50.5	1994
Iwate Ichinohe, Tohoku Shinkansen, Honshu, Japan	Rail	25.8	2002
Lærdal, Lærdal–Aurland, Sogn og Fjordane, Norway	Road	24.5	2000
Shimizu, Joetsu Shinkansen, Honshu, Japan	Rail	22.2	1982
Simplon II; I, Brig, Switzerland–Iselle, Italy	Rail	19.8;19.8	1922; '06
Vereina, Selfranga–Sagliains, Switzerland	Rail	19.1	1999
Shin-Kanmon, Sanyo Shinkansen [Honshu–Kyushu], Japan	Rail	18.7	1975
Appennino, 'Direttissima' Bologna–Florence, Italy	Rail	18.5	1934
Qinling I-II, Xi'an–Ankang Line, Shaanxi, China	Rail	18.5	2002
Gotthard (Road), Göschenen–Airolo, Switzerland	Road	16.9	1980
Rokko, Sanyo Shinkansen [Osaka–Kobe], Honshu, Japan	Rail	16.3	1972
Furka Base, Oberwald–Realp, Switzerland	Rail	15.4	1982
Haruna, Joetsu Shinkansen, Honshu, Japan	Rail	15.4	1982
Severomuysk, Baikal-Amur Line, Russian Federation	Rail	15.3	2001
Gorigamine, Hokuriku Shinkansen, Japan	Rail	15.2	1997
Monte Santomarco, Páola–Cosenza, Italy	Rail	15.0	1987
Gotthard (Rail), Andermatt–Airolo, Switzerland	Rail	15.0	1882
Nakayama, Joetsu Shinkansen, Japan	Rail	14.9	1982
Mount Macdonald, Rogers Pass, Glacier Nat. Park, BC, Canada	Rail	14.7	1988
Lötschberg, Kandersteg–Goppenstein, Switzerland	Rail	14.6	1913
Romeriksporten, Oslo–Gardermoen Airport, Norway	Rail	14.6	1999
Dayaoshan, Hengyang–Guangzhou Line, Guangdong, China	Rail	14.3	1987
Arlberg, Langen–St Anton, Austria	Road	14.0	1978

11: World Monuments Fund

The World Monuments Fund (http://wmf.org) is a New York-based non-profit organisation dedicated to the conservation of culturally and historically significant works of art and architecture around the world. The Fund calls attention to imperiled cultural heritage sites by publishing a list every two years of the world's 100 most endangered sites. The 2006 list is shown below.

• UNITED STATES & CANADA
Ennis Brown House, Los Angeles, CA
Hanging Flume, Montrose County, CO
Bluegrass cultural landscape, central KY
Cyclorama Center, Gettysburg, PA
Mount Lebanon Shaker Village, New Lebanon, NY
Dutch Reformed Church, Newburgh, NY
2 Columbus Circle, New York, NY
Ellis Island Baggage and Dormitory Building, New York, NY

• LATIN AMERICA & THE CARIBBEAN
Pimería Alta Missions, Sonora, Mexico
San Nicolás Obispo, Morelia, Mexico
Mexico City historic centre, Mexico
Chalcatzingo, Morelos, Mexico
San Juan Bautista Cuauhtinchan, Puebla, Mexico
Naranjo, El Petén, Guatemala
San Miguel Arcangel and Santa Cruz de Roma, Oanchimalco and Huizucar, El Salvador
Panama Canal area, Panama
Finca Vigia (Hemingway's House), San Francisco de Paula, Cuba
La Guaira historic city, Venezuela
Túcume archaeological site, Lambayeque, Peru
Cajamarquilla, Lima, Peru
Presbitero Maestro Cemetery, Lima, Peru
Quinta Heeren, Lima, Peru
Revash funerary complex, near Chachapoyas, Peru
Convent of San Francisco and Historic Olinda, Olinda, Brazil
Cerros Pintados, Tarapacá, Chile
Tulor Village, Antofagasta, Chile

• EUROPE (including Turkey)
Sandviken Bay, Bergen, Norway

Helsinki-Malmi Airport, Finland
St Vincent's Street Church, Glasgow, Scotland
St Mary's Church, Stow, Lincolnshire
Wonderul Barn, Kildare, Ireland
Segovia Aqueduct, Spain
Teatro Capitolio, Lisbon, Portugal
Santa Maria in Stelle Hypogeum, Verona, Italy
Civita di Bagnoregio, Bagnoregio, Italy
Cimitero Acattolico, Rome, Italy
Temple of Portunus, Rome, Italy
Academy of Hadrian's Villa, Tivoli, Italy
Portici Royal Palace, Naples, Italy
Murgia del Trulli, Puglia, Italy
Jerusalem Hospital of the Teutonic Order, Malbork, Poland
Mausoleum of Karol Scheibler, Lodz, Poland
Lednicke-Rovne Historical Park, Slovak Republic
Novi Dvori Castle, Zapresic, Croatia
St Blaise Church, Dubrovnik, Croatia
Mehmed-Pasha Sokolovic Bridge, Visegrad, Bosnia-Herzegovina
Subotica Synagogue, Serbia
Prizren historic centre, Serbia
Treskavec Monastery and Church, FYR of Macedonia
Oradea Fortress, Romania
Helike archaeological site, Achaia, Greece
Little Hagia Sophia, Istanbul, Turkey
Aphrodisias, near Denizli, Turkey
Riga Cathedral, Latvia

• RUSSIAN FEDERATION
Melnikov's House-Studio, Moscow
Narkomfin Building, Moscow
Semenovskoe-Otrada, Moscow region

• AFRICA
Sabil Ruqayya Dudu, Cairo, Egypt
Tarabay al-Sharify, Cairo, Egypt
Suakin, Sudan
Luxor West Bank, Egypt
Asmara historic city centre and theatre, Eritrea
Massawa historic town, Eritrea
Kidane-Mehret Church, Senafe, Eritrea
Tarrafal Concentration Camp, Cape Verde

Chinguetti Mosque, Mauritania
Old Fourah Bay College, Freetown, Sierra Leone
Benin City earthworks, Nigeria
Bafut Palace, Bafut, Cameroon
Mtwapa heritage site, Kilifi, Kenya
Richtersveld cultural landscape, northern Cape Province, South Africa

• ASIA
Amrit archaeological site, Syria
Shayzar Castle, Syria
Tell Mozan (Ancient Urkesh), NE Syria
Tripoli International Fairground, Lebanon
Chehabi Citadel, Hasbaya, Lebanon
Tell Balatah (Shechem or Ancient Nablus), Nablus, Palestine NRA
Jvari Monastery, Mtshekta, Georgia
Cultural heritage sites countrywide, Iraq
Bam, Iran
Haji Piyada Mosque, Balkh, Afghanistan
Thatta monuments, Pakistan
Mian Nasir Mohamed Graveyard, Dadu district, Pakistan
Guru Lhakhang and Sumda Chung Temples, Ladakh, India
Dhangkar Gompa, Himachal Pradesh, India
Watson's Hotel, Mumbai, India
Dalhousie Square, Kolkata, India
Sonargaon-Panam City, Bangladesh
Patan Royal Palace complex, Nepal
Tianshui traditional houses, Gansu, China
Qikou Town, Shanxi, China
Cockcrow Post Town, Huailai, Hebei, China
Lu Mansion, Dongyang, Zhejiang, China
Stone Towers of southwest China, China
Tuanshan Historical Village, Yunnan, China
Chom Phet cultural landscape, Luang Prabang, Laos
Omo Hada, Nias, Indonesia

• AUSTRALASIA & OCEANIA
Dampier Rock Art Complex, Burrup Peninsula, WA, Australia
Pulemelei Mound, Palauli, Letolo Plantation, Samoa

• ANTARCTICA
Sir Ernest Shackleton's Expedition Hut

The listings above refer to a selection of related themes.
For more information, see the Contents (2-5).

12: City Nicknames

Thousands of cities world-wide have a nickname, and many have more than one. This list has limited itself to a selection of important cities, and to a maximum of four nicknames for each.

Nicknames can have several origins. Some date back centuries, while others are recent and often fanciful inventions by marketing companies or tourist offices. Many refer to a real or imagined pre-eminence in agricultural or industrial production, others to qualities of architecture, location or nightlife that the city sees itself as possessing. Some may have been given to one city by another in a spirit of rivalry, friendly or otherwise. These are often obsure to anyone not from that area, and occasionally strikingly offensive, and so have generally not been included here. Apologies to any city where a particularly uncomplimentary nickname has slipped in by mistake.

Two of the most popular types of nicknames are, firstly, a comparison with a more famous city such as Athens, Paris or Venice because of similar characteristics; and secondly, the claim to be the 'World capital of...' In some cases this refers more to past glory than present reality. The world capitals which have not been included here include those of fruitcake, hubcaps, rhubarb pie, snacks, polar bears, fire hydrants, curtains, gumboots, horseradish sauce and barbed wire. Whatever the reason for a nickname, and however accurate it may be, each gives a clue as to how a city sees itself, or how it would wish others to do so.

Aberdeen, Scotland	Granite City; Silver City
Abidjan, Côte d'Ivoire	Paris of Africa
Adelaide, SA, Australia	City of Churches
Akron, OH, USA	Rubber City
Albuquerque, NM, USA	Duke City
Alexandria, Egypt	Pearl of the Mediterranean
Allentown, PA, USA	Cement Town; Truck Capital of the World
Alleppey, India	Venice of the East
Amsterdam, The Netherlands	Venice of the North; Gateway to Europe
Anchorage, AK, USA	City of Lights; Anchortown; The End of the World
Ancona, Italy	Princess of the Adriatic; Doric City
Annapolis, MD, USA	Crabtown; Sailing Capital of the World; Naptown
Aosta, Italy	The Rome of the Alps
Århus, Denmark	World's Smallest Metropolis
Asheville, NC, USA	Paris of the South
Atlanta, GA, USA	Athens of the South; Phoenix City of the South; Gate City of the South; Dogwood City
Auckland, New Zealand	City of Sails, Queen City; Big Smoke
Augusta, GA, USA	Home of the Masters; Garden City
Austin, TX, USA	Live Music Capital of the World; City of the Violet Crown
Ávila, Spain	City of Saints and Stones
Bacolod, the Philippines	City of Smiles
Baguio, the Philippines	Summer Capital of the Philippines; City of Pines
Baltimore, MD, USA	Monument City; Charm City; City That Reads; Mob Town
Bangalore, India	India's Silicon Valley; City of Gardens
Bangkok, Thailand	Venice of the East
Bangor, Wales	Athens of Wales
Bari, Italy	Small Paris
Barranquilla, Colombia	The Sandy, Curramba the Beautiful
Basra, Iraq	Venice of the Middle East
Bayamón, Puerto Rico	City of the Cowboys
Beijing, China	The Forbidden City
Beirut, Lebanon	Paris of the Middle East
Belgrade, Serbia	White City
Benares, India	Luminous City
Bérgamo, Italy	City of Garibaldi's Thousand
Berkeley, CA, USA	Athens of the West
Berlin, Germany	Spree-Athens; Grey City
Berne, Switzerland	Zürich West

Billings, MT, USA	Star of the Big Sky Country; Magic City; City Beneath the Rimrocks
Birmingham, AL, USA	Magic City; Pittsburgh of the South
Birmingham, England	Venice of the North; Brum; City of a Thousand Trades
Bogotá, Colombia	Athens of South America
Boise, ID, USA	City of Trees
Bologna, Italy	The Fat One; The Learned One; The Red One
Bolzano, Italy	Door to the Dolomites
Bordeaux, France	Wine Capital of the World
Boston, MA, USA	Puritan City; Cradle of Liberty; Athens of America; Beantown
Braga, Portugal	City of the Bishops
Brandon, MN, Canada	Paris of the Prairies
Bremen, Germany	Key to the World
Bréscia, Italy	Lioness of Italy
Bridgeport, CT, USA	Park City
Brighton, England	Liberal City
Brisbane, QL, Australia	River City; Brisvegas
Bruges, Belgium	Venice of the North
Bucharest, Romania	Little Paris
Budapest, Hungary	Pearl of the Danube
Buenos Aires, Argentina	Paris of Latin America; Queen of the Plata
Buffalo, NY, USA	Bison City; Nickel City; Queen City of the Great Lakes; City of Good Neighbors
Bydgoszcz, Poland	Venice of the North
Caguas, Puerto Rico	Country City
Calgary, AL, Canada	Stampede City; Canada's Oil Capital; Cowtown; Gateway to the Rockies
Cali, Colombia	The Sultaness of the Valley
Cambridge (and area), England	Silicon Fen
Cambridge, MA, USA	Moscow on the Charles
Campbell River, BC, Canada	Salmon Capital of the World
Campinas, Brazil	Brazilian Silicon Valley
Canberra, AC, Australia	Bush Capital
Cape Town, South Africa	Mother City
Carolina, Puerto Rico	Giant City
Caserta, Italy	Versailles of Italy
Casper, WY, USA	Oil Capital of the Rockies; Ghost Town
Cebu, the Philippines	Queen City of the South
Cedar Rapids, IA, USA	City of Five Seasons
Charleston, SC, USA	Palmetto City; America's Most Historic City; Marina City; Holy City
Charleston, WV, USA	Chemicalville
Charlotte, NC, USA	Queen City; Hornet's Nest
Chattanooga, TN, USA	Scenic City; Dynamo of Dixie
Chengdu, China	Brocade City; City of Hibiscus
Cheyenne, WY, USA	Magic City of the Plains
Chicago, IL, USA	Windy City; Second City; City of Big Shoulders; Hog Butcher to the World
Christchurch, New Zealand	Garden City
Cincinnati, OH, USA	Queen City of the West; Porkopolis
Clarksville, TN, USA	Gateway to the New South; Queen City; ClarksVegas
Clearwater, FL, USA	Lightning Capital of the World
Cleveland, OH, USA	Forest City; Mistake on the Lake
Cody, WY, USA	Rodeo Capital of the World
Colorado Springs, CO, USA	Pikes Peak City
Columbus, IN, USA	Athens of the Prairie
Columbus, OH, USA	Crossroads of Ohio; Cowtown
Coober Pedy, SA, Australia	Opal Capital of the World
Corpus Christi, TX, USA	Sparkling City by the Sea
Coventry, England	Concrete Block
Cracow, Poland	Royal Capital City
Cuernavaca, Mexico	City of Eternal Springs
Dakar, Senegal	Paris of Africa
Dalian, China	Hong Kong of the North
Dallas, TX, USA	The Texas Star; Big D; Cowtown
Dallas-Fort Worth, TX, USA	Metroplex
Dayton, OH, USA	Gem City; Birthplace of Aviation

Denver, CO, USA	Mile-High City; Gateway to the Rockies; Queen City of the Plains; Convention City
Detroit, MI, USA	Motor City (Motor-Town/Motown); Hitsville USA; Amityville; Hockeytown
Dodge City, KS, USA	Cowboy Capital of the World
Dresden, Germany	Florence on the Elbe
Dublin, Ireland	Fair City; The Pale
Dubrovnik, Croatia	Pearl of the Adriatic
Dunedin, New Zealand	Edinburgh of the South
Durham, NC, USA	Bull City; City of Medicine
Edinburgh, Scotland	Athens of the North; Auld Reekie
Edmonton, AL, Canada	Nashville of the North; City of Champions; Gateway to the North; Canada's Festival City
El Paso, TX, USA	Sun City Texas; City with a Legend
Erfurt, Germany	Thuringian Rome
Eskilstuna, Sweden	Smith City
Florence, Italy	City of Lilies; Athens of Italy
Fort Lauderdale, FL, USA	Venice of America; Fort Leatherdale
Fort Wayne, IN, USA	Summit City; City of Churches
Fort Worth, TX, USA	Where The West Begins; Cowtown
Frankfurt, Germany	Mainhattan; Bankfurt
Fredericton, NB, Canada	City of Stately Elms
Fresno, CA, USA	Garden of the Sun; California's New Frontier; Raisin Capital of the World
Gaeta, Italy	Venice of the Tyrrhenian
Galway, Ireland	Venice of the West; City of the Tribes
Genoa, Italy	The Superb
Ghadamis, Libya	Pearl of the Desert
Glasgow, Scotland	Second City of the Empire; Shipbuilding Capital of the World; Dear Green Place
Gothenburg, Sweden	Little London
Grand Rapids, MI, USA	Furniture City; Valley City
Green Bay, WI, USA	Titletown USA
Guadalajara, Mexico	The Tapatian Pearl
Hague, The, The Netherlands	City of Peace and Justice
Hamburg, Germany	Gateway to the World; Venice of the North
Hamilton, New Zealand	Hamilton
Hamilton, OT, Canada	Steeltown
Harbin, China	Paris of the East
Havana, Cuba	Paris of the Caribbean
Helsinki, Finland	White City of the North
Hershey, PA, USA	Chocolate Town USA; The Sweetest Place on Earth
Ho Chi Minh City, Vietnam	Paris of the Orient
Hollywood (West), CA, USA	Boystown; Creative City
Hollywood, CA, USA	Tinseltown; Showbusiness Capital of the World; Hollyweird
Hong Kong, China	Pearl of the Orient; Asia's World City
Houston, TX, USA	Magnolia City; Space City; Bayou City; Oil Capital of the World
Hyderabad, India	Cyberabad
Indianapolis, IN, USA	Crossroads of America; Naptown; Railroad City; Circle City
Isfahan, Iran	Half of the World
Jackson, MS, USA	Chimneyville
Jacksonville, FL, USA	Bold New City of the South; River City by the Sea; Where Florida Begins
Japiur, India	Pink City
Jeddah, Saudi Arabia	Paris of Arabia
Jerusalem, Israel	City of David; City of Peace; Holy City
Jodhpur, India	Blue City
Johannesburg, South Africa	Egoli (City of Gold)
Jönköping, Sweden	Jerusalem of Småland
Kansas City, MO, USA	City of Fountains; Heart of America; Cowtown
Knoxville, TN, USA	Marble City
Kolkata (Calcutta), India	City of Love; City of Palaces
Kristianstad, Sweden	Little Paris

City	Nickname
Kuching, Malaysia	Cat City
Lahti, Finland	Finland's Chicago
Las Vegas (downtown), NV, USA	The Strip; Glitter Gulch
Las Vegas, NV, USA	Entertainment Capital of the World; City of Lights; America's Playground; Sin City
León, Mexico	Shoe Capital of Mexico
Lexington, KY, USA	Horse Capital of the World
Lima, Peru	City of the Kings
Lisbon, Portugal	White City; City with a Future
Little Rock, AR, USA	City of Roses
Livingston (and area), Scotland	Silicon Glen
London (City of), England	The City; The Square Mile
London, England	Big Smoke; Great Wen
London, OT, Canada	Forest City
Londonderry, Northern Ireland	Maiden City
Los Angeles, CA, USA	Big Orange; City of the Angels; Entertainment Capital of the World; City of Flowers & Sunshine
Louisville, KY, USA	Derby City; Falls City; River City; City of Beautiful Churches
Lubbock, TX, USA	Hub of the Plains
Macau, China	Monte Carlo of the East
Madison, WI, USA	Four Lake City; Mad City
Madurai, India	Athens of the East
Manchester, England	Venice of the North
Manchester, NH, USA	Queen City
Manila, the Philippines	Pearl of the Orient; City by the Bay
Mar del Plata, Argentina	Queen of the Coast; La Feliz (The Happy)
Mayagüez, Puerto Rico	Sultan of the West
Mazatlán, Mexico	Pearl of the Pacific
Medellín, Colombia	Orchid City; La Bella Villa
Melbourne, VI, Australia	Paris on the Yarra
Memphis, TN, USA	Home of the Blues; Birthplace of Rock 'n' Roll; Bluff City; River City
Mérida, Mexico	White City
Mexicali, Mexico	City That Captured the Sun
Mexico City, Mexico	City of Palaces
Miami Beach, FL, USA	America's Riviera; Sun and Fun Capital of the World
Miami, FL, USA	Little Cuba; Gateway to the Americas; Capital of Latin America; Magic City
Milan, Italy	Fashion Capital of the World; Factory of the Future; Moral Capital of Italy; Drinkable City
Milwaukee, WI, USA	Cream City; Brew/Beer City; City of Festivals; Flour City
Minneapolis, MN, USA	City of Lakes; Minneapple; Mill City; Flour City
Minneapolis-St Paul, MN, USA	Twin Cities
Mobile, AL, USA	Azalea City; City of Five Flags
Moncton, NB, Canada	Hub City; Monkeytown
Monterrey, Mexico	Sultaness of the North
Montréal, QU, Canada	City of Saints
Mopti, Mali	Venice of Mali
Moscow, Russian Federation	The Third Rome; Big Village
Munich, Germany	Village of a Million Inhabitants; World City with Heart
Nantes, France	Venice of the West
Naples, Italy	Capital of the South
Nashville, TN, USA	Music City USA; Country Music Capital of the World; Athens of the South; Protestant Vatican
New Orleans, LA, USA	Big Easy; Crescent City; Queen of the Mississippi; City That Time Forgot
New York (Lower Manhattan), NY, USA	Silicon Alley
New York, NY, USA	Big Apple; Empire City; City That Never Sleeps; Capital of the World
Newark, NJ, USA	Brick City; Renaissance City
Newcastle upon Tyne, England	The Toon; Georgieland (refers to the Tyneside conurbation)
Niagara Falls, OT, Canada	Honeymoon Capital of the World
Nijmegen, The Netherlands	Oldest City of The Netherlands
Norrköping, Sweden	Peking
Nouméa, New Caledonia	Paris of the Pacific
Oakland, CA, USA	Oaktown
Oklahoma City, OK, USA	Renaissance City
Oporto, Portugal	The Invincible
Orange County, CA, USA	Biotech Beach
Orlando, FL, USA	City Beautiful
Ottawa, OT, Canada	Venice of the North; Silicon Valley of the North; Bytown
Oxford, England	City of Dreaming Spires; Silicon Spires
Paris, France	City of Light; City of Love
Pasadena, CA, USA	City of Roses; Crown City
Penang, Malaysia	Pearl of the Orient
Pensacola, FL, USA	City of Five Flags
Perth, WA, Australia	City of Lights
Petra, Jordan	Rose Red City
Philadelphia, PA, USA	City of Brotherly Love; Philly; Quaker City
Phoenix, AZ, USA	Valley of the Sun; Desert Storm
Pittsburgh, PA, USA	Steel City; Iron City; Birmingham of America; City of Champions
Ponce, Puerto Rico	City of the Lions; Senior City
Port Elizabeth, South Africa	Friendly City; Windy City
Portland, ME, USA	Forest City; Hill City
Portland, OR, USA	City of Roses; Rip City; Bridgetown; Little Beirut; Stumptown
Portsmouth, England	Pompey
Prague, Czech Republic	Golden City; City of 100 Spires; Heart of Europe; Rome of the North
Pretoria, South Africa	Jacaranda City
Providence, RI, USA	Beehive of Industry
Puebla, Mexico	City of Angels; City of Sweet Potatoes; City of Tiles
Qom, Iran	Iran's Vatican
Québec, QU, Canada	Gibraltar of North America; Le Grande Village; La Vieille Capital
Queenstown, New Zealand	Extreme Sports Capital of the World
Raleigh, NC, USA	City of Oaks; Raleighwood
Recife, Brazil	Venice of Brazil
Regina, SA, Canada	Queen City
Reno, NV, USA	Biggest Little City in the World; Neon Babylon
Richmond, VA, USA	Capital of the Confederacy; City of Seven Hills; Easy to Love; Fist City
Riga, Latvia	Paris of the East
Rio de Janeiro, Brazil	Marvellous City
Rochester, NY, USA	Flower City; Kodak City; Snapshot City
Rome, Italy	Eternal City; City of the Seven Hills; City of Love; City of Cats
Rosario, Argentina	Chicago of Argentina
Sacramento, CA, USA	Big Tomato; Camelia Capital of the World; Almond Capital of the World; River City
St John, NB, Canada	Port City
St Louis, MO, USA	Gateway to the West; Mound City; City with a Future
St Paul, MN, USA	Moscow on the Mississippi
St Petersburg, Russian Fed.	Venice of the North; Northern Palmyra
Salem, MA, USA	City of Witches
Salem, OR, USA	Cherry City
San Antonio, TX, USA	Alamo City; Mission City; River City; Venice of the West
San Diego, CA, USA	Plymouth of the West; America's Finest City; The Place Where California Began; The First Great City of the 21st Century
San Francisco (southern bay area), CA, USA	Silicon Valley
San Francisco, CA, USA	Golden Gate City; Shaky Town; City by the Bay; Baghdad by the Bay
San Jose, CA, USA	Garden City; Capital of Silicon Valley
São Paulo, Brazil	Brazil's Locomotive; City That Never Sleeps; Land of Fog
Saskatoon, SA, Canada	City of Bridges; Saskabush
Scarborough, England	Queen of the Yorkshire Coast
Seattle, WA, USA	Emerald City; Jet City; Queen City of the Pacific Northwest
Sète, France	Venice of the South
Shanghai, China	Paris of the Orient
Sheffield, England	Steel City; People's Republic of South Yorkshire
Shibam, Yemen	Manhattan of the Desert
Shiraz, Iran	Athens of Iran; Paris of Iran; City of Roses
Singapore	Lion City
Sioux Falls, SD, USA	Gateway to the Plains
Sitka, AK, USA	The Natural Place to Visit; Paris of the Pacific
Spokane, WA, USA	Lilac City; Spokavegas; The Can; Skybridge City
Springfield, MA, USA	City of Firsts; Birthplace of Basketball
Springfield, MO, USA	Gateway to the Ozarks; Birthplace of Route 66
Stockholm, Sweden	Venice of the North; The Oak
Stockton, CA, USA	California's Sunrise Seaport; Asparagus Capital of the World
Suzhou, China	Venice of the East
Sydney, NS, Australia	Harbour City; Emerald City
Syracuse, NY, USA	Salt City; Central City; City of Bridges; Typewriter City
Tabriz, Iran	City of Uprising
Tacoma, WA, USA	City of Destiny; Tacyoma; America's Number One Wired City
Tai O, Hong Kong, China	Venice of Hong Kong
Tampa, FL, USA	America's Next Greatest City
Tampere, Finland	Manchester of the North
Táranto, Italy	City of the Two Seas
Tarpon Springs, FL, USA	Venice of the South
Taxco, Mexico	Silver Capital of the World
Te Puke, New Zealand	Kiwi Fruit Capital of the World
Tehran, Iran	City of 72 Nations
Tel Aviv, Israel	City That Never Stops
Tijuana, Mexico	Television Capital of the World
Tikal, Guatemala	City That Time Forgot
Toledo, OH, USA	Glass City; Frog Town; Corn City
Toronto, OT, Canada	Queen City; Hogtown; Festival City; Hollywood North
Tromsø, Norway	Paris of the North
Tucson, AZ, USA	The Old Pueblo
Tulsa, OK, USA	Oil Capital of the World
Turin, Italy	Capital of the Alps; First Capital of Italy; Regal City
Udaipur, India	Venice of the East
Umeå, Sweden	City of Birches
Ushuaia, Argentina	The End of the World
Vancouver, BC, Canada	Rainy City; Brollywood; Terminal City; VanCity
Västerås, Sweden	Cucumber City
Venice, Italy	Bride of the Sea; Queen of the Adriatic; La Serenissima
Victoria, BC, Canada	Whale-watching Capital of the World; Little England; Garden City
Vilnius, Lithuania	Athens of the North
Warsaw, Poland	Paris of the North; Phoenix City; Biggest Village in Poland
Washington DC, USA	News Capital of the World; Capital City; Our City, Our Future
Wellington, New Zealand	Harbour Capital; Windy City; Wellywood
Wichita, KS, USA	Emerald City; Air Capital of the World
Wilmington, DE, USA	Chemical Capital of the World
Windsor, OT, Canada	Tijuana North; Sin City Canada
Winnipeg, MN, Canada	Winterpeg
Zákinthos, Greece	Venice of the South
Zamboanga, the Philippines	City of Flowers

108 | **Appendices**

Countries A-Z: Afghanistan-Benin

▶ **See also...** pages 116 for notes relating to this section; Contents (2-5) for details of all maps and charts in this Atlas

These pages provide exact data on a variety of themes, some of which are addressed in maps or charts elsewhere in this atlas. Information is provided here for every country in the world, not just for those in Europe. The matter of deciding what is and what is not a country is by no means clear-cut, but no political or other subjective stance has been adopted. Many countries have dependencies, overseas possessions, offshore island groups and the like; for various reasons (mainly connected with the availability, reliability or relevance of statistical data) some have been listed separately, some have had their figures amalgamated with those for their mother country and some have been excluded altogether. As a general, rule, but not infallible, rule, where 'T' appears in the Military Spending column, this indicates that the country has a dependence of some kind on another state (which takes responsibility for its defence). For more information on countries worldwide and related matters, consult the latest edition of the Columbus *World Travel Atlas*, *World Travel Dictionary* or *World Travel Guide*.

Throughout, n/a means that, at the time of going to press, data was not available, not reliable or not relevant. In the case of mobile telephone lines and internet usage, it may in a few instances also mean that the country did not have a network or service. Some countries have more than one capital city or have recently changed their capital or its name. These are referred to in the notes at the foot of the chart on page 116. These notes also specify inclusions and exclusions for offshore islands and the like for some of the more important countries.

The *italic* numbers in the second row for each country (preceded by a •) give the world ranking for that category in descending order (highest figure number 1). The top 10 countries in each category have their ranking figure in **bold**. Countries whose figures are equal according to whatever rounding has been used have been ranked equally. As data is not always available for all 226 countries, the figures at the bottom of the chart give the lowest ranking figure in that category; as this can be shared by two or more countries, it may therefore not always represent the total number of countries covered.

Country (Map Ref)	Code	Capital	Area ('000 sq km)	Population ('000, 2004)	Pop. Density (/sq km, 2004)	Int'l Arrivals 1997 ('000)	Int'l Arrivals 2004 ('000)	Visitor Receipts (US$m, 2004)	Int'l Departures ('000, 2004)	Visitor Expenditure (US$m, 2004)	Hotel Bedrooms (2003)	Gross Nat'l Income (US$m, 2004)	GNI per Person (US$, 2004)	GDP Growth (%, 1997–2006)	Energy Production (Mt, 2004)	Energy Consumption (Mt, 2004)	Energy Cons. (t/person, 2004)	Fixed Tel. (/100, 2004)	Mobile Tel. (/100, 2004)	Internet (/100, 2004)	Agric. Land (%, 2004)	Total Health Spending (%, 2002)	Life Expectancy (yrs)	Military Spending (%)
Afghanistan (M4)	.af	Kabul	652.10 •41	29,929 •38	45.9 •150	n/a	n/a	n/a	n/a	n/a	n/a	5,543 •122	185 •217	15.3 •**2**	0.21 •131	0.48 •159	0.02 •209	0.20 •220	2.41 •188	0.10 •204	58.3 •44	8.0 •42	41.5 •210	2.8 •40
Albania (J3)	.al	Tirana	28.70 •142	3,563 •130	124.2 •80	19 •192	42 •144	673 •75	n/a	n/a	4,161 •114	6,641 •114	1,864 •136	5.4 •40	1.39 •106	2.44 •119	0.68 •137	8.30 •142	35.80 •88	2.35 •160	39.7 •103	6.1 •87	72.0 •87	1.2 •120
Algeria (J4)	.dz	Algiers	2,381.70 •11	32,532 •37	13.7 •194	635 •85	1,234 •71	179 •–	n/a	n/a	n/a	73,676 •49	2,265 •119	4.1 •68	176.64 •16	33.29 •42	1.02 •114	7.08 •149	14.48 •128	2.61 •156	16.8 •170	4.3 •150	70.5 •111	3.3 •31
American Samoa (A6)	.as	Pago Pago	0.20 •211	58 •205	289.4 •40	26 •184	n/a	n/a	n/a	n/a	n/a	500 •191	8,638 •68	n/a	0.00 •–	0.21 •176	3.62 •48	25.86 •85	4.14 •174	n/a	24.9 •149	n/a	76.0 •55	T •–
Andorra (J3)	.ad	Andorra la Vella	0.45 •196	71 •200	156.8 •65	2,347 •47	2,791 •54	n/a	n/a	n/a	n/a	1,900 •159	26,932 •23	n/a	0.00 •–	n/a	n/a	52.30 •26	61.63 •56	16.42 •81	55.6 •52	6.5 •71	81.0 •**4**	T •–
Angola (J6)	.ao	Luanda	1,246.70 •23	11,827 •69	9.5 •204	45 •174	194 •121	n/a	n/a	n/a	9,244 •83	14,441 •83	1,221 •148	9.5 •**6**	48.99 •37	3.37 •111	0.28 •160	0.67 •203	6.68 •156	1.22 •174	46.0 •83	5.0 •124	40.0 •213	4.7 •17
Anguilla (F5)	.ai	The Valley	0.16 •215	13 •219	82.8 •106	43 •177	54 •141	97 •103	69 •109	n/a	759 •139	30 •220	2,263 •121	n/a	0.00 •–	n/a	n/a	47.69 •39	13.85 •131	n/a	0.0 •–	n/a	77.0 •47	T •–
Antigua & Barbuda (F5)	.ag	St John's	0.44 •197	69 •202	156.2 •66	240 •129	245 •115	n/a	n/a	n/a	7,731 •86	800 •179	11,641 •59	3.7 •81	0.00 •180	0.19 •180	2.75 •68	49.35 •35	70.13 •49	25.97 •58	31.7 •122	4.8 •133	72.5 •77	M •–
Argentina (F7)	.ar	Buenos Aires	2,780.40 •**8**	39,538 •31	14.2 •192	2,764 •41	3,353 •47	2,563 •46	3,088 •39	2,964 •31	174,629 •15	142,338 •35	3,600 •100	2.2 •142	91.17 •25	66.76 •28	1.69 •88	22.76 •96	35.35 •89	16.10 •82	63.7 •25	8.9 •29	74.5 •63	1.2 •120
Armenia (L3)	.am	Yerevan	29.80 •141	2,983 •135	100.1 •92	23 •188	169 •78	n/a	n/a	n/a	5,034 •107	3,424 •142	1,148 •150	7.7 •13	0.95 •110	4.31 •99	1.44 •96	9.09 •140	6.66 •157	4.91 •131	46.9 •77	5.8 •99	68.5 •127	2.7 •45
Aruba (F5)	.aw	Oranjestad	0.18 •213	72 •199	397.6 •22	650 •81	728 •85	n/a	n/a	n/a	n/a	323 •200	4,513 •88	n/a	0.00 •169	0.34 •169	4.72 •27	35.03 •60	73.61 •46	33.33 •43	10.4 •188	n/a	79.5 •17	–
Australia (P7)	.au	Canberra	7,682.30 •**6**	20,090 •52	2.6 •220	4,318 •28	5,200 •27	12,952 •**10**	3,388 •37	9,407 •17	204,461	541,173 •18	26,937 •22	3.6 •85	256.53 •**9**	128.46 •18	6.39 •18	58.55 •19	82.76 •33	65.28 •19	58.1 •45	9.5 •19	80.5 •**7**	1.9 •77
Austria (J3)	.at	Vienna	83.90 •115	8,185 •89	97.6 •95	16,647 •11	19,373 •**10**	15,412 •**9**	5,060 •27	11,416 •14	282,614 •**10**	262,147 •22	32,029 •15	2.2 •142	12.37 •63	36.38 •40	4.44 •31	46.20 •41	97.36 •12	47.52 •30	40.5 •100	7.7 •49	79.0 •24	0.8 •144
Azerbaijan (L3)	.az	Baku	86.60 •113	7,912 •91	91.4 •102	306 •120	n/a	n/a	n/a	n/a	5,107	7,828 •104	989 •161	11.4 •**4**	22.77 •53	15.86 •66	2.00 •80	12.28 •124	17.44 •125	4.89 •132	54.2 •61	3.7 •167	65.0 •146	1.9 •77
Bahamas (F4)	.bs	Nassau	13.90 •159	302 •175	21.7 •179	1,618 •56	1,561 •64	1,884 •54	n/a	n/a	15,393 •71	4,684 •131	15,521 •42	3.2 •108	0.00 •–	1.21 •136	4.01 •41	44.14 •48	58.68 •61	29.34 •49	1.0 •213	6.9 •66	72.0 •87	M •–
Bahrain (L4)	.bh	Manama	0.71 •187	688 •161	969.5 •**10**	1,611 •57	n/a	740 •73	n/a	n/a	n/a	8,834 •99	12,834 •55	5.2 •42	11.19 •67	10.22 •77	14.85 •**5**	25.92 •84	87.92 •24	20.67 •72	14.1 •176	4.4 •146	74.0 •70	5.1 •15
Bangladesh (N4)	.bd	Dhaka	148.40 •93	144,320 •**7**	972.5 •**9**	182 •136	271 •112	67 •110	n/a	n/a	4,565 •110	61,230 •52	424 •188	5.6 •36	10.90 •68	15.37 •67	0.11 •179	0.61 •205	2.03 •193	0.22 •198	61.2 •35	3.1 •179	63.0 •154	1.2 •120
Barbados (F5)	.bb	Bridgetown	0.43 •198	279 •178	648.5 •13	472 •95	552 •95	810 •69	n/a	n/a	6,210 •97	2,507 •151	8,990 •67	2.4 •133	0.08 •141	0.55 •157	1.97 •82	50.09 •31	73.85 •44	55.35 •18	44.2 •88	6.9 •66	74.5 •63	M •–
Belarus (K3)	.by	Minsk	207.60 •85	10,300 •78	49.6 •145	254 •126	68 •138	287 •93	n/a	524 •54	n/a	20,856 •73	2,025 •131	6.8 •23	2.14 •99	30.76 •45	2.99 •63	32.24 •65	22.73 •114	24.98 •59	43.0 •91	6.4 •75	69.0 •126	1.2 •120
Belgium (J3)	.be	Brussels	30.50 •139	10,364 •77	339.8 •28	6,037 •23	6,710 •28	9,120 •18	7,268 •18	13,954 •11	63,220 •34	322,837 •18	31,149 •18	2.2 •142	12.25 •64	67.02 •27	6.47 •15	46.44 •40	88.32 •23	40.62 •37	49.8 •69	9.1 •26	78.5 •30	1.3 •113
Belize (E5)	.bz	Belmopan	23.00 •153	281 •177	12.2 •196	146 •142	231 •118	n/a	n/a	n/a	5,050 •105	1,115 •171	3,967 •94	5.7 •35	0.02 •151	0.32 •171	1.14 •107	12.92 •107	35.12 •91	13.41 •86	6.6 •199	5.2 •115	68.0 •131	2.0 •73
Benin (J5)	.bj	Porto Novo	112.60 •100	7,649 •93	67.9 •121	148 •141	174 •–	n/a	n/a	n/a	n/a	3,667 •141	479 •184	4.6 •58	0.02 •151	0.64 •153	0.08 •187	1.00 •194	5.33 •161	1.38 •170	29.9 •128	4.7 •137	53.0 •185	1.8 •83

•: Ranking (top 10 in **bold**). **n/a**: Not available, not relevant or not reliable. **T**: See note on page 41. **M**: See note on page 41. For more information, see pages 202 & 210.

▶ *See also...* pages 108 & 116 for notes relating to this section; Contents (2-5) for details of all maps and charts in this Atlas

Appendices 109
Countries A-Z: Bermuda-Congo

Country (Map Ref pp.14-15)	Internet code	Capital	Area '000 sq km	Population '000 (2004)	Population Density people/sq km (2004)	International Arrivals 1997 '000	International Arrivals 2004 '000	Visitor Receipts US$ million (2004)	International Departures '000	Visitor Expenditure US$ million (2004)	Hotel Bedrooms (2003)	Gross Nat'l Income US$ million (2004)	GNI per Person US$ (2004)	GDP Growth Av. annual % 1997-2006	Energy Production Mill tonnes oil equiv (2004)	Energy Consumption Mill tonnes oil equiv (2004)	Energy Consumption Tonnes oil equiv/person (2004)	Fixed Tel. Lines Lines/100 people (2004)	Mobile Tel. Lines Lines/100 people (2004)	Internet Usage Subscribers/100 people (2004)	Agricultural Land % of national area (2002)	Total Health Spending % of GNI (2004)	Life Expectancy Years	Military Spending % of GNI
Bermuda F4	.bm	Hamilton	0.05 •221	65 •203	1,307.3 **•6**	380 •104	272 •111	354 •90	n/a —	232 •68	3,100 •122	2,710 •149	41,459 **•4**	n/a —	0.00 —	0.20 •178	3.08 •61	86.15 **•4**	79.03 •37	62.90 **•10**	18.9 •167	n/a —	n/a —	T —
Bhutan N4	.bt	Thimphu	46.50 •142	2,232 •142	48.0 •149	5 •200	9 •152	12 •114	n/a —	n/a —	1,239 •136	677 •186	303 •204	8.2 •12	0.52 •119	0.46 •161	0.21 •167	3.88 •169	2.45 •187	0.04 •207	12.5 •183	4.5 •144	62.5 •155	1.8 •83
Bolivia F8	.bo	note[9]	1,098.60 •28	8,858 •86	8.1 •208	355 •112	405 •105	n/a —	672 •61	126 •73	20,611 •58	8,656 •101	977 •163	3.0 •117	8.72 •76	4.70 •93	0.53 •141	6.97 •150	20.07 •116	3.90 •139	33.6 •118	7.0 •62	65.0 •146	1.7 •88
Bosnia-Herzegovina J3	.ba	Sarajevo	51.10 •127	4,430 •119	86.7 •104	76 •160	190 •122	490 •82	n/a —	n/a —	n/a —	7,841 •103	1,770 •138	9.1 **•7**	4.36 •84	5.51 •89	1.24 •102	22.17 •106	27.40 •106	5.38 •127	41.5 •95	9.2 •24	72.5 •77	2.9 •35
Botswana K7	.bw	Gaborone	581.70 •47	1,640 •147	2.8 •218	607 •88	1,202 •73	549 •77	n/a —	n/a —	3,589 •119	7,490 •107	4,567 •86	5.5 •39	0.58 •116	1.30 •130	0.79 •128	7.96 •145	33.31 •96	3.50 •143	44.7 •87	6.0 •92	36.5 •217	4.1 •26
Brazil G6	.br	Brasília	8,547.40 **•5**	186,113 **•5**	21.8 •177	2,850 •42	4,725 •39	3,222 •42	2,293 •42	2,871 •33	n/a —	552,096 •13	2,966 •103	2.4 •133	178.37 •14	220.81 **•10**	1.19 •106	23.46 •93	36.32 •85	12.18 •90	30.8 •125	7.9 •45	69.5 •123	1.6 •93
British Virgin Is. F5	.vg	Road Town	0.13 •217	23 •214	174.2 •63	244 •128	332 •108	n/a —	n/a —	n/a —	2,705 •126	265 •203	11,703 •57	n/a —	0.00 —	0.02 •204	0.87 •124	50.87 •30	34.78 •93	17.39 •78	58.8 •42	n/a —	76.5 •53	T —
Brunei O5	.bn	Bandar Seri Begawan	5.80 •169	372 •173	64.2 •130	643 •83	n/a —	n/a —	n/a —	n/a —	n/a —	6,842 •111	18,375 •38	2.1 •149	21.78 •54	2.36 •120	6.34 •17	25.57 •86	17.74 •123	15.30 •83	3.3 •206	3.5 •171	77.0 •47	6.1 •11
Bulgaria K3	.bg	Sofia	111.00 •102	7,450 •95	67.1 •122	2,980 •37	4,630 •40	2,168 •49	3,403 •36	963 •45	5,127 •104	21,326 •71	2,862 •104	3.1 •112	9.73 •74	22.22 •57	2.98 •64	35.13 •59	60.94 •57	28.35 •51	48.0 •74	7.4 •56	72.5 •77	2.6 •47
Burkina H5	.bf	Ouagadougou	274.10 •74	13,492 •63	49.2 •146	138 •145	n/a —	n/a —	n/a —	n/a —	n/a —	4,436 •135	329 •200	5.6 •36	0.04 •146	0.45 •162	0.03 •202	0.61 •205	2.97 •185	0.40 •192	37.9 •109	4.3 •150	45.0 •201	1.3 •113
Burundi K6	.bi	Bujumbura	27.80 •145	7,795 •92	280.4 •42	11 •198	n/a —	n/a —	n/a —	n/a —	n/a —	669 •187	86 •224	2.4 •133	0.04 •146	0.19 •180	0.02 •208	0.34 •212	0.90 •204	0.35 •195	78.0 **•9**	3.0 •182	42.5 •208	5.9 •12
Cambodia O5	.kh	Phnom Penh	181.00 •89	13,636 •62	75.3 •116	219 •130	1,055 •79	n/a —	n/a —	n/a —	n/a —	4,430 •136	325 •201	7.0 •19	0.01 •158	0.21 •176	0.02 •210	0.26 •217	3.52 •180	0.28 •196	29.3 •134	12.0 **•2**	53.5 •184	2.5 •53
Cameroon J5	.cm	Yaoundé	475.40 •53	16,988 •58	35.7 •162	42 •178	n/a —	n/a —	n/a —	n/a —	n/a —	13,138 •89	773 •170	4.2 •66	4.38 •83	1.91 •125	0.11 •178	0.59 •207	9.43 •148	1.02 •175	19.3 •166	4.6 •140	47.5 •196	1.5 •102
Canada D2	.ca	Ottawa	9,970.60 **•2**	32,805 •35	3.3 •214	17,669 **•9**	19,150 •11	12,843 •12	17,739 **•10**	16,017 **•9**	n/a —	905,629 **•8**	27,606 •21	2.5 •128	460.91 **•5**	337.11 **•7**	10.28 **•9**	64.27 •15	46.72 •75	62.36 •12	6.8 •198	9.6 •16	80.0 **•10**	1.2 •120
Cape Verde H5	.cv	Praia	4.00 •172	418 •171	104.6 •90	45 •175	157 •124	109 •102	n/a —	78 •75	n/a —	852 •177	2,037 •130	7.2 •17	0.00 —	0.06 •195	0.14 •173	15.56 •110	13.94 •130	5.30 •129	17.4 •169	5.0 •124	70.0 •116	0.7 •147
Cayman Is. E5	.ky	George Town	0.26 •205	44 •208	170.3 •64	381 •103	260 •113	n/a —	n/a —	n/a —	n/a —	1,391 •166	31,421 •17	n/a —	0.00 —	0.13 •185	2.95 •65	86.36 **•3**	38.64 •81	22.50 •64	11.6 •186	n/a —	80.0 **•10**	T —
Central African Rep. K5	.cf	Bangui	622.40 •43	4,238 •121	6.8 •210	17 •193	n/a —	n/a —	n/a —	n/a —	n/a —	1,226 •169	289 •206	1.6 •159	0.02 •151	0.15 •184	0.04 •200	0.26 •217	1.53 •198	0.23 •197	8.3 •193	3.9 •161	42.5 •208	1.3 •113
Chad J5	.td	Ndjaména	1,284.00 •21	9,657 •82	7.5 •209	27 •182	n/a —	n/a —	n/a —	n/a —	n/a —	2,277 •154	236 •213	8.4 **•10**	2.03 •100	0.07 •191	0.01 •211	0.15 •222	1.39 •201	0.68 •184	37.9 •109	6.5 •71	45.5 •198	1.4 •109
Channel Is. I3	.gg .je	note[10]	0.20 •212	156 •190	780.2 •11	n/a —	n/a —	n/a —	n/a —	n/a —	n/a —	6,190 •119	39,669 **•7**	n/a —	n/a —	n/a —	n/a —	86.00 **•5**	83.33 •32	42.00 •35	n/a —	n/a —	80.0 **•10**	T —
China: Hong Kong SAR[1] O4	.hk	-	1.10 •180	6,899 •98	6,271.5 **•4**	11,273 •13	21,811 **•7**	9,007 •19	n/a —	13,258 •12	52,362 •39	183,516 •29	26,602 •25	4.1 •68	0.00 —	21.82 •61	3.16 •59	54.42 •25	118.77 **•2**	50.32 •21	6.4 •201	n/a —	79.5 •17	n/a —
China: Macau SAR[1] O4	.mo	-	0.02 •222	449 •167	22,459.9 **•1**	3,836 •33	8,323 •24	7,452 •20	n/a —	156 •80	9,185 •84	6,717 •113	14,953 •44	n/a —	0.00 —	0.66 •151	1.47 •95	37.38 •56	92.94 •17	32.24 •45	0.0 **•1**	n/a —	82.0 **•1**	n/a —
Chile F7	.cl	Santiago	736.90 •39	15,981 •60	21.7 •180	1,644 •55	1,785 •61	1,091 •61	2,100 •47	892 •47	42,936 •44	78,407 •48	4,906 •82	4.1 •68	8.39 •77	27.59 •49	1.73 •86	21.53 •99	62.08 •54	27.90 •54	20.2 •161	8.6 •99	77.0 •47	3.5 •30
China O4	.cn	Beijing	9,536.70 **•3**	1,306,314 **•1**	137.0 •73	23,770 **•6**	41,761 **•4**	25,739 **•7**	20,222 **•9**	19,100 **•7**	992,804 **•4**	1,676,846 **•6**	1,284 •146	8.4 **•10**	1,102.52 **•2**	1,137.06 **•2**	0.87 •123	23.98 •91	25.76 •110	7.23 •113	57.9 •47	5.8 •99	71.5 •95	2.3 •60
Colombia F5	.co	Bogotá	1,141.70 •26	42,954 •28	37.6 •159	639 •84	744 •84	1,032 •63	1,177 •57	1,290 •41	54,820 •38	90,626 •44	2,110 •128	2.2 •142	76.55 •29	28.83 •47	0.67 •138	17.14 •108	22.95 •113	8.94 •103	40.2 •101	8.1 •40	72.5 •77	4.4 •18
Comoros L6	.km	Moroni	1.90 •177	671 •162	353.3 •26	26 •184	n/a —	n/a —	n/a —	n/a —	n/a —	328 •199	489 •180	2.4 •133	0.00 —	0.04 •198	0.04 •198	1.66 •185	0.25 •211	1.01 •176	78.9 **•7**	2.9 •183	64.0 •151	3.0 •34
Congo J6	.cg	Brazzaville	341.80 •63	3,602 •128	10.5 •200	27 •182	n/a —	n/a —	n/a —	n/a —	n/a —	2,974 •147	826 •165	3.5 •91	13.11 •61	0.38 •165	0.11 •180	0.36 •211	10.05 •147	0.94 •178	29.9 •128	2.2 •187	54.0 •183	1.4 •109

•: Ranking (top 10 in bold). **n/a:** Not available, not relevant or not reliable. **T:** See note on page 41. **M:** See note on page 41. For more information, see pages 202 & 210.

▶ *See also...* pages 108 & 116 for notes relating to this section; Contents (2-5) for details of all maps and charts in this Atlas

Country / Map Ref. (pp14-15)	Internet code	Capital	Area '000 sq km	Population '000 (2004)	Population Density People/sq km (2004)	International Arrivals 1997 '000 (1997)	International Arrivals 2004 '000 (2004)	Visitor Receipts US$ million (2004)	International Departures '000	Visitor Expenditure US$ million (2004)	Hotel Bedrooms (2003)
Congo, Dem. Rep. K6	.zr	Kinshasa	2,344.90 • **12**	60,764 • 20	25.9 • 174	30 • 179	30 • 148	1 • 117	n/a • –	n/a • –	5,829 • 100
Cook Is. A6	.ck	Avarua	0.23 • 210	21 • 215	93.0 • 99	50 • 171	83 • 136	n/a • –	10 • 90	n/a • –	1,152 • 137
Costa Rica E5	.cr	San José	51.10 • 128	4,016 • 123	78.6 • 112	811 • 74	1,453 • 67	1,357 • 58	373 • 70	404 • 58	35,003 • 52
Côte d'Ivoire I5	.ci	note 11	320.80 • 68	17,298 • 57	53.9 • 142	274 • 122	n/a • –	n/a • –	n/a • –	n/a • –	n/a • –
Croatia J3	.hr	Zagreb	56.50 • 126	4,496 • 117	79.6 • 111	4,178 • 31	7,912 • 25	6,973 • 23	n/a • –	841 • 48	77,113 • 29
Cuba F4	.cu	Havana	110.90 • 103	11,347 • 72	102.3 • 91	1,153 • 63	2,017 • 58	n/a • –	113 • 82	n/a • –	43,696 • 43
Cyprus 2 K4	.cy	Nicosia	9.30 • 166	780 • 158	83.9 • 105	2,088 • 52	2,349 • 55	2,096 • 50	629 • 63	208 • 70	46,706 • 41
Czech Rep. J3	.cz	Prague	78.90 • 117	10,241 • 79	129.8 • 76	4,976 • 27	6,061 • 33	4,169 • 37	36,074 • **5**	2,271 • 39	97,282 • 23
Denmark J3	.dk	Copenhagen	43.10 • 133	5,432 • 108	126.0 • 78	2,158 • 51	3,358 • 46	5,669 • 29	5,564 • 25	n/a • –	41,729 • 45
Djibouti L5	.dj	Djibouti	23.20 • 149	477 • 165	20.5 • 181	20 • 191	n/a • –	n/a • –	n/a • –	n/a • –	n/a • –
Dominica F5	.dm	Roseau	0.75 • 184	69 • 201	92.0 • 100	65 • 167	n/a • –	n/a • –	n/a • –	n/a • –	n/a • –
Dominican Republic F5	.do	Santo Domingo	48.40 • 130	9,050 • 84	187.0 • 57	2,211 • 50	3,450 • 45	3,180 • 43	321 • 72	n/a • –	56,378 • 35
East Timor P6	.tp	Dili	14.60 • 158	1,041 • 155	71.3 • 119	n/a • –	n/a • –	n/a • –	n/a • –	n/a • –	n/a • –
Ecuador F6	.ec	Quito	275.80 • 73	13,364 • 64	48.5 • 148	529 • 92	793 • 83	367 • 89	613 • 64	391 • 59	38,237 • 47
Egypt K4	.eg	Cairo	997.70 • 30	77,506 • 15	77.7 • 114	3,656 • 34	7,051 • 26	6,125 • 26	3,644 • 34	1,257 • 43	136,510 • 18
El Salvador E5	.sv	San Salvador	21.00 • 152	6,705 • 99	319.3 • 32	387 • 102	966 • 80	337 • 91	940 • 58	240 • 67	4,578 • 109
Equatorial Guinea J5	.gq	Malabo	28.10 • 144	529 • 164	18.8 • 185	n/a • –	n/a • –	n/a • –	n/a • –	n/a • –	n/a • –
Eritrea K5	.er	Asmara	93.70 • 109	4,670 • 115	49.8 • 144	410 • 100	87 • 134	73 • 106	n/a • –	n/a • –	4,139 • 115
Estonia K3	.ee	Tallinn	45.20 • 132	1,333 • 151	29.5 • 169	730 • 77	1,750 • 63	806 • 70	2,075 • 48	365 • 61	12,445 • 74
Ethiopia L5	.et	Addis Ababa	1,104.30 • 27	73,053 • 16	66.2 • 126	139 • 144	n/a • –	n/a • –	n/a • –	n/a • –	3,497 • 120
Falkland Is. G8	.fk	Stanley	12.20 • 160	3 • 225	0.2 • 225	n/a • –	n/a • –	n/a • –	n/a • –	n/a • –	n/a • –
Faroe Is. I2	.fo	Tórshavn	1.40 • 179	47 • 207	33.5 • 164	n/a • –	n/a • –	n/a • –	n/a • –	n/a • –	n/a • –
Fiji Is. R6	.fj	Suva	18.30 • 155	893 • 156	48.8 • 147	359 • 110	507 • 99	n/a • –	104 • 83	n/a • –	6,142 • 98
Finland K2	.fi	Helsinki	338.10 • 64	5,223 • 111	15.4 • 189	1,832 • 54	2,840 • 53	2,060 • 51	5,585 • 24	n/a • –	55,767 • 37
France 3 J3	.fr	Paris	549.10 • 49	60,656 • 21	110.5 • 85	66,591 • **1**	75,121 • **1**	40,842 • **3**	17,426 • 11	28,636 • **5**	603,279 • **7**
French Guiana G5	.gf	Cayenne	85.50 • 114	196 • 184	2.3 • 222	68 • 164	n/a • –	n/a • –	n/a • –	n/a • –	n/a • –

Country	Gross Nat'l Income US$ billion (2004)	GNI per Person US$ (2004)	GDP Growth Av. annual % 1997-2006	Energy Production Mil. tonnes oil equiv. (2004)	Energy Consumption Mil tonnes oil equiv. (2004)	Energy Consumption Tonnes oil equiv./person (2004)	Fixed Tel. Lines Lines/100 people (2004)	Mobile Tel. Lines Lines/100 people (2004)	Internet Usage Subscribers/100 people (2004)	Agricultural Land % of national area (2002)	Total Health Spending % of GNI (2004)	Life Expectancy Years (2004)	Military Spending % of GNI (2003)
Congo, Dem. Rep.	6,416 • 117	106 • 223	0.9 • 169	2.78 • 94	2.01 • 122	0.03 • 204	0.02 • 223	1.89 • 194	0.09 • 205	9.7 • 189	4.0 • 159	44.5 • 205	1.0 • 134
Cook Is.	531 • 189	24,827 • 27	n/a • –	0.00 • –	0.02 • 204	0.95 • 119	29.52 • 73	7.14 • 155	17.14 • 79	25.3 • 146	4.6 • 140	71.0 • 99	T • –
Costa Rica	18,969 • 78	4,723 • 84	4.5 • 59	2.22 • 97	4.25 • 100	1.06 • 109	31.62 • 69	21.73 • 115	23.54 • 61	56.1 • 50	9.3 • 21	77.5 • 41	M • –
Côte d'Ivoire	13,263 • 88	767 • 168	1.0 • 168	3.40 • 90	2.53 • 117	0.15 • 171	1.43 • 188	9.07 • 149	1.78 • 165	23.6 • 155	6.2 • 81	45.5 • 198	1.5 • 102
Croatia	29,700 • 61	6,606 • 75	3.6 • 85	4.32 • 85	9.95 • 78	2.21 • 79	42.74 • 51	58.37 • 63	29.51 • 48	55.6 • 52	7.4 • 56	74.5 • 63	2.1 • 66
Cuba	25,501 • 66	2,247 • 123	3.7 • 81	3.76 • 88	11.78 • 74	1.04 • 111	6.78 • 151	0.67 • 206	1.32 • 171	60.1 • 39	7.5 • 55	77.0 • 47	n/a • –
Cyprus 2	13,633 • 85	17,475 • 40	3.5 • 91	0.00 • –	2.83 • 114	3.63 • 47	51.84 • 27	79.37 • 36	36.93 • 41	1.1 • 212	7.0 • 62	78.5 • 30	1.5 • 102
Czech Rep.	93,155 • 42	9,096 • 66	2.2 • 142	28.70 • 49	43.46 • 38	4.24 • 37	33.58 • 62	105.64 • **5**	49.97 • 25	54.2 • 61	7.0 • 62	75.5 • 59	2.2 • 63
Denmark	219,422 • 27	40,392 • **6**	2.0 • 153	29.41 • 47	22.17 • 58	4.08 • 39	64.46 • 14	95.51 • 15	60.41 • 14	61.9 • 31	8.8 • 31	77.5 • 41	1.5 • 102
Djibouti	739 • 183	1,550 • 141	2.2 • 142	0.00 • –	0.66 • 151	1.38 • 100	1.63 • 186	5.07 • 164	1.32 • 171	56.1 • 50	6.3 • 77	54.5 • 182	4.3 • 20
Dominica	261 • 204	3,781 • 98	0.9 • 169	0.01 • 158	0.05 • 197	0.72 • 135	29.40 • 74	58.68 • 61	28.75 • 50	29.3 • 134	6.4 • 75	73.5 • 75	M • –
Dominican Republic	18,443 • 79	2,038 • 129	4.9 • 48	0.35 • 125	7.27 • 83	0.80 • 127	10.65 • 134	28.82 • 101	9.10 • 102	76.3 • 12	6.1 • 87	68.5 • 127	1.1 • 129
East Timor	506 • 190	486 • 181	4.0 • 73	n/a • –	n/a • –	n/a • –	n/a • –	n/a • –	n/a • –	19.6 • 162	9.7 • 13	58.0 • 176	n/a • –
Ecuador	28,783 • 63	2,154 • 127	2.6 • 126	24.69 • 50	9.73 • 80	0.73 • 134	12.22 • 126	26.86 • 108	4.73 • 133	29.7 • 130	4.8 • 133	71.0 • 99	2.4 • 57
Egypt	90,129 • 45	1,163 • 149	4.9 • 48	67.62 • 32	58.06 • 29	0.75 • 132	13.52 • 117	10.92 • 143	5.57 • 126	3.4 • 205	4.9 • 128	67.0 • 137	2.6 • 47
El Salvador	15,613 • 81	2,329 • 117	2.5 • 128	0.89 • 111	2.98 • 113	0.44 • 146	13.42 • 119	27.71 • 105	8.88 • 104	81.0 • **5**	8.0 • 42	70.0 • 116	0.7 • 147
Equatorial Guinea	323 • 201	611 • 171	34.8 • **1**	11.47 • 66	1.24 • 134	2.34 • 75	1.77 • 181	10.95 • 142	0.99 • 177	11.9 • 185	1.8 • 191	51.0 • 190	2.5 • 53
Eritrea	806 • 178	173 • 219	1.4 • 163	0.00 • –	0.24 • 175	0.05 • 196	9.30 • 139	4.74 • 168	11.84 • 91	61.7 • 32	5.1 • 119	59.5 • 169	19.4 • **1**
Estonia	9,435 • 98	7,079 • 71	6.5 • 25	3.07 • 92	5.59 • 87	4.19 • 38	33.95 • 61	96.00 • 13	51.22 • 20	15.4 • 173	5.1 • 119	71.0 • 99	1.9 • 77
Ethiopia	7,747 • 105	106 • 222	4.4 • 61	0.52 • 119	1.94 • 123	0.03 • 207	0.63 • 204	0.25 • 211	0.16 • 201	27.1 • 141	5.7 • 107	50.0 • 192	4.3 • 20
Falkland Is.	32 • 217	10,785 • 61	n/a • –	0.00 • –	0.01 • 207	3.33 • 55	80.00 • **6**	n/a • –	50.00 • 23	92.8 • **1**	n/a • –	0.0 • –	T • –
Faroe Is.	1,008 • 173	21,464 • 32	n/a • –	0.02 • 151	0.26 • 173	5.53 • 22	49.76 • 34	85.78 • 28	66.47 • **5**	2.1 • 211	n/a • –	79.5 • 17	T • –
Fiji Is.	2,281 • 153	2,553 • 108	2.5 • 128	0.16 • 134	0.68 • 148	0.76 • 131	12.35 • 123	13.31 • 134	7.20 • 114	25.1 • 147	4.2 • 158	68.5 • 127	2.2 • 63
Finland	171,024 • 30	32,742 • 14	3.6 • 85	10.49 • 70	30.48 • 46	5.84 • 20	45.40 • 44	95.63 • 14	63.00 • **9**	6.6 • 199	7.3 • 59	78.5 • 30	1.2 • 120
France 3	1,858,731 • **5**	30,644 • 19	1.7 • 156	128.38 • 21	281.05 • **8**	4.63 • 28	56.04 • 22	73.72 • 45	41.37 • 36	54.3 • 59	9.7 • 13	80.0 • **10**	2.6 • 47
French Guiana	2,282 • 152	11,672 • 58	n/a • –	0.00 • –	0.36 • 167	1.84 • 84	30.22 • 72	53.55 • 67	20.77 • 70	0.3 • 215	n/a • –	77.5 • 41	n/a • –

•: *Ranking* (top 10 in **bold**). **n/a:** Not available, not relevant or not reliable. **T:** See note on page 41. **M:** See note on page 41. For more information, see pages 202 & 210.

▶ See also... pages 108 & 116 for notes relating to this section; Contents (2-5) for details of all maps and charts in this Atlas

Appendices **111**

Countries A-Z: French Polynesia-Israel

Country (Map Ref.)	Internet code	Capital	Area '000 sq km	Population '000 (2004)	Population Density people/sq km (2004)	International Arrivals 1997 '000	International Arrivals 2004 '000	Visitor Receipts US$ million (2004)	International Departures '000 (2004)	Visitor Expenditure US$ million (2004)	Hotel Bedrooms (2003)	Gross Nat'l Income US$ million (2004)	GNI per Person US$ (2004)	GDP Growth Av. annual % 1997-2006	Energy Production Mil tonnes oil equiv. (2004)	Energy Consumption Mil tonnes oil equiv. (2004)	Energy Consumption Tonnes oil equiv./person (2004)	Fixed Tel. Lines /100 people (2004)	Mobile Tel. Lines /100 people (2004)	Internet Usage Subscribers/100 people (2004)	Agricultural Land % of national area (2002)	Total Health Spending % of GNI (2002)	Life Expectancy Years (2004)	Military Spending % of GNI (2003)
French Polynesia (B7)	.pf	Papeete	4.20 •171	270 •180	64.4 •129	180 •137	212 •119	n/a	n/a	n/a	3,221 •121	3,794 •138	14,027 •50	n/a	0.02 •151	0.27 •172	1.00 •115	21.48 •100	29.24 •100	18.15 •75	10.8 •187	n/a	76.0 •55	T —
Gabon (J6)	.ga	Libreville	267.70 •76	1,394 •150	5.2 •212	167 •—	236 •75	n/a	n/a	n/a	n/a	5,415 •123	3,884 •96	4.7 •53	13.30 •59	0.98 •140	0.70 •136	3.17 •173	36.20 •86	2.96 •153	19.3 •165	4.3 •150	57.5 •177	0.3 •162
Gambia, The (H5)	.gm	Banjul	10.70 •164	1,595 •148	149.1 •70	85 •156	n/a	n/a	n/a	n/a	n/a	414 •193	260 •208	4.7 •53	0.00 •—	0.10 •188	0.06 •189	2.89 •177	11.97 •138	3.35 •146	63.2 •27	7.3 •59	57.5 •177	0.6 •152
Georgia (L3)	.ge	Tbilisi	69.70 •121	4,677 •114	67.1 •123	313 •118	n/a	n/a	n/a	n/a	n/a	4,683 •132	1,001 •159	6.0 •30	1.96 •101	3.49 •109	0.75 •133	13.47 •118	16.57 •126	3.46 •144	43.1 •90	3.8 •163	71.0 •99	1.1 •129
Germany (J3)	.de	Berlin	357.00 •62	82,431 •14	230.9 •50	15,837 •12	20,137 •9	27,657 •5	74,600 •1	72,271 •1	892,302 •5	2,488,974 •3	30,194 •20	1.2 •165	132.43 •19	356.03 •5	4.32 •34	66.15 •12	86.42 •27	42.67 •33	47.5 •75	10.9 •7	79.0 •24	1.4 •109
Ghana (I5)	.gh	Accra	238.50 •81	21,946 •50	92.0 •101	325 •115	n/a	n/a	n/a	n/a	n/a	8,090 •102	369 •197	4.8 •50	1.53 •105	3.14 •112	0.14 •174	1.47 •187	7.93 •152	1.72 •166	61.5 •33	5.6 •109	58.5 •175	0.7 •147
Gibraltar (I4)	.gi	Gibraltar	0.01 •225	28 •213	4,647.3 •5	n/a	n/a	n/a	n/a	n/a	n/a	498 •192	17,860 •39	n/a	0.00 •—	1.32 •129	n/a	87.50 •2	35.00 •92	22.14 •65	0.0 •—	n/a	80.0 •10	T —
Greece (K4)	.gr	Athens	132.00 •96	10,668 •75	80.8 •107	10,070 •16	13,787 •16	12,872 •11	2,874 •32	n/a	330,970 •9	183,917 •28	17,239 •41	3.4 •98	10.38 •71	35.57 •41	3.33 •54	57.84 •29	84.77 •29	17.81 •77	64.0 •23	9.5 •19	78.5 •30	4.1 •26
Greenland (G2)	.gl	Nuuk	2,166.10 •14	56 •206	0.0 •226	n/a	n/a	n/a	n/a	n/a	n/a	764 •181	13,552 •53	n/a	0.00 •—	0.20 •178	3.57 •49	44.89 •46	35.15 •90	66.32 •6	0.1 •216	n/a	78.0 •39	T —
Grenada (F5)	.gd	St George's	0.34 •202	90 •196	263.2 •46	111 •148	134 •126	30 •111	n/a	n/a	1,758 •131	397 •194	4,436 •89	3.4 •98	0.00 •—	0.09 •189	1.00 •115	31.75 •68	42.05 •78	7.77 •110	37.6 •111	5.7 •107	67.5 •135	M —
Guadeloupe (F5)	.gp	note 12	1.70 •178	449 •168	263.9 •45	660 •80	n/a	n/a	n/a	n/a	7,603 •—	6,006 •120	13,385 •54	n/a	0.00 •—	0.67 •149	1.49 •94	48.73 •—	71.04 •48	17.83 •76	28.2 •—	n/a	78.5 •30	n/a
Guam (O5)	.gu	Agaña	0.54 •191	169 •188	312.2 •33	1,382 •60	1,160 •75	770 •72	n/a	n/a	7,227 •93	3,120 •146	18,509 •36	n/a	0.00 •—	1.00 •139	5.92 •19	50.89 •29	19.29 •119	47.88 •29	40.1 •102	n/a	78.5 •30	T —
Guatemala (E5)	.gt	Guatemala City	108.90 •104	12,014 •68	110.3 •86	576 •89	1,182 •74	658 •62	649 •50	n/a	17,519 •64	26,945 •64	2,243 •124	3.3 •103	1.95 •102	4.35 •97	0.36 •151	8.94 •141	25.02 •111	5.97 •123	41.4 •97	4.8 •133	66.5 •140	0.5 •156
Guinea (I5)	.gn	Conakry	245.90 •78	9,453 •83	38.4 •158	17 •193	45 •143	30 •—	n/a	n/a	n/a	3,681 •140	389 •195	3.7 •81	0.11 •137	0.56 •156	0.06 •193	1.44 •199	0.53 •186	0.34 •212	49.8 •69	5.8 •99	52.0 •187	2.9 •35
Guinea-Bissau (I5)	.gw	Bissau	36.10 •137	1,413 •149	39.2 •156	n/a	n/a	n/a	n/a	n/a	n/a	250 •207	177 •218	-0.3 •175	0.00 •—	0.13 •185	0.09 •183	0.82 •196	1.99 •164	0.10 •215	45.1 •85	6.3 •77	46.5 •197	3.1 •32
Guyana (G5)	.gy	Georgetown	215.00 •84	765 •160	3.6 •213	76 •160	122 •127	372 •—	n/a	n/a	n/a	765 •180	1,000 •160	1.1 •167	0.00 •—	0.60 •155	0.78 •129	13.39 •120	13.64 •132	18.90 •73	8.1 •194	5.6 •109	62.5 •155	0.9 •138
Haiti (F5)	.ht	Port-au-Prince	27.80 •146	8,122 •90	292.1 •39	149 •140	836 •82	93 •—	n/a	n/a	n/a	3,380 •143	416 •192	0.9 •169	0.06 •144	0.67 •149	0.08 •188	1.71 •182	4.87 •166	6.09 •122	57.3 •48	7.6 •52	53.0 •185	0.9 •138
Honduras (E5)	.hn	Tegucigalpa	112.10 •101	7,168 •96	63.9 •131	307 •119	672 •87	396 •87	210 •69	n/a	18,590 •62	7,321 •108	1,021 •157	3.4 •98	0.44 •121	2.52 •118	0.35 •154	5.57 •157	10.10 •146	3.18 •152	26.1 •143	6.2 •81	67.0 •137	0.4 •159
Hungary (J3)	.hu	Budapest	93.00 •110	10,007 •81	107.6 •87	2,887 •39	12,212 •17	4,061 •38	14,283 •14	2,884 •34	64,091 •33	83,315 •46	8,326 •70	4.0 •73	9.73 •74	26.86 •50	2.68 •69	35.43 •58	86.43 •26	26.74 •56	63.1 •28	7.8 •48	72.5 •77	1.8 •83
Iceland (I2)	.is	Reykjavik	103.00 •105	297 •176	2.9 •217	202 •—	372 •88	372 •—	n/a	n/a	7,330 •92	11,199 •96	37,740 •8	3.50 •108	2.50 •95	3.50 •108	11.78 •8	65.01 •13	99.00 •10	77.00 •2	22.1 •159	9.9 •11	80.0 •10	M —
India [19] (M4)	.in	New Delhi	3,065.00 •7	1,080,264 •2	352.5 •27	2,374 •45	3,457 •44	4,739 •35	5,351 •26	5,072 •24	91,720 •25	674,580 •11	624 •170	6.0 •30	253.66 •11	350.75 •6	0.32 •156	4.07 •170	4.37 •170	3.24 •151	55.1 •55	6.1 •87	61.5 •158	2.1 •66
Indonesia (O6)	.id	Jakarta	1,919.40 •16	241,974 •4	126.1 •77	5,185 •25	5,322 •37	4,798 •34	3,507 •28	n/a	263,014 •11	248,007 •23	1,025 •156	2.7 •124	216.96 •12	117.97 •20	0.49 •144	4.49 •162	13.48 •133	6.52 •120	23.3 •156	3.2 •177	66.5 •140	1.5 •102
Iran (L4)	.ir	Tehran	1,648.00 •18	68,018 •18	41.3 •153	764 •76	1,506 •65	n/a	n/a	n/a	n/a	153,984 •33	2,264 •120	4.8 •50	281.68 •6	150.98 •16	2.22 •78	21.97 •98	7.88 •108	6.16 •158	37.1 •112	6.0 •92	69.5 •123	3.8 •28
Iraq (L4)	.iq	Baghdad	438.30 •58	26,075 •44	59.5 •137	15 •197	n/a	n/a	n/a	n/a	n/a	#VALUE!	n/a	n/a	71.44 •31	24.40 •53	0.94 •120	4.00 •168	2.22 •191	0.14 •202	23.0 •157	1.5 •192	55.5 •180	n/a
Ireland (I3)	.ie	Dublin	70.30 •120	4,016 •124	57.1 •137	5,587 •24	6,982 •27	4,279 •36	4,929 •28	5,200 •23	n/a	137,761 •37	34,306 •34	7.7 •13	0.88 •112	15.20 •44	3.78 •44	49.94 •16	93.49 •16	29.63 •47	62.7 •44	7.3 •59	78.5 •30	1.0 •134
Israel [20] (K4)	.il	Jerusalem	21.90 •151	6,277 •101	286.6 •41	2,010 •53	n/a	2,383 •47	3,299 •38	2,976 •30	46,368 •42	118,124 •37	18,819 •34	n/a	0.20 •132	22.28 •56	3.55 •50	43.72 •49	105.25 •6	46.63 •32	25.6 •145	9.1 •26	80.0 •10	9.1 •4

*: Ranking (top 10 in **bold**).   n/a: Not available, not relevant or not reliable.   M: See note on page 41.   T: See note on page 41.   For more information, see pages 202 & 210.

112 Appendices

Countries A-Z: Italy-Mali

▶ *See also...* pages 108 & 116 for notes relating to this section; Contents (2-5) for details of all maps and charts in this Atlas

Country	Map Ref (pp 14-15)	Internet code	Capital	Area '000 sq km	Population '000 (2004)	Population Density people/sq km (2004)	International Arrivals 1997 '000	International Arrivals 2004 '000	Visitor Receipts US$m (2004)	International Departures '000 (2004)	Visitor Expenditure US$m (2004)	Hotel Bedrooms (2003)	Gross Nat'l Income US$ billion (2004)	GNI per Person US$ (2004)	GDP Growth av. annual % 1997-2006	Energy Production Mt oil equiv (2004)	Energy Consumption Mt oil equiv (2004)	Energy Consumption t oil equiv/person (2004)	Fixed Tel. Lines /100 (2004)	Mobile Tel. Lines /100 (2004)	Internet Usage /100 (2004)	Agricultural Land % (2004)	Total Health Spending % GNI (2004)	Life Expectancy years (2004)	Military Spending % GNI (2003)
Italy	J3	.it	Rome	301.30 •71	58,103 •23	192.8 •55	34,692 •4	37,071 •5	35,658 •4	26,817 •7	20,544 •6	999,722 •3	1,503,562 •7	25,878 •26	1.2 •165	31.19 •45	199.05 •12	3.43 •52	44.75 •45	108.19 •4	49.78 •26	51.2 •67	8.5 •35	81.0 •4	1.9 •77
Jamaica	F5	.jm	Kingston	11.40 •162	2,736 •138	240.0 •49	1,192 •62	1,415 •68	1,437 •57	n/a •–	287 •64	20,827 •57	7,738 •106	2,829 •106	1.3 •164	0.05 •145	3.84 •106	1.40 •99	14.60 •113	82.21 •34	39.87 •38	46.7 •81	6.0 •92	72.5 •77	0.4 •159
Japan	P4	.jp	Tokyo	377.80 •61	127,417 •10	337.3 •29	4,218 •30	6,138 •32	11,294 •13	13,296 •15	38,129 •4	1,562,867 •2	4,749,910 •2	37,278 •9	0.9 •169	98.56 •23	560.53 •4	4.40 •33	46.00 •43	71.58 •47	50.20 •22	13.7 •177	7.9 •45	81.5 •2	1.0 •134
Jordan	K4	.jo	Amman	91.90 •111	5,760 •105	62.7 •133	1,127 •64	2,853 •52	826 •67	1,533 •51	n/a •–	19,698 •61	11,629 •92	2,019 •132	4.4 •61	0.37 •123	5.96 •85	1.03 •112	11.00 •131	28.41 •104	10.69 •98	12.8 •181	9.3 •21	71.0 •99	8.9 •6
Kazakhstan	M3	.kz	Astana	2,717.30 •9	15,186 •61	5.6 •211	1,471 •59	2,374 •41	n/a •–	2,374 •41	n/a •–	11,104 •77	33,780 •60	2,224 •125	7.1 •18	104.38 •22	52.22 •33	3.44 •51	16.23 •109	17.91 •122	2.60 •157	76.1 •13	3.5 •171	61.5 •158	1.1 •129
Kenya	K5	.ke	Nairobi	582.60 •46	33,830 •34	58.1 •138	907 •70	1,132 •77	495 •81	n/a •–	n/a •–	n/a •–	14,987 •82	443 •186	2.8 •123	1.00 •108	3.84 •106	0.11 •177	0.92 •195	7.85 •153	4.63 •135	45.6 •84	4.9 •128	49.5 •193	1.7 •88
Kiribati	A6	.ki	Bairiki	0.72 •186	103 •195	143.2 •71	5 •200	n/a •–	n/a •–	n/a •–	n/a •–	n/a •–	95 •215	922 •164	4.2 •66	0.00 •–	0.01 •207	0.10 •182	5.11 •158	0.59 •207	2.35 •160	48.1 •73	8.0 •42	64.5 •150	T •–
Korea, DPR (North)	P3	.kp	Pyongyang	122.80 •98	22,912 •47	186.6 •58	n/a •–	n/a •–	n/a •–	n/a •–	n/a •–	n/a •–	11,047 •97	482 •183	n/a •–	20.45 •55	22.04 •59	0.96 •118	4.10 •166	n/a •–	n/a •–	22.4 •158	4.6 •140	66.5 •140	n/a •–
Korea, Rep. (South)	P4	.kr	Seoul	99.40 •107	48,641 •24	489.3 •19	3,908 •32	5,818 •35	5,697 •28	7,086 •19	9,499 •16	56,196 •36	673,036 •12	13,837 •52	4.7 •53	33.93 •42	215.84 •11	4.44 •32	55.31 •23	76.09 •41	65.68 •7	19.5 •163	5.0 •124	76.5 •53	2.5 •53
Kuwait	L4	.kw	Kuwait City	17.80 •156	2,336 •140	131.2 •75	79 •159	91 •132	180 •98	n/a •–	377 •60	7,618 •89	43,052 •58	18,433 •37	3.0 •117	130.29 •20	23.45 •54	10.04 •10	19.47 •103	78.34 •38	23.50 •62	8.5 •191	3.8 •163	77.5 •41	9.0 •5
Kyrgyzstan	M3	.kg	Bishkek	199.90 •86	5,146 •112	25.7 •175	87 •155	n/a •–	n/a •–	n/a •–	n/a •–	n/a •–	2,050 •157	398 •193	5.6 •36	3.46 •89	4.63 •94	0.90 •122	8.18 •144	5.17 •162	5.16 •130	54.3 •59	4.3 •150	63.5 •152	2.9 •35
Laos	O5	.la	Vientiane	236.80 •82	6,217 •102	26.3 •173	193 •134	236 •117	119 •101	n/a •–	n/a •–	12,289 •76	2,239 •155	360 •198	6.2 •28	1.11 •107	1.24 •134	0.20 •168	1.30 •190	3.53 •179	0.36 •194	7.9 •195	2.9 •183	59.0 •172	2.1 •66
Latvia	K3	.lv	Riga	64.60 •124	2,290 •141	35.5 •163	635 •75	1,080 •78	267 •94	2,286 •43	377 •60	n/a •–	12,570 •90	5,489 •87	6.8 •23	0.54 •118	3.90 •103	1.70 •87	28.45 •77	67.22 •51	n/a •–	38.3 •107	5.1 •119	71.0 •99	1.7 •88
Lebanon	K4	.lb	Beirut	10.50 •165	3,826 •126	364.4 •25	558 •90	1,278 •70	1,278 •59	n/a •–	n/a •–	16,202 •69	22,668 •69	5,925 •78	3.0 •117	0.26 •129	5.74 •86	1.50 •93	17.75 •105	25.01 •112	16.90 •80	31.5 •124	11.5 •3	70.0 •116	4.3 •20
Lesotho	K7	.ls	Maseru	30.40 •141	2,031 •144	66.8 •124	144 •143	n/a •–	n/a •–	144 •143	n/a •–	n/a •–	1,336 •167	658 •169	2.0 •153	0.09 •139	0.17 •183	0.08 •186	2.07 •180	8.83 •150	2.39 •159	76.9 •11	6.2 •81	37.5 •216	2.6 •47
Liberia	I5	.lr	Monrovia	99.10 •108	2,900 •136	29.3 •170	n/a •–	n/a •–	n/a •–	n/a •–	n/a •–	n/a •–	391 •196	135 •221	n/a •–	0.00 •–	0.18 •182	0.06 •190	0.21 •219	1.40 •200	0.03 •208	26.6 •142	2.1 •188	41.5 •210	7.5 •8
Libya	J4	.ly	Tripoli	1,775.50 •17	5,766 •104	3.2 •215	50 •171	n/a •–	n/a •–	n/a •–	n/a •–	12,405 •75	25,257 •68	4,381 •90	3.5 •91	83.91 •26	18.15 •65	3.15 •60	13.56 •116	2.30 •189	3.62 •141	8.7 •190	3.3 •175	63.5 •152	2.0 •73
Liechtenstein	J3	.li	Vaduz	0.16 •216	34 •210	210.7 •52	57 •170	50 •171	n/a •–	n/a •–	n/a •–	591 •141	1,252 •168	37,133 •10	n/a •–	n/a •–	n/a •–	n/a •–	n/a •–	n/a •–	n/a •–	56.3 •49	n/a •–	79.5 •17	T •–
Lithuania	K3	.lt	Vilnius	65.30 •123	3,597 •129	55.1 •140	1,012 •67	1,800 •60	817 •68	3,502 •35	639 •51	7,694 •87	19,727 •75	5,485 •81	5.9 •32	4.63 •81	10.95 •75	3.04 •62	23.80 •92	99.29 •9	28.09 •52	53.4 •65	5.9 •96	72.0 •87	1.6 •93
Luxembourg	J3	.lu	Luxembourg	2.60 •174	469 •166	180.2 •60	778 •75	874 •81	3,666 •41	n/a •–	3,347 •29	7,626 •88	25,302 •67	53,998 •13	5.2 •42	0.04 •146	4.46 •96	9.51 •13	79.75 •1	119.38 •1	59.00 •15	24.0 •152	6.2 •81	79.0 •24	0.9 •138
Macedonia, FYR	K3	.mk	Skopje	25.70 •148	2,045 •143	79.6 •110	121 •147	165 •123	72 •107	n/a •–	55 •76	6,825 •94	4,855 •127	2,374 •113	2.4 •133	1.56 •104	2.77 •115	1.35 •101	25.19 •89	37.23 •82	7.70 •111	48.3 •76	6.8 •69	72.0 •87	2.5 •53
Madagascar	L8	.mg	Antananarivo	587.00 •45	18,040 •56	30.7 •167	101 •151	n/a •–	n/a •–	n/a •–	n/a •–	9,325 •94	5,181 •122	287 •207	3.2 •108	0.14 •136	0.92 •144	0.05 •197	0.33 •214	1.87 •195	0.50 •187	46.9 •77	2.1 •188	57.0 •179	1.4 •109
Malawi	K6	.mw	Lilongwe	118.50 •99	12,707 •65	107.2 •88	207 •131	414 •104	n/a •–	n/a •–	n/a •–	n/a •–	1,922 •158	151 •220	5.9 •32	0.32 •126	0.61 •154	0.05 •198	0.75 •200	1.80 •196	0.37 •193	36.2 •114	9.8 •12	35.0 •219	0.8 •144
Malaysia	O5	.my	Kuala Lumpur	329.80 •66	23,953 •44	72.6 •117	6,211 •22	15,703 •13	8,198 •20	32,201 •6	n/a •–	144,380 •16	117,132 •38	4,890 •83	4.4 •61	93.04 •24	57.85 •30	2.42 •73	17.38 •66	57.12 •66	38.62 •40	23.9 •153	3.8 •163	72.5 •77	2.8 •40
Maldives	M6	.mv	Malé	0.30 •204	349 •174	1,163.7 •8	366 •108	617 •90	479 •83	44 •87	n/a •–	8,557 •85	752 •182	2,154 •126	6.9 •20	0.00 •–	0.85 •145	2.44 •72	9.60 •138	34.53 •94	5.79 •124	43.6 •89	5.8 •99	65.0 •146	5.5 •13
Mali	I5	.ml	Bamako	1,248.60 •22	11,415 •71	9.1 •205	75 •162	113 •129	113 •129	n/a •–	n/a •–	3,907 •116	4,335 •137	380 •196	5.2 •42	0.17 •133	0.38 •165	0.03 •203	0.68 •202	3.60 •177	0.45 •190	28.0 •140	4.5 •144	45.0 •201	1.9 •77

*: Ranking (top 10 in **bold**). •: ___ M: See note on page 41. M: See note on page 41. T: See note on page 41. n/a: Not available, not relevant or not reliable. For more information, see pages 202 & 210.

▶ See also... pages 108 & 116 for notes relating to this section; Contents (2-5) for details of all maps and charts in this Atlas

Appendices 113

Countries A-Z: Malta-Niue

Country	Map Ref.	Capital	Internet code	Military Spending % of GNI (2003)	Life Expectancy Years (2004)	Total Health Spending % of GNI (2004)	Agricultural Land % of national area (2004)	Internet Usage Subscribers/100 people (2004)	Mobile Tel. Lines /100 (2004)	Fixed Tel. Lines /100 (2004)	Energy Consumption Tonnes oil equiv./person (2004)	Energy Consumption Mill tonnes oil equiv. (2004)	Energy Production Mill tonnes oil equiv. (2004)	GDP Growth Av. annual % 1997-2006	GNI per Person US$ (2004)	Gross Nat'l Income US$ mn (2004)	Hotel Bedrooms (2003)	Visitor Expenditure US$ mn (2004)	International Departures 000 (2004)	Visitor Receipts US$ mn (2004)	International Arrivals 2004 000	International Arrivals 1997 000	Population Density People/sq km (2004)	Population 000 (2004)	Area 000 sq km
Malta	J4	Valletta	.mt	0.7 •147	78.5 •30	9.6 •16	31.6 •123	75.25 •4	76.52 •40	51.63 •28	2.46 •71	0.98 •140	0.00 •–	2.5 •128	12,328 •56	4,913 •126	n/a	256 •65	174 •77	779 •71	1,156 •76	1,111 •66	1,245.4 •7	399 •172	0.32 •203
Marshall Is.	R5	Majuro	.mh	T –	61.5 •158	10.6 •8	77.3 •10	3.51 •142	1.11 •203	8.27 •143	n/a	note 1	0.00 •–	n/a	2,404 •112	142 •210	n/a	n/a	n/a	n/a	7 •153	6 •199	328.2 •30	59 •204	0.18 •214
Martinique	F5	Fort-de-France	.mq	n/a	79.0 •24	n/a	30.0 •127	27.09 •55	74.78 •43	44.47 •47	1.66 •90	0.72 •146	0.00 •–	n/a	14,659 •47	6,346 •118	6,766 •95	n/a	n/a	n/a	471 •100	513 •93	393.5 •24	433 •170	1.10 •181
Mauritania	I5	Nouakchott	.mr	1.6 •93	50.5 •191	3.9 •161	38.6 •106	0.47 •189	17.53 •124	1.31 •189	0.40 •147	1.25 •133	0.01 •158	7.4 •15	392 •191	1,210 •170	n/a	n/a	n/a	n/a	n/a	24 •187	3.0 •216	3,087 •133	1,030.70 •29
Mauritius	L7	Port Louis	.mu	0.2 •163	72.5 •77	3.5 •171	55.4 •54	14.60 •84	41.36 •79	28.69 •75	1.06 •110	1.30 •130	0.03 •150	5.0 •45	4,656 •85	5,730 •121	9,647 •81	255 •66	161 •79	853 •66	719 •86	536 •91	615.3 •15	1,231 •152	2.00 •176
Mayotte	L6	Dzaoudzi	.yt	T –	61.5 •158	6.1 •87	54.9 •56	n/a	n/a	6.24 •154	n/a	n/a	0.00 •–	n/a	4,550 •87	881 •175	n/a	n/a	n/a	n/a	n/a	n/a	523.3 •18	194 •185	0.37 •200
Mexico	D4	Mexico City	.mx	0.5 •156	74.5 •63	6.5 •71	54.9 •56	13.38 •87	36.64 •84	17.22 •107	1.60 •91	169.79 •13	254.19 •10	3.5 •91	6,620 •74	703,080 •10	496,292 •8	6,959 •22	11,044 •17	10,753 •14	20,618 •8	19,351 •8	54.0 •141	106,203 •11	1,967.20 •15
Micronesia, Fed. States	O5	Palikir	.fm	T –	69.5 •123	7.0 •62	67.1 •21	n/a	n/a	10.81 •133	n/a	n/a	0.00 •–	n/a	2,331 •115	252 •206	n/a	n/a	n/a	n/a	19 •150	17 •193	154.4 •67	108 •194	0.70 •188
Moldova	K3	Chisinău	.md	0.4 •159	67.0 •137	7.0 •62	75.0 •14	9.52 •100	18.46 •121	20.25 •101	0.97 •117	4.34 •98	0.09 •140	3.3 •103	575 •175	2,563 •150	2,559 •127	135 •100	67 •85	95 •104	24 •149	21 •190	132.2 •74	4,455 •118	33.70 •138
Monaco	J3	Monaco-Ville	.mc	T –	81.5 •2	11.0 •6	0.0 •–	50.00 •23	60.31 •59	105.31 •1	n/a	n/a	0.00 •–	n/a	26,844 •24	870 •176	2,212 •130	n/a	n/a	n/a	246 •114	259 •124	16,204.5 •2	32 •211	0.002 •226
Mongolia	O3	Ulan Bator	.mn	2.1 •66	65.5 •145	6.3 •77	83.4 •3	7.60 •112	12.98 •136	5.62 •156	0.84 •126	2.35 •121	1.72 •103	4.4 •61	532 •179	1,484 •165	n/a	134 •72	n/a	n/a	n/a	82 •157	1.8 •223	2,791 •137	1,565.00 •19
Montserrat	F5	Plymouth[13]	.ms	T –	79.0 •24	n/a	29.4 •133	n/a	n/a	n/a	2.22 •77	0.02 •204	0.00 •–	n/a	2,248 •122	21 •221	n/a	n/a	n/a	n/a	10 •151	19 •193	93.4 •98	9 •222	0.10 •223
Morocco[21]	I4	Rabat	.ma	4.2 •24	71.0 •99	4.6 •140	42.6 •92	11.71 •92	31.23 •98	4.38 •164	0.38 •150	12.39 •73	0.32 •127	3.3 •103	1,421 •143	46,518 •56	75,284 •30	568 •53	1,694 •50	3,921 •40	5,501 •36	3,072 •36	71.3 •118	32,726 •36	458.70 •55
Mozambique	K7	Maputo	.mz	1.3 •113	45.0 •201	5.8 •99	60.6 •36	0.73 •176	3.73 •176	0.42 •209	0.21 •164	4.16 •102	3.92 •86	8.5 •9	243 •211	4,710 •130	n/a	n/a	n/a	n/a	n/a	n/a	24.3 •176	19,407 •54	799.40 •35
Myanmar (Burma)[14]	N4	Yangon[14]	.mm	2.3 •60	59.5 •169	2.2 •188	16.1 •172	0.12 •203	0.17 •214	0.79 •198	0.10 •181	4.58 •95	10.14 •72	n/a	293 •205	13,785 •84	17,039 •65	477 •57	136 •100	95 •104	242 •116	189 •135	69.5 •120	46,997 •26	676.60 •40
Namibia	J7	Windhoek	.na	2.8 •40	51.5 •189	6.7 •70	47.1 •76	3.73 •140	14.23 •129	6.36 •153	0.62 •139	1.26 •132	0.36 •124	3.5 •91	2,370 •114	4,813 •128	2,749 •125	87 •74	n/a	403 •86	n/a	502 •94	2.5 •221	2,031 •145	824.30 •34
Nauru	R6	Yaren District	.nr	T –	61.5 •158	7.6 •52	0.0 •–	0.02 •209	11.54 •139	14.62 •112	4.62 •29	0.06 •195	0.00 •–	n/a	2,452 •110	32 •218	n/a	n/a	n/a	n/a	n/a	n/a	652.4 •12	13 •220	0.02 •223
Nepal	N4	Kathmandu	.np	1.6 •93	60.5 •166	5.2 •115	34.2 •116	0.48 •188	0.47 •208	1.69 •183	0.06 •194	1.55 •128	0.57 •117	3.7 •81	236 •212	6,538 •116	20,063 •60	258 •74	n/a	258 •?	360 •107	422 •97	196.6 •54	27,677 •40	140.80 •95
Netherlands[15]	J3	Amsterdam[15]	.nl	1.6 •93	78.5 •30	8.8 •31	46.9 •77	61.63 •13	91.21 •18	48.44 •38	6.12 •18	100.47 •22	63.20 •34	2.3 •139	31,397 •17	515,148 •15	88,146 •26	16,539 •8	16,463 •12	10,081 •16	9,646 •20	7,841 •18	395.4 •23	16,407 •59	41.50 •134
Netherlands Antilles	F5	Willemstad	.an	T –	76.0 •55	n/a	8.3 •192	n/a	90.09 •20	37.23 •57	17.59 •4	3.87 •105	0.00 •–	1.7 •156	9,793 •63	2,154 •158	1,472 •133	n/a	n/a	919 •64	705 •78	705 •78	274.9 •43	220 •181	0.80 •183
New Caledonia	R7	Nouméa	.nc	T –	74.0 •70	n/a	13.4 •178	n/a	50.19 •69	22.98 •69	3.24 •58	0.70 •147	0.08 •142	n/a	14,587 •48	3,158 •145	n/a	n/a	78 •84	136 •100	100 •130	105 •149	11.6 •199	216 •182	18.60 •154
New Zealand	R7	Wellington	.nz	1.1 •129	79.5 •17	8.5 •35	63.7 •25	81.95 •1	77.52 •39	46.11 •42	5.42 •23	21.87 •60	17.12 •56	3.1 •112	20,435 •33	82,465 •47	20,072 •59	2,360 •38	1,374 •54	4,951 •33	2,348 •56	1,497 •58	14.9 •191	4,035 •122	270.50 •75
Nicaragua	E5	Managua	.ni	0.9 •138	70.5 •111	7.9 •45	58.0 •46	2.20 •162	13.00 •135	3.77 •171	0.29 •159	0.29 •159	0.22 •130	3.8 •79	815 •166	4,452 •134	4,418 •112	n/a	562 •65	n/a	615 •91	358 •111	41.8 •151	5,465 •107	130.70 •97
Niger	J5	Niamey	.ne	1.1 •129	41.5 •210	4.0 •159	13.0 •180	0.19 •199	1.19 •202	0.19 •221	0.03 •205	0.40 •163	0.11 •137	3.6 •85	233 •214	2,836 •148	1,472 •133	n/a	n/a	n/a	n/a	44 •176	10.3 •201	12,163 •66	1,186.40 •25
Nigeria	J5	Abuja (9)	.ng	1.2 •120	45.5 •198	4.7 •137	78.2 •8	1.39 •169	7.20 •154	0.81 •197	0.19 •169	24.62 •59	140.10 •18	4.1 •68	419 •191	53,983 •54	n/a	611 •?	n/a	611 •87	1,472 •?	611 •87	139.4 •72	128,766 •9	923.80 •32
Niue	A6	Alofi	.nu	T –	71.0 •99	9.7 •15	30.4 •126	n/a	20.00 •117	20.00 •117	0.50 •143	0.00 •211	0.00 •–	n/a	1,847 •137	54 •224	n/a	n/a	n/a	n/a	3 •154	2 •204	8.3 •207	2 •226	0.26 •206

*: Ranking (top 10 in **bold**).   **n/a**: Not available, not relevant or not reliable.   **T**: See note on page 41.   **M**: See note on page 41.   For more information, see pages 202 & 210.

▶ **See also...** pages 108 & 116 for notes relating to this section; Contents (2-5) for details of all maps and charts in this Atlas

Country	Map Ref. (pp.14-15)	Internet code	Capital	Military Spending % of GNI (2003)	Life Expectancy Years (2004)	Total Health Spending % of GNI (2004)	Agricultural Land % of national area (2004)	Internet Usage Subscribers/100 people (2004)	Mobile Tel. Lines /100 people (2004)	Fixed Tel. Lines /100 people (2004)	Energy Consumption t oil equiv./person (2004)	Energy Consumption Mt oil equiv. (2004)	Energy Production Mt oil equiv. (2004)	GDP Growth Av. annual % 1997-2006	GNI per Person US$ (2004)	Gross Nat'l Income US$m (2004)	Hotel Bedrooms (2003)	Visitor Expenditure US$m (2004)	International Departures 000 (2004)	Visitor Receipts US$m (2004)	Visitor Arrivals 2004 000	International Arrivals 1997 000	Population Density /sq km (2004)	Population 000 (2004)	Area 000 sq km
Northern Mariana Is.	Q5	.mp	Saipan	T –	76.0 •55	n/a –	28.4 •138	n/a –	3.75 •175	26.25 •82	n/a –	n/a –	0.00 •	n/a –	1,456 •142	117 •212	4,231 •113	n/a –	n/a –	n/a –	525 •97	685 •79	174.7 •62	80 •198	0.46 •194
Norway	J2	.no	Oslo	2.0 •73	79.5 •17	9.6 •16	3.2 •207	39.37 •39	90.89 •19	48.64 •37	9.69 •12	44.51 •36	260.06 •8	3.0 •117	51,904 •2	238,398 •25	67,114 •32	8,428 •19	2,588 •40	3,087 •44	3,600 •42	2,702 •42	14.2 •193	4,593 •116	323.80 •67
Oman	L5	.om	Muscat	12.2 •2	74.0 •70	3.4 •174	3.5 •204	10.14 •99	33.32 •95	10.05 •136	3.25 •57	9.75 •79	59.36 •36	4.0 •73	6,832 •72	20,508 •74	6,473 •96	n/a –	n/a –	n/a –	n/a –	376 •105	9.7 •203	3,002 •134	309.50 •70
Pakistan	M4	.pk	Islamabad	4.4 •18	62.0 •157	3.2 •177	34.1 •117	1.31 •173	3.29 •182	2.95 •176	0.29 •158	47.69 •35	31.62 •43	4.5 •59	558 •176	90,663 •43	36,451 •49	1,275 •42	n/a –	186 •97	648 •89	375 •106	204.0 •53	162,420 •6	796.10 •36
Palau	P5	.pw	Koror	T –	68.0 •131	9.1 •26	17.7 •168	n/a –	5.00 •165	33.50 •63	n/a –	n/a –	n/a –	n/a –	6,748 •73	137 •211	5,919 •99	n/a –	n/a –	n/a –	89 •133	74 •163	39.8 •155	20 •217	0.51 •192
Palestine NAR[4]	K4	.ps	Jerusalem[16]	n/a –	72.5 •77	n/a –	61.5 •33	4.34 •138	26.44 •109	9.70 •137	n/a –	n/a –	n/a –	n/a –	1,002 •158	3,771 •139	n/a –	n/a –	n/a –	n/a –	n/a –	201 •133	606.8 •16	3,762 •127	6.20 •168
Panama	E5	.pa	Panama City	1.2 •120	75.5 •59	8.9 •29	29.5 •132	9.46 •101	26.98 •107	11.85 •129	1.59 •92	4.99 •90	0.72 •115	4.1 •68	4,289 •91	13,468 •86	16,766 •68	n/a –	n/a –	685 •74	652 •88	421 •98	41.6 •152	3,140 •132	75.50 •118
Papua New Guinea	Q6	.pg	Port Moresby	0.6 •152	60.5 •166	4.3 •150	2.3 •209	2.91 •154	0.27 •210	1.13 •193	0.21 •166	1.17 •137	2.95 •93	0.6 •174	588 •173	3,262 •144	2,830 •124	n/a –	n/a –	18 •113	59 •140	66 •166	12.0 •198	5,545 •106	462.80 •54
Paraguay	G7	.py	Asunción	0.9 •138	72.0 •87	8.4 •38	61.0 •36	2.49 •158	29.38 •99	4.73 •160	1.68 •89	10.64 •76	13.13 •60	1.7 •156	1,064 •155	6,752 •112	4,899 •108	499 •56	153 •81	70 •108	309 •109	395 •101	15.6 •188	6,348 •100	406.80 •59
Peru	F6	.pe	Lima	1.3 •113	70.5 •111	4.4 •146	24.4 •151	11.61 •93	14.75 •127	7.39 •147	0.51 •142	14.22 •69	10.04 •73	3.4 •98	2,329 •116	65,043 •50	123,252 •19	620 •52	889 •59	1,078 •72	1,203 •72	649 •82	21.7 •178	27,926 •39	1,285.20 •20
Philippines	P5	.ph	Manila	0.9 •138	68.0 •131	2.9 •183	40.7 •99	5.32 •128	39.85 •80	4.16 •165	0.36 •153	31.30 •44	10.63 •69	3.8 •79	1,103 •154	96,930 •41	21,409 •55	1,315 •40	1,803 •49	2,012 •52	2,291 •57	2,223 •49	292.9 •38	87,857 •12	300.00 •72
Poland	J3	.pl	Warsaw	2.0 •73	75.0 •62	6.1 •87	58.7 •43	23.35 •63	59.91 •60	31.85 •67	2.37 •74	91.20 •23	75.82 •30	4.2 •66	6,027 •77	232,398 •26	68,588 •31	3,906 •27	38,730 •4	5,828 •27	14,290 •15	19,520 •7	123.3 •81	38,558 •32	312.70 •69
Portugal[5]	I3	.pt	Lisbon	2.1 •66	77.5 •41	9.3 •21	44.9 •86	28.03 •55	98.41 •11	40.25 •55	2.64 •70	27.92 •48	4.58 •79	2.5 •128	14,176 •34	149,790 •34	105,986 •21	2,767 •35	n/a –	7,788 •21	11,617 •15	10,172 •15	115.0 •82	10,566 •76	91.90 •112
Puerto Rico	F5	.pr	San Juan	T –	n/a –	n/a –	32.8 •120	22.12 •66	68.82 •50	28.53 •76	3.34 •53	13.07 •71	0.07 •143	n/a –	1,142 •152	4,468 •133	12,788 •73	n/a –	1,272 •55	3,024 •45	3,541 •43	3,242 •35	439.5 •21	3,911 •125	8.90 •167
Qatar	L4	.qa	Doha	10.0 •3	74.5 •63	3.1 •179	6.2 •202	22.00 •67	65.38 •52	25.45 •87	14.37 •6	12.40 •72	77.43 •27	9.9 •5	22,583 •30	19,490 •77	3,858 •117	512 •55	333 •71	n/a –	498 •80	435 •96	75.7 •115	863 •157	11.40 •163
Réunion	L7	.re	Saint-Denis	n/a –	74.5 •63	n/a –	19.5 •163	26.08 •57	75.51 •42	41.04 •53	1.42 •98	1.10 •138	0.15 •135	n/a –	11,268 •60	8,755 •100	2,910 •123	n/a –	n/a –	448 •85	430 •103	374 •107	310.8 •34	777 •159	2.50 •175
Romania	K3	.ro	Bucharest	2.4 •57	71.5 •95	6.3 •77	62.2 •30	20.76 •71	47.13 •73	20.25 •101	1.89 •83	42.12 •39	29.02 •48	2.4 •133	2,862 •105	63,910 •51	97,320 •22	n/a –	6,497 •20	505 •79	3,739 •41	2,957 •38	94.5 •97	22,330 •49	236.40 •83
Russian Federation	M2	.ru	Moscow	4.3 •20	65.0 •146	6.2 •81	12.7 •182	11.10 •95	51.61 •68	27.47 •78	5.07 •25	726.61 •3	1,230.03 •3	4.7 •53	3,398 •101	487,335 •15	177,200 •14	15,730 •14	20,468 •8	5,226 •20	9,164 •21	7,463 •10	8.4 •206	143,420 •8	17,075.40 •1
Rwanda	K6	.rw	Kigali	2.8 •40	44.5 •205	5.3 •114	70.2 •16	0.45 •190	1.64 •197	0.27 •215	0.04 •199	0.34 •169	0.02 •151	6.4 •26	222 •215	1,875 •160	1,680 •132	n/a –	n/a –	n/a –	104 •150	n/a –	320.9 •31	8,441 •88	26.30 •147
St Helena	I7	.sh	Jamestown	n/a –	78.0 •39	n/a –	29.3 •134	7.14 •115	n/a –	31.43 •68	0.01 •207	0.01 •207	0.00 •207	n/a –	2,413 •111	18 •222	n/a –	n/a –	n/a –	n/a –	n/a –	n/a –	62.2 •134	7 •223	0.12 •218
St Kitts & Nevis	F5	.kn	Basseterre	M –	70.5 •111	5.5 •112	38.2 •108	21.41 •68	20.00 •117	50.00 •32	1.03 •113	0.04 •198	0.00 •198	3.2 •108	9,164 •65	357 •197	3,749 •118	n/a –	n/a –	n/a –	n/a –	88 •154	149.8 •69	39 •209	0.26 •207
St Lucia	F5	.lc	Castries	M –	72.0 •87	5.0 •124	32.5 •121	36.67 •42	62.00 •55	31.95 •66	0.78 •130	0.13 •185	0.00 •185	2.1 •149	4,245 •92	706 •184	n/a –	n/a –	n/a –	325 •92	298 •110	248 •127	268.2 •44	166 •189	0.62 •190
St Pierre et Miquelon	G3	.pm	St Pierre	M –	n/a –	n/a –	12.4 •184	n/a –	n/a –	68.57 •11	4.29 •35	0.03 •202	0.00 •202	n/a –	15,402 •43	108 •214	n/a –	n/a –	n/a –	n/a –	n/a –	n/a –	29.2 •171	7 •224	0.24 •208
St Vincent & the Gren.	F5	.vc	Kingstown	M –	70.0 •116	5.9 •96	41.1 •98	6.61 •119	47.07 •74	13.72 •115	0.59 •140	0.07 •191	0.01 •158	3.5 •91	3,369 •102	396 •195	939 •138	n/a –	n/a –	n/a –	87 •134	65 •167	301.4 •37	118 •191	0.39 •199
Samoa	S6	.ws	Apia	T –	70.0 •116	6.2 •81	46.3 •82	3.33 •147	5.76 •160	7.29 •148	0.40 •148	0.07 •191	0.07 •151	3.3 •103	1,878 •135	333 •198	683 •140	n/a –	n/a –	n/a –	98 •131	68 •164	63.3 •132	177 •187	2.80 •173
San Marino	J3	.sm	San Marino	T –	81.0 •4	7.7 •49	16.4 •171	49.31 •27	57.93 •65	71.03 •9	n/a –	n/a –	0.00 •	n/a –	22,611 •29	653 •188	n/a –	n/a –	n/a –	n/a –	42 •146	28 •181	481.3 •20	29 •212	0.06 •220

▶ *See also...* pages 108 & 116 for notes relating to this section; Contents (2-5) for details of all maps and charts in this Atlas

Appendices 115

Countries A-Z: São Tome-Tonga

Military Spending % of GNI (2003)	Life Expectancy Years (2004)	Total Health Spending % of GNI (2004)	Agricultural Land % of national area (2004)	Internet Usage Subscribers/100 people (2004)	Mobile Tel. Lines Lines/100 people (2004)	Fixed Tel. Lines Lines/100 people (2004)	Energy Consumption Tonnes oil equiv/person (2004)	Energy Consumption Mil tonnes oil equiv (2004)	Energy Production Mil tonnes oil equiv (2004)	GDP Growth Av. annual % 1997-2006	GNI per Person US$ (2004)	Gross Nat'l Income US$ billion (2004)	Hotel Bedrooms (2003)	Visitor Expenditure US$ million (2004)	International Departures '000	Visitor Receipts US$ million (2004)	International Arrivals 2004 '000	International Arrivals 1997 '000	Population Density people/sq km (2004)	Population '000 (2004)	Area '000 sq km	Capital	Internet Code	Country / Map Ref (pp 14-15)
0.8 •144	59.0 •172	11.1 •**5**	54.9 •56	12.20 •89	3.17 •183	4.59 •161	0.21 •165	0.04 •198	0.00 •198	3.3 •103	320 •202	60 •216	n/a •–	n/a •–	n/a •–	n/a •–	n/a •–	5 •200	187.4 •56	187 •186	1.00 •182	São Tomé	.st	São Tomé e Príncipe J6
8.7 •**7**	71.0 •99	4.3 •150	n/a •–	6.36 •121	36.82 •83	14.83 •111	5.39 •24	142.180 •17	580.17 •**4**	3.4 •98	9,167 •64	242,180 •24	81,197 •28	4,406 •26	4,104 •31	6,542 •24	8,580 •22	n/a •–	12.0 •197	26,418 •43	2,200.00 •13	Riyadh	.sa	Saudi Arabia L4
1.5 •102	55.5 •180	5.1 •119	41.5 •95	4.66 •134	10.85 •144	2.37 •179	0.14 •175	1.64 •126	0.04 •146	5.4 •40	595 •172	6,967 •109	10,268 •80	n/a •–	n/a •–	n/a •–	363 •106	314 •117	59.7 •136	11,706 •70	196.20 •87	Dakar	.sn	Senegal I5
1.8 •83	72.5 •77	8.1 •40	54.7 •58	18.61 •74	58.01 •64	32.94 •64	1.78 •85	19.23 •63	13.34 •58	2.0 •153	2,005 •133	21,715 •95	37,101 •48	55 •77	50 •86	220 •95	580 •92	298 •121	106.0 •89	10,829 •74	102.20 •106	Belgrade	.yu	Serbia & Montenegro 22
4.2 •24	72.0 •87	5.2 •115	15.4 •173	24.69 •60	60.78 •58	26.16 •83	4.94 •26	0.40 •163	0.00 •–	0.7 •173	8,437 •69	685 •185	2,435 •129	n/a •–	n/a •–	172 •99	121 •128	130 •146	176.5 •61	81 •197	0.46 •195	Victoria	.sc	Seychelles L6
1.7 •88	38.0 •215	2.9 •183	39.0 •105	0.06 •199	2.28 •190	0.48 •208	0.06 •191	0.35 •168	0.00 •–	5.0 •45	190 •216	1,113 •172	1,457 •134	n/a •–	n/a •–	13 •88	44 •144	23 •188	80.0 •108	5,867 •103	73.30 •119	Freetown	.sl	Sierra Leone I5
5.2 •14	61.5 •158	4.3 •150	3.0 •208	56.12 •16	89.47 •21	43.20 •50	9.92 •11	43.92 •37	0.00 •–	4.1 •68	23,724 •28	104,994 •39	35,930 •50	4,221 •30	n/a •–	5,090 •32	8,328 •23	6,531 •21	6,808.8 •**3**	4,426 •120	0.65 •189	Singapore	.sg	Singapore O5
1.9 •77	74.0 •70	5.9 •96	49.6 •71	42.27 •34	79.39 •35	23.22 •77	3.69 •46	20.04 •62	7.07 •79	3.6 •85	6,427 •76	34,907 •59	35,853 •51	745 •49	408 •68	901 •65	1,401 •69	814 •72	110.8 •84	5,431 •109	49.00 •129	Bratislava	.sk	Slovak Rep. K3
1.5 •102	77.0 •47	8.3 •39	24.9 •149	47.96 •28	87.09 •25	40.68 •54	3.82 •43	7.68 •82	7.55 •78	3.6 •85	14,696 •46	29,555 •62	15,534 •70	911 •46	2,114 •46	1,630 •55	1,499 •66	974 •68	99.1 •94	2,011 •146	20.30 •153	Ljubljana	.si	Slovenia J3
M •–	71.0 •99	4.8 •133	4.2 •203	0.61 •185	0.31 •209	1.31 •190	0.13 •176	0.07 •191	0.00 •–	-0.5 •176	483 •182	260 •205	n/a •–	n/a •–	n/a •–	4 •116	16 •196	n/a •–	18.9 •184	538 •163	28.40 •143	Honiara	.sb	Solomon Is. R6
n/a •–	44.0 •207	n/a •–	69.1 •19	1.67 •167	4.17 •173	1.67 •184	0.03 •206	0.26 •173	0.00 •–	n/a •–	#VALUE!	n/a •–	n/a •–	n/a •–	n/a •–	n/a •–	n/a •–	n/a •–	13.5 •195	8,592 •87	637.70 •42	Mogadishu	.so	Somalia L5
1.6 •93	49.0 •194	8.7 •33	81.7 •**4**	7.89 •107	43.13 •77	10.40 •135	2.76 •67	122.54 •19	147.89 •17	3.1 •112	3,728 •99	165,326 •31	52,329 •40	5,692 •23	4,094 •32	5,648 •30	6,678 •29	5,170 •26	36.2 •161	44,344 •27	1,224.70 •24	note 17	.za	South Africa K7
1.2 •120	79.5 •17	7.6 •52	59.8 •40	33.18 •44	89.46 •22	41.52 •52	3.82 •42	154.30 •15	37.99 •39	3.1 •112	21,210 •31	875,817 •**9**	740,747 •**6**	12,156 •15	n/a •–	45,248 •**2**	53,599 •**3**	39,553 •**3**	79.9 •109	40,341 •29	504.80 •51	Madrid	.es	Spain 6 I4
2.7 •45	71.5 •95	3.7 •167	36.0 •115	1.44 •168	11.37 •141	5.10 •159	0.24 •161	4.90 •91	0.75 •114	4.7 •53	978 •162	19,618 •76	16,973 •66	296 •62	561 •66	513 •78	566 •93	366 •108	305.9 •36	20,065 •53	65.60 •122	note 18	.lk	Sri Lanka N5
2.4 •57	59.5 •169	4.9 •128	53.4 •64	3.30 •150	3.04 •184	2.98 •175	0.09 •185	3.46 •110	12.85 •62	8.7 •**8**	452 •185	18,152 •80	n/a •–	n/a •–	n/a •–	n/a •–	n/a •–	n/a •–	16.0 •187	40,187 •30	2,505.80 •**10**	Khartoum	.sd	Sudan K5
0.7 •147	66.0 •143	8.6 •34	0.5 •214	6.83 •118	48.48 •71	18.52 •104	2.24 •76	0.98 •140	0.96 •109	3.2 •108	2,276 •118	997 •174	n/a •–	n/a •–	30 •179	n/a •–	138 •125	61 •169	2.7 •219	438 •169	163.80 •91	Paramaribo	.sr	Surinam G5
1.7 •88	34.5 •220	6.0 •92	80.1 •**6**	3.32 •148	10.43 •145	4.43 •163	0.47 •145	0.53 •158	0.28 •128	2.9 •122	1,633 •140	1,859 •162	1,339 •135	n/a •–	n/a •–	n/a •–	459 •101	269 •123	65.4 •127	1,138 •153	17.40 •157	Mbabane	.sz	Swaziland K7
1.8 •83	80.5 •**7**	9.2 •24	7.0 •197	75.46 •**7**	108.47 •**3**	71.54 •**8**	5.78 •21	52.01 •30	30.27 •46	2.7 •124	35,504 •11	321,401 •19	96,372 •24	12,579 •16	n/a •–	6,167 •25	3,003 •49	2,388 •44	20.0 •182	9,002 •85	450.00 •56	Stockholm	.se	Sweden J2
1.0 •134	80.5 •**7**	11.2 •**4**	36.9 •113	47.20 •31	84.63 •31	70.97 •**10**	4.25 •36	31.86 •43	15.97 •57	1.5 •160	47,541 •**3**	356,052 •17	139,969 •17	8,797 •18	n/a •–	10,309 •15	6,578 •30	10,600 •14	182.2 •59	7,489 •94	41.10 •135	Bern	.ch	Switzerland J3
7.1 •**9**	71.5 •95	5.1 •119	74.3 •15	4.39 •137	12.87 •137	14.60 •113	1.13 •108	22.69 •55	36.99 •40	3.0 •117	1,145 •151	21,125 •75	16,966 •67	2,220 •48	3,997 •33	2,220 •48	3,032 •48	891 •71	99.6 •93	18,449 •55	185.20 •88	Damascus	.sy	Syria K4
2.6 •47	77.0 •47	5.6 •109	25.0 •148	53.81 •19	100.31 •**8**	59.63 •18	4.56 •30	104.43 •21	11.89 •65	4.3 •65	13,849 •51	317,070 •20	21,896 •54	5,923 •22	n/a •–	4,040 •39	2,950 •50	2,372 •46	632.4 •14	22,894 •48	36.20 •136	Taipei	.tw	Taiwan P4
2.2 •63	61.0 •165	3.3 •175	29.7 •130	0.08 •206	0.73 •205	3.75 •172	0.90 •121	6.45 •86	3.92 •86	7.4 •15	248 •210	1,779 •163	n/a •–	n/a •–	n/a •–	n/a •–	n/a •–	2 •204	50.1 •143	7,164 •97	143.10 •94	Dushanbe	.tj	Tajikistan M4
2.1 •66	45.0 •201	4.9 •128	42.4 •93	0.88 •179	4.35 •172	0.42 •209	0.05 •195	1.94 •123	0.79 •113	6.4 •26	314 •203	11,560 •93	10,525 •79	n/a •–	n/a •–	595 •76	566 •93	347 •113	38.9 •157	36,766 •33	945.00 •31	Dodoma	.tz	Tanzania K6
1.3 •113	70.0 •116	4.4 •146	39.3 •104	11.25 •94	44.18 •76	10.97 •132	1.22 •104	78.09 •25	39.81 •38	2.6 •126	2,473 •109	158,703 •32	n/a •–	4,517 •25	2,152 •45	10,034 •17	11,651 •18	7,294 •20	125.1 •79	64,186 •19	513.10 •50	Bangkok	.th	Thailand O5
1.6 •93	52.0 •187	10.5 •**9**	63.9 •24	4.41 •136	4.40 •169	1.21 •192	0.09 •184	0.48 •159	0.00 •–	2.3 •139	346 •199	1,868 •161	4,480 •111	n/a •–	n/a •–	n/a •–	83 •136	92 •153	95.1 •96	5,400 •110	56.80 •125	Lomé	.tg	Togo J5
M •–	71.0 •99	6.9 •66	69.5 •18	2.88 •155	3.38 •181	11.29 •130	0.36 •152	0.04 •198	0.00 •–	2.1 •149	1,654 •139	186 •208	n/a •–	n/a •–	n/a •–	n/a •–	41 •147	26 •184	149.9 •68	112 •192	0.75 •185	Nuku'alofa	.to	Tonga S6

116 | **Appendices**
Countries A-Z: Trinidad & Tobago-Zimbabwe

▶ See also... pages 108 for notes relating to this section; Contents (2-5) for details of all maps and charts in this Atlas

Each cell shows *value* and *•rank*. T = See note 10 in bold. M = See note on page 41. n/a = Not available, not relevant or not reliable.

Country (Map Ref / Internet code)	Capital	Military Spending % of GNI (2003)	Life Expectancy Years (2004)	Total Health Spending % of GNI (2004)	Agricultural Land % of national area (2002)	Internet Usage Subscribers/100 (2004)	Mobile Tel. Lines /100 (2004)	Fixed Tel. Lines /100 (2004)	Energy Consumption tonnes oil/person (2004)	Energy Consumption Mil. tonnes oil (2004)	Energy Production Mil. tonnes oil (2004)	GDP Growth Av. annual % 1997-2006	GNI per Person US$ (2004)	Gross Nat'l Income US$ billion (2004)	Hotel Bedrooms (2003)	Visitor Expenditure US$ million (2004)	International Departures 000	Visitor Receipts US$ million 2004	International Arrivals 2004 000	International Arrivals 1997 000	Population Density people/sq km (2004)	Population 000 (2004)	Area 000 sq km
Trinidad & Tobago (F5, .tt)	Port of Spain	0.6 •152	70.0 •116	3.7 •167	25.9 •144	12.24 •88	49.82 •70	24.58 •90	12.35 •7	13.28 •70	31.51 •44	6.9 •20	10,567 •62	11,360 •94	5,378 •102	n/a •77	n/a •90	n/a •117	443 •102	324 •116	210.8 •51	1,075 •154	5.10 •170
Tunisia (J4, .tn)	Tunis	1.6 •93	72.0 •87	5.8 •99	59.7 •41	8.40 •106	35.86 •87	12.11 •127	0.85 •125	8.56 •81	6.25 •80	5.0 •45	2,611 •107	26,301 •81	110,009 •20	326 •62	2,274 •44	1,910 •53	5,998 •34	4,263 •29	65.2 •128	10,075 •80	154.50 •92
Turkey (K4, .tr)	Ankara	4.9 •16	70.5 •111	6.5 •71	53.5 •63	14.13 •85	47.99 •72	26.45 •81	1.20 •105	83.32 •24	22.81 •52	3.9 •76	3,858 •97	268,741 •21	201,510 •13	2,524 •37	5,928 •21	15,888 •8	16,826 •12	9,040 •17	89.4 •103	69,661 •17	779.50 •37
Turkmenistan (L4, .tm)	Ashgabat	2.9 •35	60.5 •166	4.3 •150	66.8 •22	0.73 •182	0.19 •213	7.73 •146	3.73 •45	18.46 •64	65.16 •33	11.7 •3	1,336 •145	6,615 •115	n/a	n/a	n/a	n/a	n/a	257 •125	10.1 •202	4,952 •113	488.10 •52
Turks & Caicos Is. (F4, .tc)	Cockburn Town	T	74.5 •63	n/a •–	2.3 •209	n/a •–	8.10 •151	27.14 •80	0.24 •163	0.01 •207	0.00 •–	n/a •–	5,692 •79	117 •213	2,473 •128	n/a	n/a	n/a	n/a	93 •152	41.1 •154	21 •216	0.50 •193
Tuvalu (R6, .tv)	Funafuti	M	61.5 •158	4.4 •146	0.0 •–	10.83 •96	n/a •–	5.83 •155	n/a •–	n/a •–	0.00 •–	n/a •–	1,117 •153	13 •223	n/a	n/a	n/a	n/a	1 •155	n/a •206	581.8 •17	12 •221	0.02 •224
Uganda (K5, .ug)	Kampala	2.3 •60	48.5 •195	7.4 •56	51.1 •68	0.75 •181	4.36 •171	0.27 •215	0.03 •201	0.94 •143	0.44 •122	5.8 •34	253 •209	6,911 •110	n/a	n/a	n/a	n/a	512 •98	175 •138	113.2 •83	27,269 •41	241.00 •80
Ukraine (K3, .ua)	Kyiv (Kiev)	2.9 •35	67.5 •135	4.7 •137	68.6 •20	7.79 •109	28.52 •103	25.22 •88	3.33 •56	156.41 •14	76.81 •28	4.8 •50	1,283 •147	60,297 •53	32,572 •53	996 •44	14,795 •13	1,141 •60	15,629 •14	7,558 •19	77.8 •113	46,997 •25	603.70 •44
United Arab Emirates (L4, .ae)	Abu Dhabi	3.1 •32	73.5 •75	3.1 •179	7.3 •196	31.85 •46	84.71 •30	27.32 •75	21.14 •3	54.19 •31	178.24 •15	6.2 •28	18,729 •35	48,007 •55	38,402 •46	n/a	n/a	1,593 •56	6,394 •31	2,476 •43	30.6 •168	2,563 •139	83.70 •116
United Kingdom[7] (I3, .uk)	London	2.8 •40	78.5 •30	7.7 •49	69.8 •17	62.88 •11	102.16 •7	56.35 •21	4.07 •40	245.87 •9	265.24 •7	2.3 •139	33,361 •13	2,016,393 •4	n/a	55,930 •3	61,424 •2	27,299 •6	27,755 •6	25,515 •5	248.2 •48	60,441 •22	243.50 •79
United States of America[8] (D3, .us)	Washington DC	3.8 •28	77.5 •41	14.6 •1	42.0 •94	55.58 •17	62.11 •53	60.60 •17	8.36 •17	2,471.07 •1	1,762.39 •1	2.2 •142	41,087 •5	12,150,931 •1	4,415,696 •1	65,635 •2	56,175 •3	74,481 •1	46,082 •2	47,752 •2	31.6 •165	295,734 •3	9,372.60 •4
United States Virgin Is. (F5, .vi)	Charlotte Amalie	T	79.0 •24	n/a •–	28.8 •137	n/a •–	n/a •–	63.86 •16	50.64 •1	5.52 •88	0.00 •–	n/a •–	14,737 •45	1,602 •164	5,044 •106	n/a	n/a	n/a	544 •96	411 •99	310.6 •35	109 •193	0.35 •201
Uruguay (G7, .uy)	Montevideo	1.6 •93	75.5 •59	10.0 •10	84.5 •2	20.98 •69	18.51 •120	30.85 •71	1.23 •103	4.20 •101	2.19 •98	1.5 •160	3,927 •95	13,414 •87	18,160 •63	495 •67	n/a	455 •84	1,756 •62	2,316 •48	19.4 •183	3,416 •131	176.20 •90
Uzbekistan (M3, .uz)	Tashkent	0.5 •156	66.0 •143	5.5 •112	60.5 •38	3.32 •148	2.05 •192	6.70 •152	1.99 •81	53.54 •32	61.64 •35	3.5 •91	442 •187	11,860 •91	7,332 •91	n/a	n/a	n/a	960 •69	400 •69	60.0 •135	26,851 •42	447.40 •57
Vanuatu (R6, .vu)	Port Vila	T	68.0 •131	3.8 •163	13.3 •179	3.46 •144	4.84 •167	3.11 •174	0.15 •172	0.03 •202	0.00 •–	1.5 •160	1,395 •144	287 •202	n/a	n/a	n/a	n/a	61 •139	50 •171	16.9 •186	206 •183	12.20 •161
Venezuela (F5, .ve)	Caracas	1.3 •113	74.0 •70	4.9 •128	23.7 •154	8.84 •105	32.17 •97	12.78 •122	2.87 •66	72.88 •26	188.88 •13	2.1 •149	4,136 •93	104,958 •40	82,366 •27	832 •60	n/a	n/a	n/a	814 •72	27.7 •172	25,375 •45	916.50 •33
Vietnam (O5, .vn)	Hanoi	2.6 •47	71.0 •99	5.2 •115	–	7.12 •116	6.01 •159	12.28 •124	0.29 •157	24.62 •51	36.46 •41	6.9 •20	540 •178	45,082 •57	n/a	n/a	n/a	n/a	2,928 •51	1,114 •65	251.8 •47	83,536 •13	331.70 •65
Wallis & Futuna (S6, .wf)	Matu Utu	T	n/a •–	n/a •–	21.9 •160	5.63 •125	n/a •–	11.88 •128	0.33 •155	0.09 •189	0.00 •–	n/a •–	1,997 •134	32 •219	n/a	n/a	n/a	n/a	n/a	n/a	66.8 •125	16 •218	0.24 •209
Western Sahara (I4, .eh)	al-Aioun	T	n/a •–	n/a •–	15.1 •175	n/a •–	n/a •–	0.73 •201	n/a •–	0.00 •–	0.00 •–	n/a •–	582 •174	159 •209	n/a	n/a	n/a	n/a	n/a	n/a	1.1 •224	273 •179	252.10 •77
Yemen (L5, .ye)	San'a	7.1 •9	59.0 •172	3.7 •167	33.0 •119	0.87 •180	5.17 •163	3.85 •170	0.19 •170	3.88 •104	23.42 •51	3.9 •76	541 •177	11,218 •95	13,280 •72	n/a	n/a	n/a	274 •117	80 •158	37.3 •160	20,727 •51	555.00 •48
Zambia (K6, .zm)	Lusaka	0.6 •152	39.0 •214	5.8 •99	46.9 •77	2.11 •163	2.75 •186	0.79 •198	0.24 •162	2.71 •116	2.25 •96	3.6 •85	422 •190	4,748 •129	5,202 •103	n/a	n/a	n/a	n/a	341 •114	15.0 •190	11,262 •73	752.60 •38
Zimbabwe (K6, .zw)	Harare	2.1 •66	36.5 •217	8.5 •35	52.6 •66	6.90 •117	3.56 •178	2.67 •178	0.39 •149	4.71 •92	3.40 •90	-4.3 •177	423 •189	5,150 •125	5,766 •101	n/a	n/a	194 •96	1,853 •59	1,281 •61	31.1 •166	12,161 •67	390.70 •60
• Lowest rank		•163	•220	•192	•216	•209	•215	•223	•211	•211	•158	•177	•224	•224	•141	•77	•90	•117	•161	•206	•226	•226	•226

•: Ranking (top 10 in **bold**). n/a: Not available, not relevant or not reliable. T: See note 10 in bold. M: See note on page 41. For more information, see pages 202 & 210.

NOTES:

1 Special Administrative Region of China.
2 Figures exclude Northern Cyprus.
3 All figures exclude overseas Départements and other dependencies listed separately here.
4 National Autonomous Region.
5 All figures include Madeira and the Azores.
6 All figures include Balearic and Canary Islands.
7 All figures exclude the Channel Islands and the Isle of Man.
8 All figures exclude overseas possessions and other dependencies listed separately here.
9 La Paz (seat of government); Sucre (judicial).
10 St Peter Port (Guernsey) & St Helier (Jersey).
11 Yamassoukro (official); Abidjan (administrative

& commercial).
12 Basse-Terre (administrative) & Pointe-à-Pitre (commercial).
13 Plymouth was largely destroyed in 1997 by volcanic eruption. A temporary administrative centre has been established at Brades.
14 Formerly called Rangoon.
15 Amsterdam (capital); The Hague (seat of government);

16 East Jerusalem has been declared the capital by the Palestinian Authority. Currently, the legislature is in Ramallah and the Palestinian Authority executive is in Gaza City.
17 Pretoria (City of Tshwane) (administrative), Cape Town (legislative), Bloemfontein (judicial). This arrangement is currently under review.

18 Colombo (administrative & commercial); Sri Jayewardenepura Kotte (legislative).
19 Population and area figures exclude the disputed territory of Jammu & Kashmir.
20 Population and area figures include the Golan Heights and East Jerusalem.
21 Population and area figures exclude Western Sahara.

21 As a result of a referendum held on 21 May 2006, Montenegro declared independence from Serbia & Montenegro on 3 June 2006, so completing the dissolution of the former state of Yugoslavia. Figures have been included in this chart for the combined republic. Montenegro has an area of 13,812 sq km and a population of 670,000. Its capital is Podgorica.

Index

INDEX TO THE ATLAS

The index lists all locations and features which appear in Europe (including the Russian Federation, Turkey and Cyprus). For countries outside Europe, refer to the 'Countries A-Z' section, which gives grid references to the World Political map on pages 28-29. The following special-subject maps and map pages are not indexed:
- World climate
- World sport
- World time
- World tourism
- Airports*
- Flight times
- Cruising
- Europe climate
- European Union
- Europe airports & high-speed rail
- Europe rail & ferries
- Europe museums & art galleries*
- London airports & connections
- UK attractions
- Belgium attractions
- The Dutch vs the Sea
- The Netherlands attractions
- Germany attractions
- France attractions
- Spain & Portugal attractions
- Italy attractions

Maps marked * include a list of locations on the page itself

GENERAL ABBREVIATIONS

Arch.	Archaeological
Hist.	Historic/Historical
I.	Island, Ile and equivalents
Int.	International
Is.	Islands, Iles and equivalents
Mem.	Memorial
Mon.	Monument
Mt	Mount/Mont
Mtn	Mountain/Montagne
Mtns	Mountains/Monts
Nac.	Nacional
Nat.	National
Naz.	Nazionale
Prov.	Provincial
St	Saint/Sankt/Sint

(all 'St' entries are treated as if spelt 'Saint' and are located in the index accordingly)

Ste	Sainte

(all 'Ste' entries are treated as if spelt 'Sainte' and are located in the index accordingly)

Vdkhr.	Vodokhranilishche

Countries and significant dependencies and possessions are shown in CAPITALS

Hyphens and some accents have been removed in certain cases for consistency and ease of viewing. The correct form appears on the maps themselves.

The following names, which appear in bold, indicate the entry is a featured location on one of the special subject maps:

Beach	Beach map
Heritage C	UNESCO map (cultural site)
Heritage N	UNESCO map (natural site)
Park L	Leisure/Theme park map
Park N	National Park map
Russ Adm	Russian administrative map
W Front	Western Front map

The following abbreviations appear occasionally to distinguish features with the same name:

[Adm]	Administrative region
[Apt]	Airport
[Riv]	River

Answers to Quizzes

Answers for UK Quiz 1

Question	Answer
1	F
2	I
3	C
4	A
5	E
6	G
7	B
8	D
9	J
10	H

Answers for UK Quiz 2

Fact	Resort
1	Brighton
2	Aberystwyth
3	St. Austell
4	Blackpool
5	Southend
6	Pwllheli
7	Ballycastle
8	St. Ives
9	Sandown
10	Scarborough

Answers for UK Quiz 3

Area	Gateway
1	D
2	G
3	I
4	B
5	C
6	G
7	A
8	E
9	F
10	J

Answers for UK Quiz 4

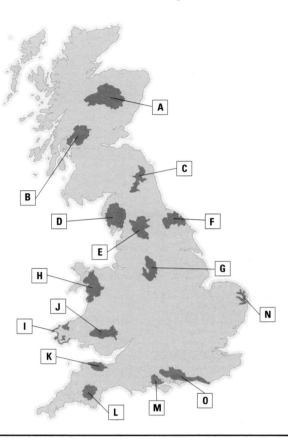

Answers for UK Quiz 5

	Airport	3-letter code
1	London Heathrow	LHR
2	Londonderry	LDY
3	Edinburgh	EDI
4	London Stansted	STN
5	Leeds Bradford	LBA
6	Birmingham	BHX
7	Cardiff	CWL
8	Glasgow International	GLA
9	Belfast City	BHD
10	Bournemouth	BOH

Answers for UK Quiz 6

Seaport	Destination
1	F
2	I
3	B
4	E
5	G
6	A
7	J
8	H
9	C
10	D

Answers for Europe Quiz 1

	Resort	Island	Country	Sea/Ocean
1	Lindos	Rhodes	Greece	Aegean
2	Kavos	Corfu	Greece	Ionian
3	Paphos	Cyprus	Greece	Mediterranean
4	Kyrenia	Cyprus	Turkey	Mediterranean
5	Alcudia	Majorca	Spain	Mediterranean
6	Funchal	Madeira	Portugal	Atlantic
7	Sliema	Malta	Malta	Mediterranean
8	Alghero	Sardinia	Italy	Mediterranean
9	Porto Vecchio	Corsica	France	Tyrrhenian
10	Molyvos	Lesbos	Greece	Aegean

Answers for Europe Quiz 2

Open-ended

Answers for Europe Quiz 3

	Airport	Nearby City	Airlines (correct at time of press)
1	Ciampino	Rome	Easyjet, Ryanair, Thomson Fly, Air Berlin, Wizz Air
2	Bratislava	Vienna	Ryanair, Easyjet, Sky Europe, Lufthansa, Czech Airlines
3	Sabiha Gokcen	Istanbul	Easyjet, Air Arabia, Condor, Pegasus, Turkish Airlines, Germanwings
4	Brescia	Verona	Ryanair, Air Alps Aviation, Gandalf Airlines
5	Beauvais	Paris	Ryanair, Blue Air, Sterling European Airlines, Wizz Air, Braathens
6	Reus	Barcelona	Ryanair, Iberia, Thompson Flights, My Travel, Air Berlin, First Choice
7	Mulhouse	Basel	Easyjet, Air France British Airways, Lufthansa, Luxair
8	Schonefeld	Berlin	Ryanair, Easyjet, Aer Lingus, Virgin Express, Germanwings
9	Treviso	Venice	Ryanair
10	Torp	Oslo	Ryanair, Coast Air, KLM

Answers for Europe Quiz 4

	Port	Body of water
1	Bergen	Norwegian Sea
2	Crete	Mediterranean Sea
3	Dubrovnik	Adriatic Sea
4	Porto	Atlantic Ocean
5	Palma de Mallorca	Mediterranean Sea
6	Istanbul	Bosporus
7	Stockhlom	Baltic Sea
8	Tromso	Norwegian Sea
9	Tallinn	Baltic Sea
10	Gibraltar	Mediterranean Sea

Answers for Europe Quiz 5

	Airport	3-letter code
1	Paris Orly	ORY
2	Faro	FAO
3	Palma, Majorca	PMI
4	Cork	ORK
5	Mikonos	JMK
6	Malaga	AGP
7	Izmir	ADB
8	Larnaca	LCA
9	Prague	PRG
10	Krakow	KRK

Answers for Europe Quiz 6

Seaport	UK destination
1	E
2	F
3	A
4	H
5	B
6	J
7	D
8	C
9	G
10	I